D0564823

O N E

They built a big coffee shop about a five-minute walk away. I'm so happy. There's plenty of space on rainy days, which makes it even better!

—ONE

Manga creator ONE began *One-Punch Man* as a webcomic, which quickly went viral, garnering over 10 million hits. In addition to *One-Punch Man*, ONE writes and draws the series *Mob Psycho 100* and *Makai no Ossan*.

Y U S U K E M U R A T A

I'm raising tomatoes. I've made all sorts of discoveries, so it's interesting.

—Yusuke Murata

A highly decorated and skilled artist best known for his work on *Eyeshield 21*, Yusuke Murata won the 122nd Hop Step Award (1995) for *Partner* and placed second in the 51st Akatsuka Award (1998) for *Samui Hanashi*.

3 1901 10098 7272

ONE-PUNCH MAN | 21

ONE + YUSUKE MURATA

★ The stories, characters and incidents mentioned in this publication are entirely fictional.

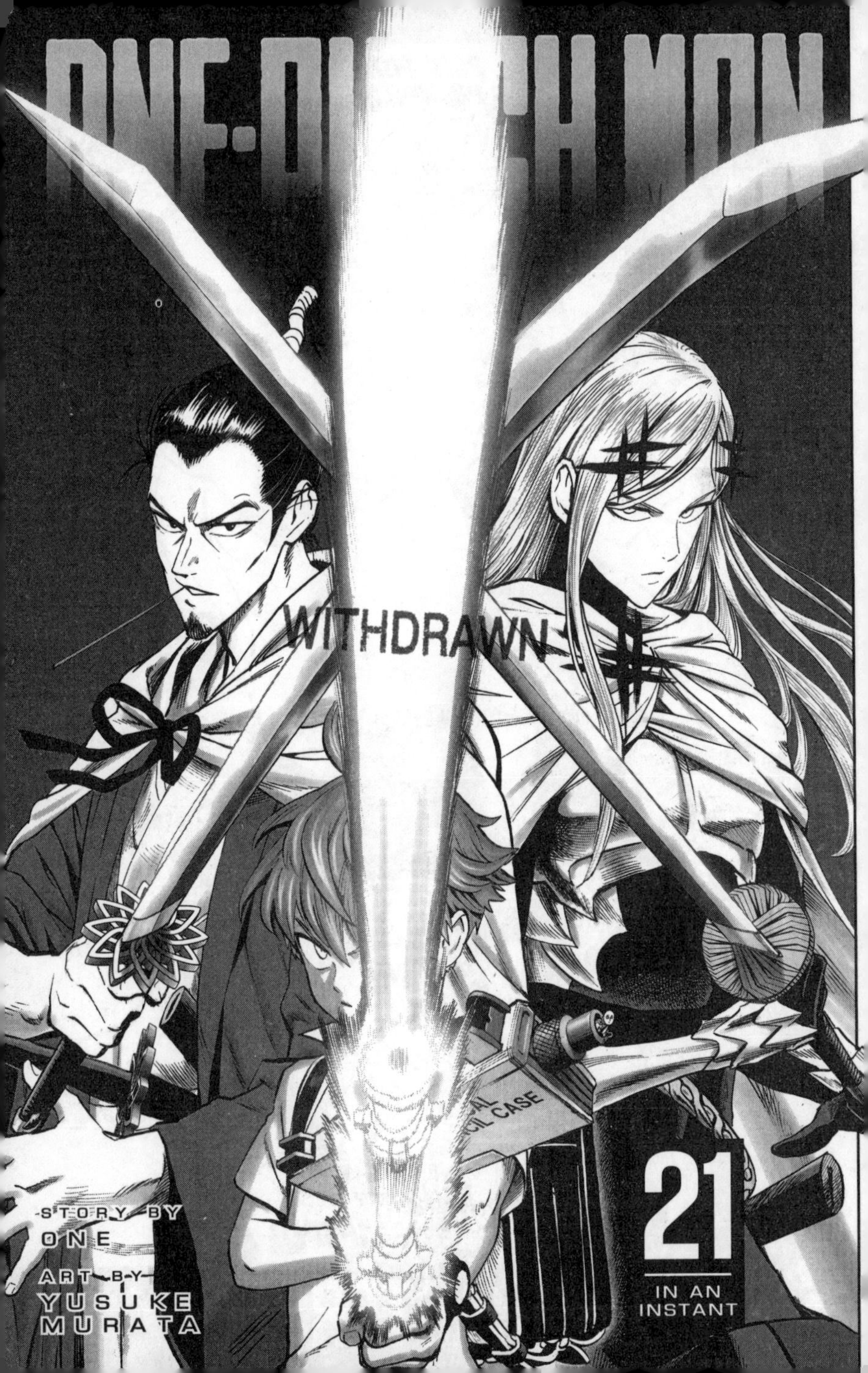
STORY BY
ONE
ART BY
YUSUKE
MURATA
21
IN AN
INSTANT

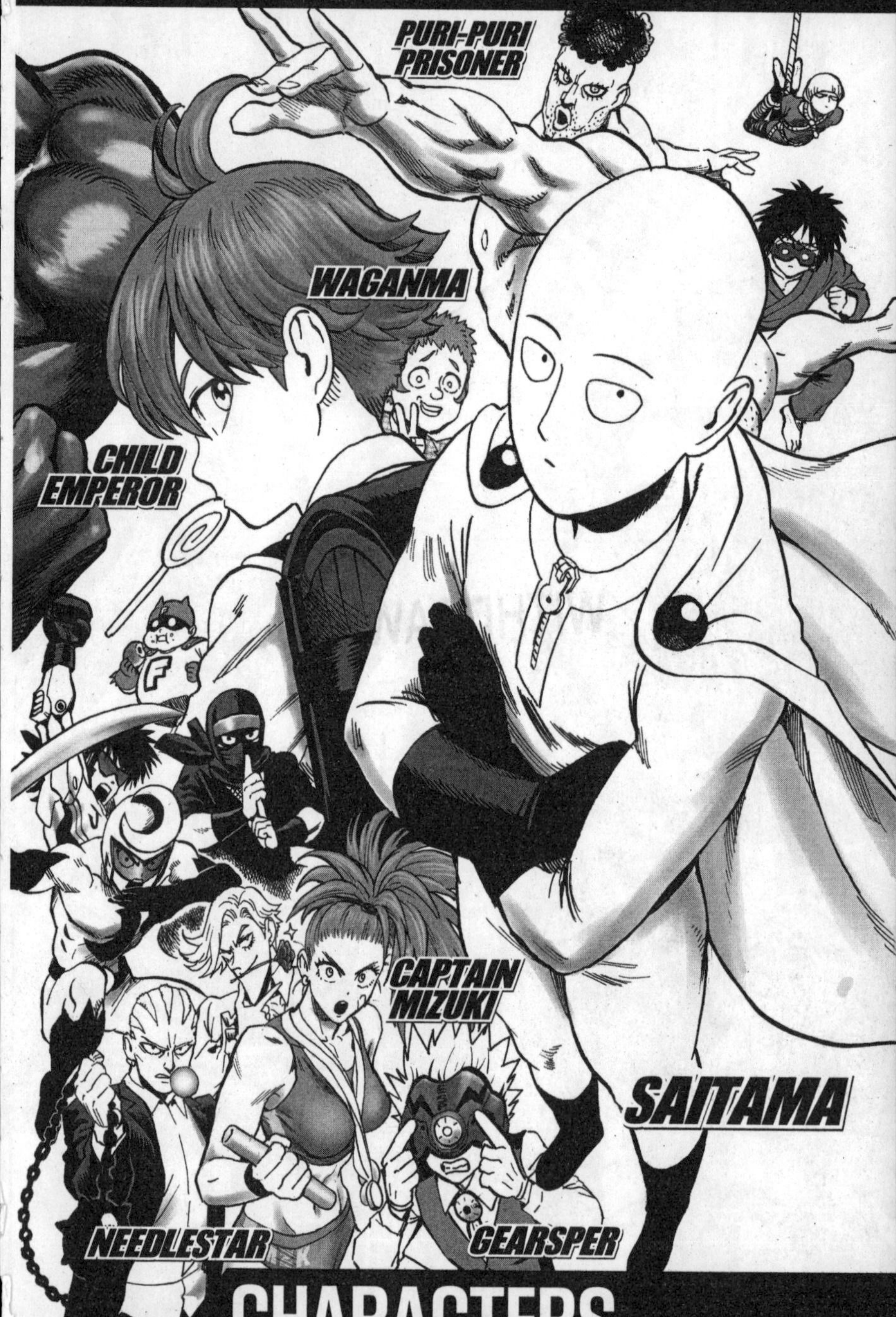
PURI-PURI PRISONER
WAGANMA
CHILD EMPEROR
CAPTAIN MIZUKI
SAITAMA
NEEDLESTAR
GEARSPER

CHARACTERS

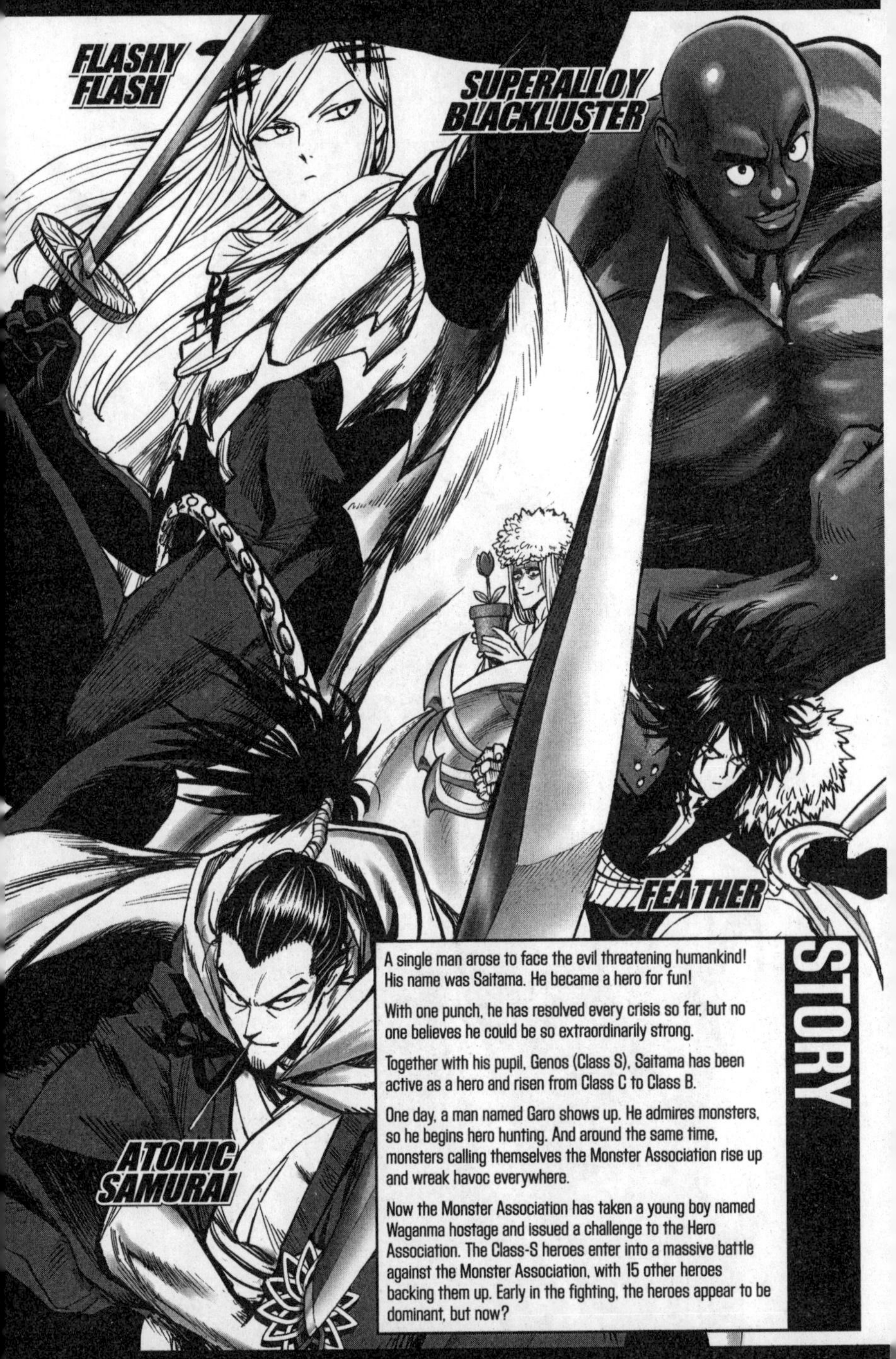
FLASHY FLASH
SUPERALLOY BLACKLUSTER
FEATHER
ATOMIC SAMURAI

STORY

A single man arose to face the evil threatening humankind! His name was Saitama. He became a hero for fun!

With one punch, he has resolved every crisis so far, but no one believes he could be so extraordinarily strong.

Together with his pupil, Genos (Class S), Saitama has been active as a hero and risen from Class C to Class B.

One day, a man named Garo shows up. He admires monsters, so he begins hero hunting. And around the same time, monsters calling themselves the Monster Association rise up and wreak havoc everywhere.

Now the Monster Association has taken a young boy named Waganma hostage and issued a challenge to the Hero Association. The Class-S heroes enter into a massive battle against the Monster Association, with 15 other heroes backing them up. Early in the fighting, the heroes appear to be dominant, but now?

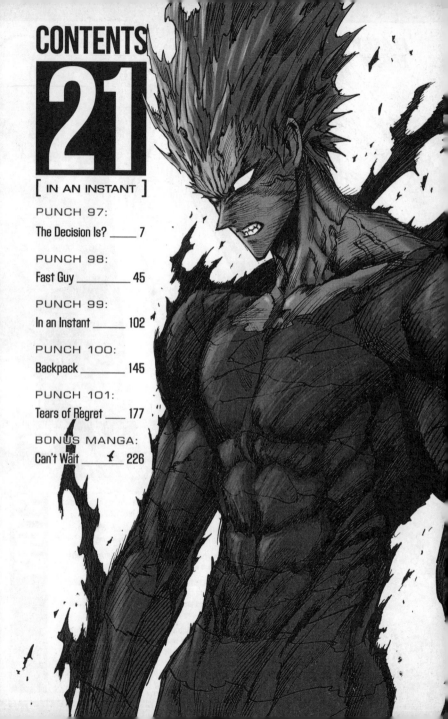

CONTENTS

21

[IN AN INSTANT]

PUNCH 97: THE DECISION IS?

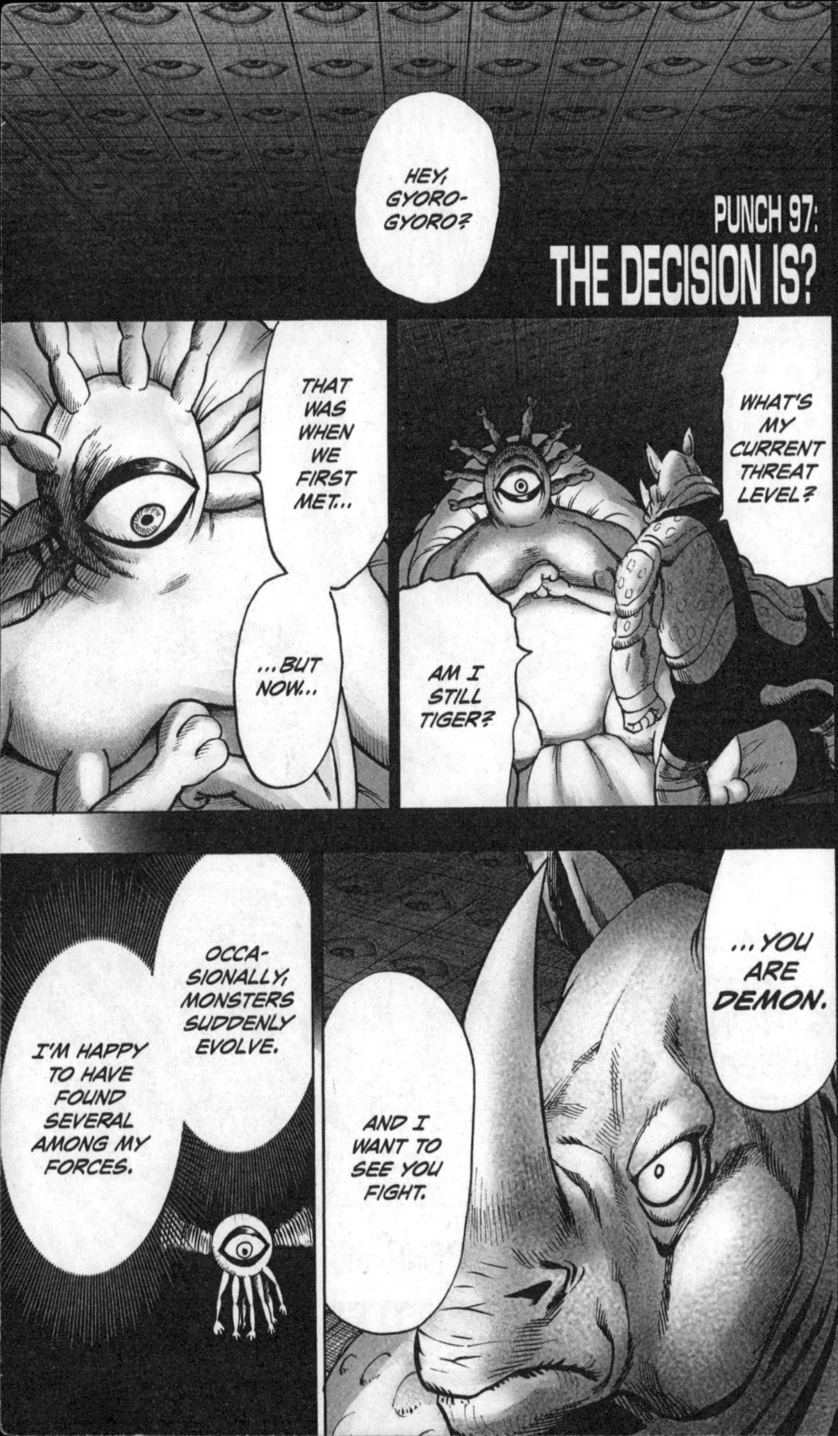
HEY, GYORO-GYORO?
WHAT'S MY CURRENT THREAT LEVEL?
AM I STILL TIGER?
THAT WAS WHEN WE FIRST MET...
...BUT NOW...
...YOU ARE DEMON.
AND I WANT TO SEE YOU FIGHT.
OCCA-SIONALLY, MONSTERS SUDDENLY EVOLVE.
I'M HAPPY TO HAVE FOUND SEVERAL AMONG MY FORCES.

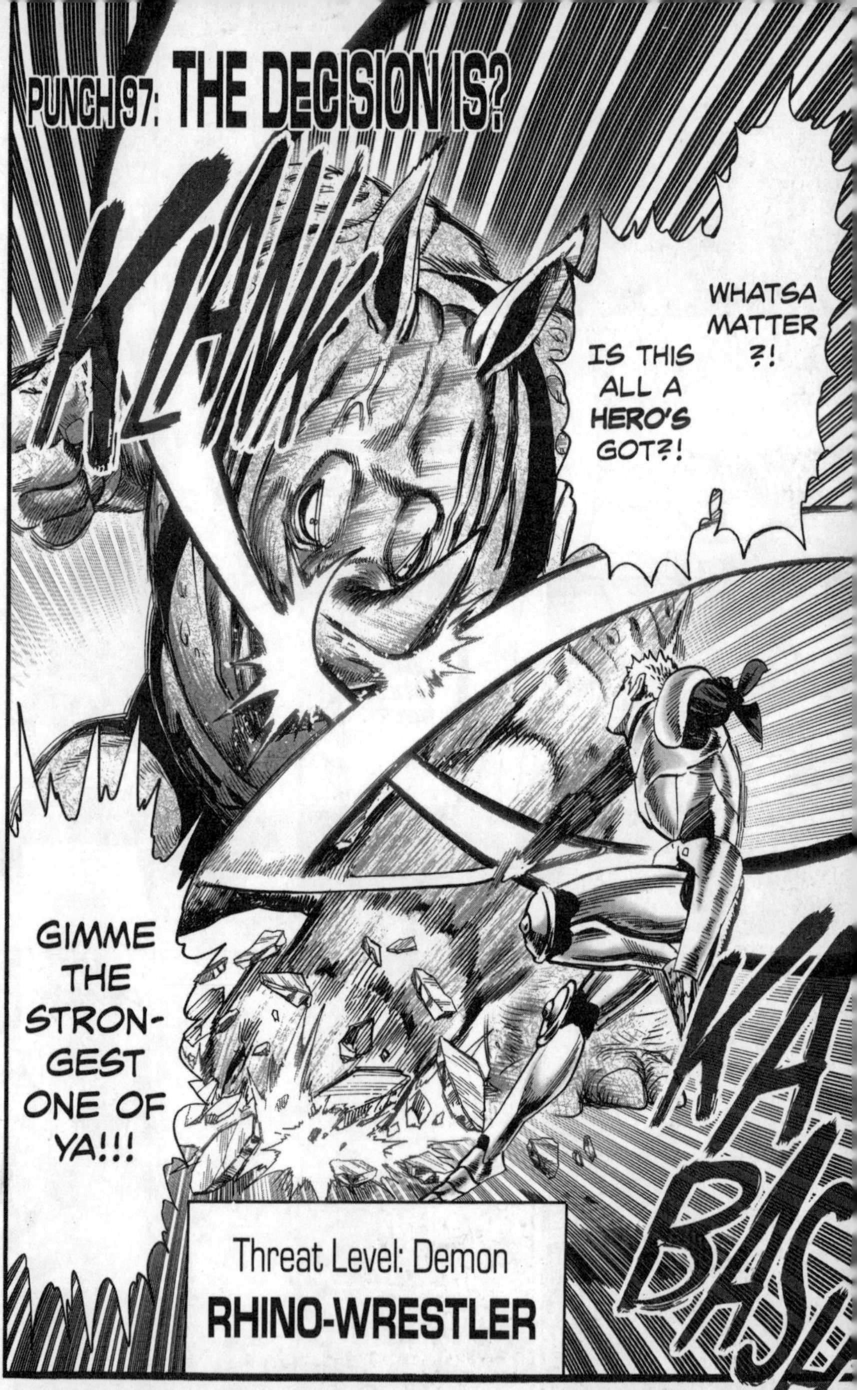
PUNCH 97: THE DECISION IS?
WHATSA MATTER ?!
IS THIS ALL A HERO'S GOT?!
GIMME THE STRON-GEST ONE OF YA!!!
Threat Level: Demon
RHINO-WRESTLER

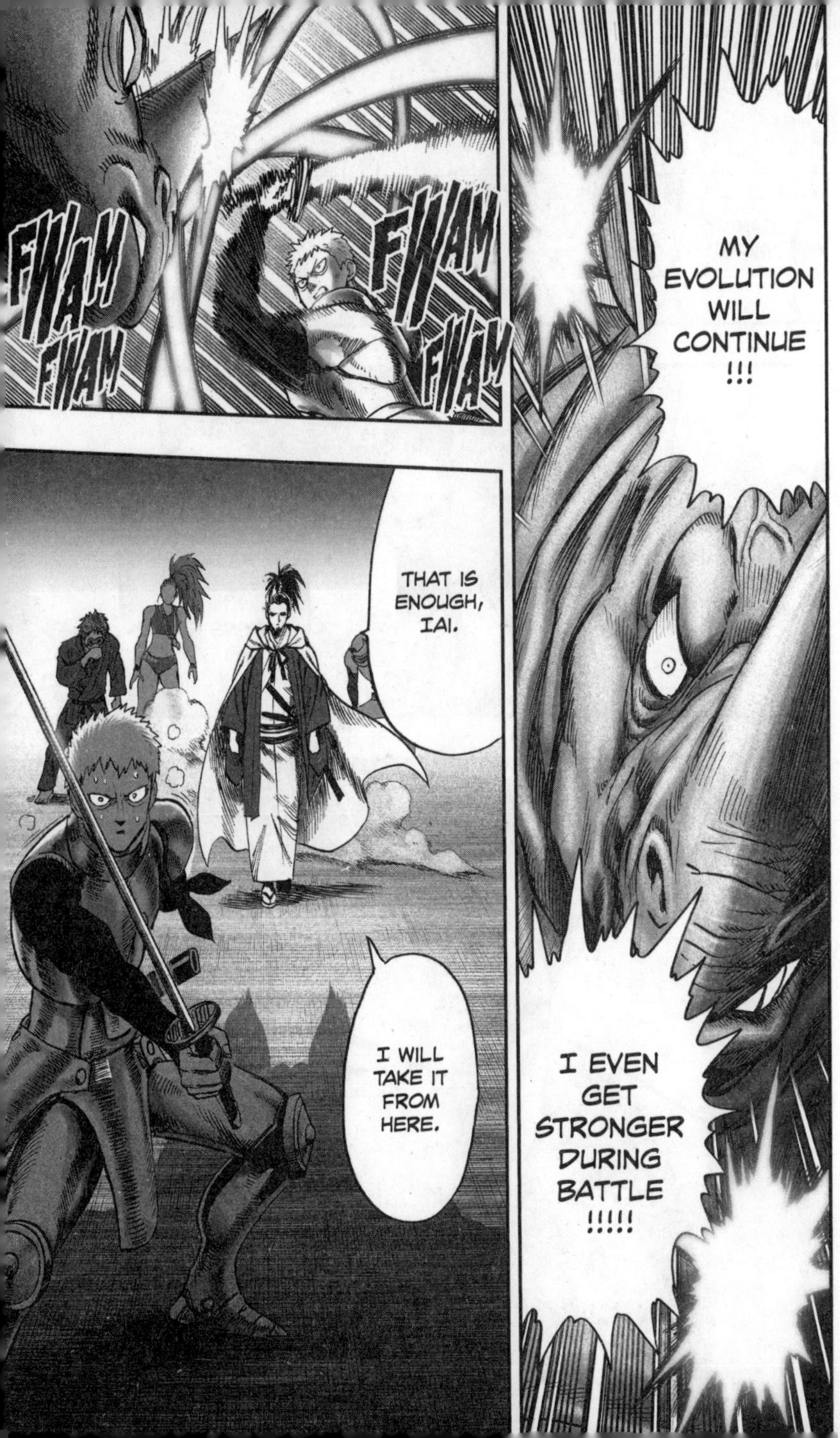
MY EVOLUTION WILL CONTINUE !!!
I EVEN GET STRONGER DURING BATTLE !!!!!
FWAM
FWAM
FWAM
FWAM
THAT IS ENOUGH, IAI.
I WILL TAKE IT FROM HERE.

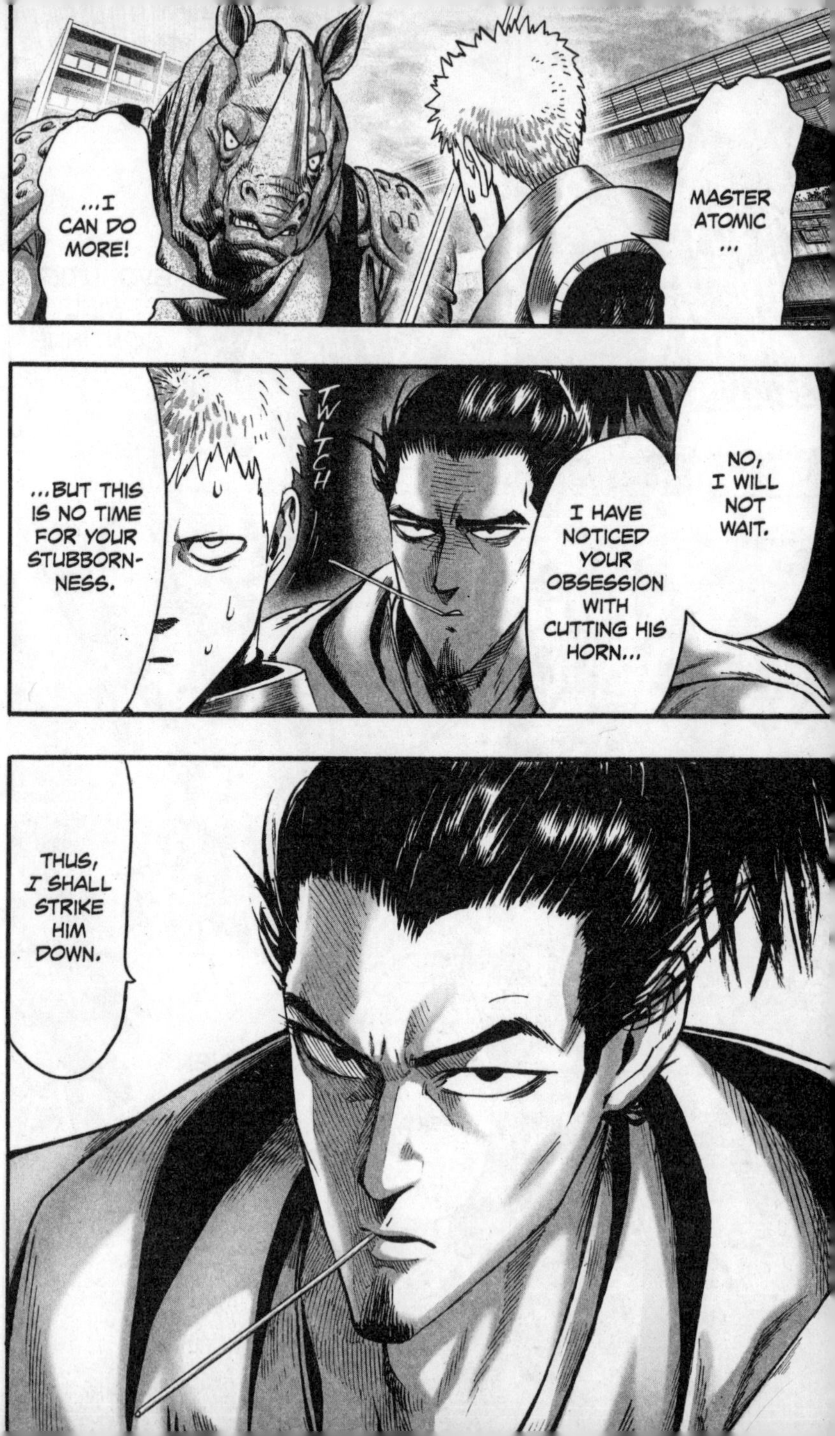
MASTER ATOMIC...
...I CAN DO MORE!
NO, I WILL NOT WAIT.
I HAVE NOTICED YOUR OBSESSION WITH CUTTING HIS HORN...
TWITCH
...BUT THIS IS NO TIME FOR YOUR STUBBORN-NESS.
THUS, I SHALL STRIKE HIM DOWN.

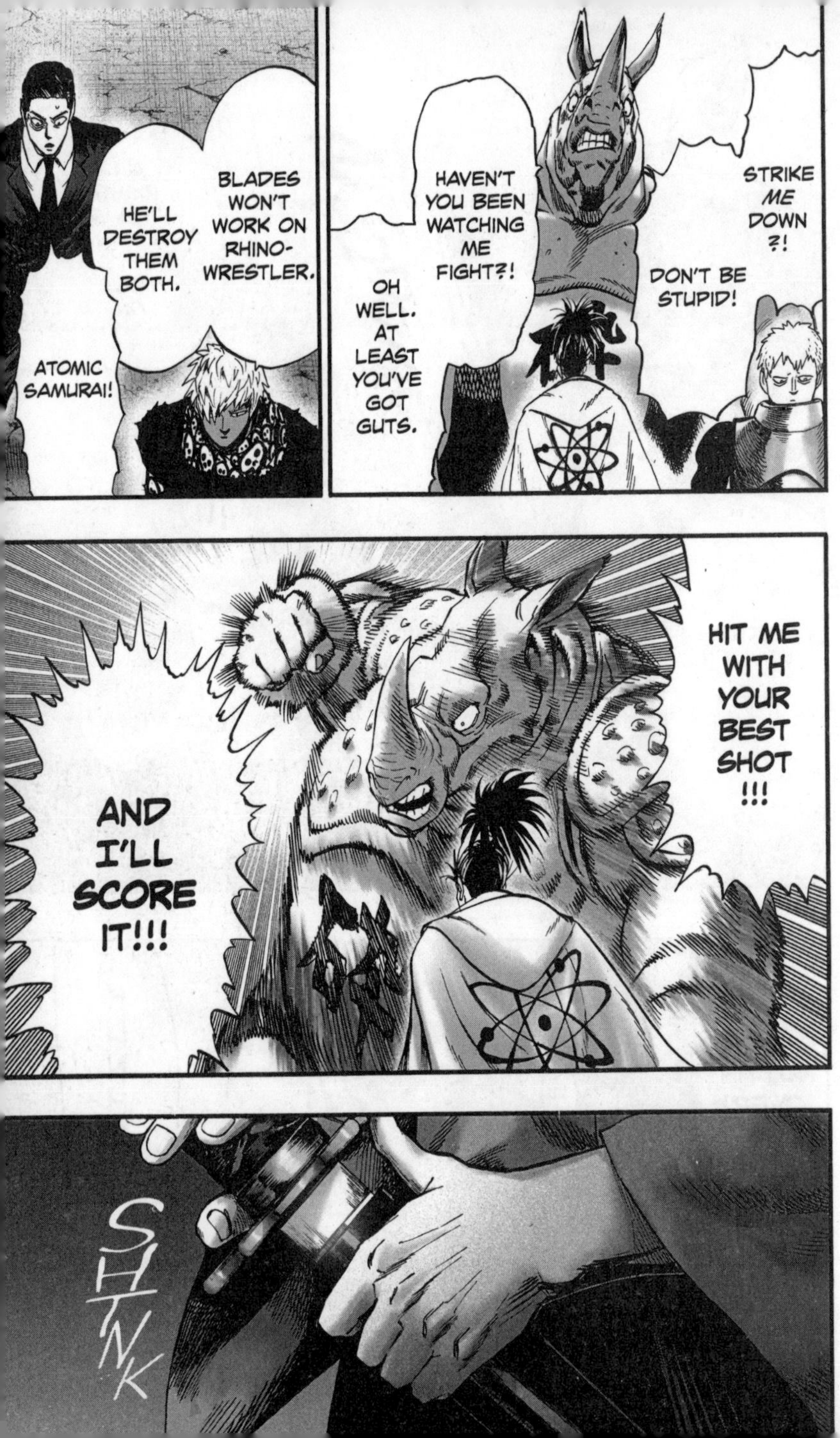
STRIKE *ME* DOWN?!
DON'T BE STUPID!
HAVEN'T YOU BEEN WATCHING ME FIGHT?!
OH WELL. AT LEAST YOU'VE GOT GUTS.
BLADES WON'T WORK ON RHINO-WRESTLER.
HE'LL DESTROY THEM BOTH.
ATOMIC SAMURAI!
HIT ME WITH YOUR BEST SHOT!!!
AND I'LL SCORE IT!!!
SHTNK

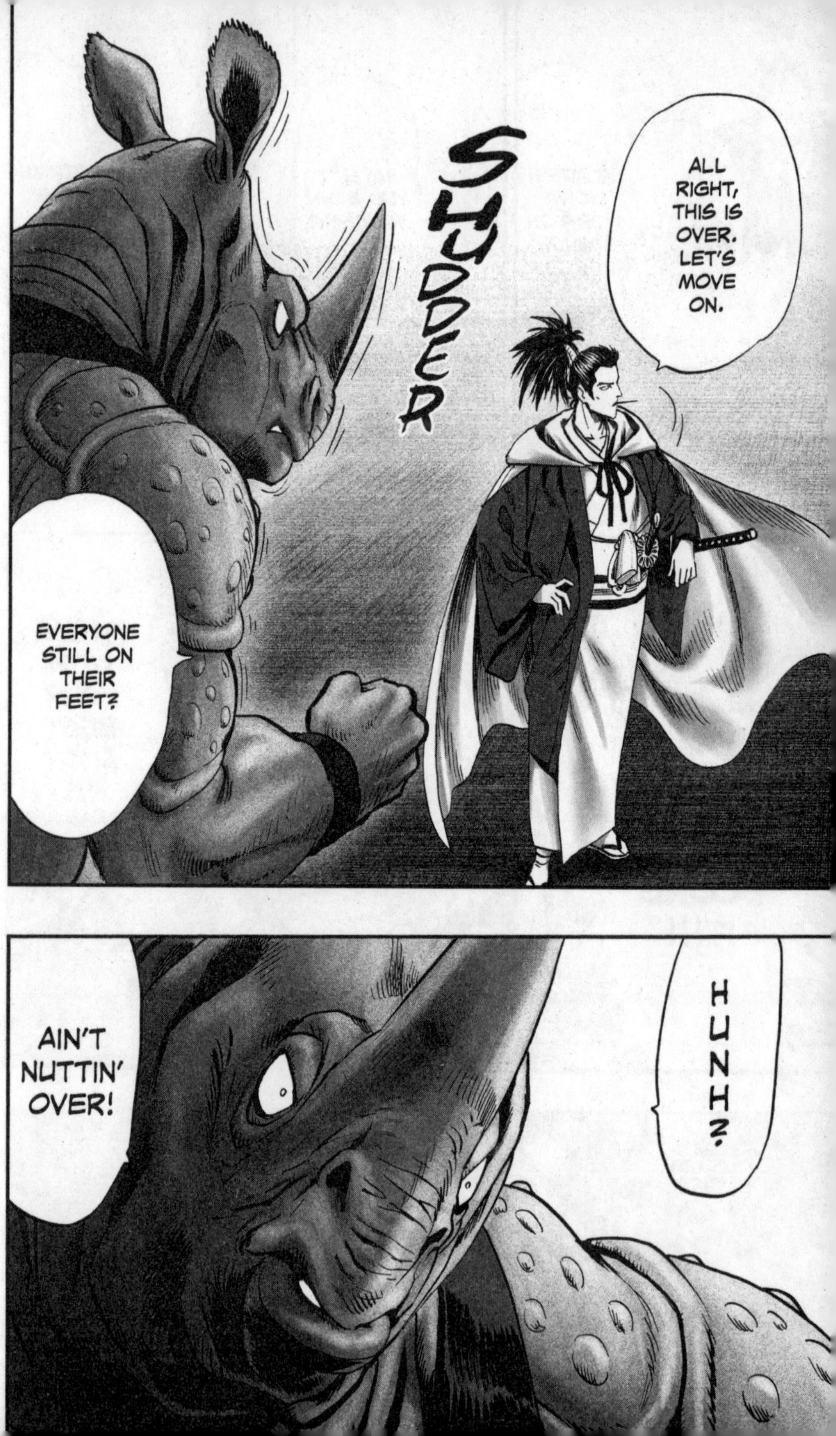
ALL RIGHT, THIS IS OVER. LET'S MOVE ON.
SHUDDER
EVERYONE STILL ON THEIR FEET?
HUNH?
AIN'T NUTTIN' OVER!

HEY!

DON'T IGNORE ME!!!

HM?

OH... RIGHT.

WHAT'S MY SCORE?

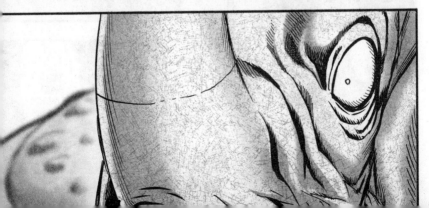

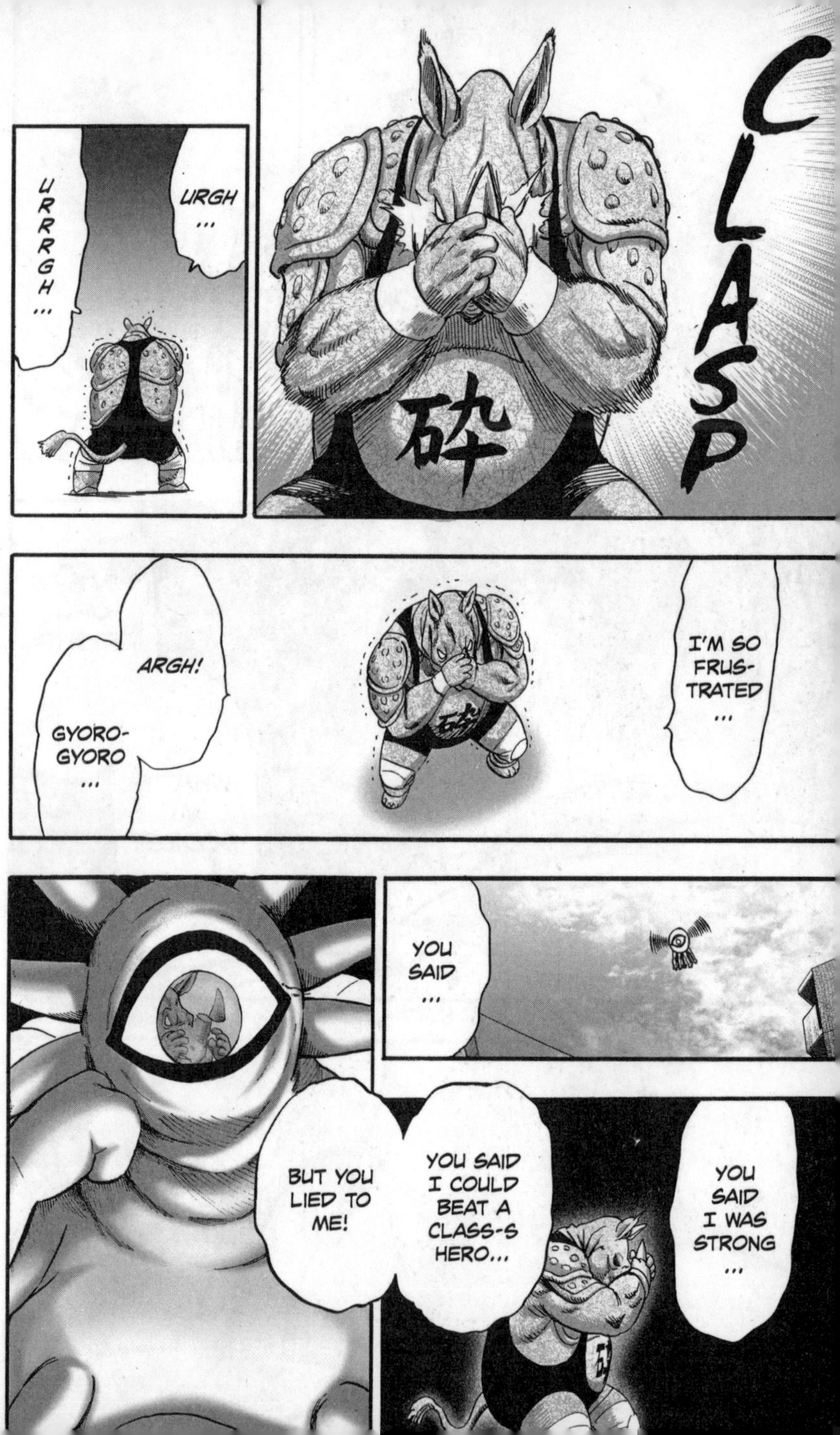
CLASP
碎
URGH...
URRRGH...
I'M SO FRUS-TRATED...
ARGH!
GYORO-GYORO...
YOU SAID...
YOU SAID I WAS STRONG...
YOU SAID I COULD BEAT A CLASS-S HERO...
BUT YOU LIED TO ME!

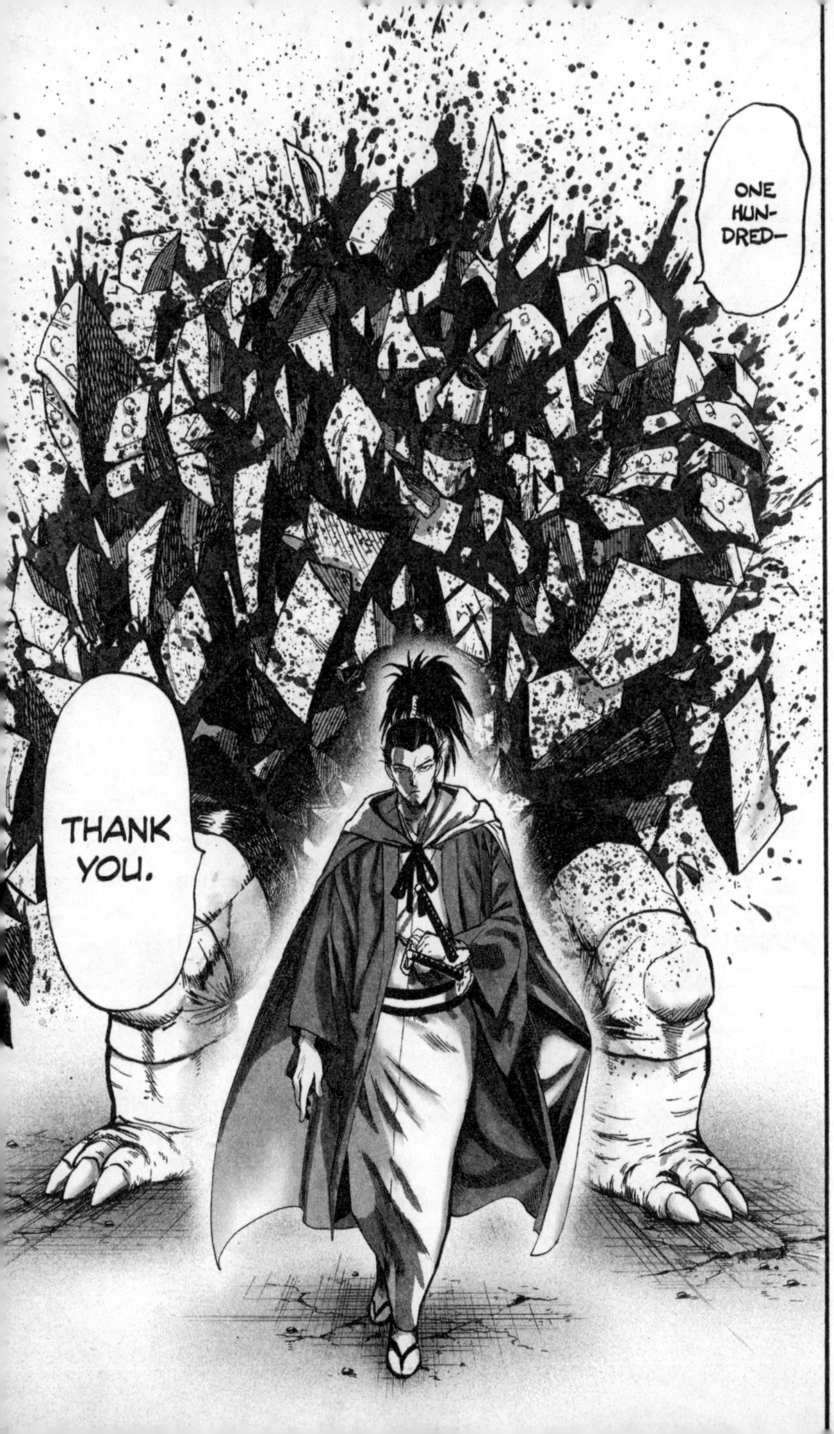
ONE HUN-DRED-
THANK YOU.

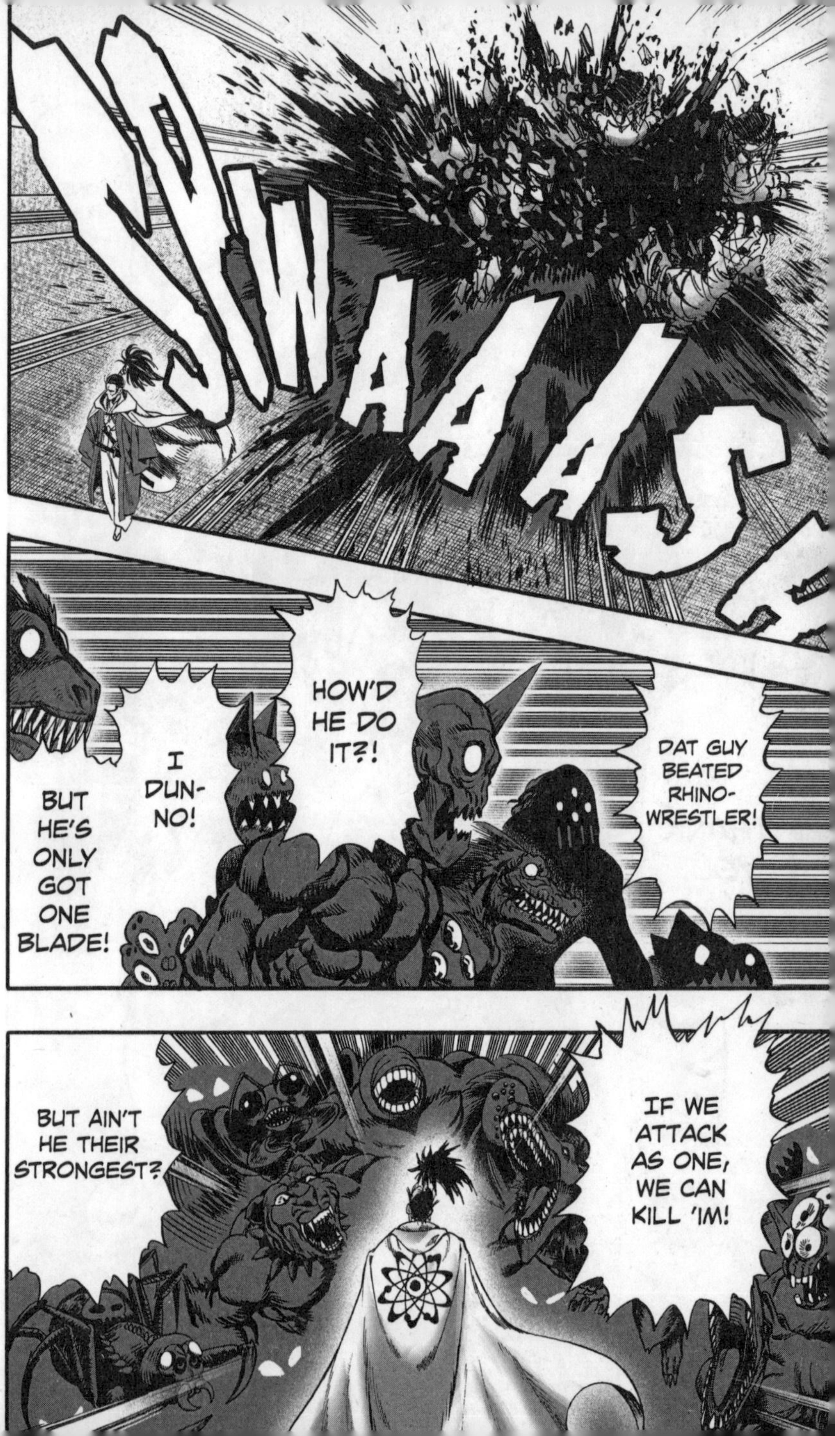
DAT GUY BEATED RHINO-WRESTLER!
HOW'D HE DO IT?!
I DUN-NO!
BUT HE'S ONLY GOT ONE BLADE!
IF WE ATTACK AS ONE, WE CAN KILL 'IM!
BUT AIN'T HE THEIR STRONGEST?

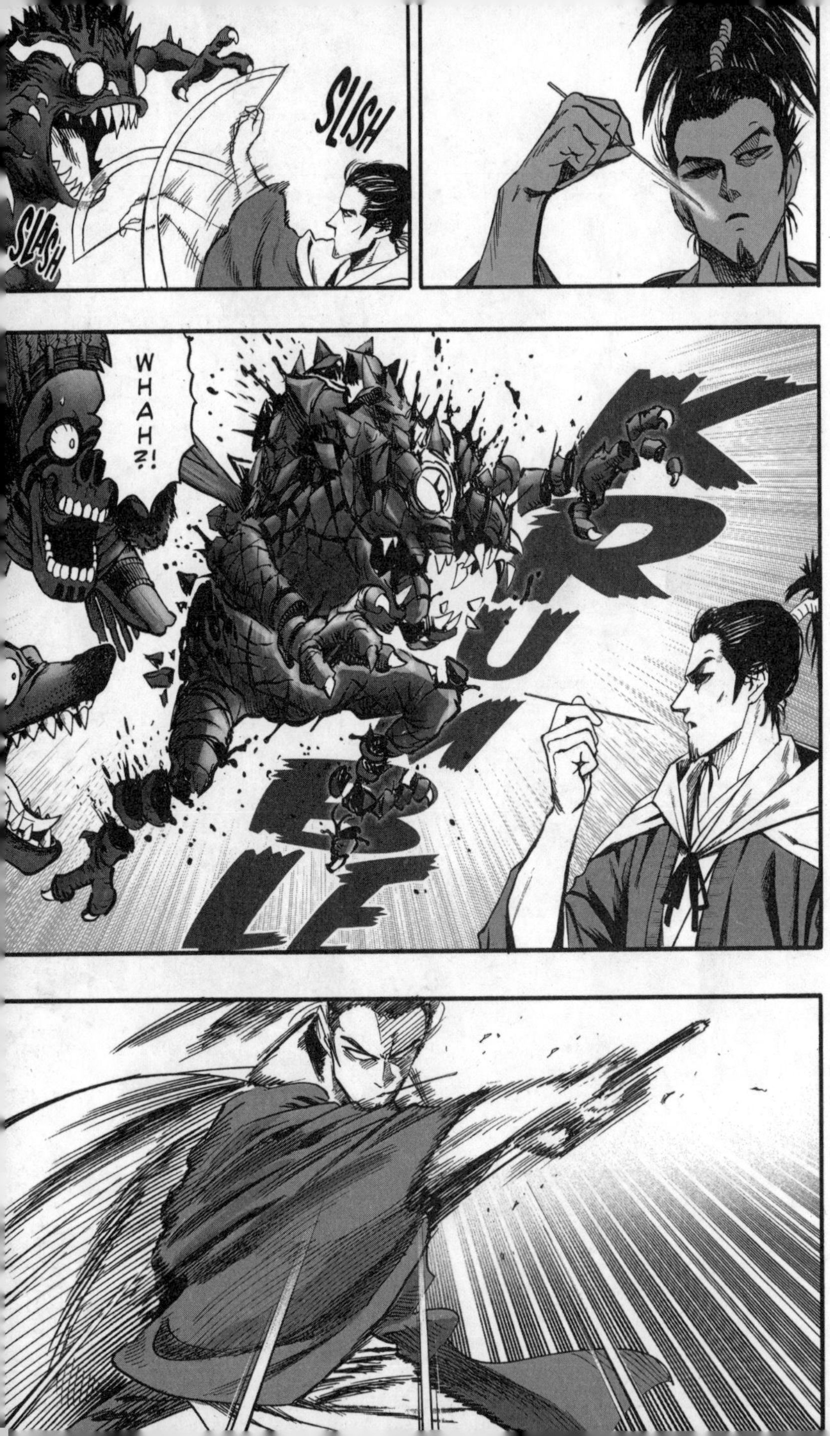
SLISH
SLASH
KRUMBLE
WHAHZ?!

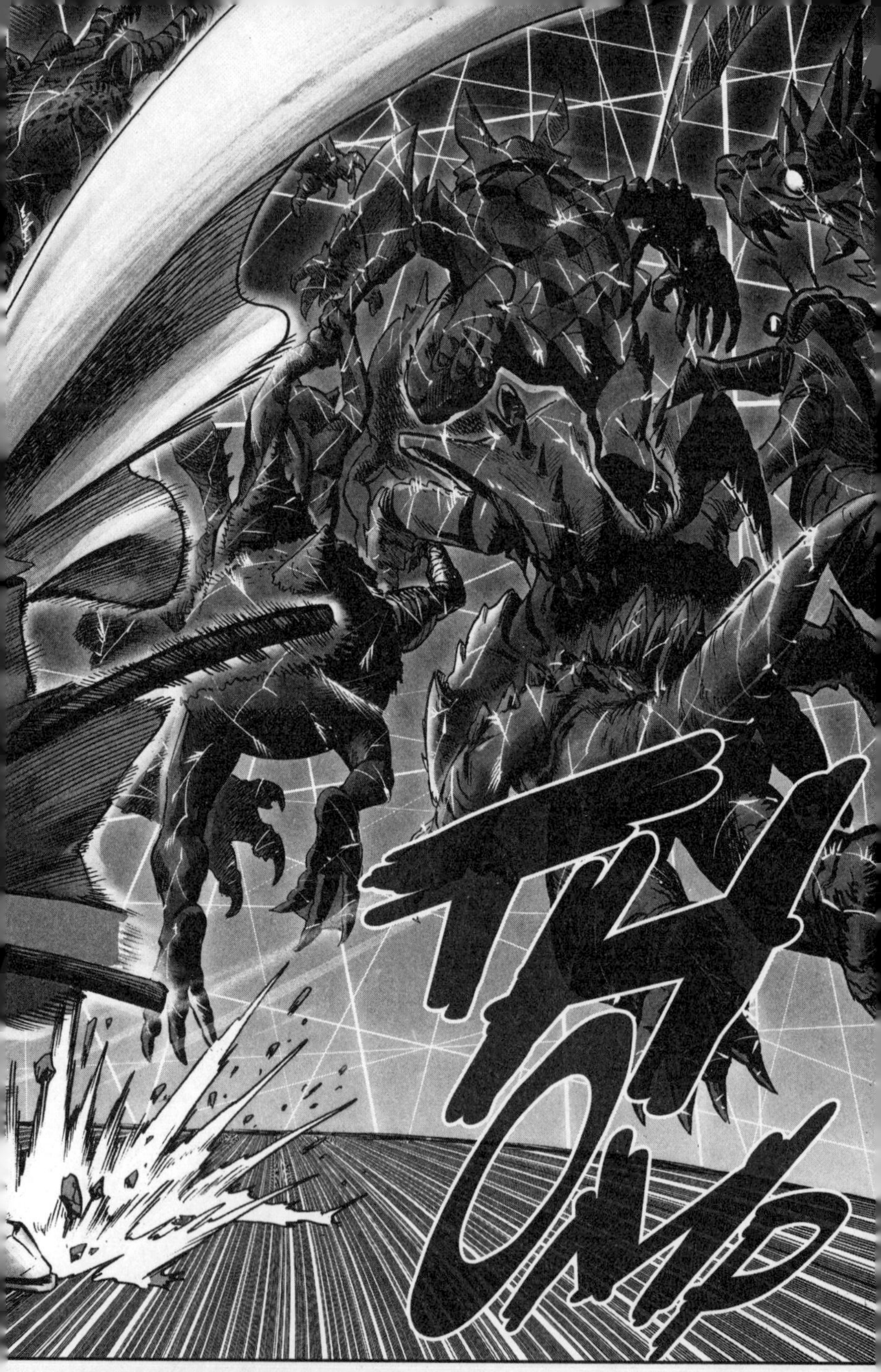
THOMP

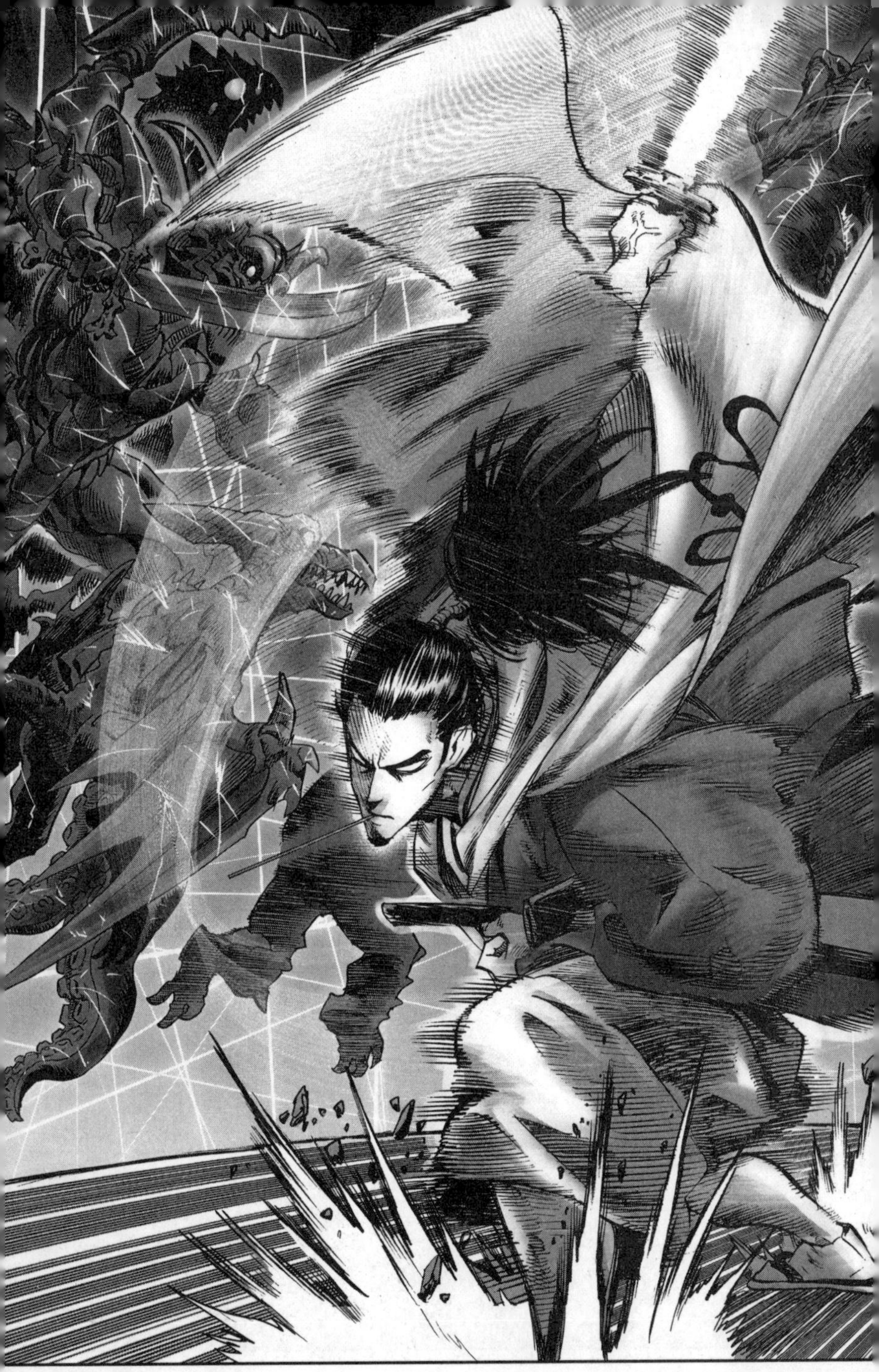

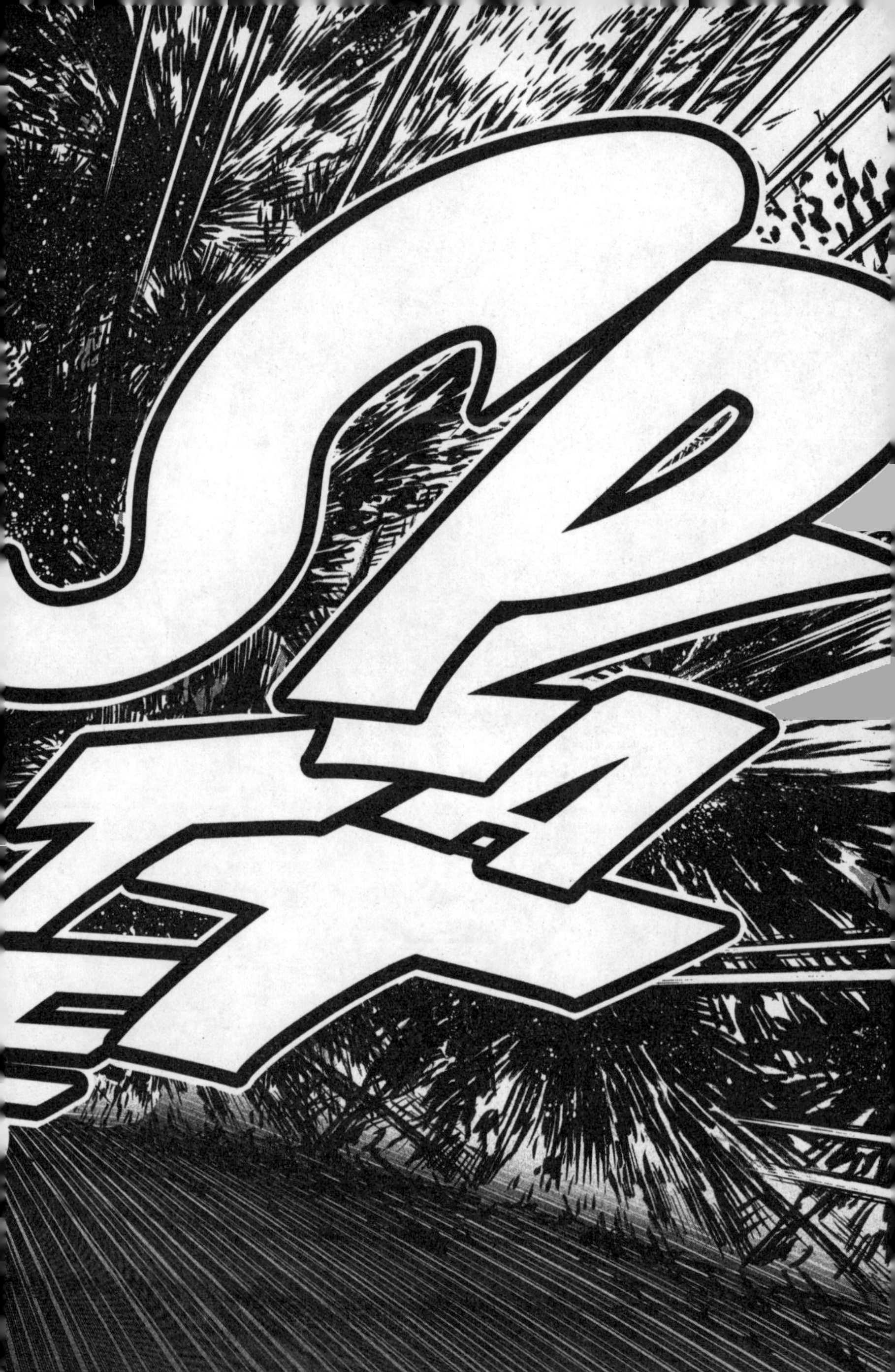

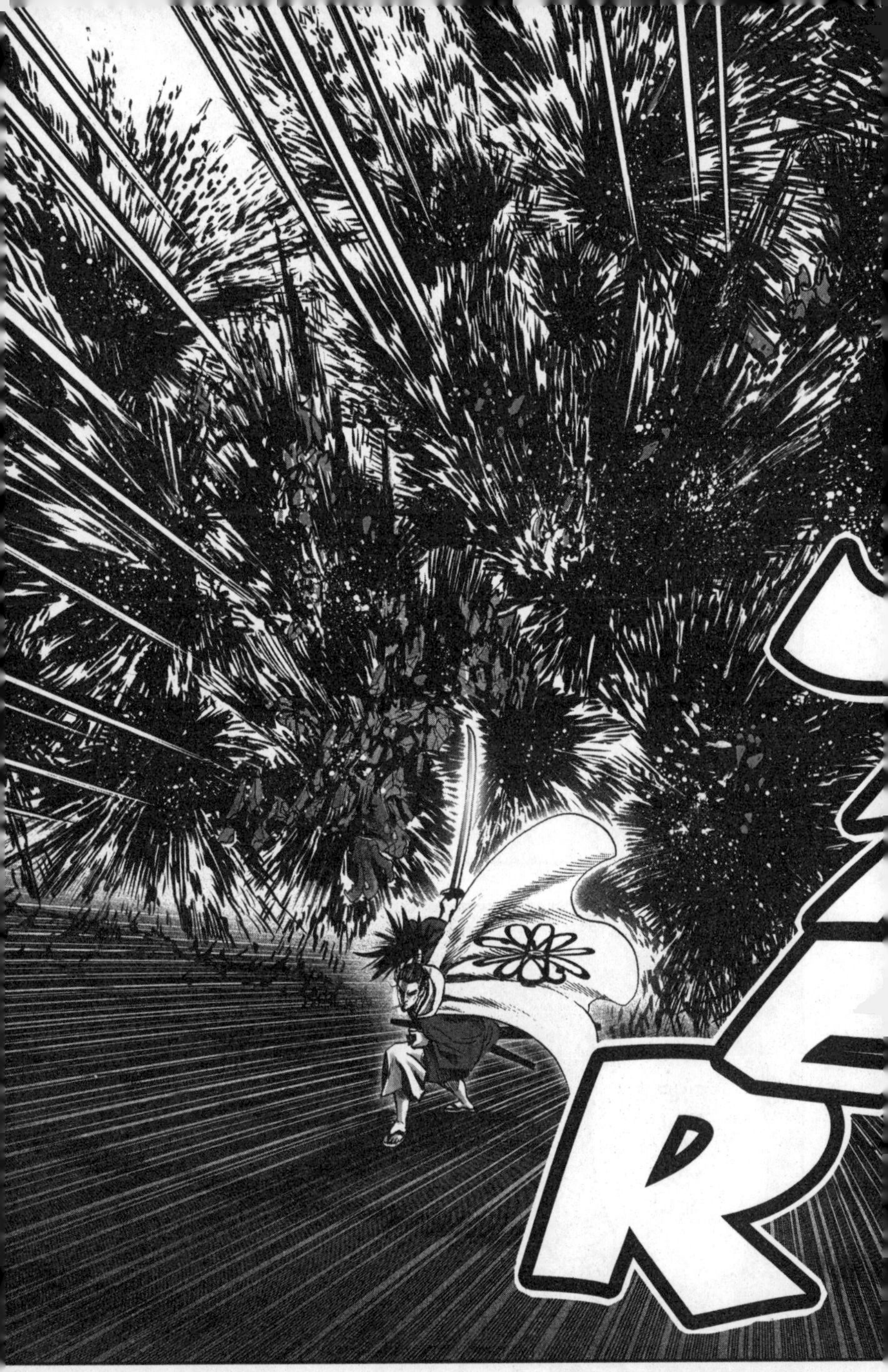

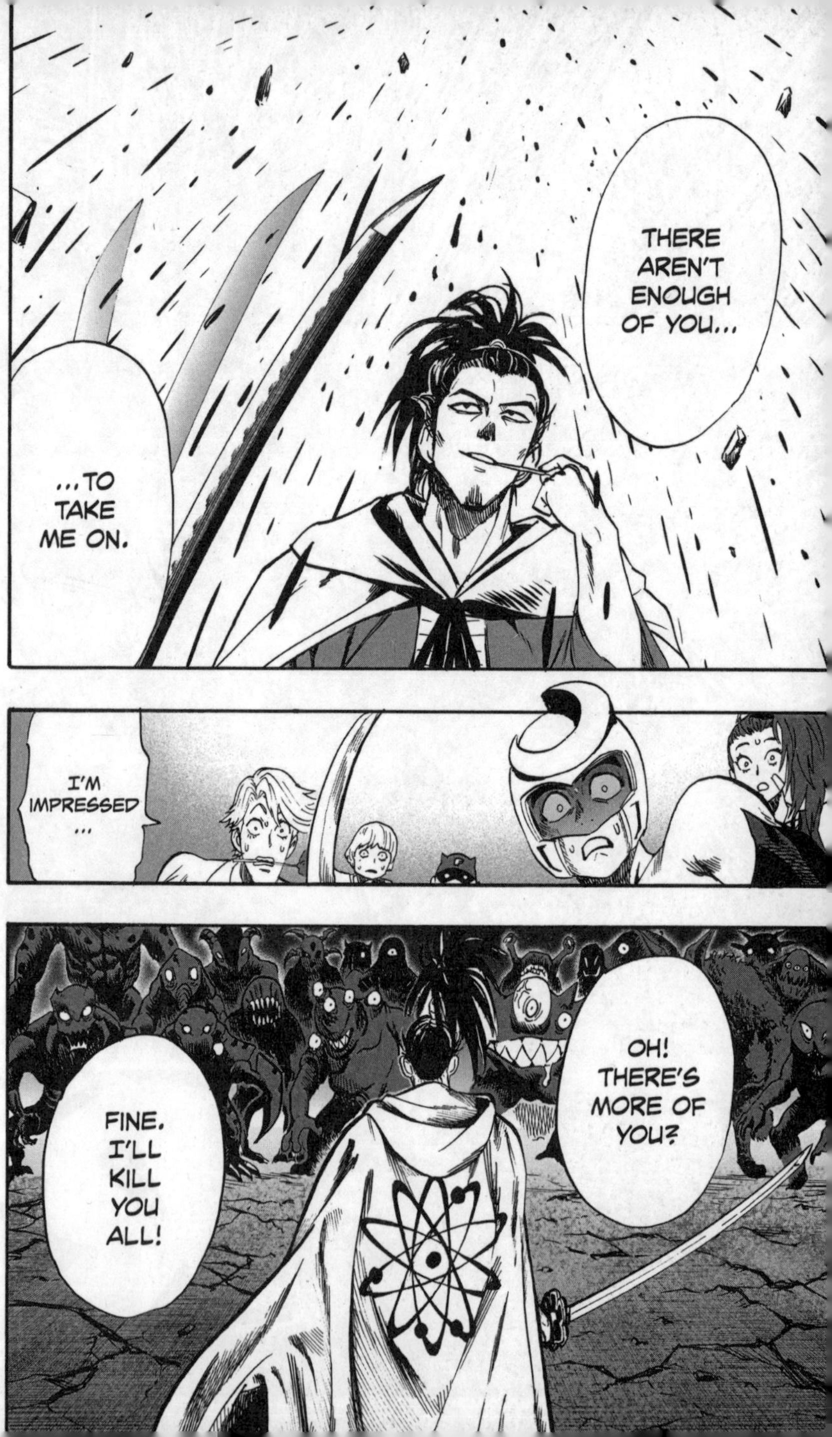
THERE AREN'T ENOUGH OF YOU...
...TO TAKE ME ON.
I'M IMPRESSED ...
OH! THERE'S MORE OF YOU?
FINE. I'LL KILL YOU ALL!

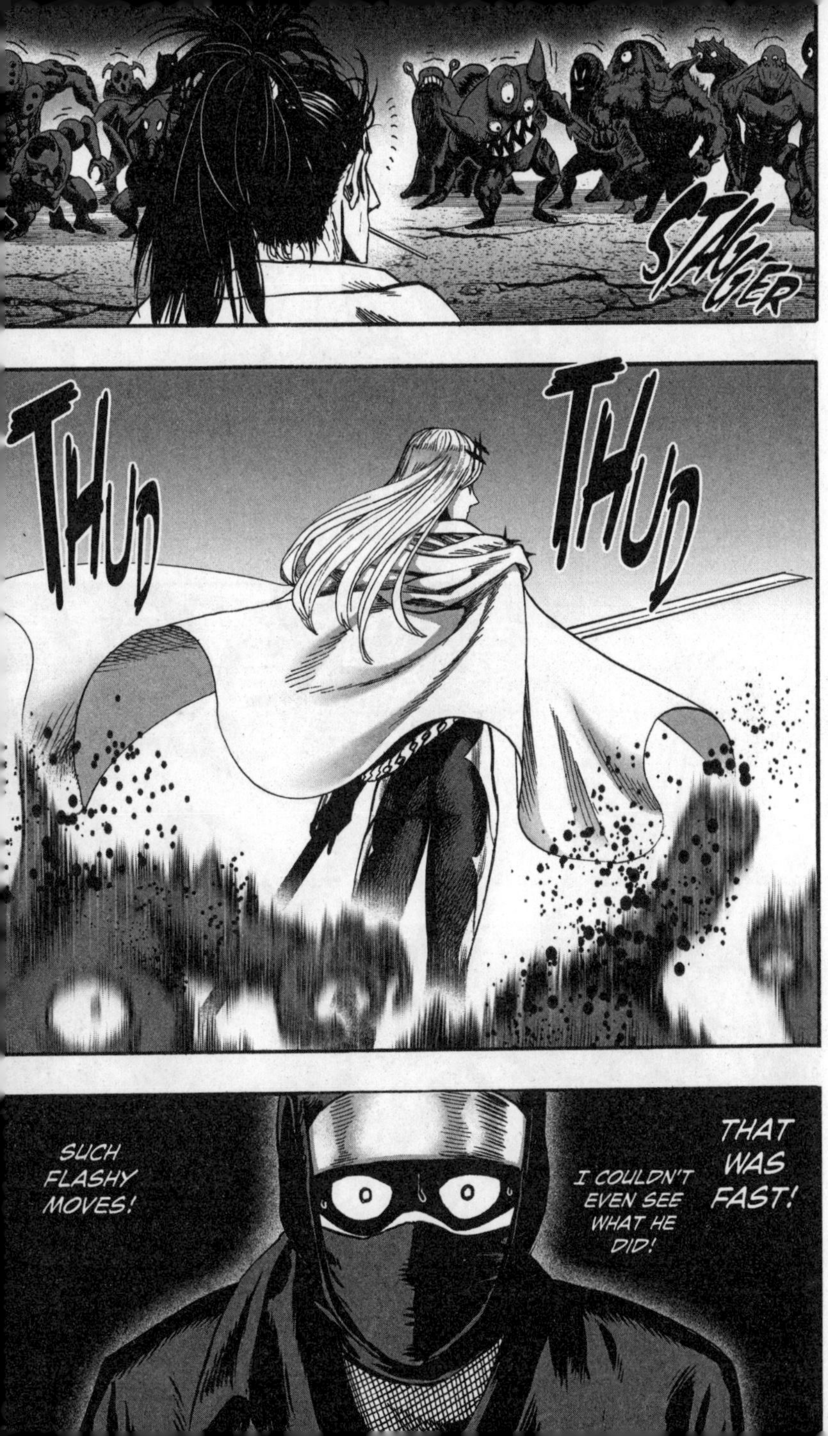
STAGGER
THUD
THUD
THAT WAS FAST!
I COULDN'T EVEN SEE WHAT HE DID!
SUCH FLASHY MOVES!

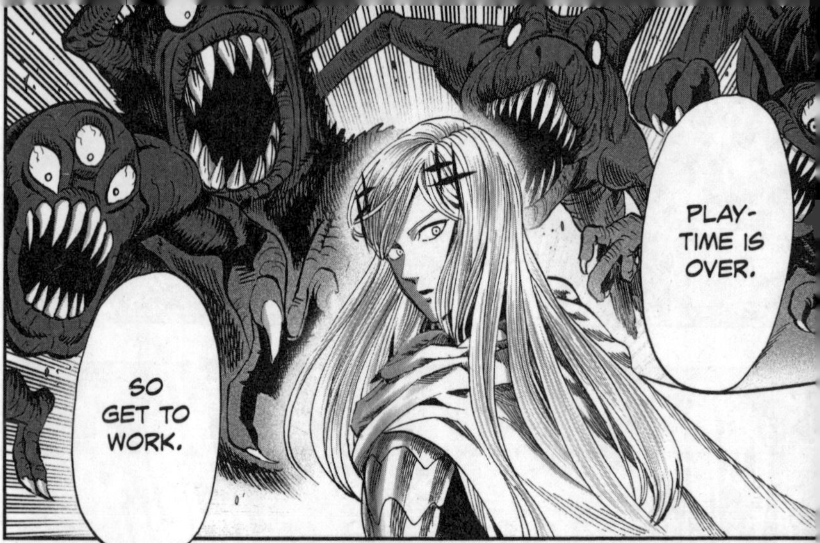
PLAY-TIME IS OVER.
SO GET TO WORK.
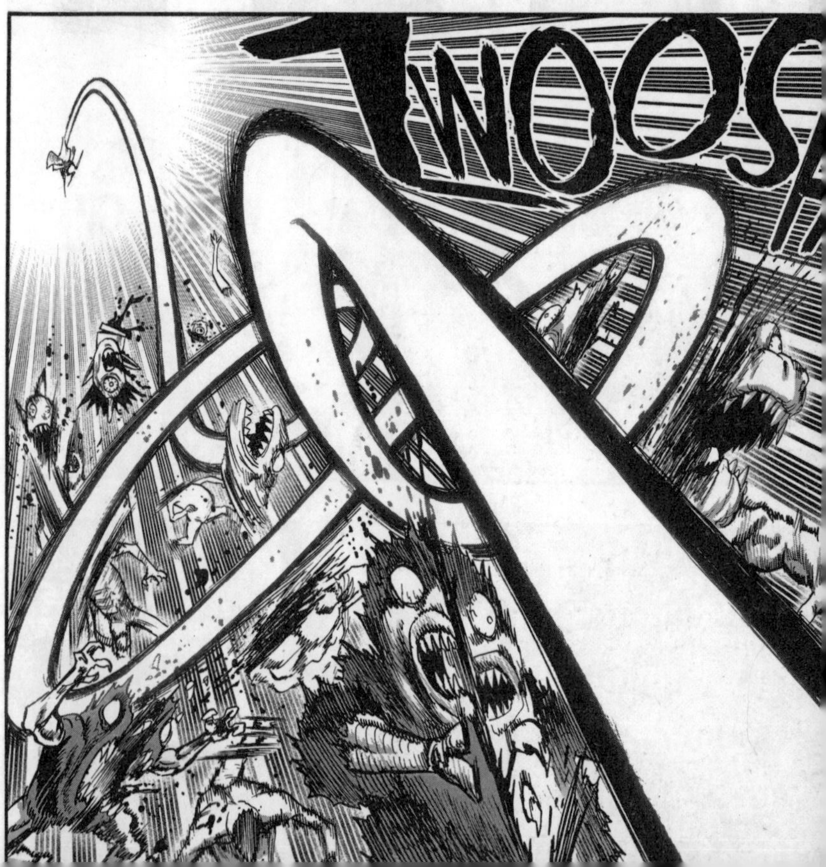
WOOS

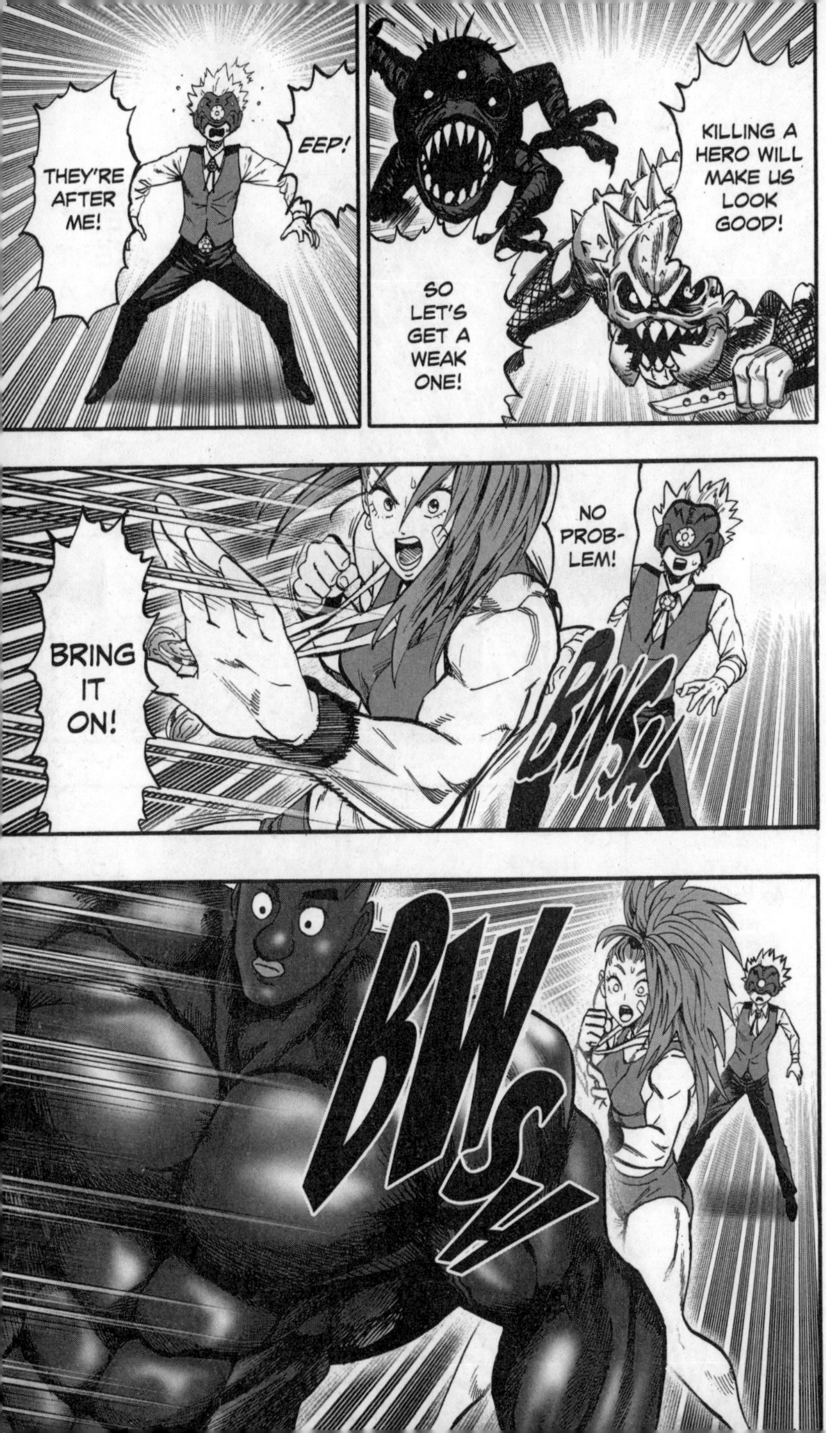
KILLING A HERO WILL MAKE US LOOK GOOD!
SO LET'S GET A WEAK ONE!
EEP!
THEY'RE AFTER ME!
NO PROB-LEM!
BRING IT ON!

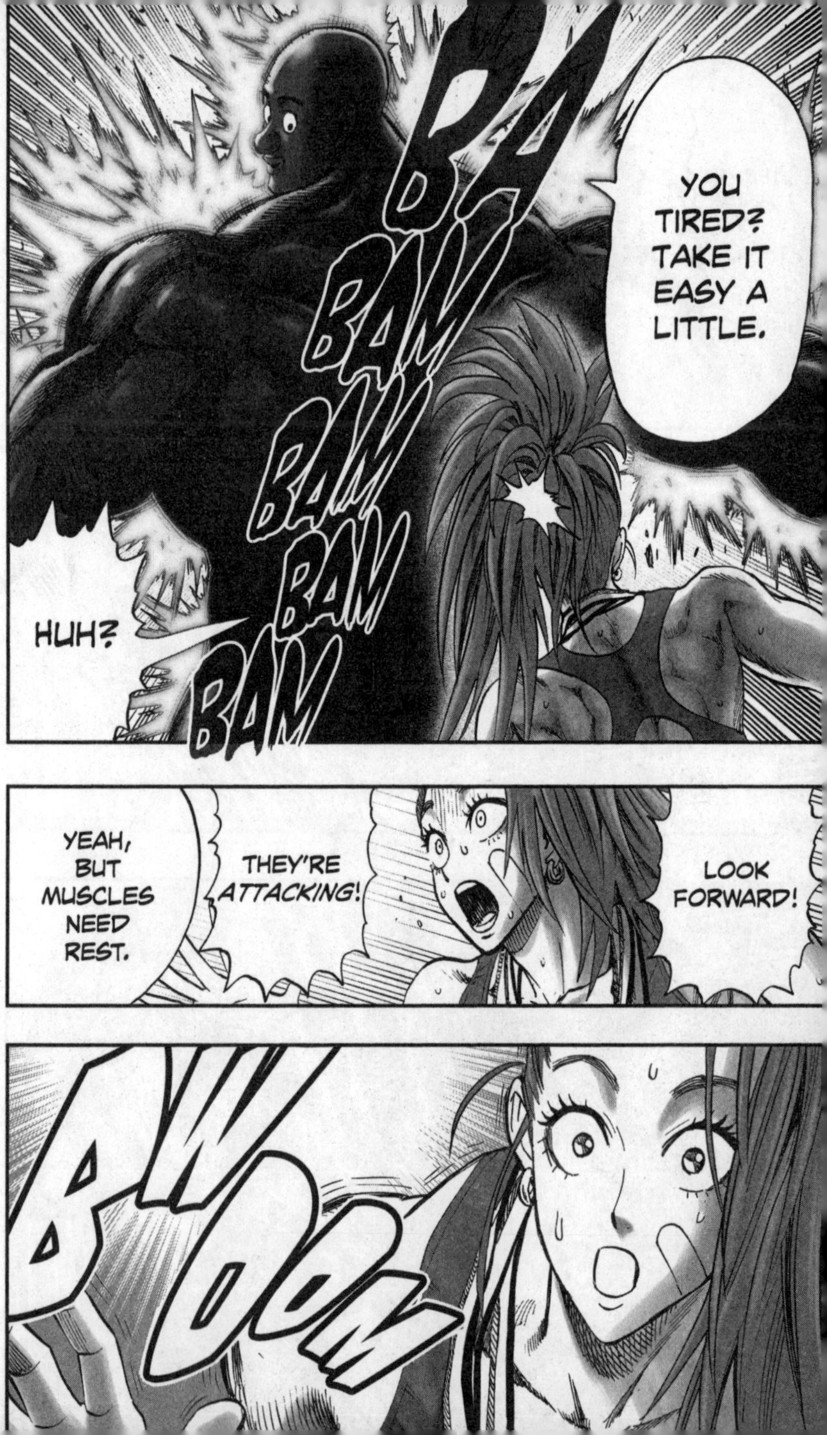
YOU TIRED? TAKE IT EASY A LITTLE.
BA BAM BAM BAM BAM BAM
HUH?
LOOK FORWARD!
THEY'RE ATTACKING!
YEAH, BUT MUSCLES NEED REST.
BWOOM

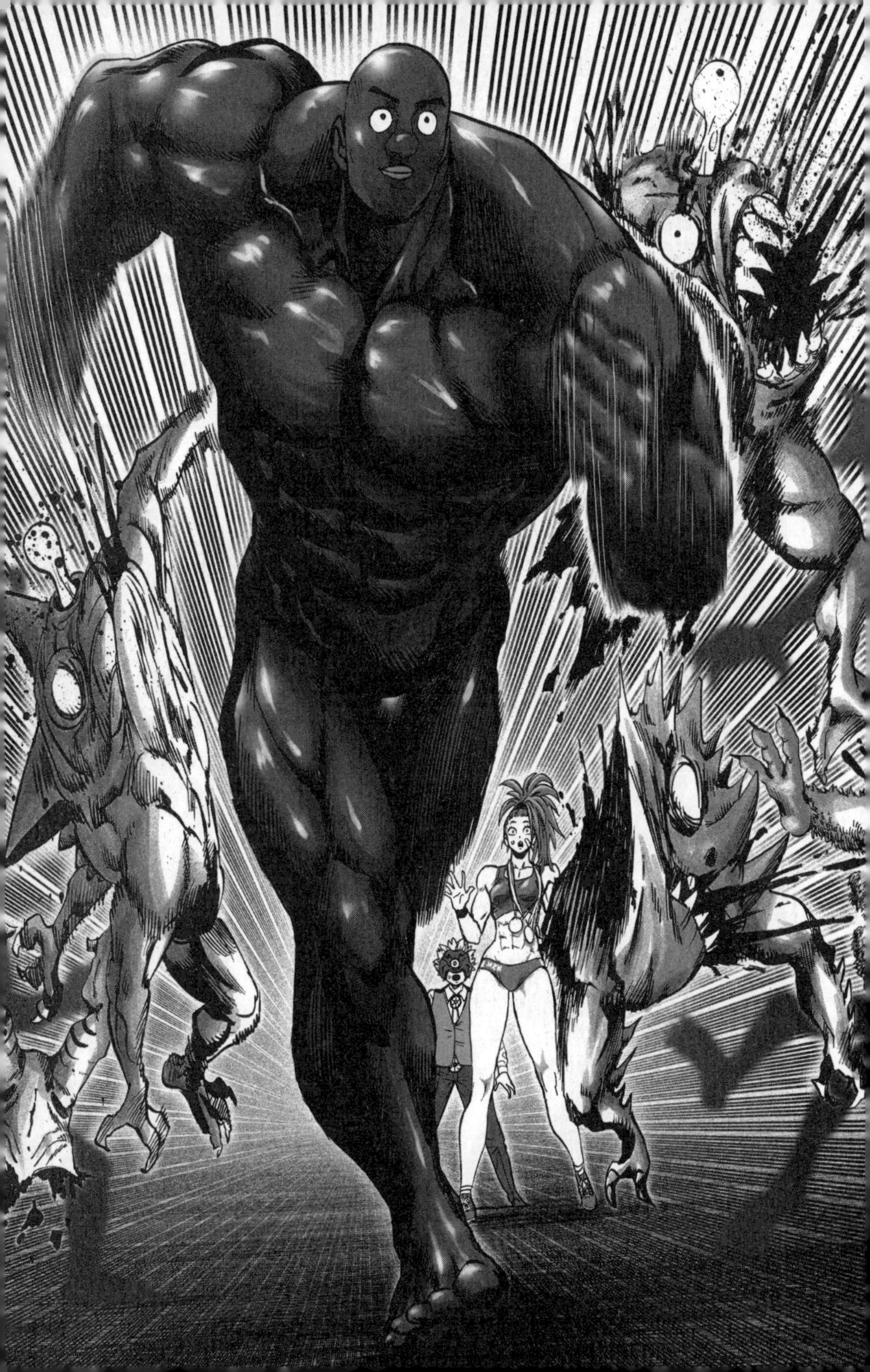

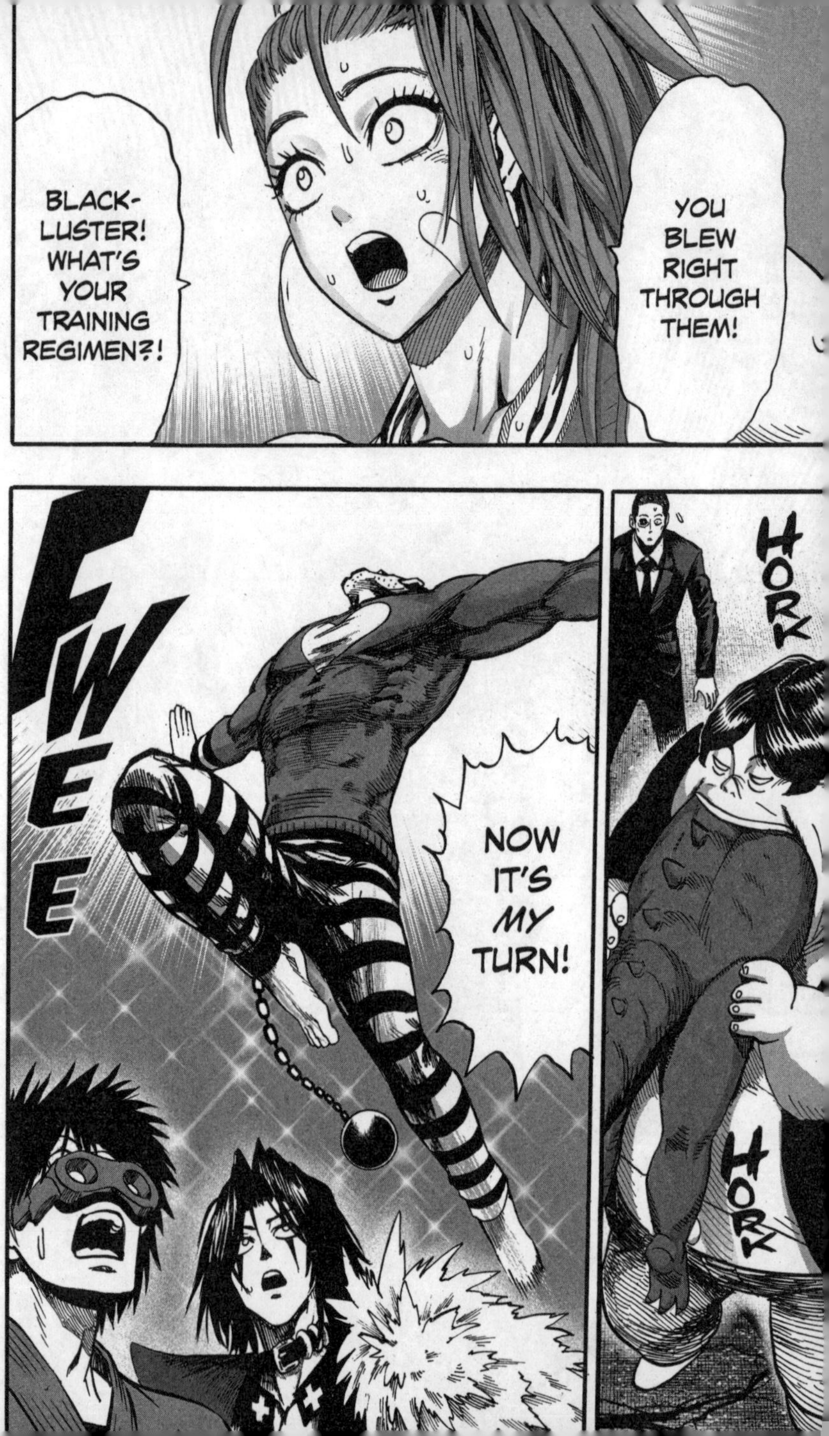
YOU BLEW RIGHT THROUGH THEM!
BLACK-LUSTER! WHAT'S YOUR TRAINING REGIMEN?!
HORK
HORK
FWEEE
NOW IT'S MY TURN!

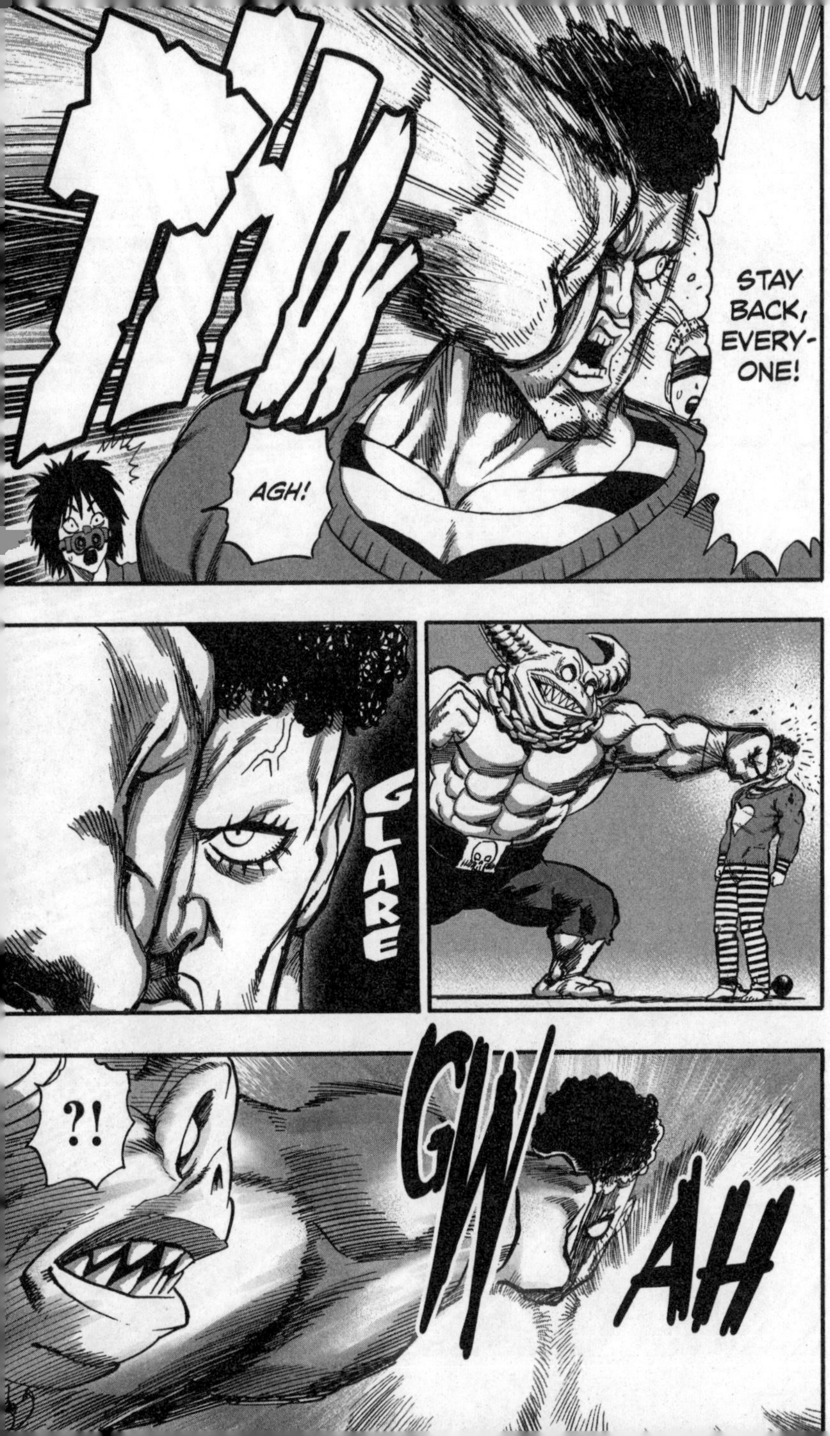
STAY BACK, EVERY-ONE!
AGH!
GLARE
GWAH
?!

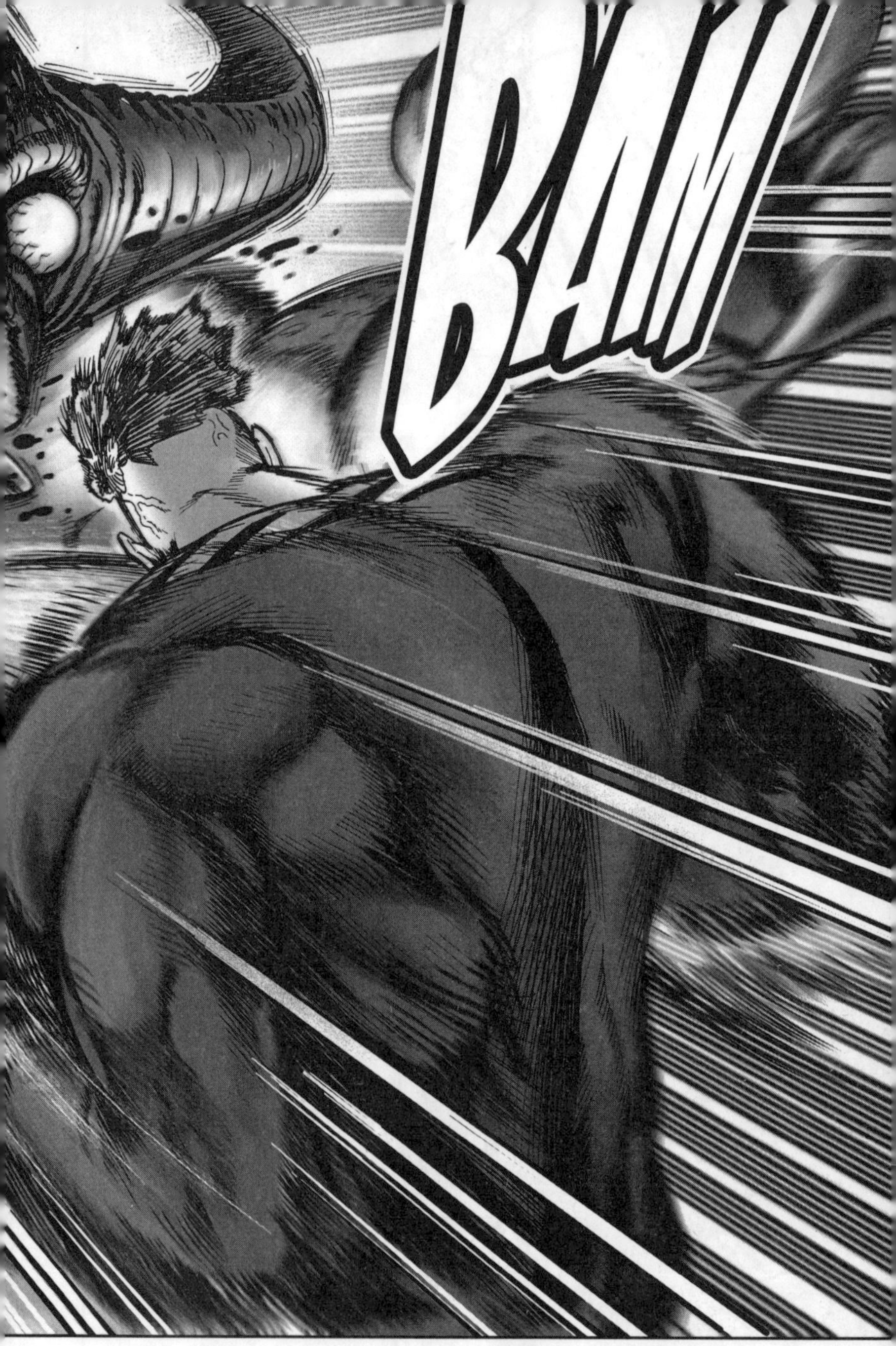
BAM

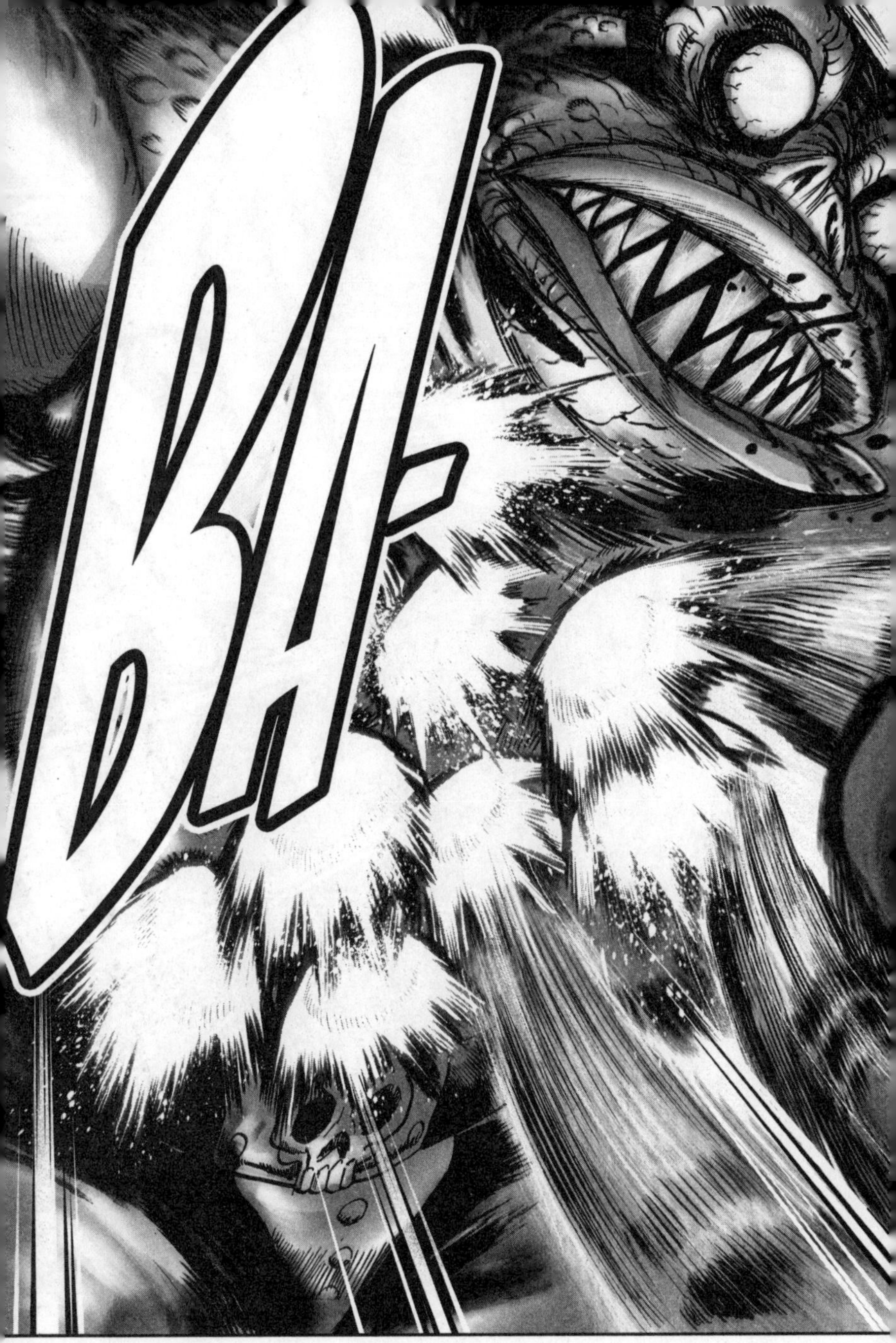

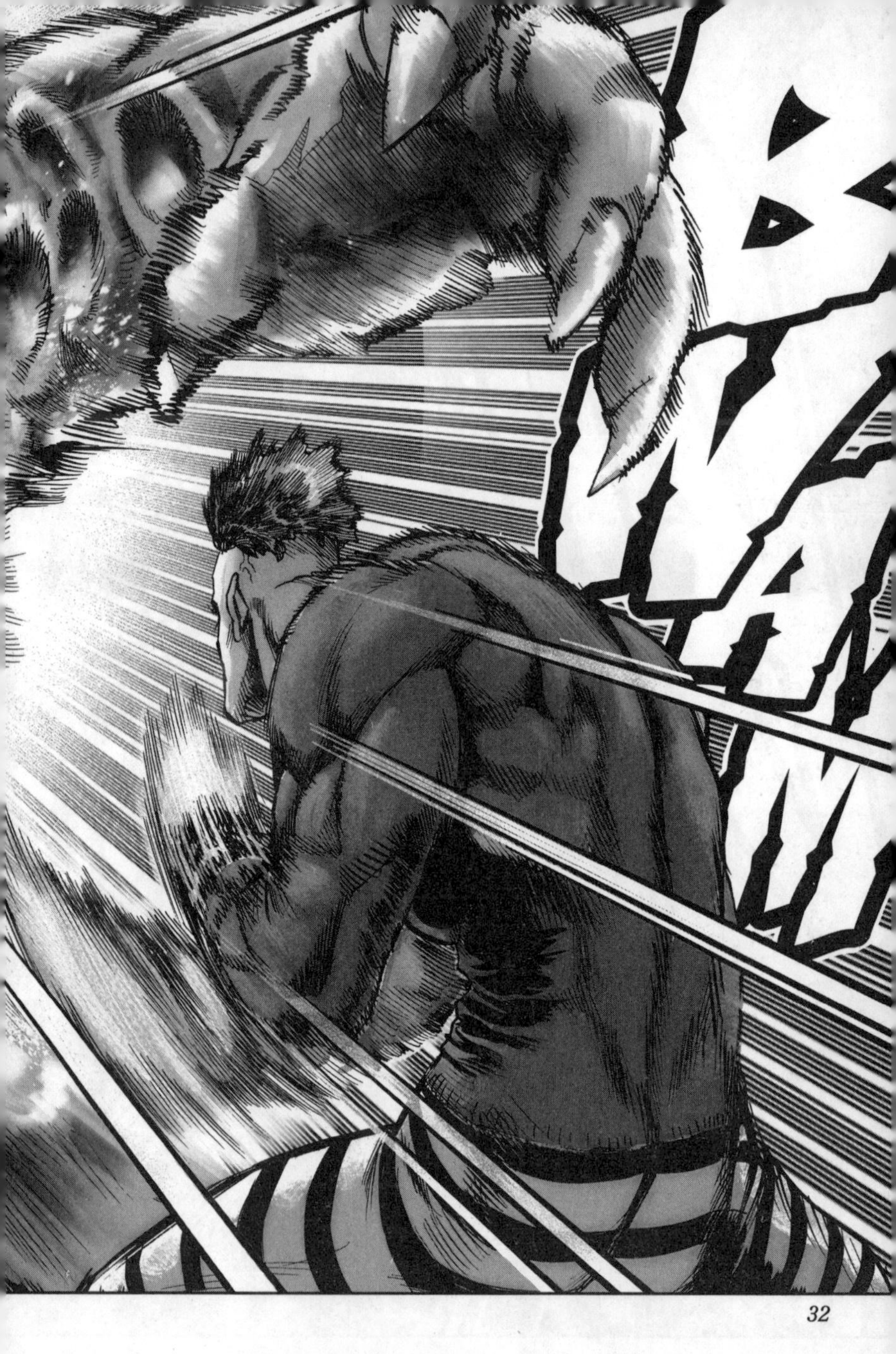

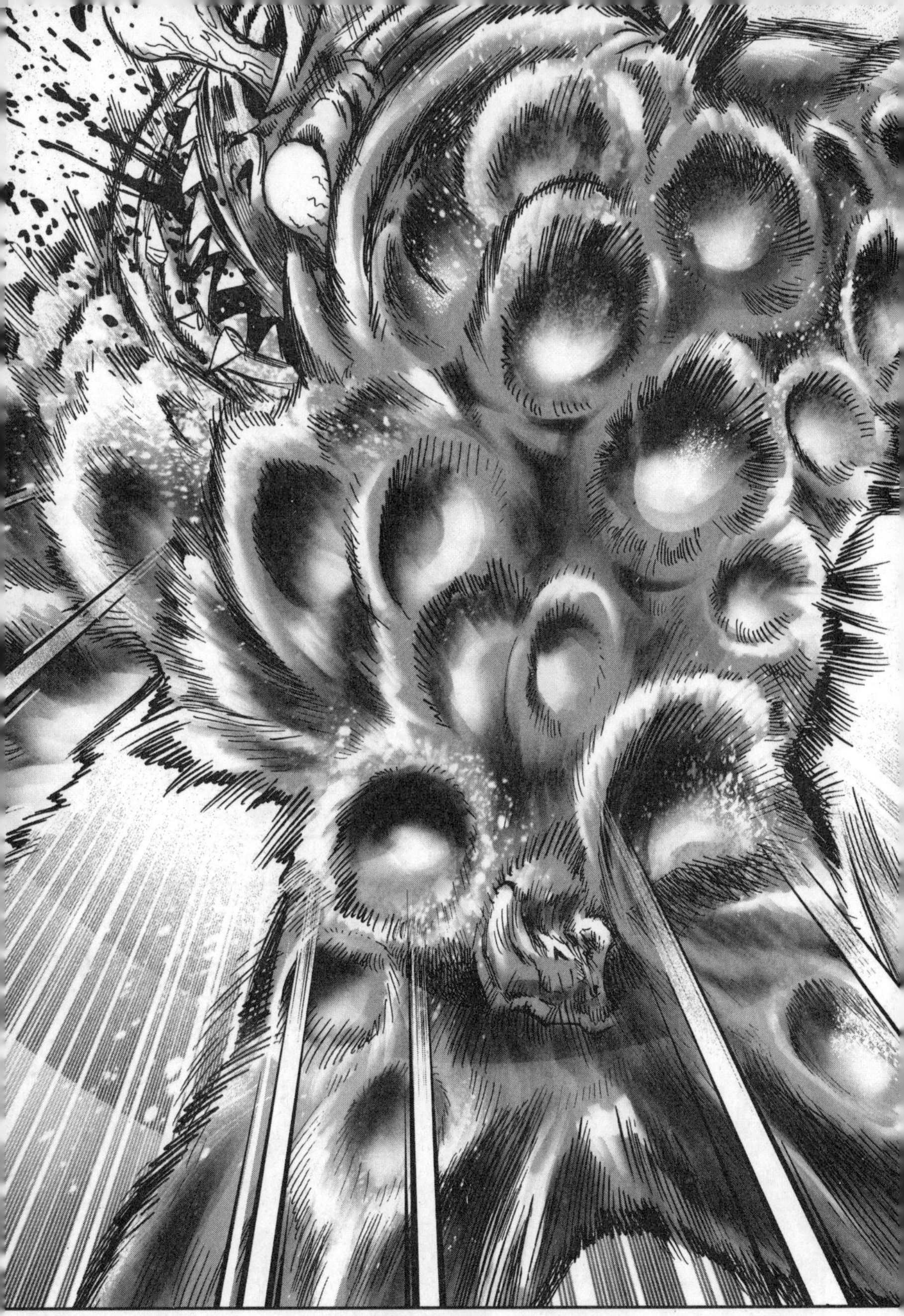

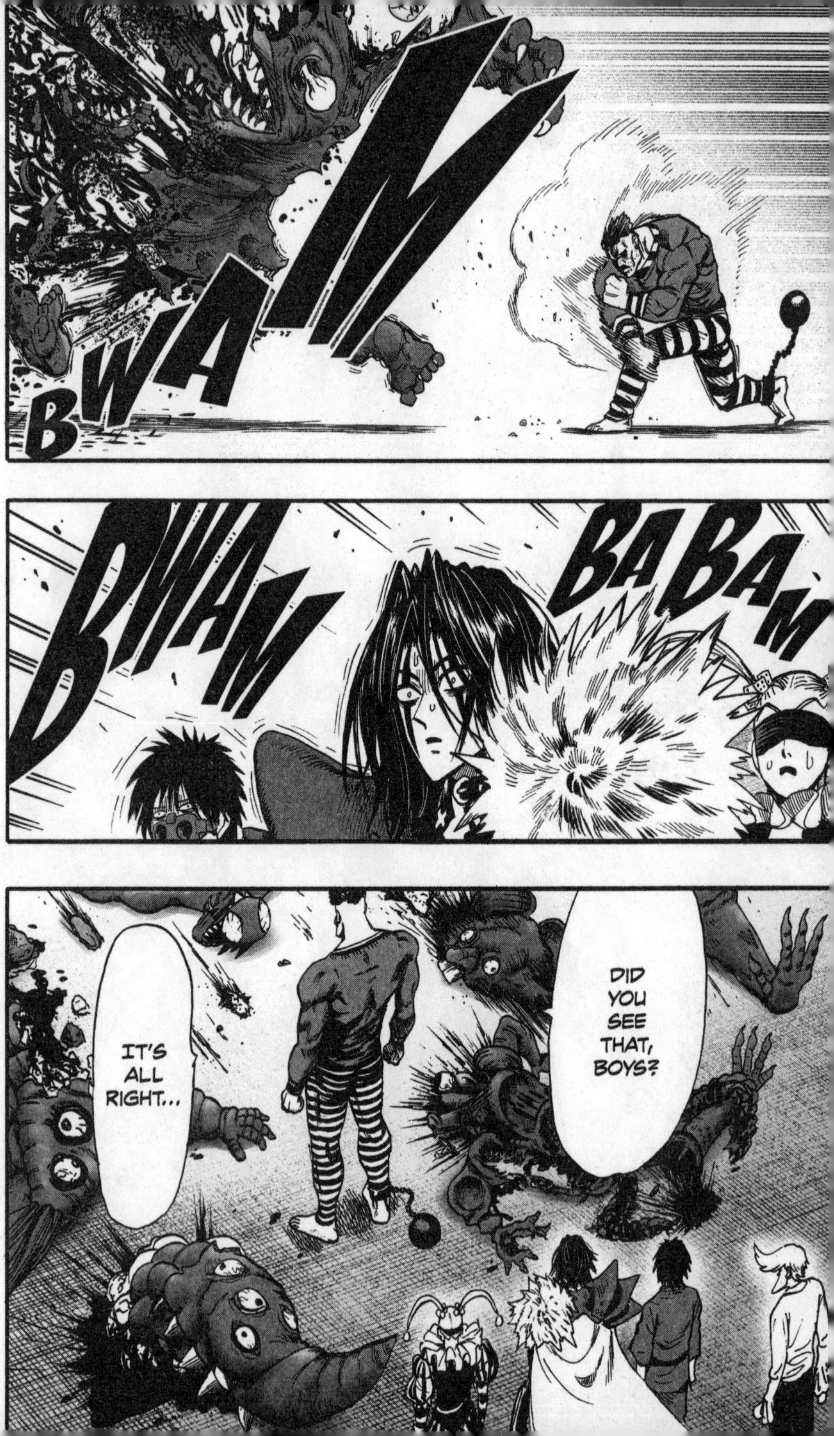
BWAM
BABAM
BWAM
DID YOU SEE THAT, BOYS?
IT'S ALL RIGHT...

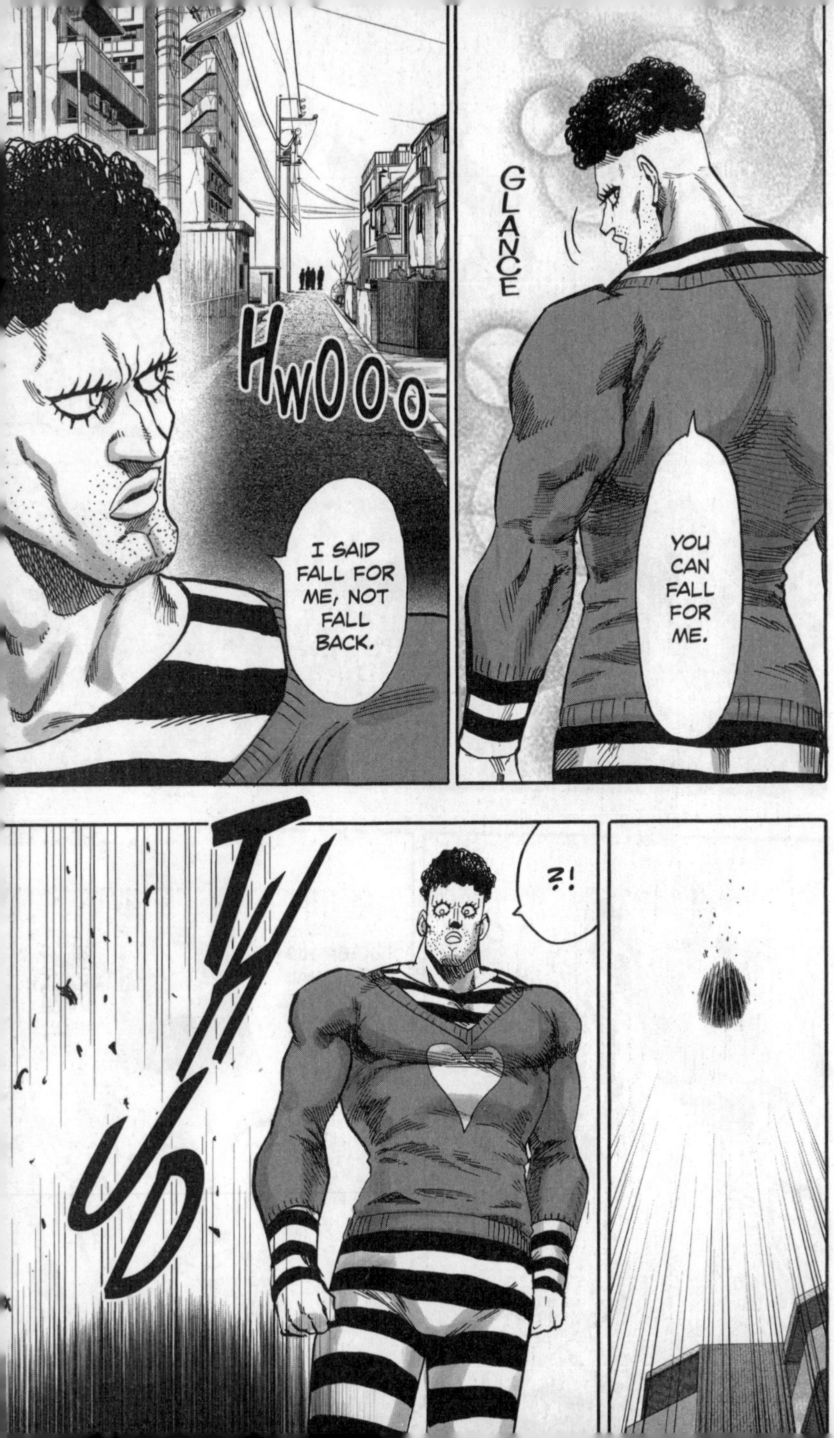
GLANCE
YOU CAN FALL FOR ME.
HWOOOO
I SAID FALL FOR ME, NOT FALL BACK.
?!
THS

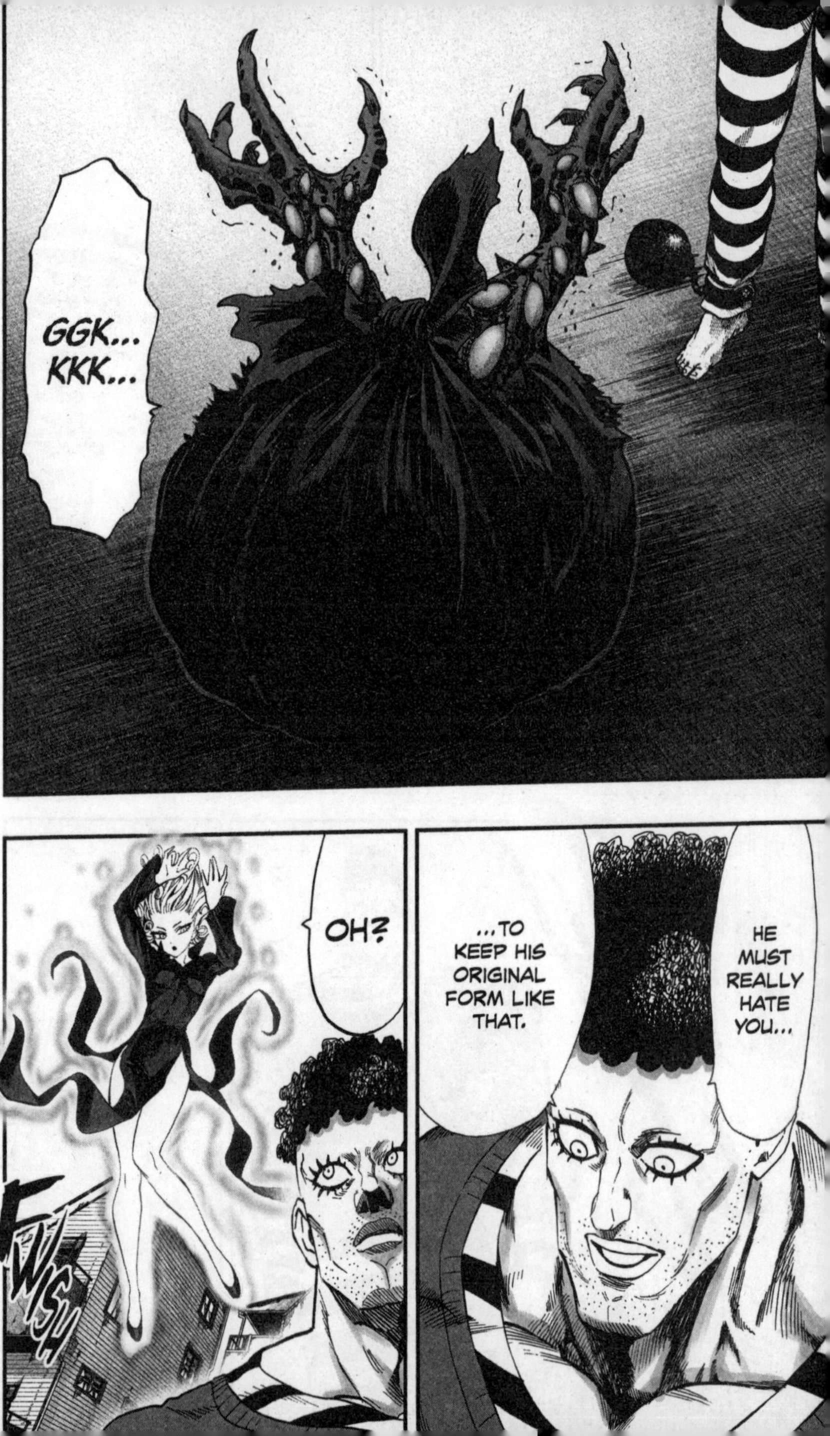
GGK... KKK...
HE MUST REALLY HATE YOU...
...TO KEEP HIS ORIGINAL FORM LIKE THAT.
OH?

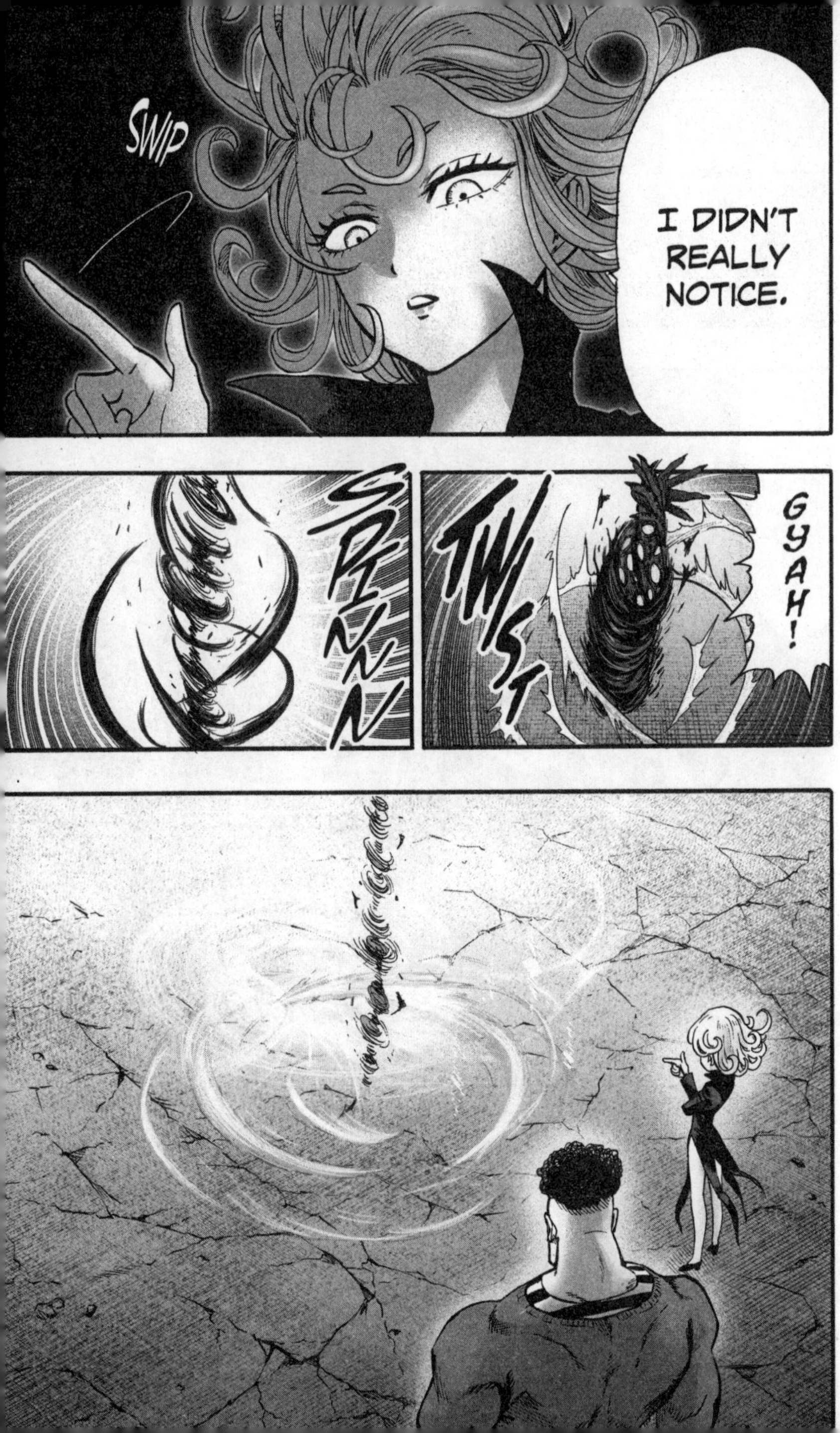
I DIDN'T REALLY NOTICE.
SWIP
GYAH!
TWIST
SPINNN

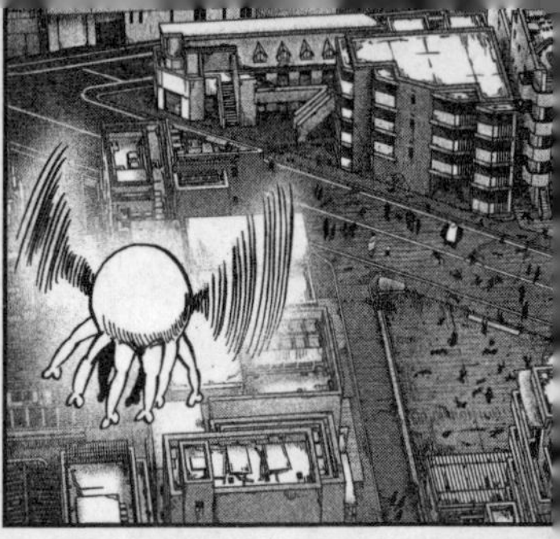

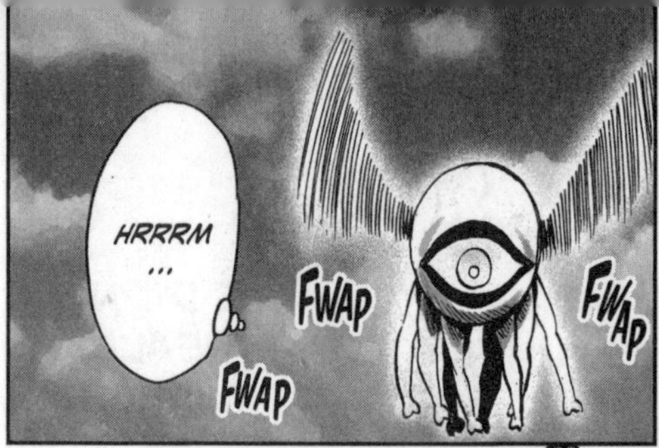
HRRRM ...
FWAP
FWAP
FWAP

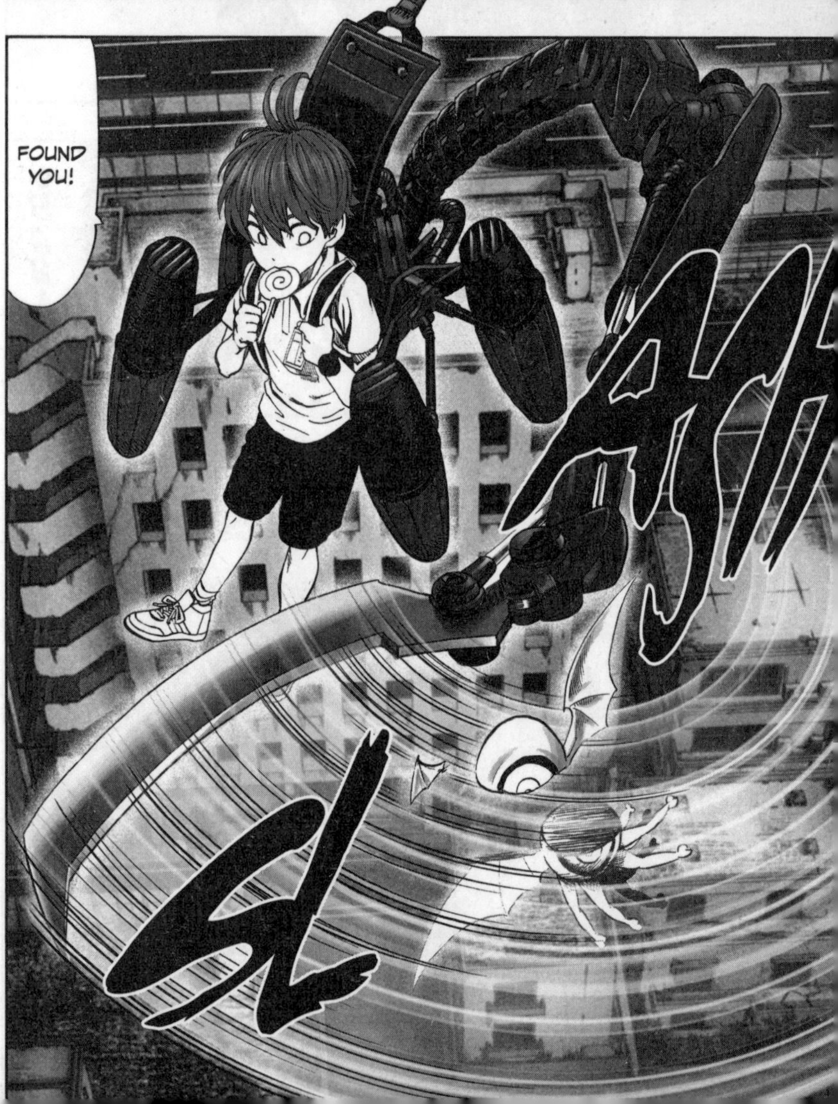
FOUND YOU!

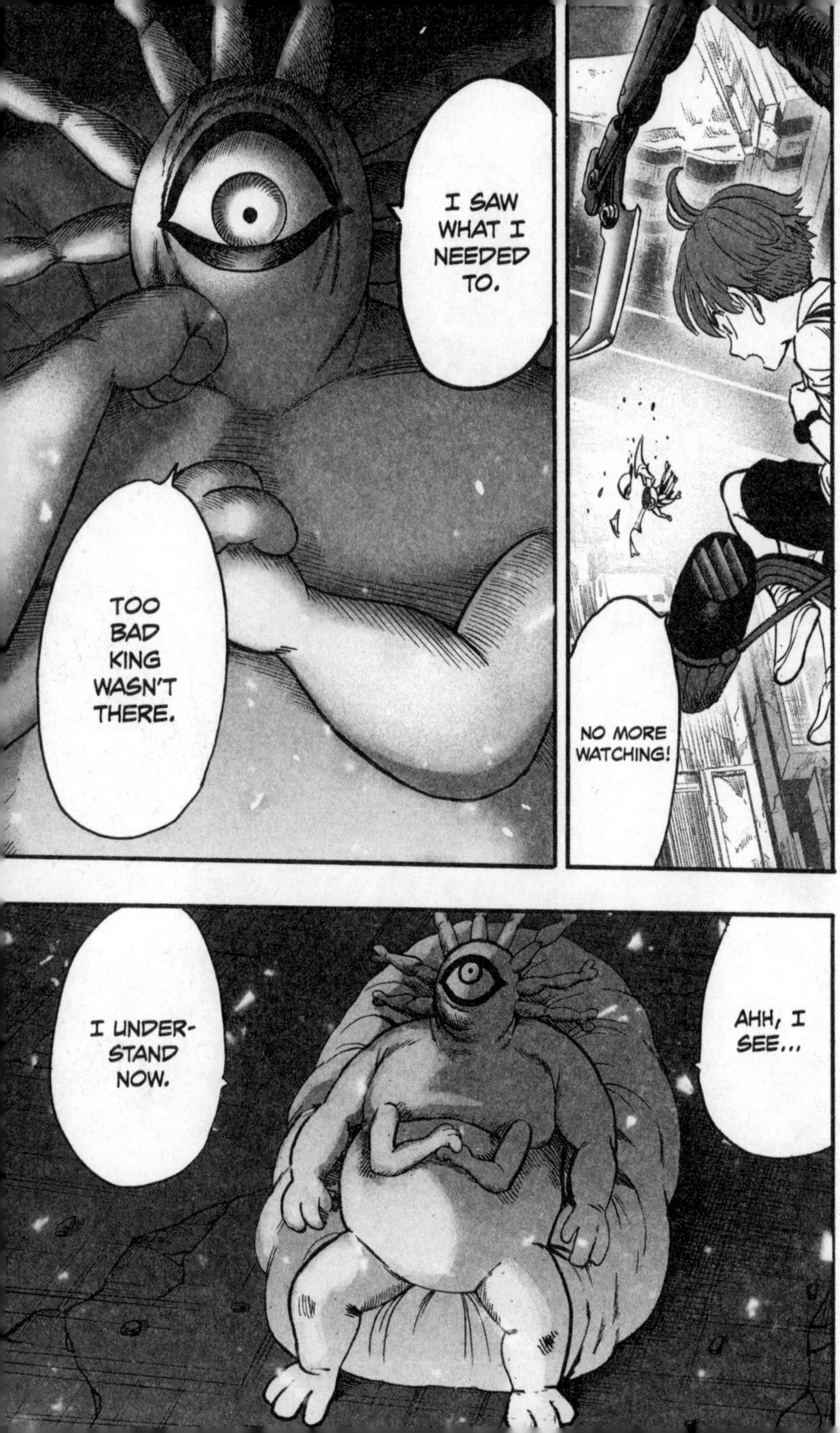
NO MORE WATCHING!
I SAW WHAT I NEEDED TO.
TOO BAD KING WASN'T THERE.
AHH, I SEE...
I UNDER-STAND NOW.

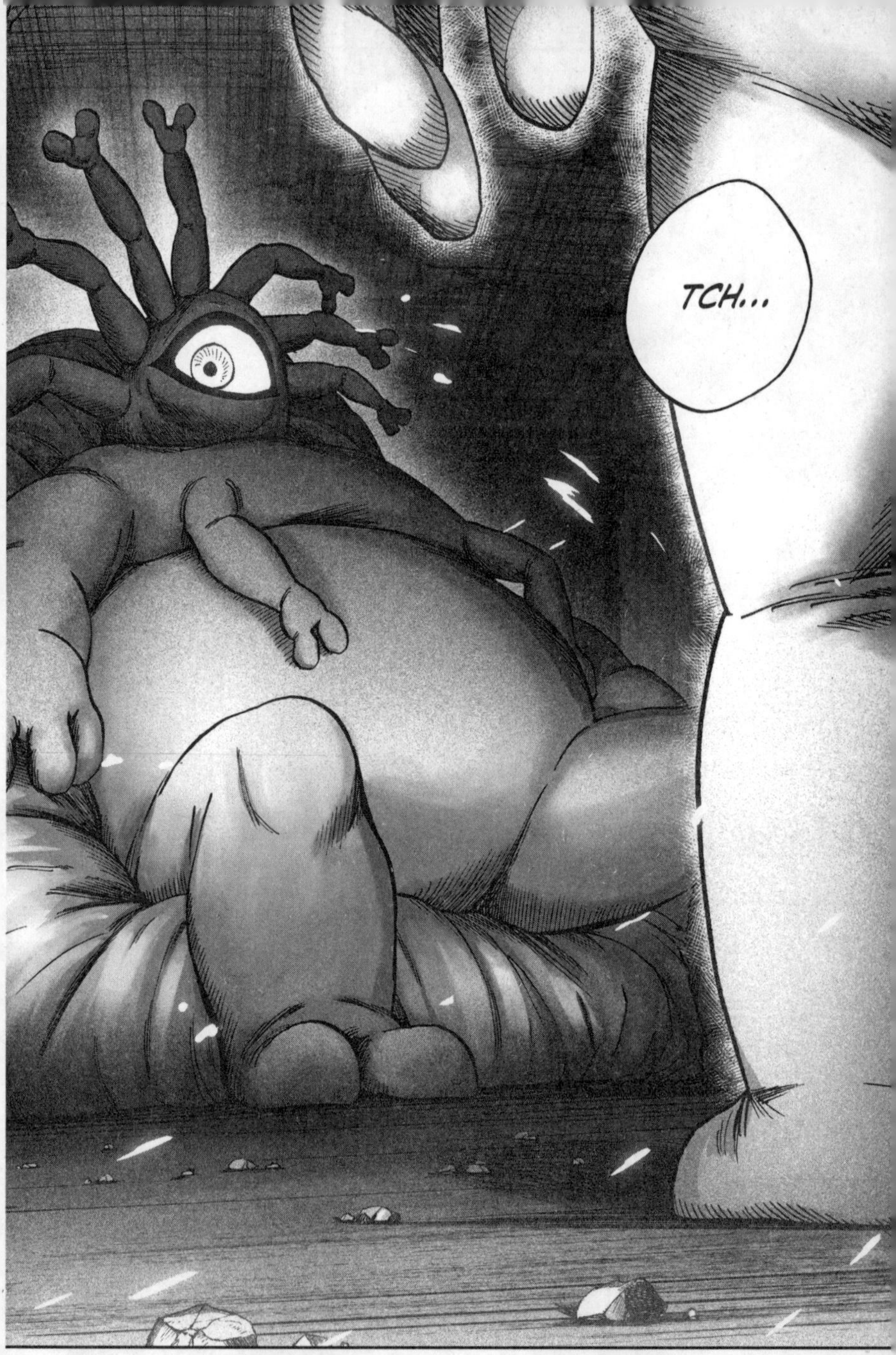
TCH...

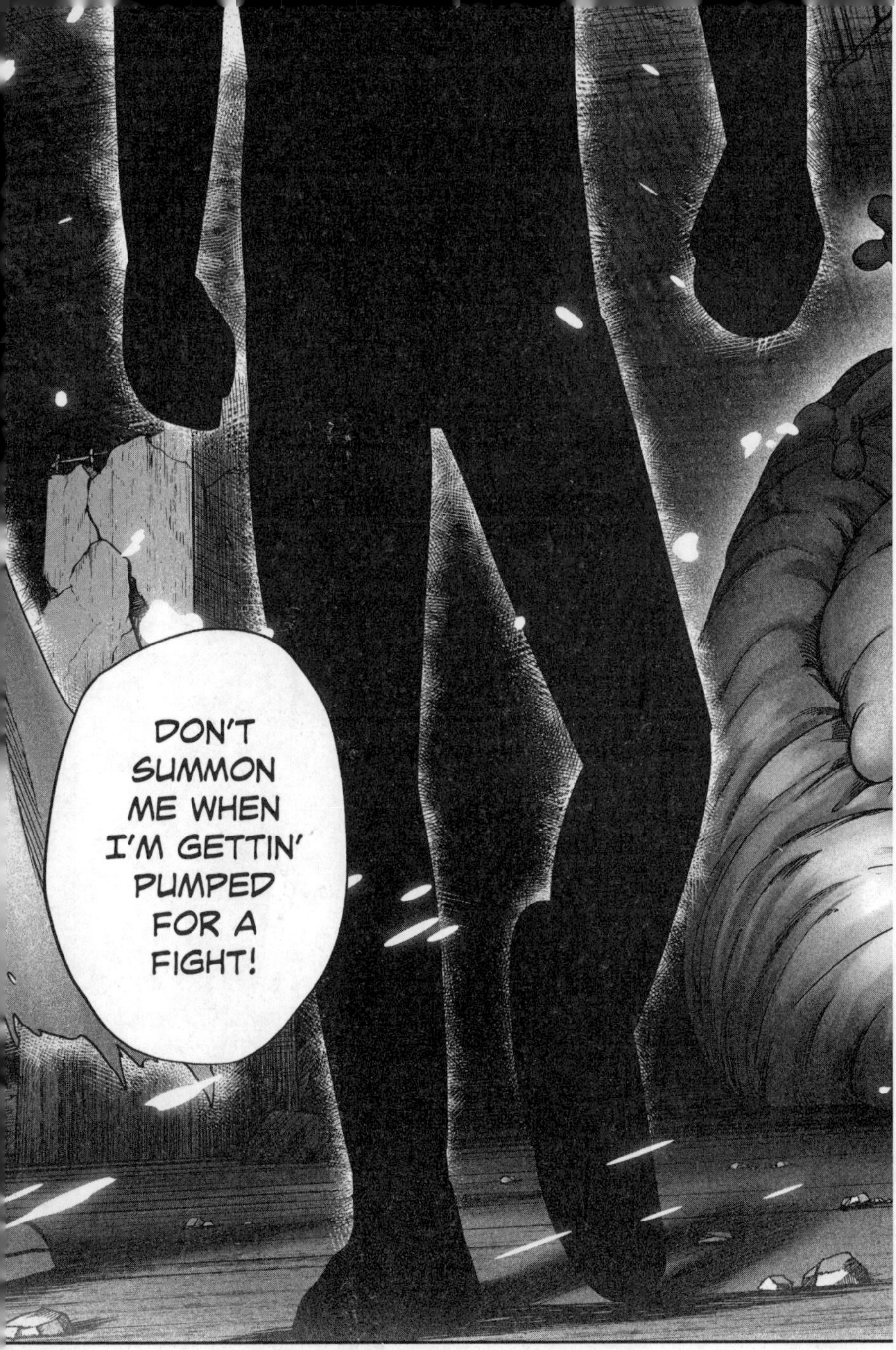
DON'T SUMMON ME WHEN I'M GETTIN' PUMPED FOR A FIGHT!

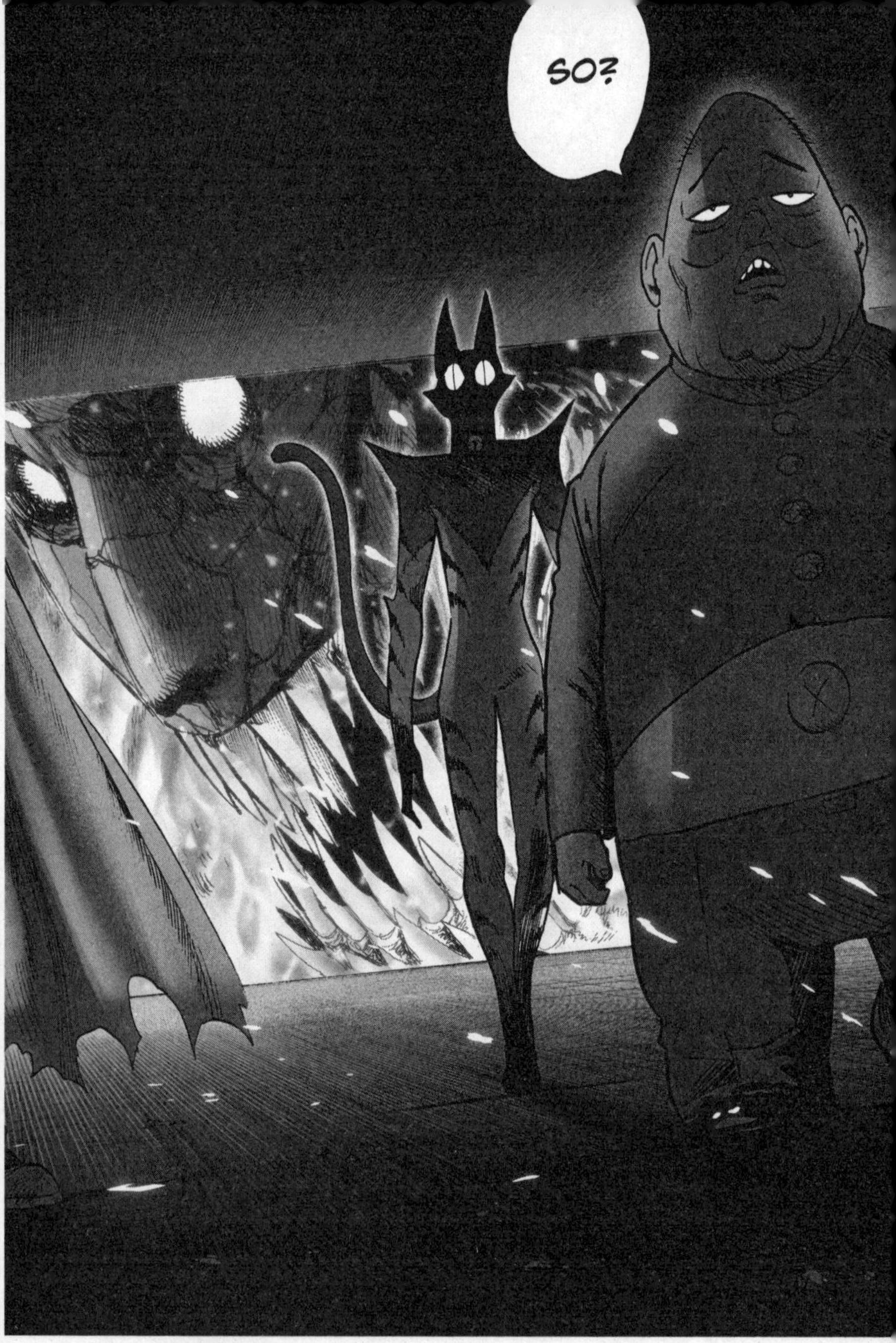
SO?

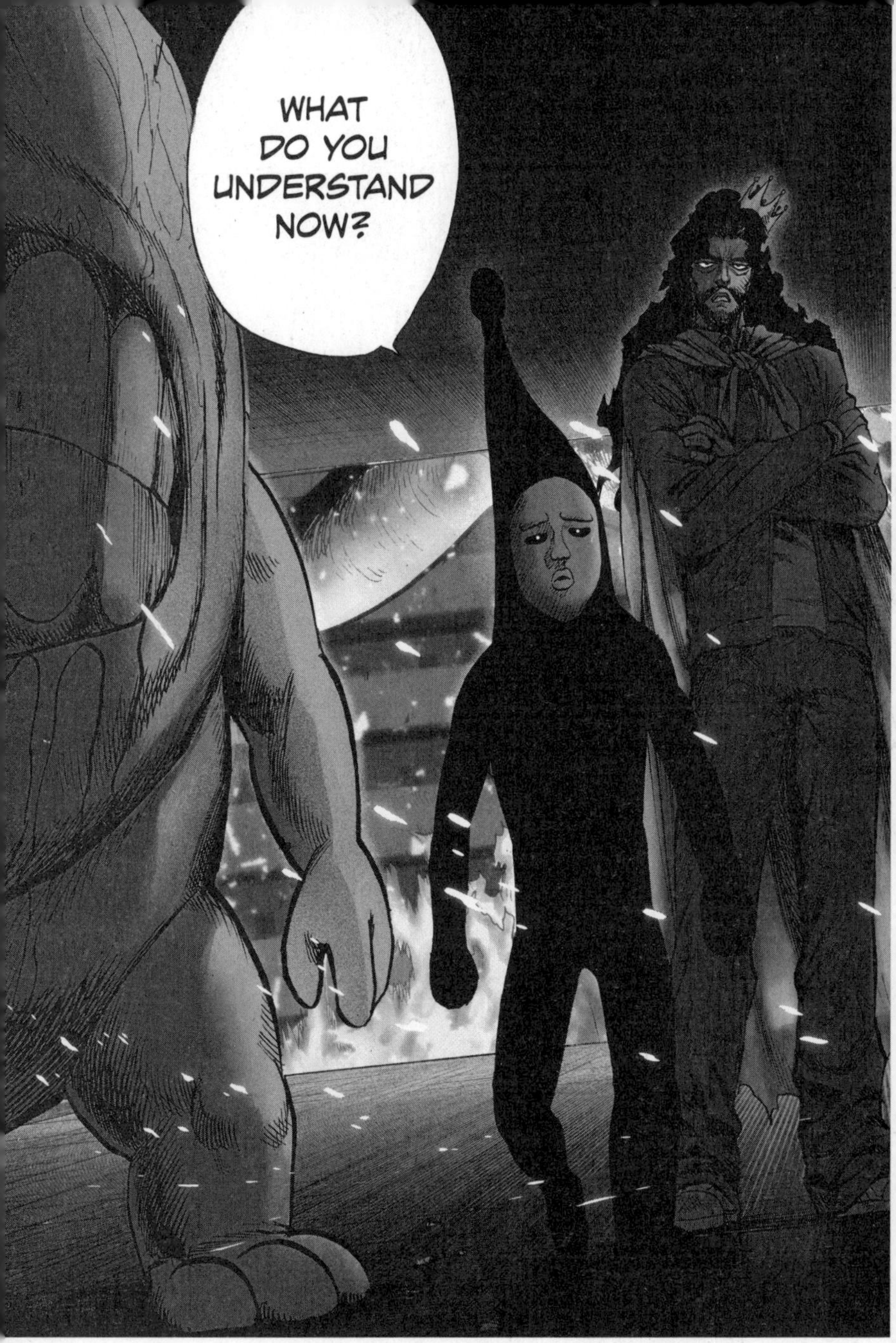
WHAT DO YOU UNDERSTAND NOW?

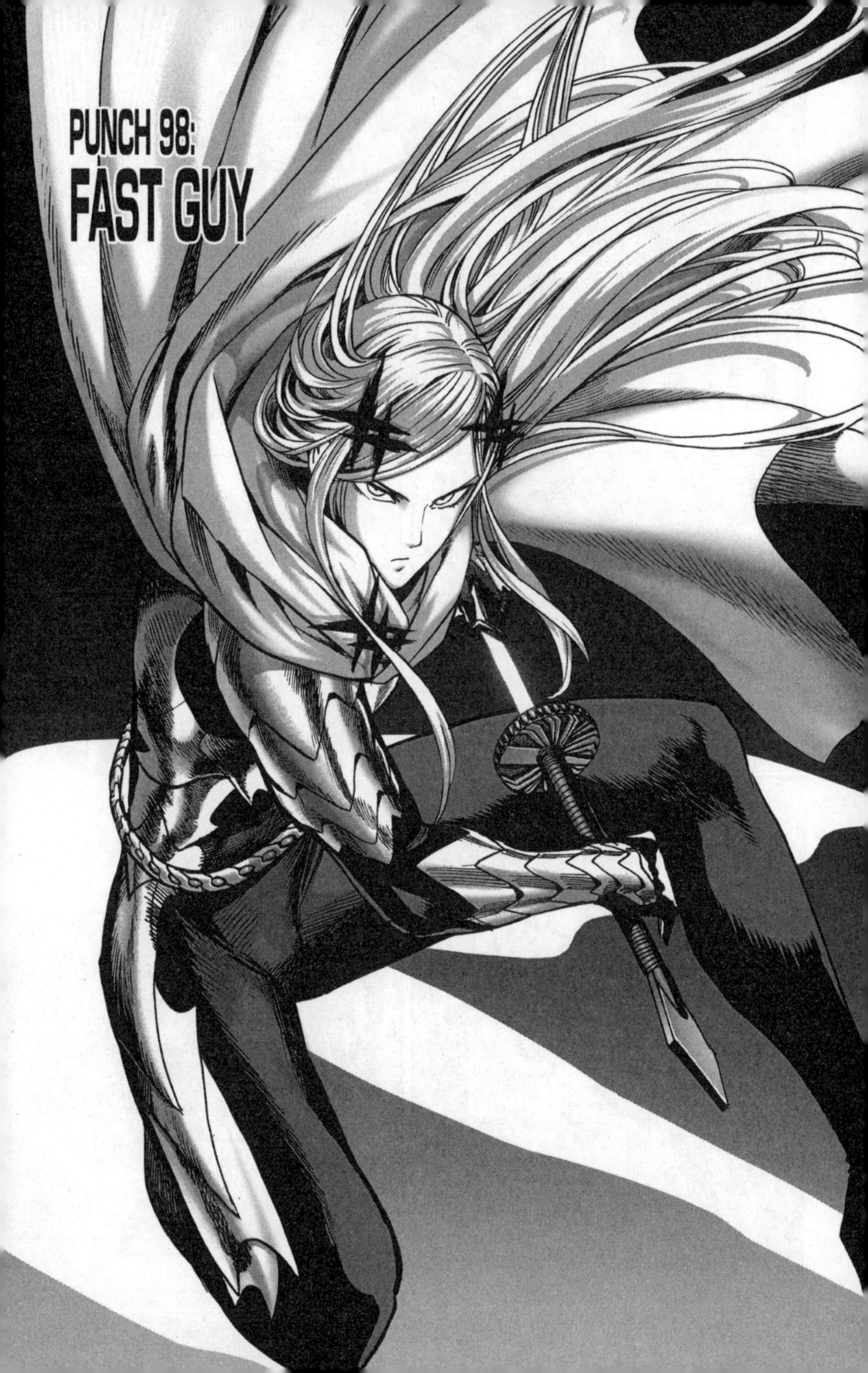
PUNCH 98:
FAST GUY

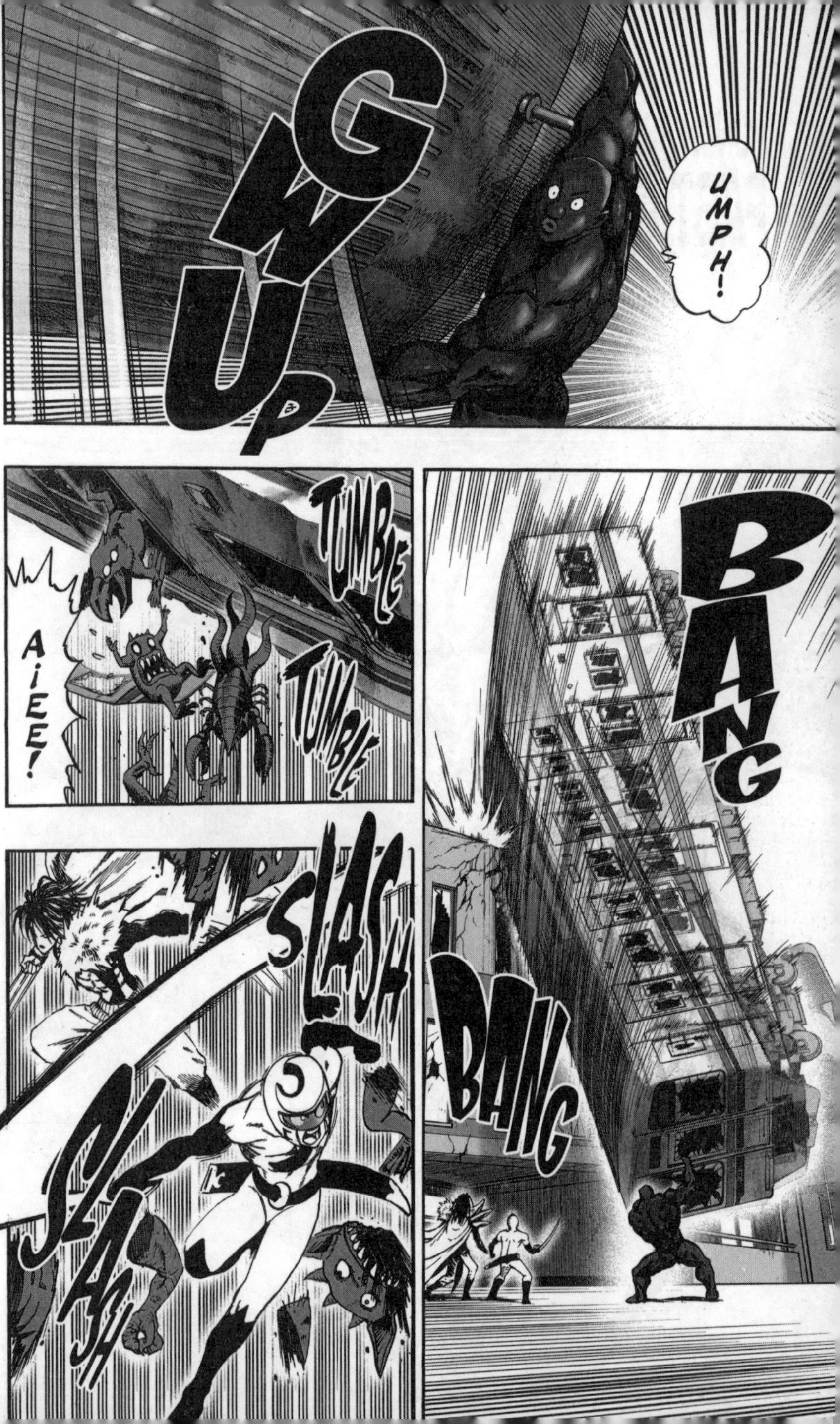

UMPH!
GWUP
BANG
BANG
TUMBLE
TUMBLE
AIEEE!
SLASH
SLASH

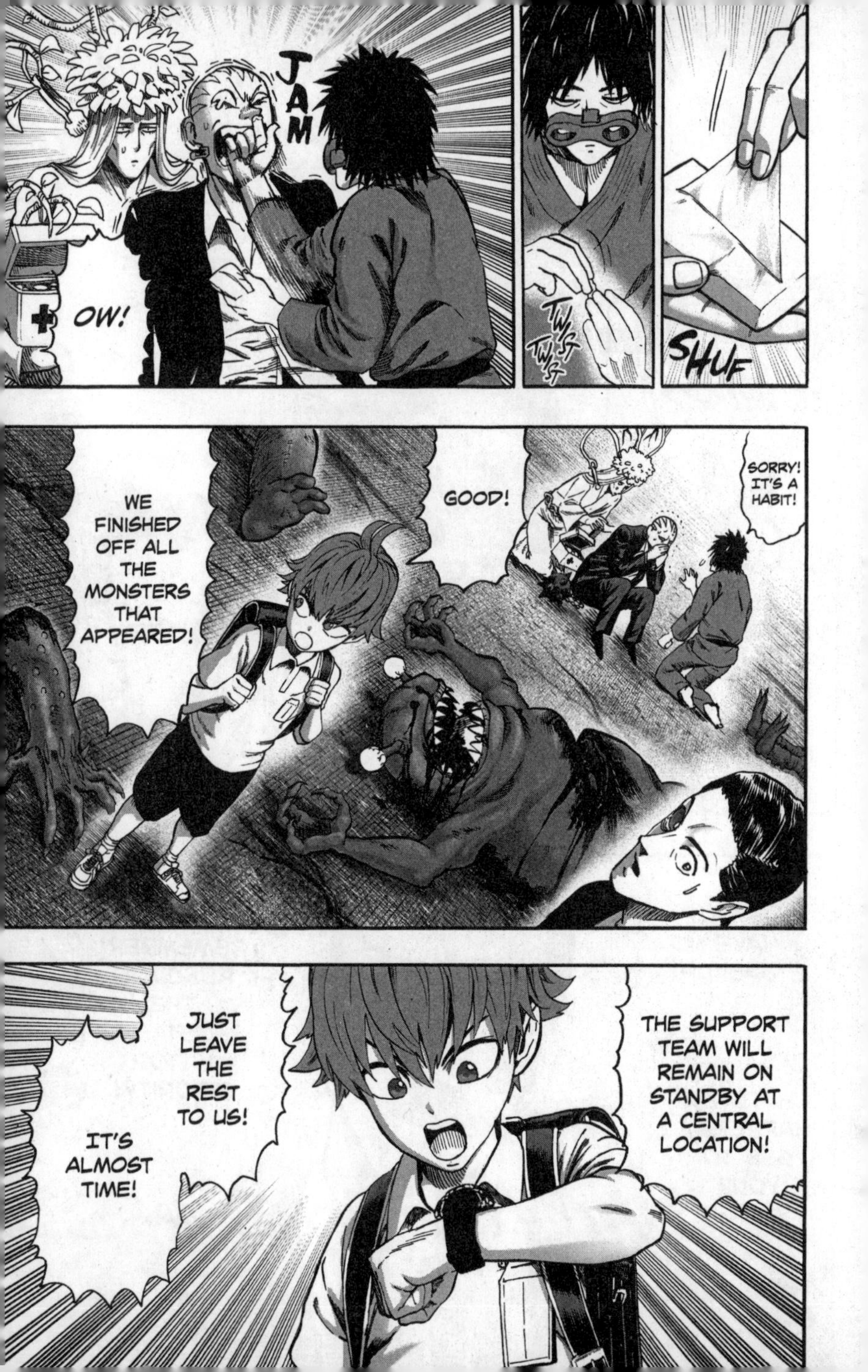
SHUF
TWIST TWIST
JAM
OW!
SORRY! IT'S A HABIT!
GOOD!
WE FINISHED OFF ALL THE MONSTERS THAT APPEARED!
THE SUPPORT TEAM WILL REMAIN ON STANDBY AT A CENTRAL LOCATION!
JUST LEAVE THE REST TO US!
IT'S ALMOST TIME!

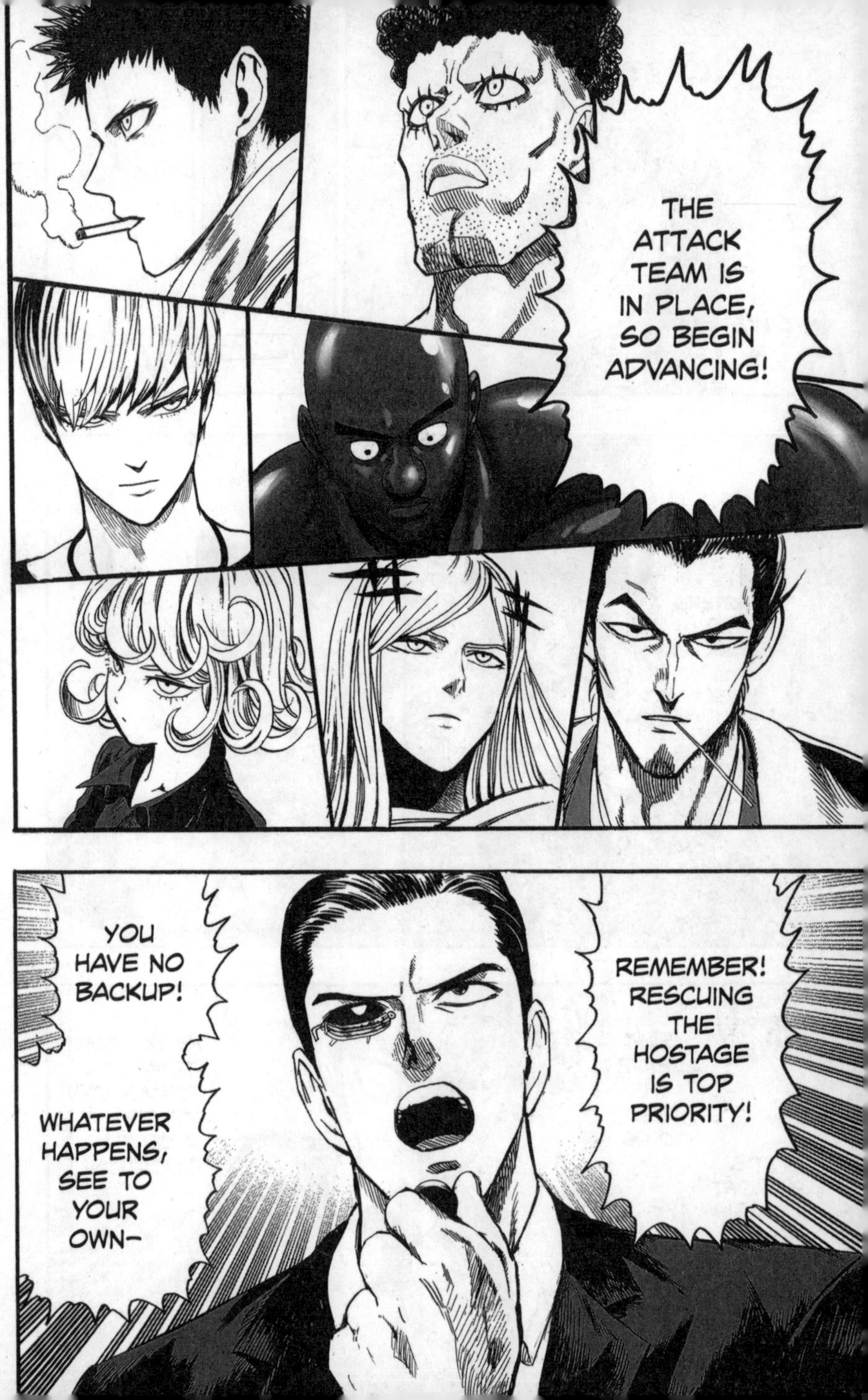
THE ATTACK TEAM IS IN PLACE, SO BEGIN ADVANCING!
REMEMBER! RESCUING THE HOSTAGE IS TOP PRIORITY!
YOU HAVE NO BACKUP!
WHATEVER HAPPENS, SEE TO YOUR OWN–

EXCUSE ME!

COULD I GET SOME HELP HERE?!

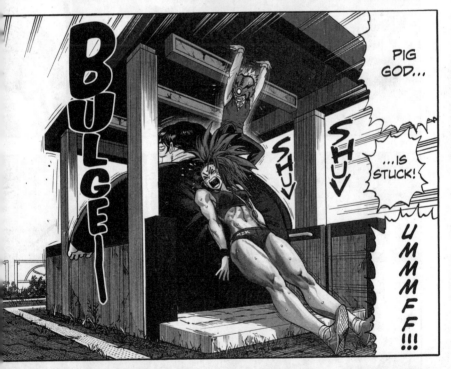

PIG GOD...

...IS STUCK!

BULGE!

SHU∨

SHU∨

UMMMFF!!!

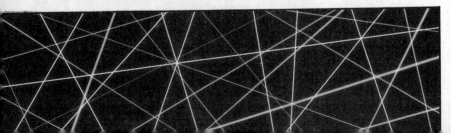

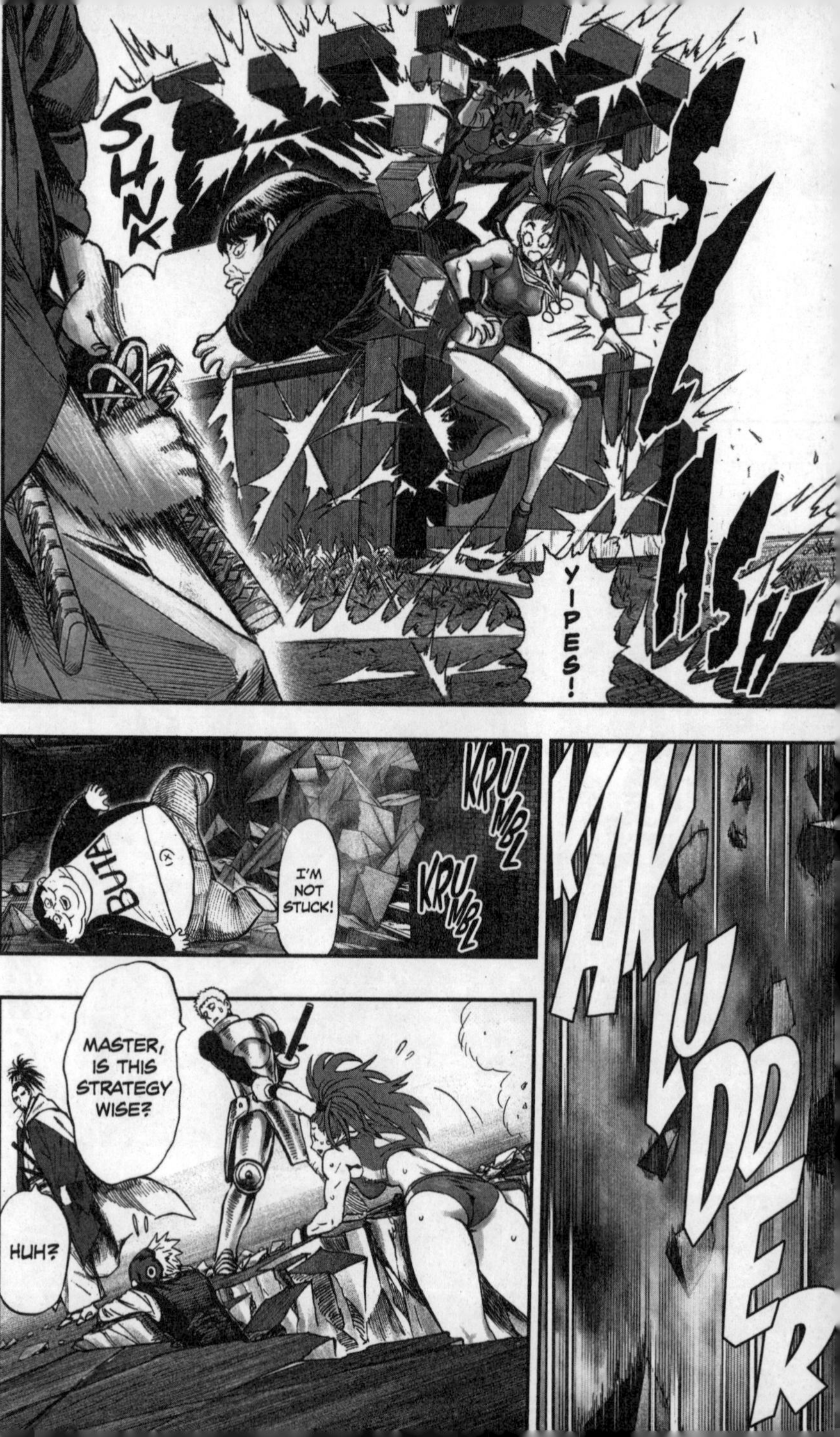
SLASH
SHUNK
YIPES!
KAKLUDDER
KRUMBL
KRUMBL
I'M NOT STUCK!
BUTA
MASTER, IS THIS STRATEGY WISE?
HUH?

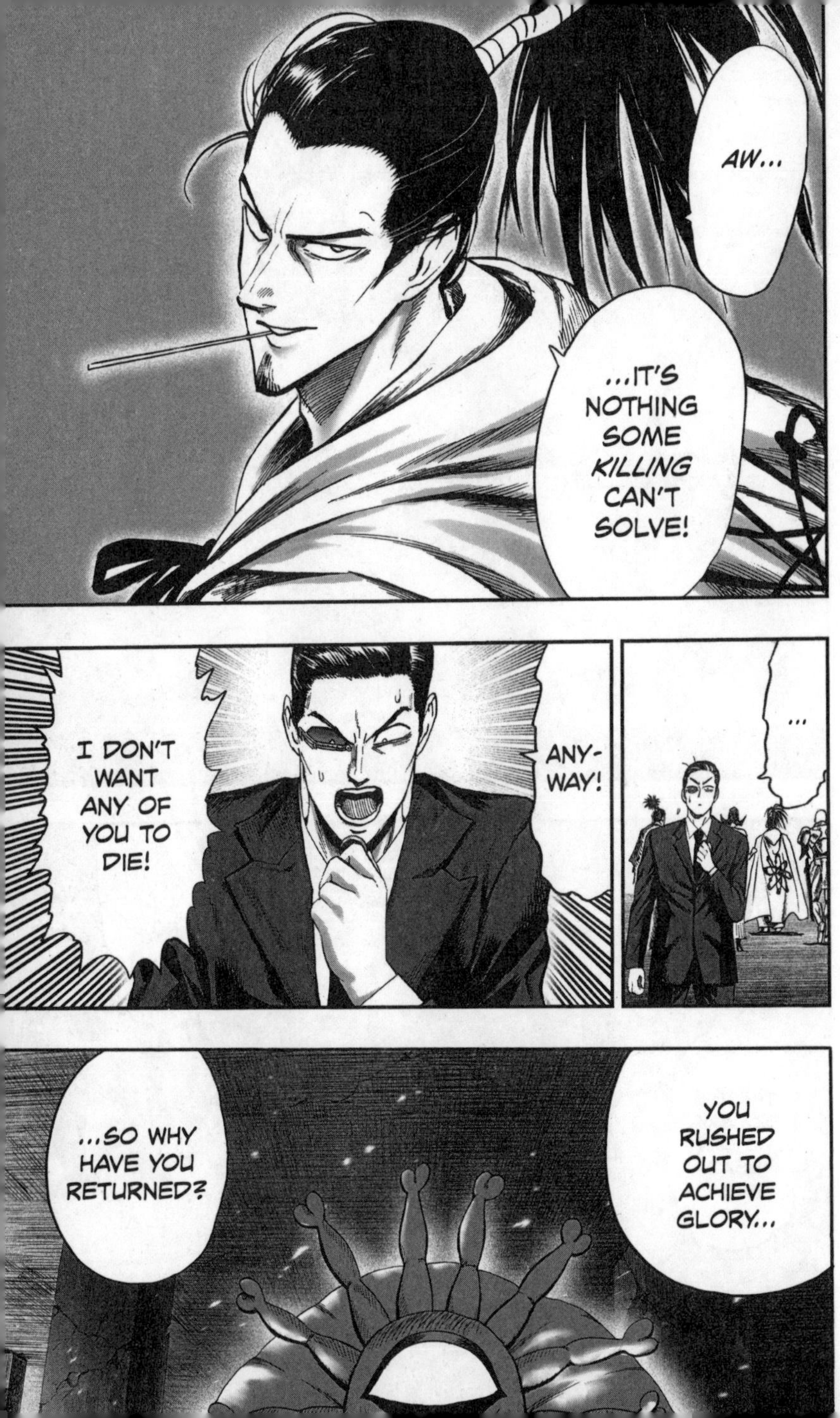
AW...
...IT'S NOTHING SOME KILLING CAN'T SOLVE!
...
ANY-WAY!
I DON'T WANT ANY OF YOU TO DIE!
YOU RUSHED OUT TO ACHIEVE GLORY...
...SO WHY HAVE YOU RETURNED?

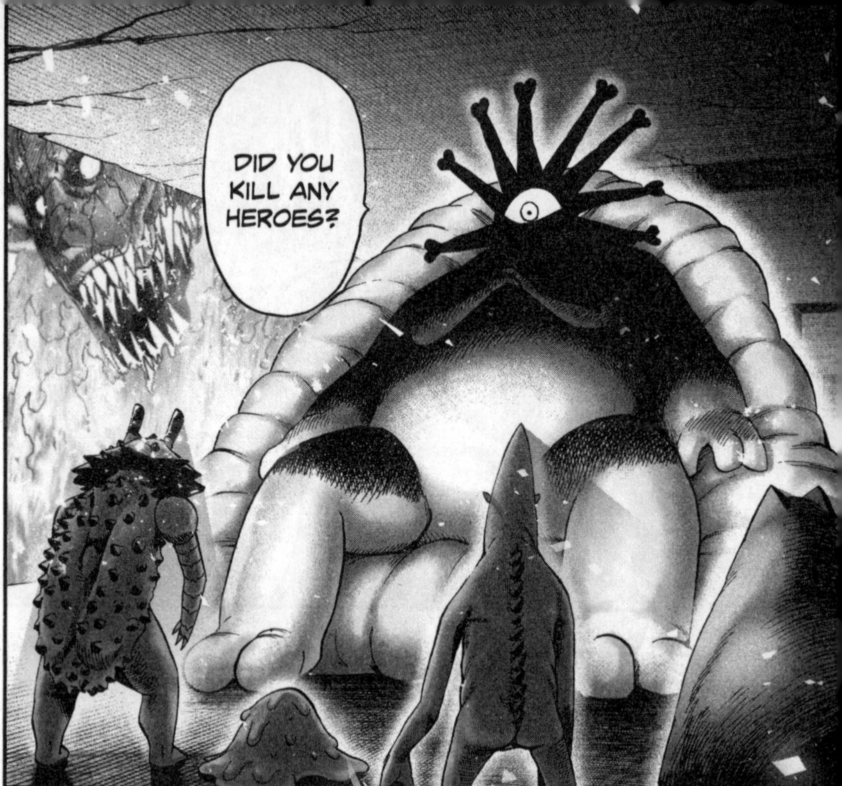
DID YOU KILL ANY HEROES?

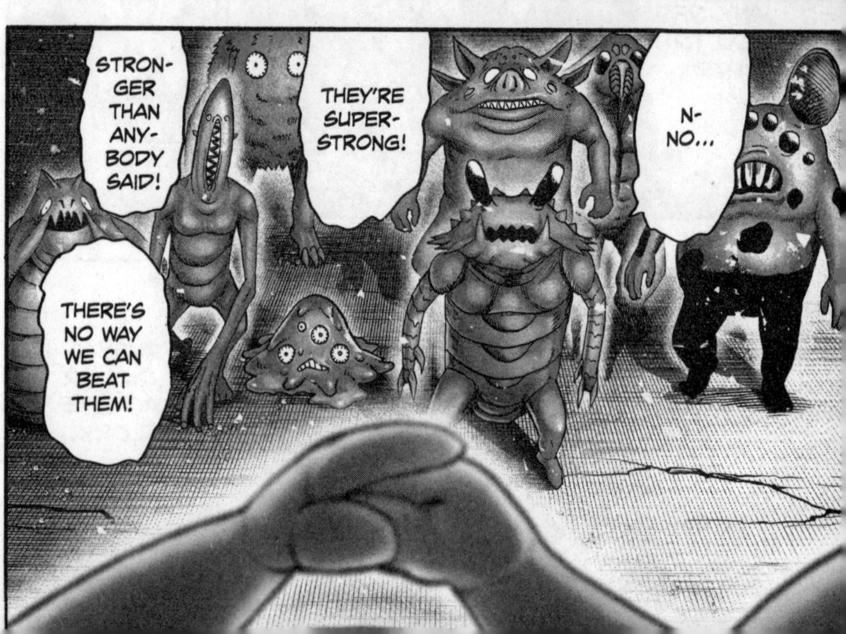
N-NO...
THEY'RE SUPER-STRONG!
STRONGER THAN ANY-BODY SAID!
THERE'S NO WAY WE CAN BEAT THEM!

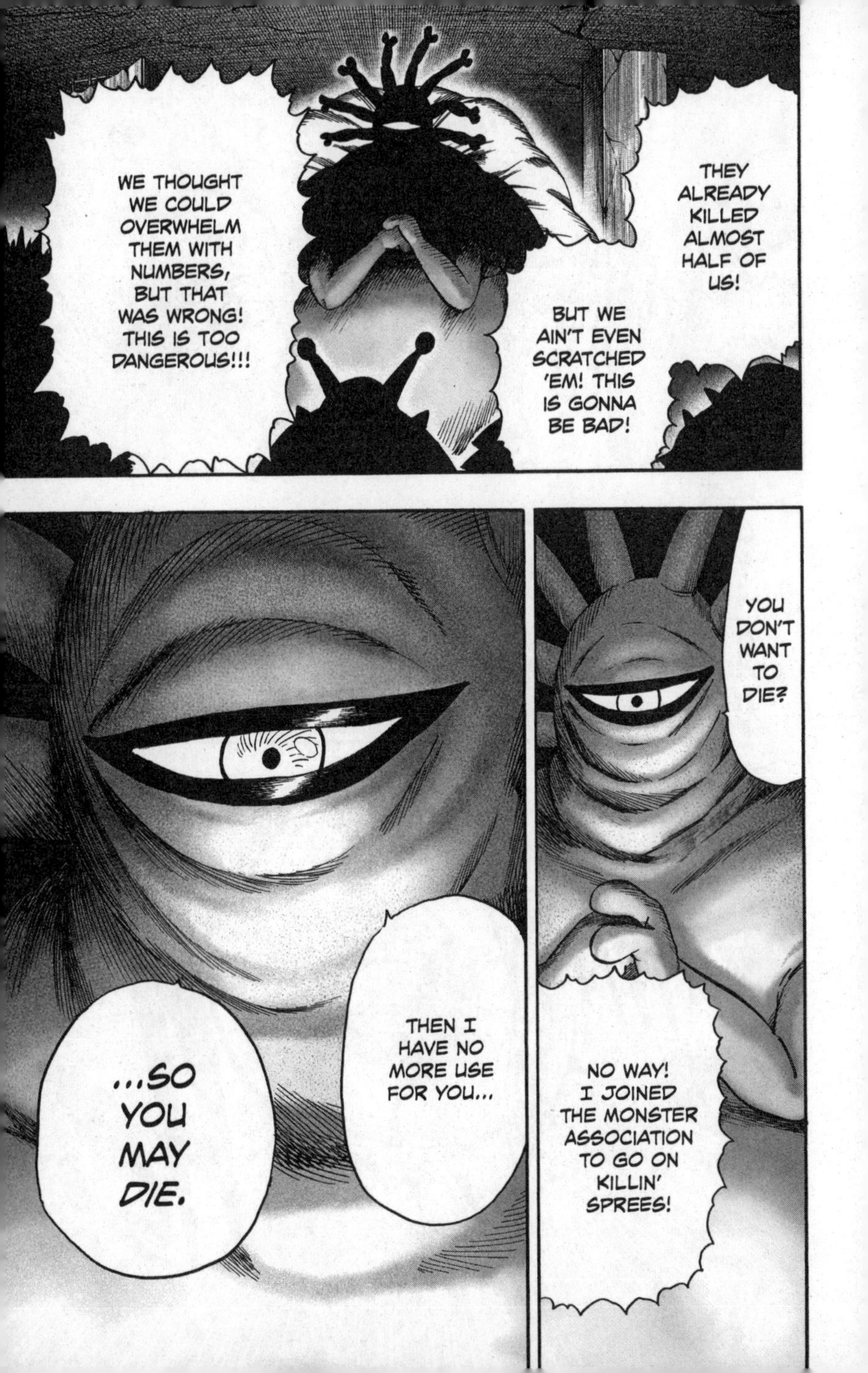
THEY ALREADY KILLED ALMOST HALF OF US!
BUT WE AIN'T EVEN SCRATCHED 'EM! THIS IS GONNA BE BAD!
WE THOUGHT WE COULD OVERWHELM THEM WITH NUMBERS, BUT THAT WAS WRONG! THIS IS TOO DANGEROUS!!!
YOU DON'T WANT TO DIE?
NO WAY! I JOINED THE MONSTER ASSOCIATION TO GO ON KILLIN' SPREES!
THEN I HAVE NO MORE USE FOR YOU...
...SO YOU MAY *DIE*.

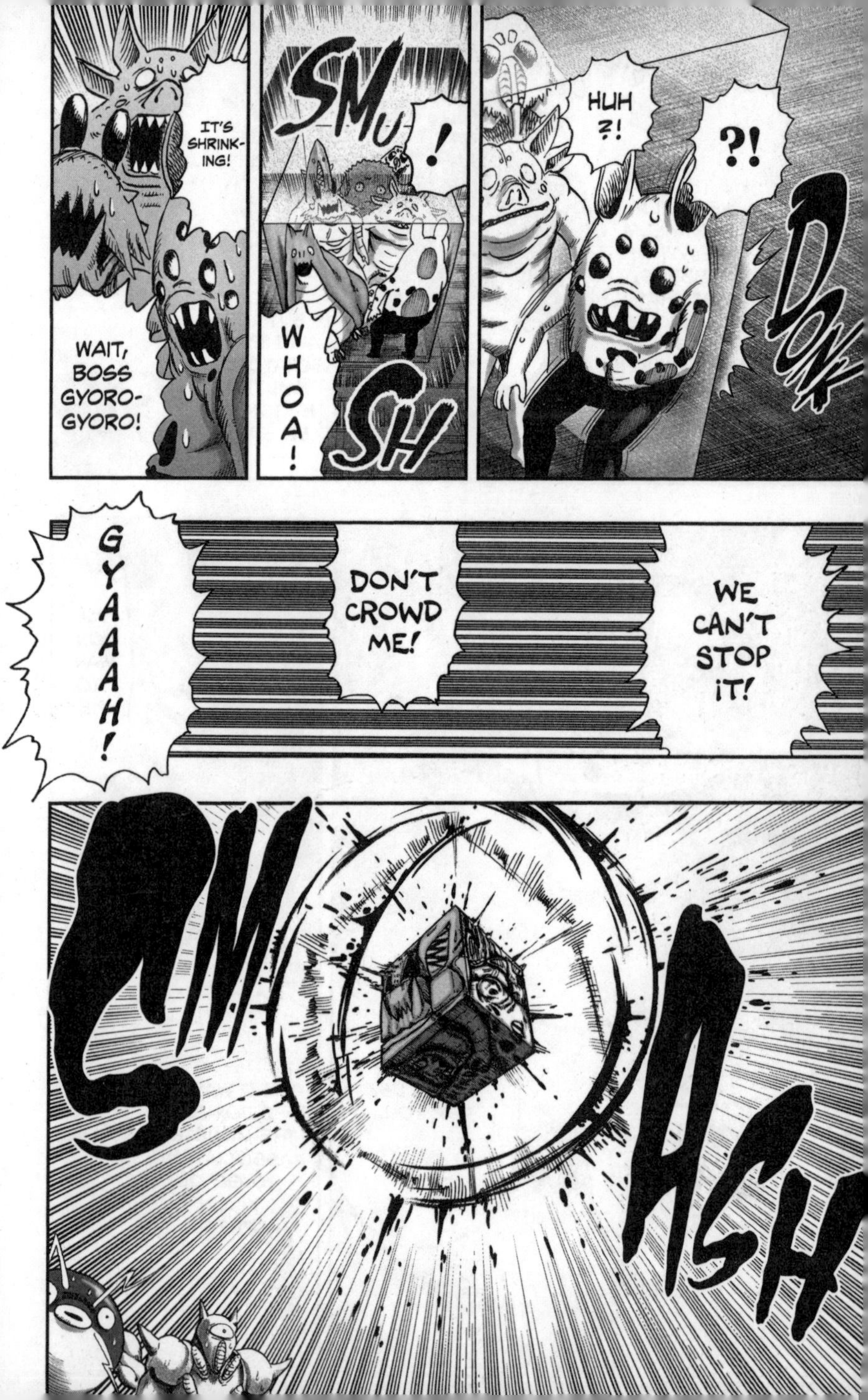
DONK
?!
HUH ?!
SMU
!
WHOA!
SH
IT'S SHRINKING!
WAIT, BOSS GYORO-GYORO!
WE CAN'T STOP IT!
DON'T CROWD ME!
GYAAAAH!
SM
ASH

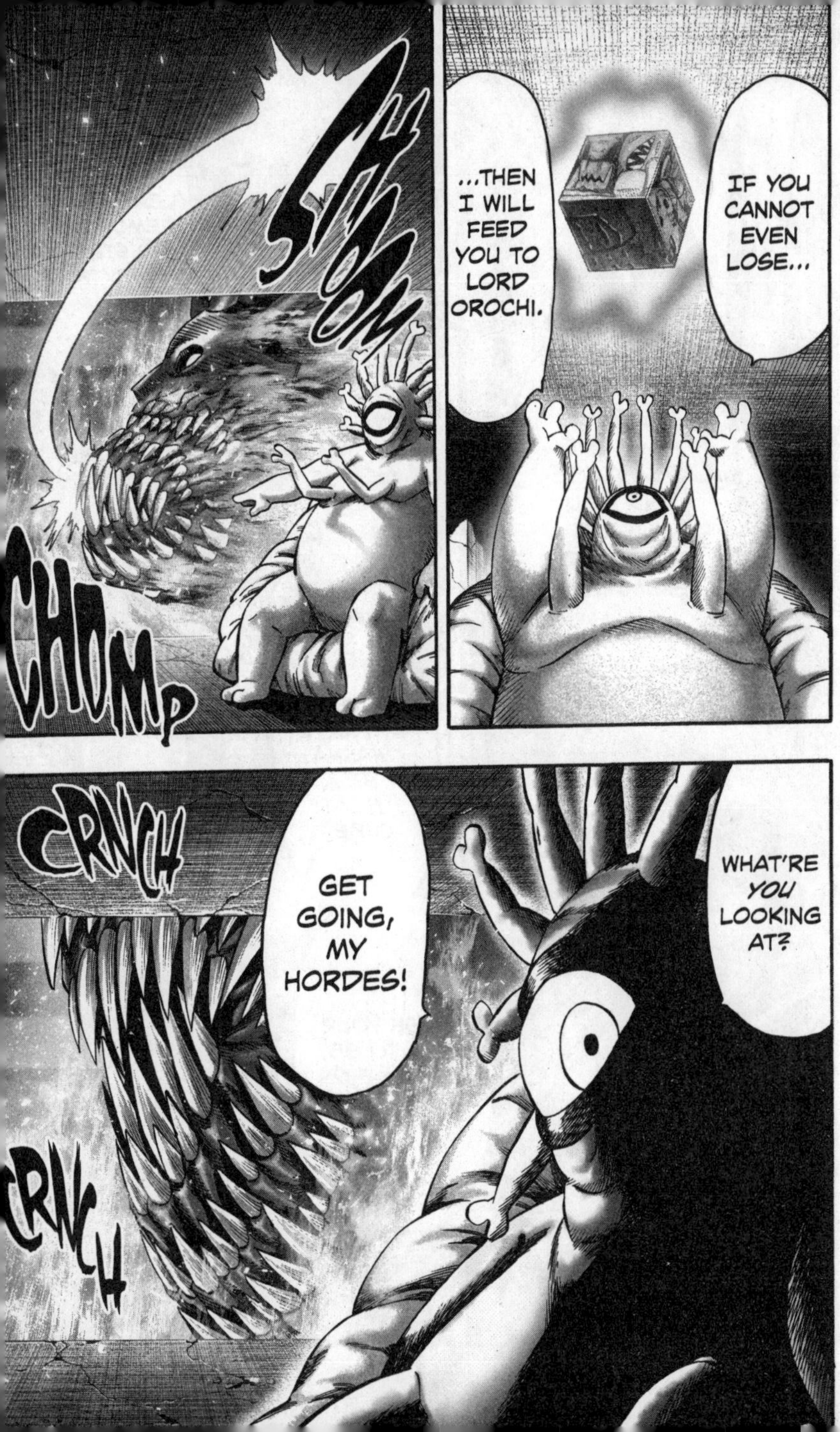
IF YOU CANNOT EVEN LOSE...
...THEN I WILL FEED YOU TO LORD OROCHI.
SHOOM
CHOMP
WHAT'RE *YOU* LOOKING AT?
GET GOING, MY HORDES!
CRNCH
CRNCH

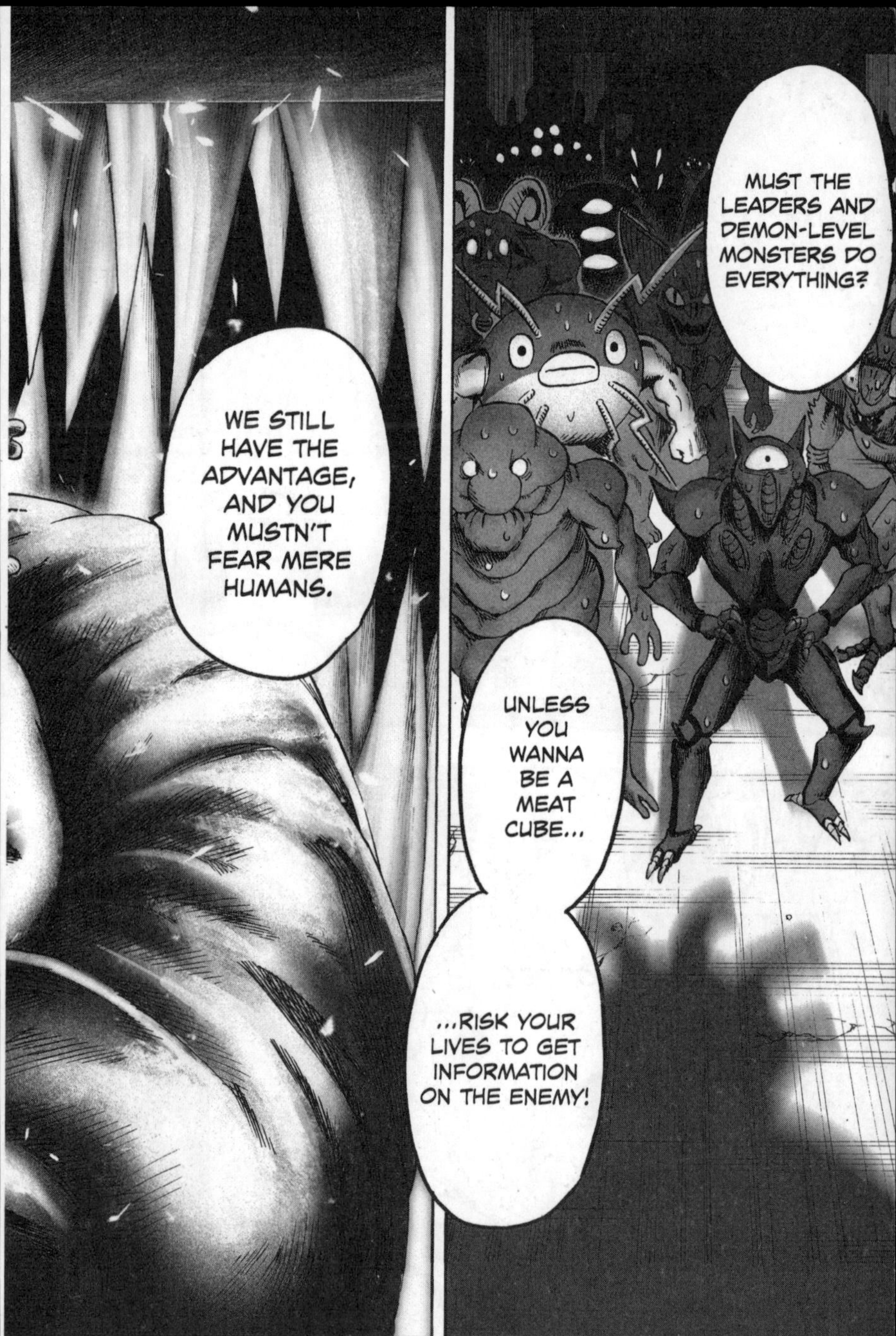
MUST THE LEADERS AND DEMON-LEVEL MONSTERS DO EVERYTHING?
UNLESS YOU WANNA BE A MEAT CUBE...
...RISK YOUR LIVES TO GET INFORMATION ON THE ENEMY!
WE STILL HAVE THE ADVANTAGE, AND YOU MUSTN'T FEAR MERE HUMANS.

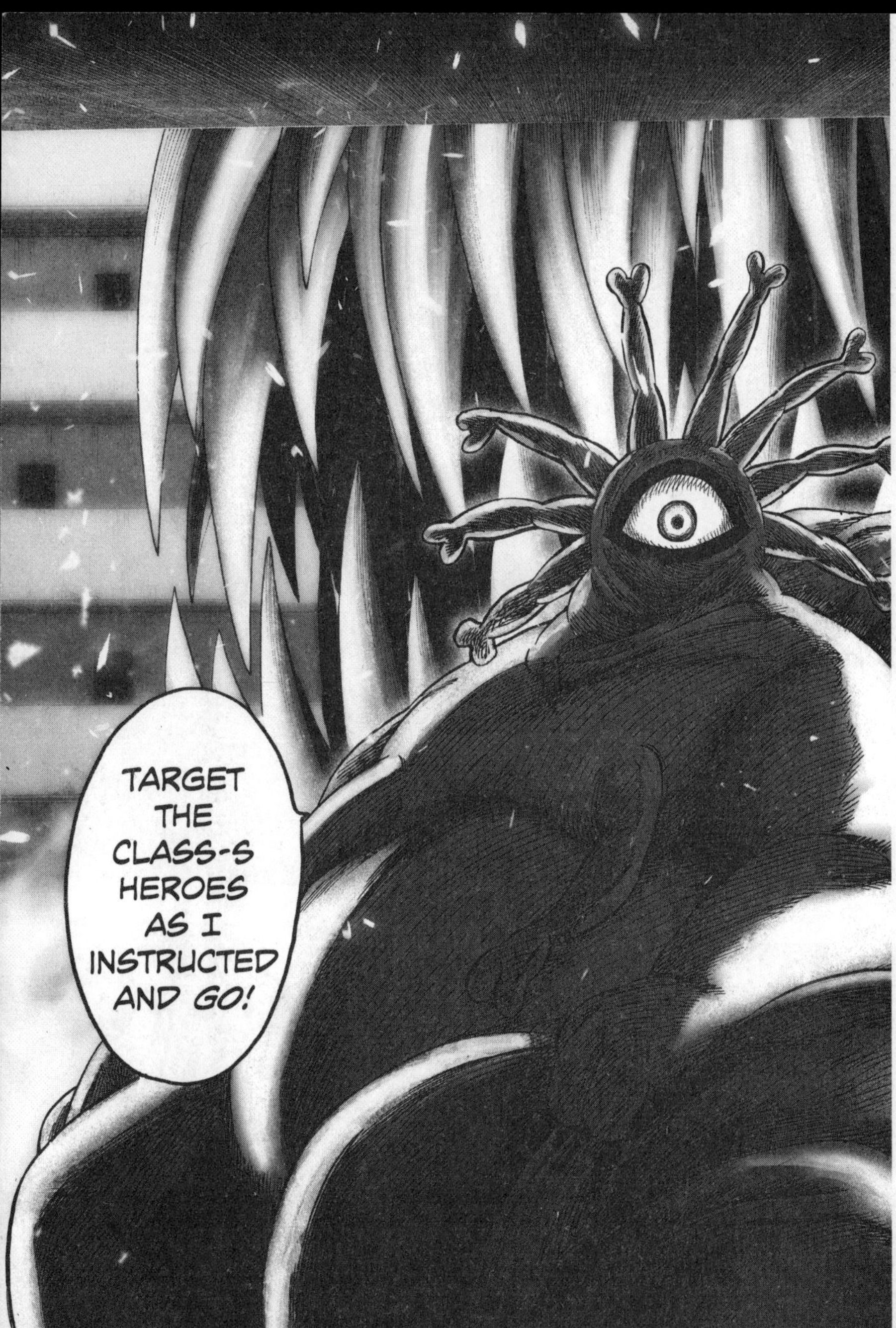
TARGET THE CLASS-S HEROES AS I INSTRUCTED AND GO!

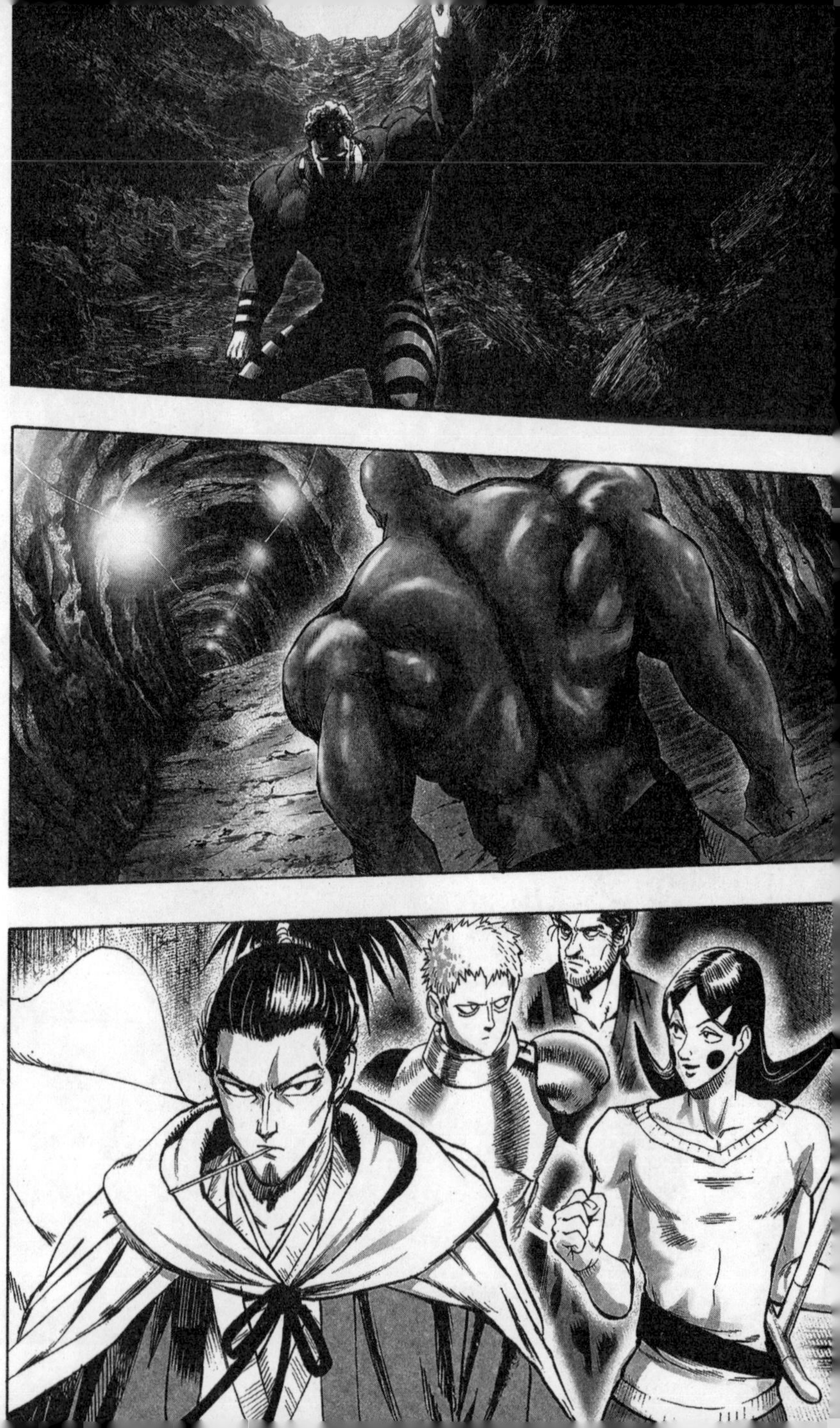

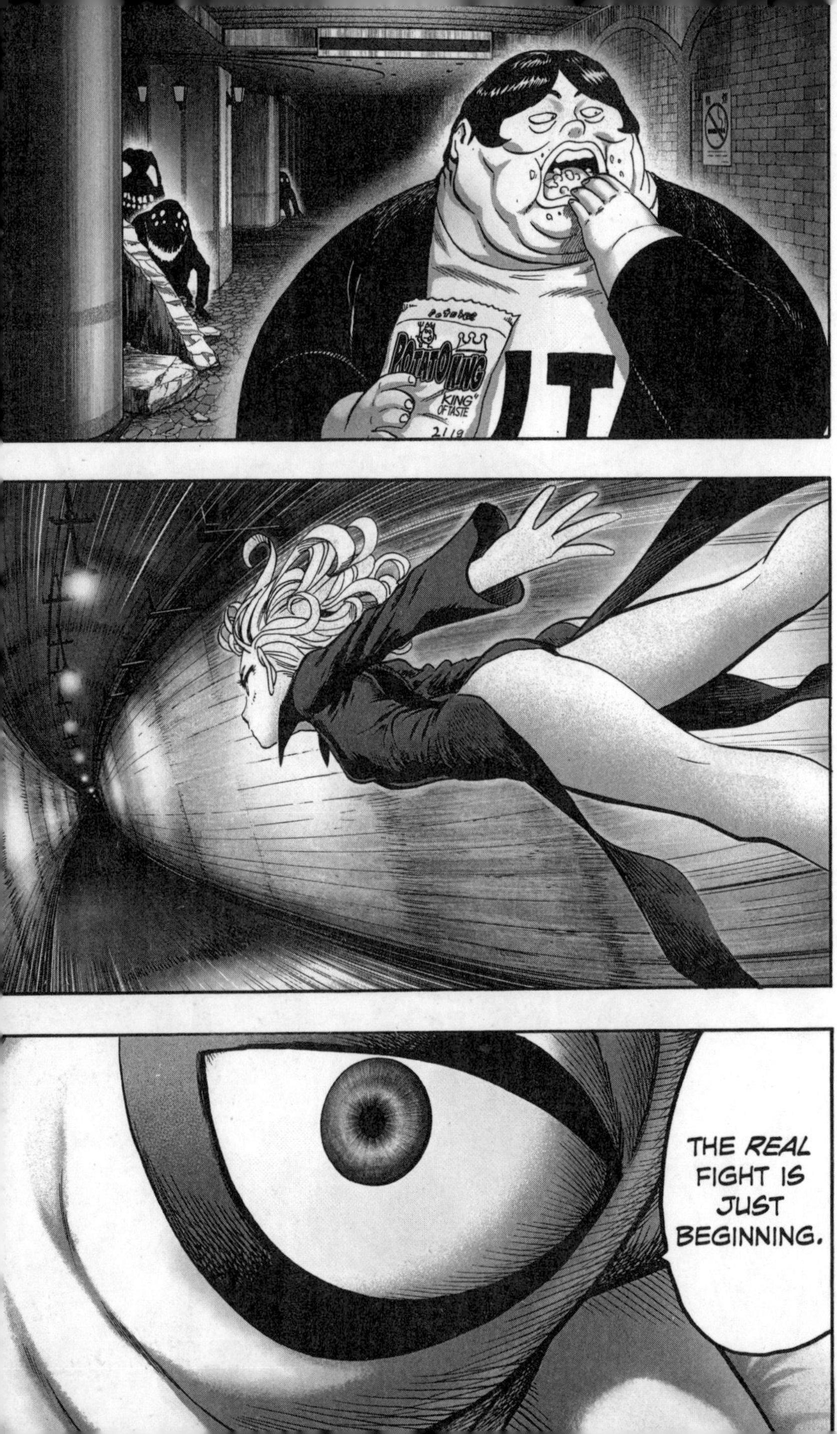
POTATO KING
KING OF TASTE
THE *REAL* FIGHT IS JUST BEGINNING.

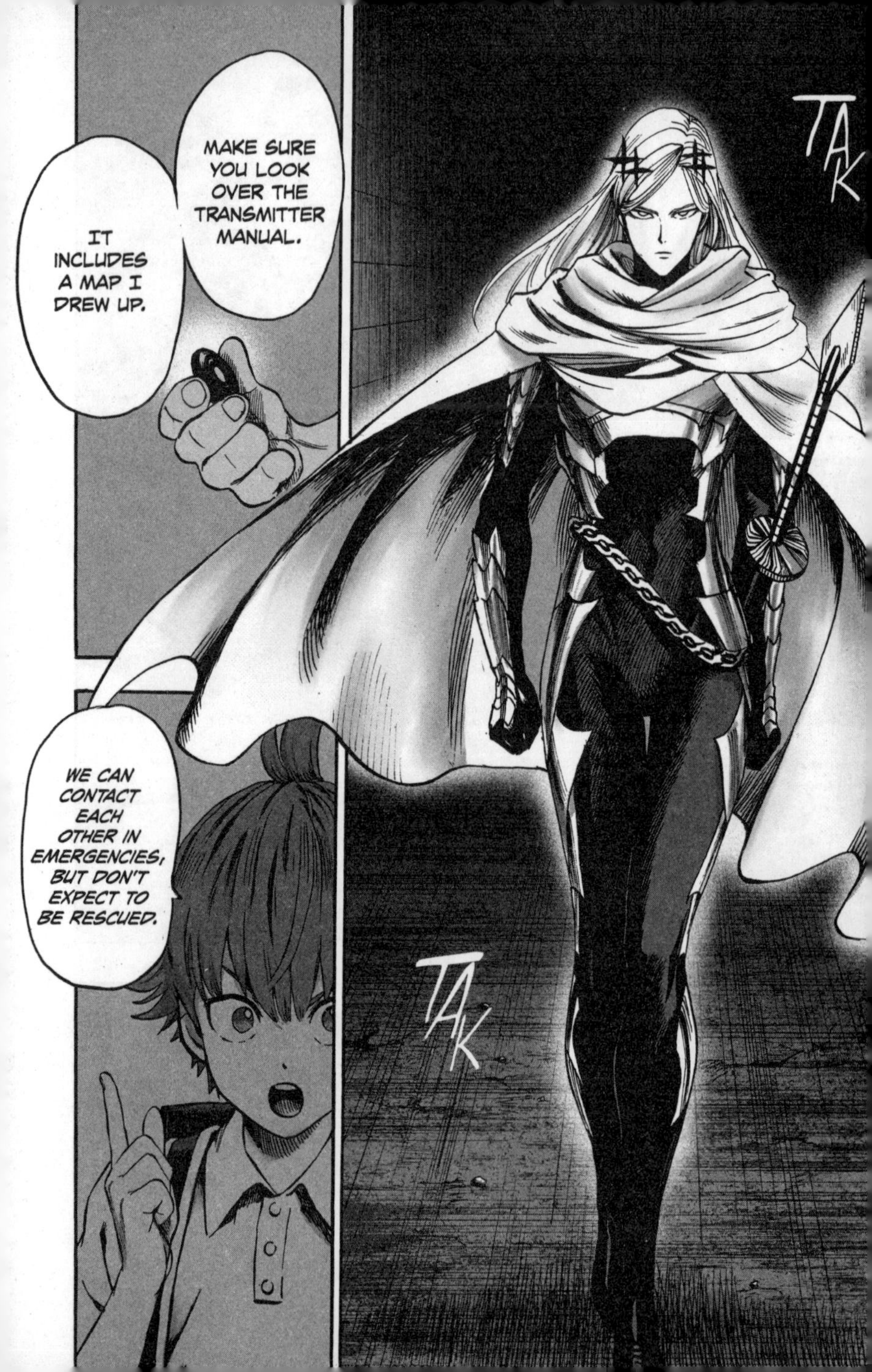
TAK
TAK
MAKE SURE YOU LOOK OVER THE TRANSMITTER MANUAL.
IT INCLUDES A MAP I DREW UP.
WE CAN CONTACT EACH OTHER IN EMERGENCIES, BUT DON'T EXPECT TO BE RESCUED.

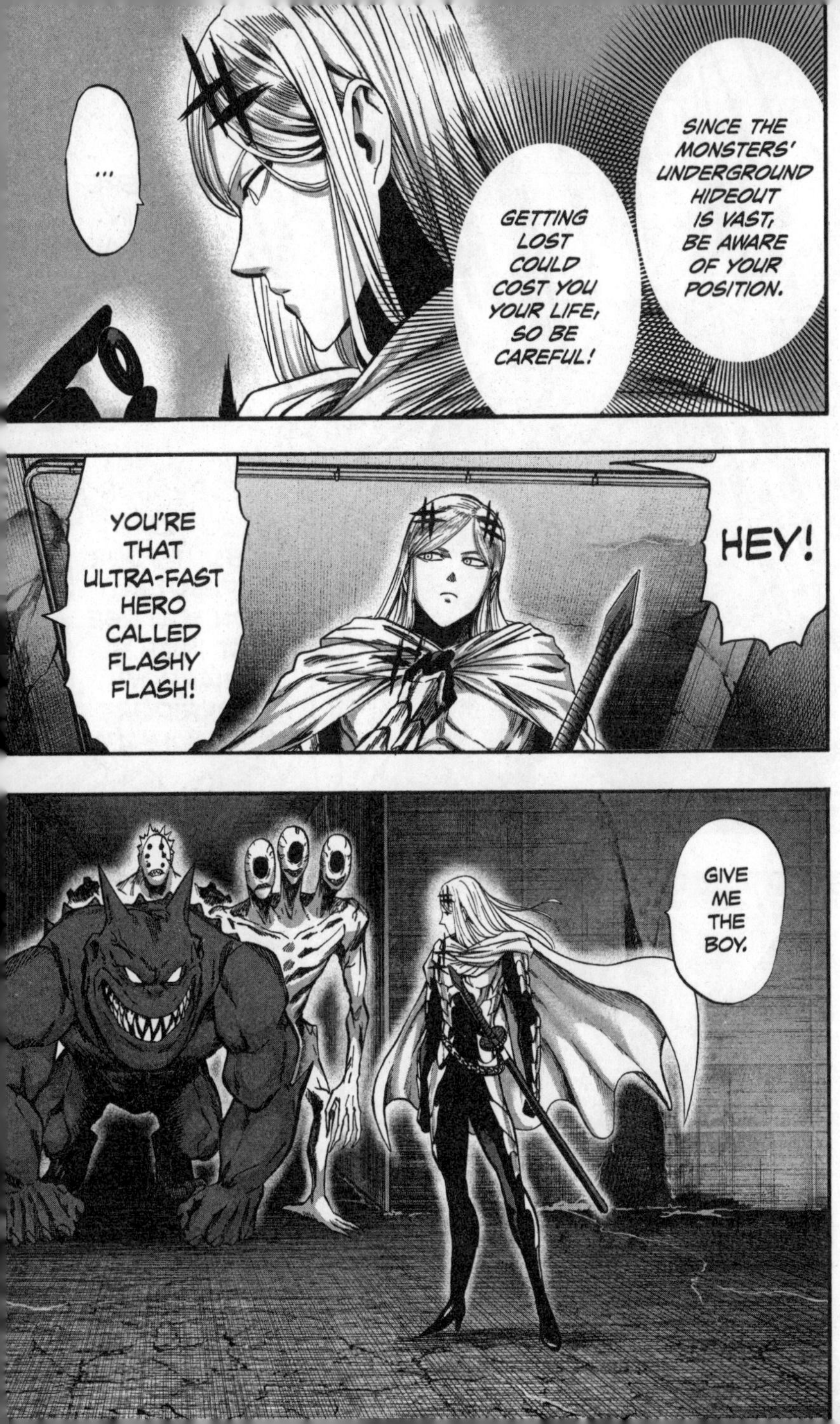
SINCE THE MONSTERS' UNDERGROUND HIDEOUT IS VAST, BE AWARE OF YOUR POSITION.
GETTING LOST COULD COST YOU YOUR LIFE, SO BE CAREFUL!
...
HEY!
YOU'RE THAT ULTRA-FAST HERO CALLED FLASHY FLASH!
GIVE ME THE BOY.

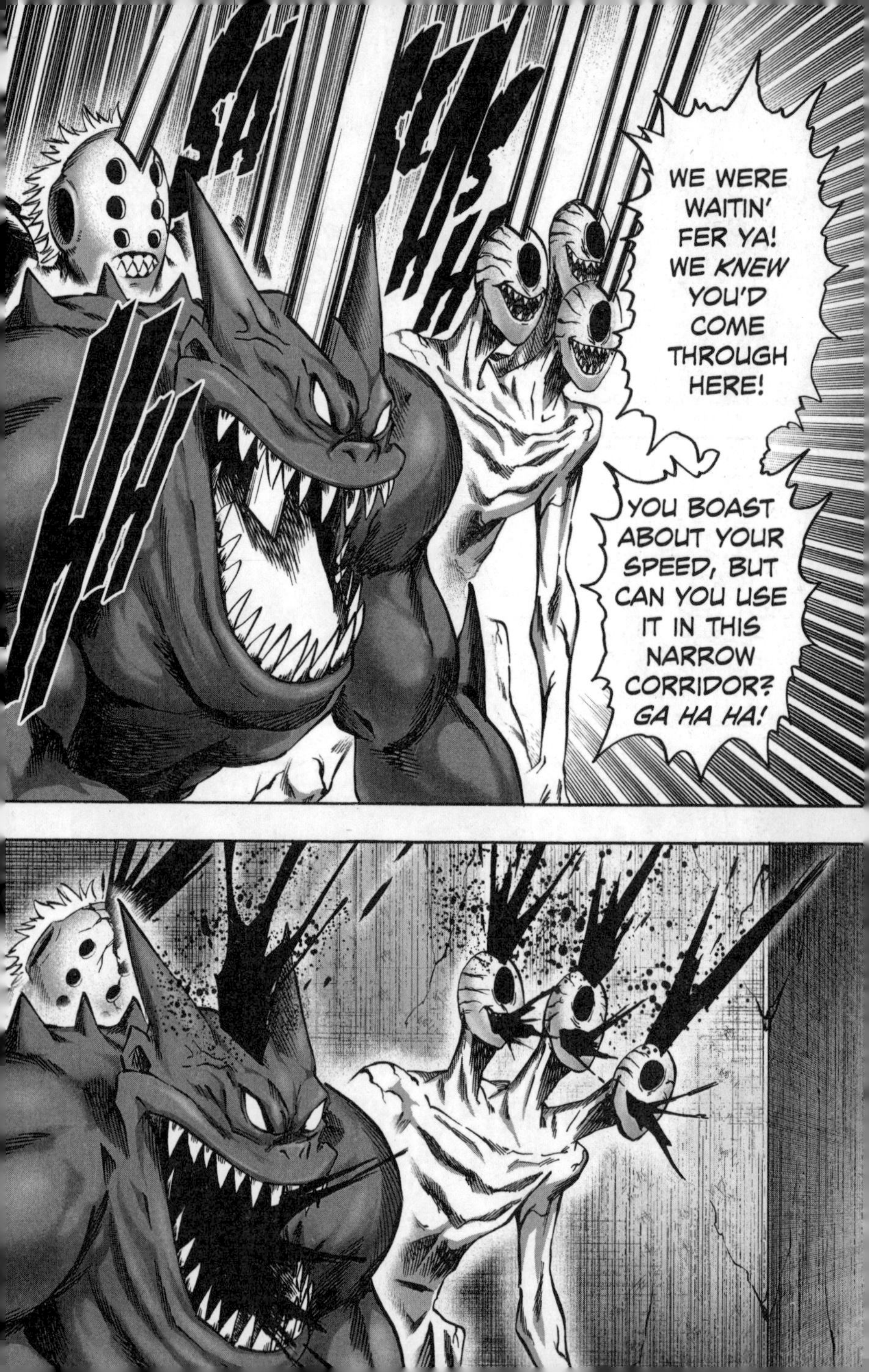
WE WERE WAITIN' FER YA! WE *KNEW* YOU'D COME THROUGH HERE!
YOU BOAST ABOUT YOUR SPEED, BUT CAN YOU USE IT IN THIS NARROW CORRIDOR? *GA HA HA!*

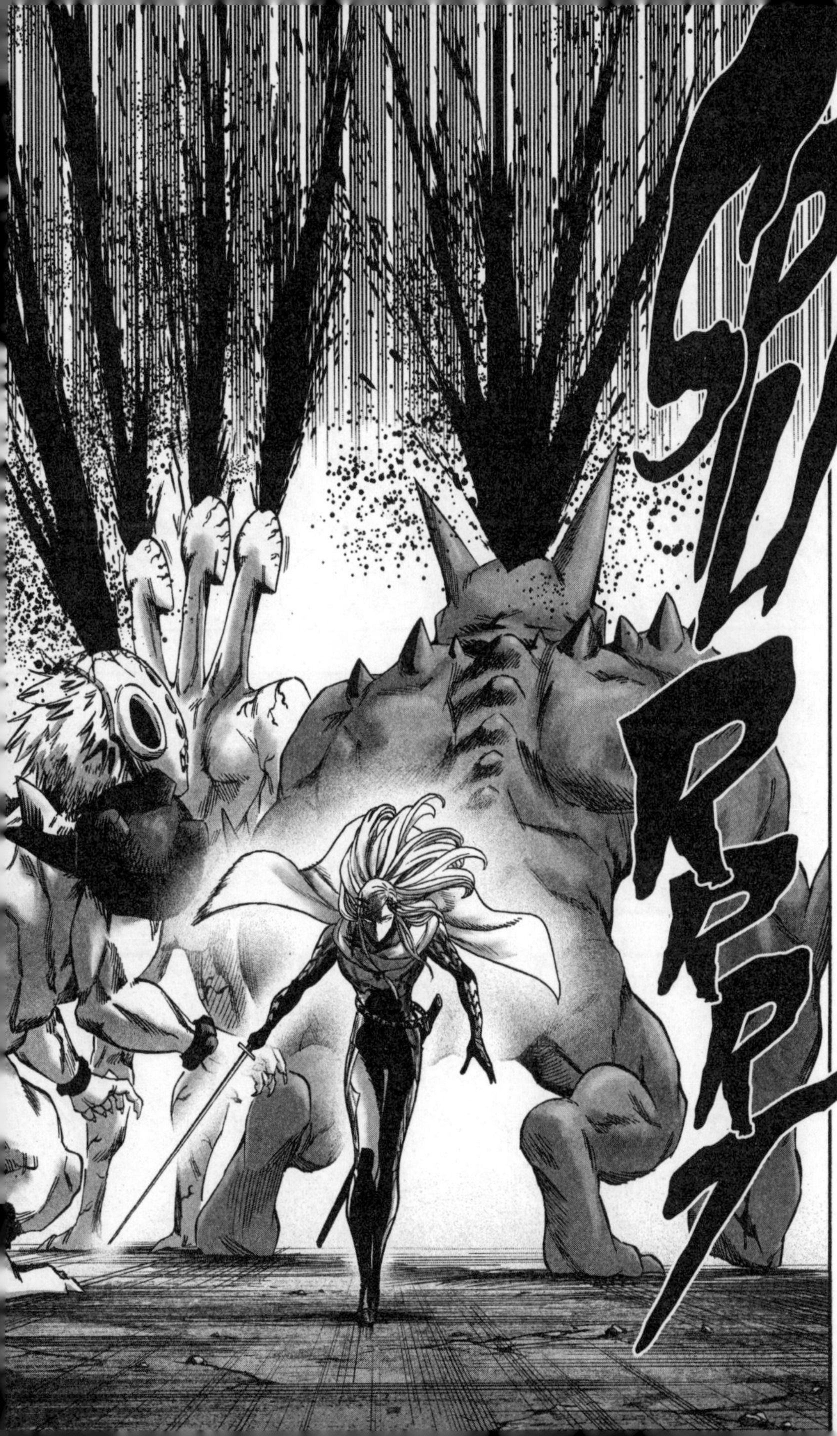

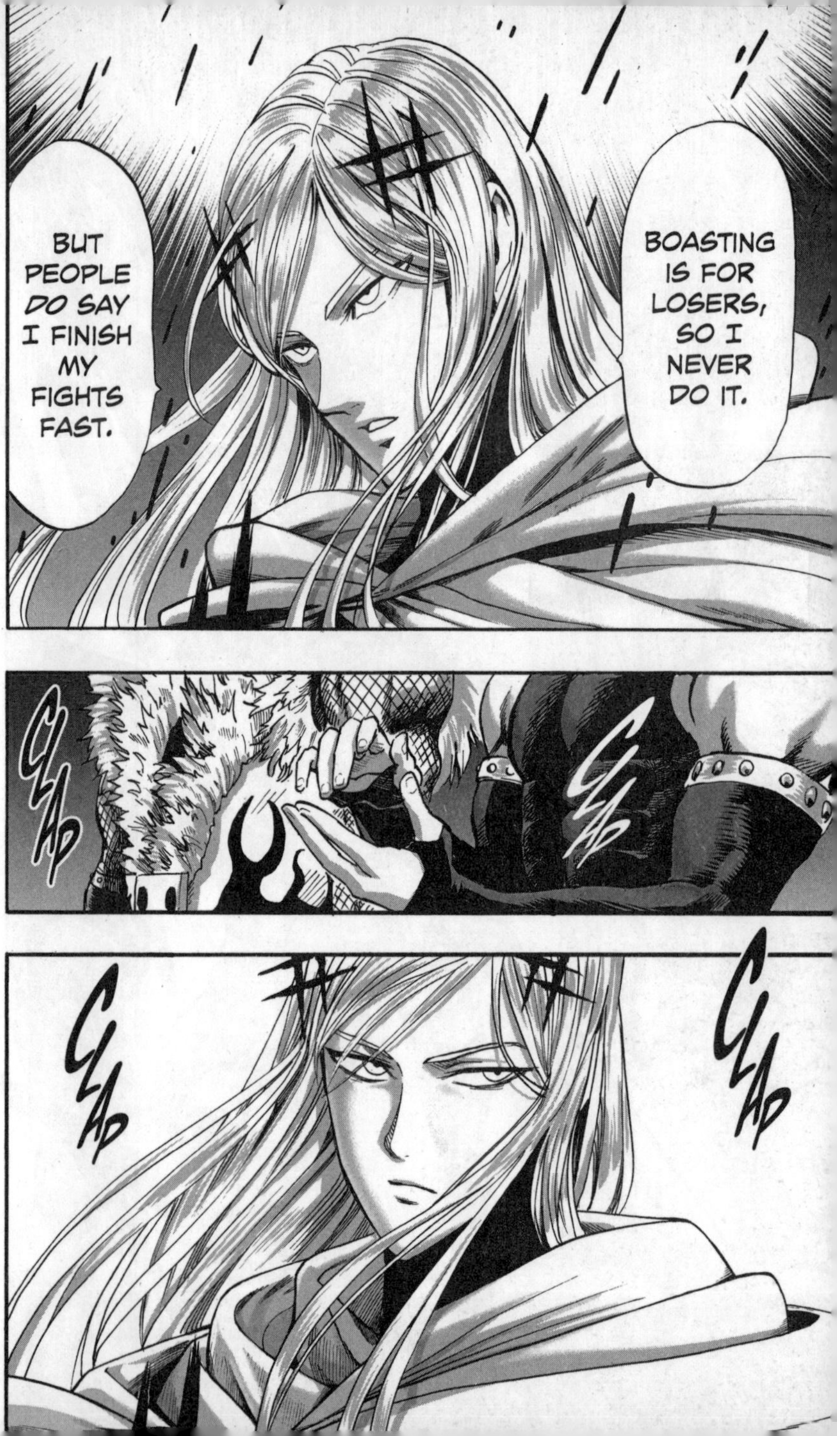
BOASTING IS FOR LOSERS, SO I NEVER DO IT.
BUT PEOPLE *DO* SAY I FINISH MY FIGHTS FAST.
CLAP
CLAP
CLAP
CLAP

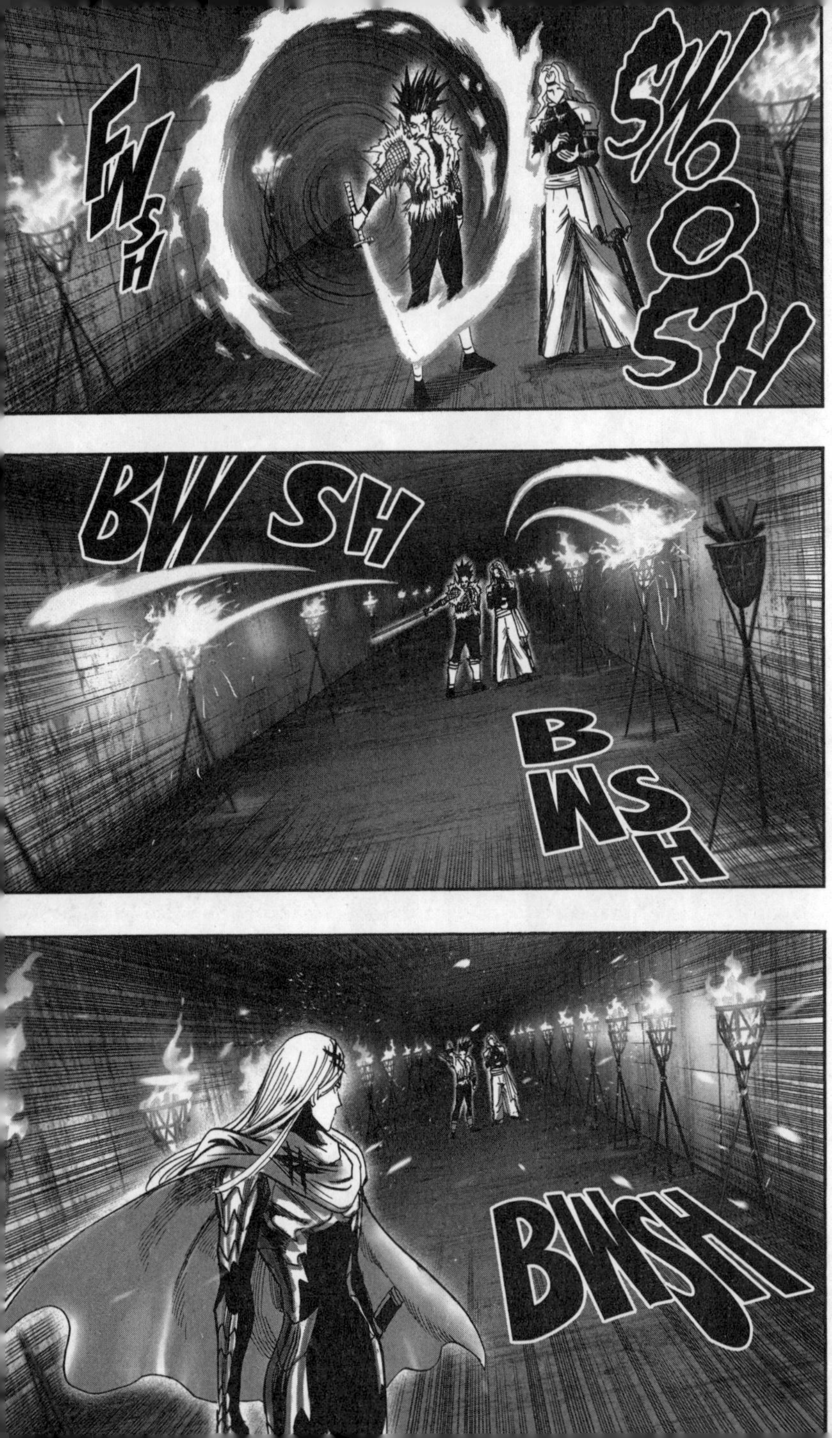
SWOOSH
FWSH
BWSH
BWSH
BWSH

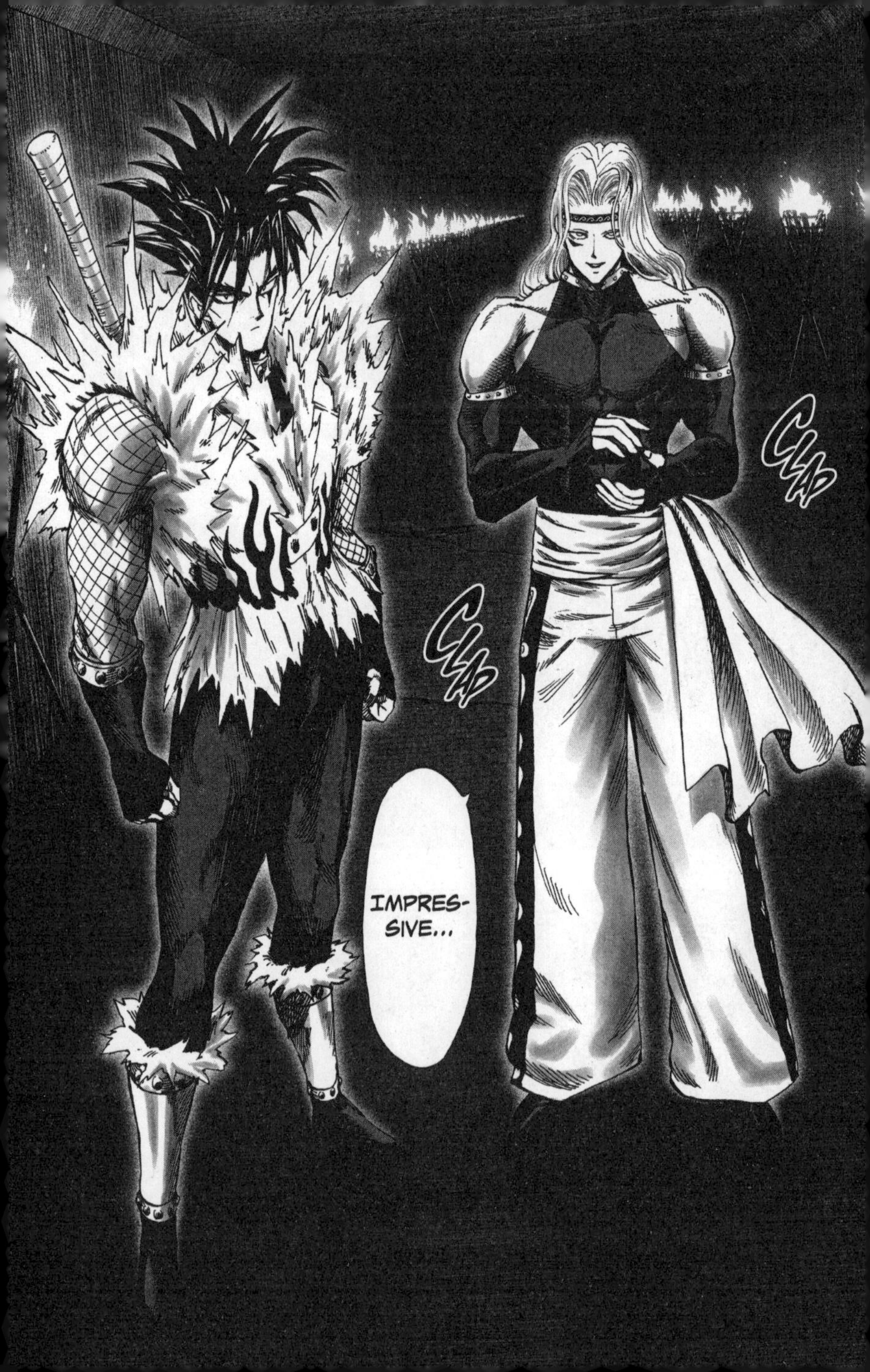
CLAP
CLAP
IMPRES-
SIVE...

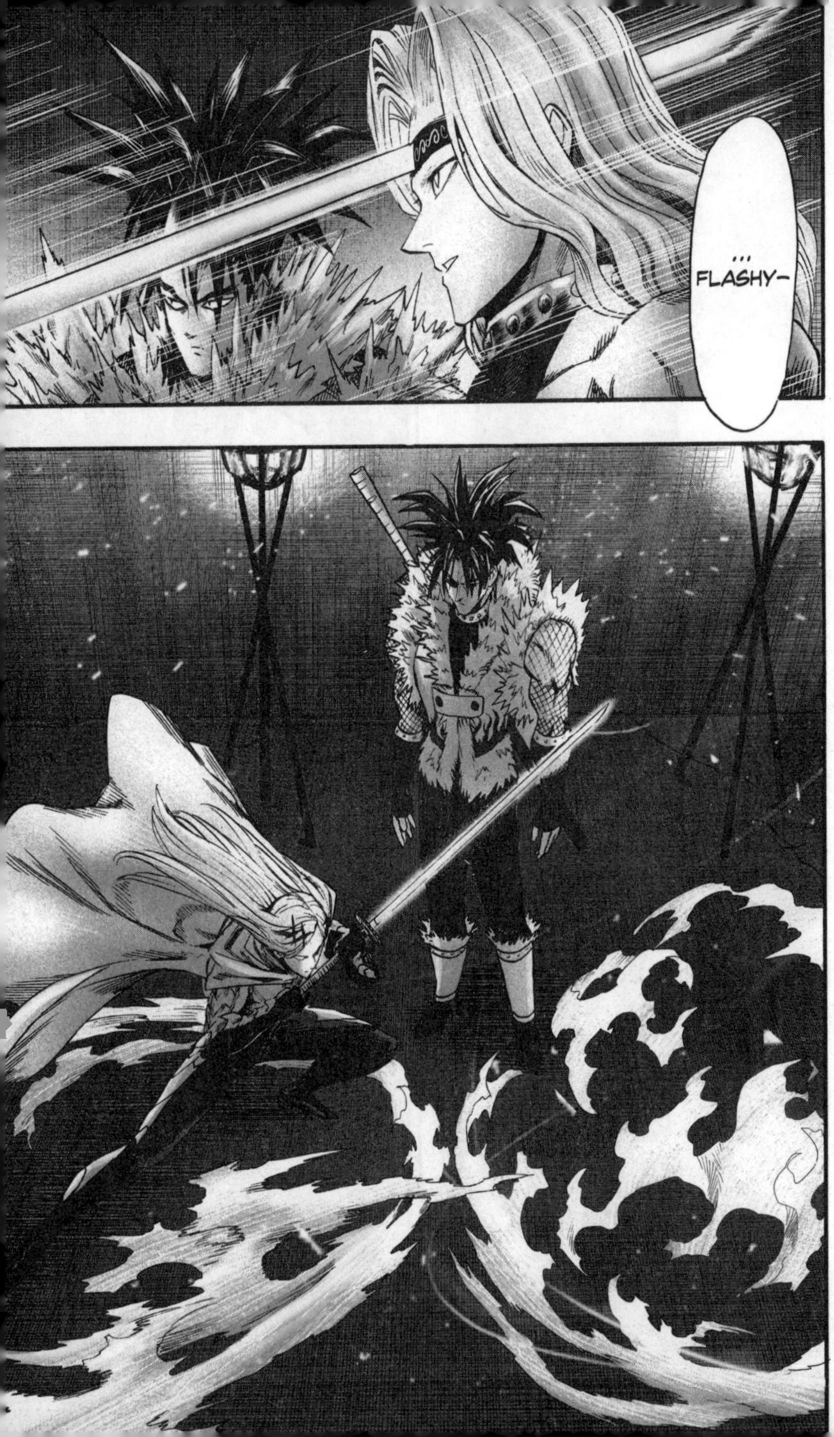
... FLASHY-

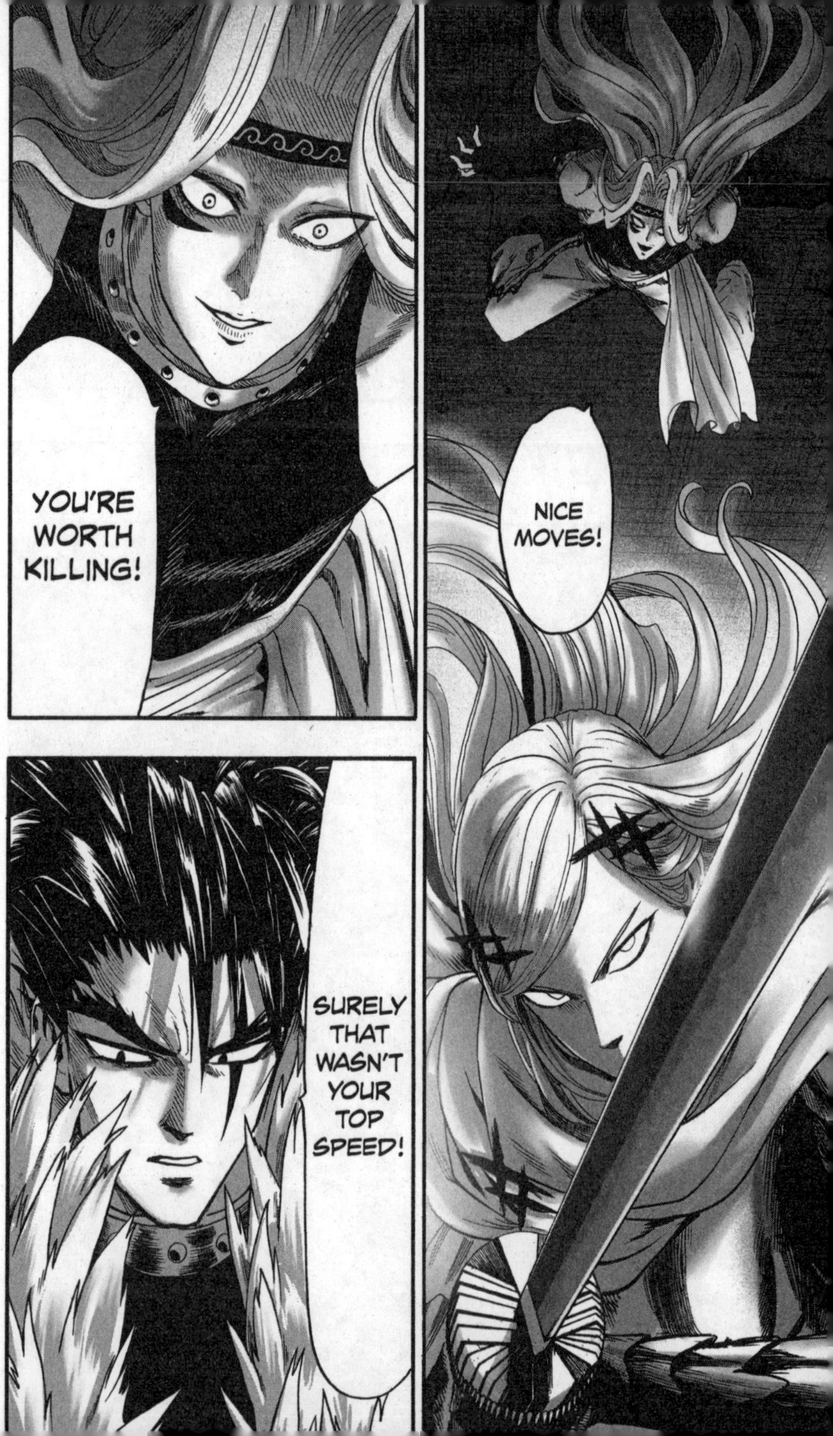
NICE MOVES!
YOU'RE WORTH KILLING!
SURELY THAT WASN'T YOUR TOP SPEED!

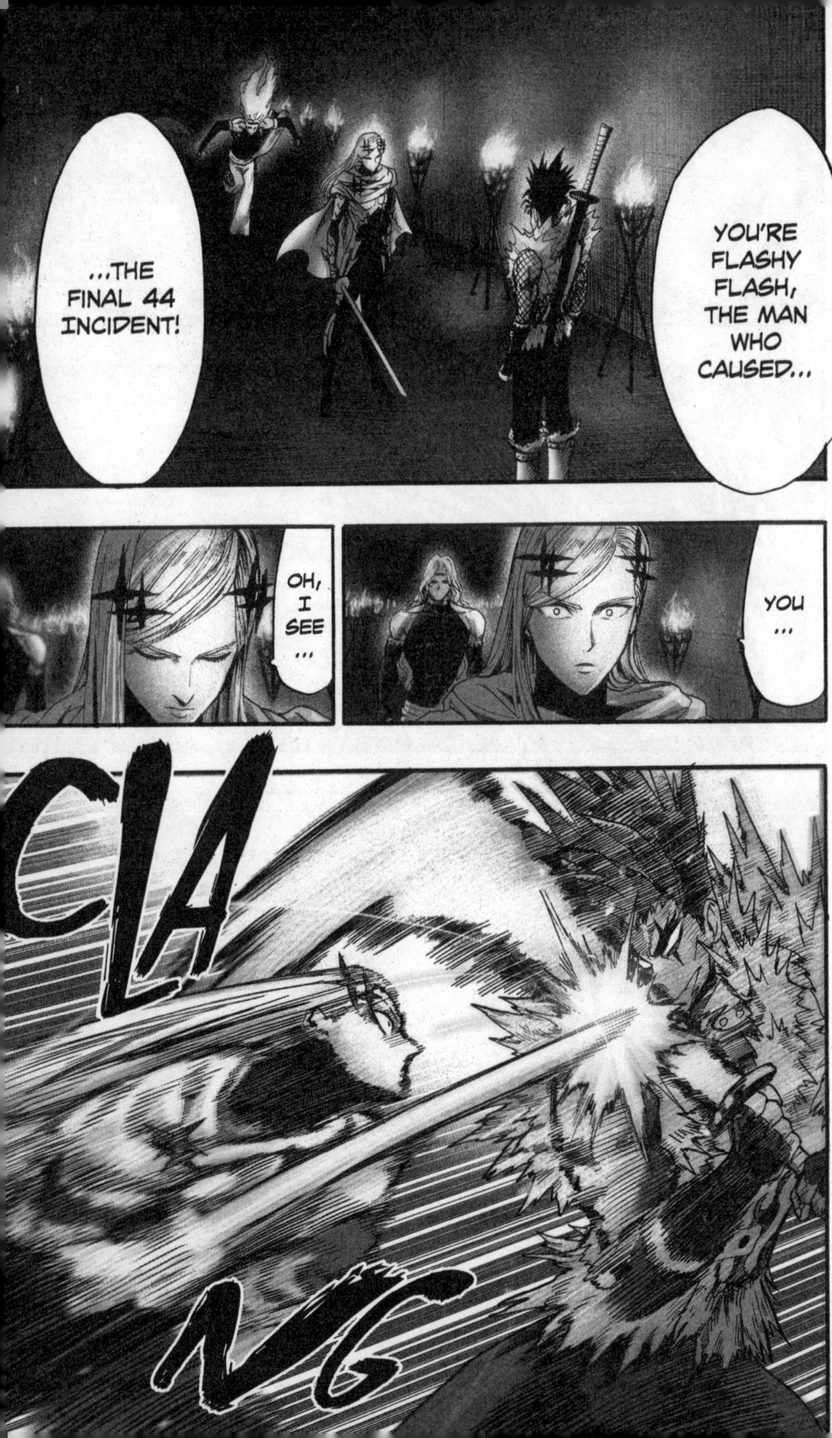
YOU'RE FLASHY FLASH, THE MAN WHO CAUSED...
...THE FINAL 44 INCIDENT!
YOU ...
OH, I SEE ...
CLANG

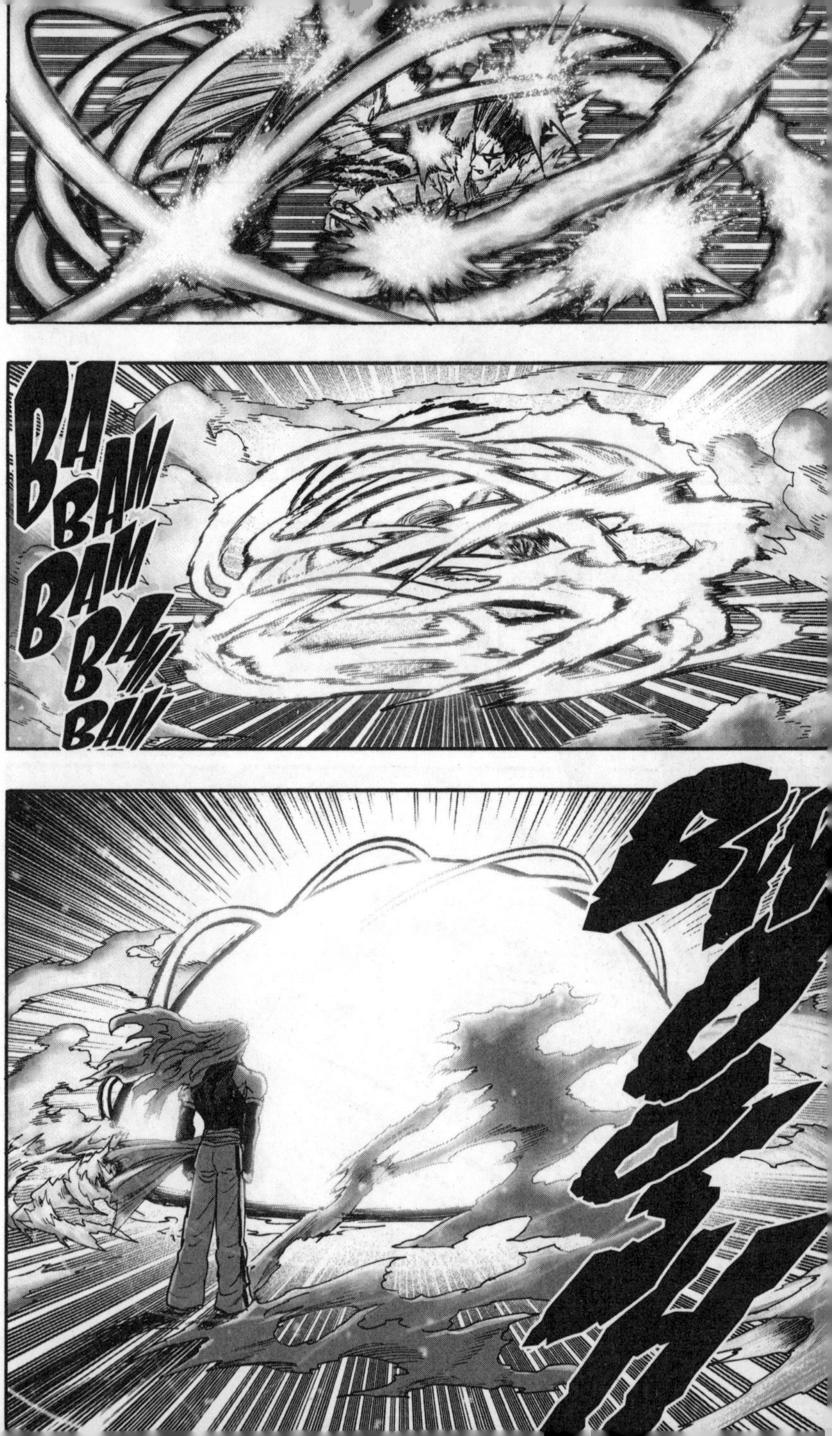
BA BAM BAM BAM BAM BAM

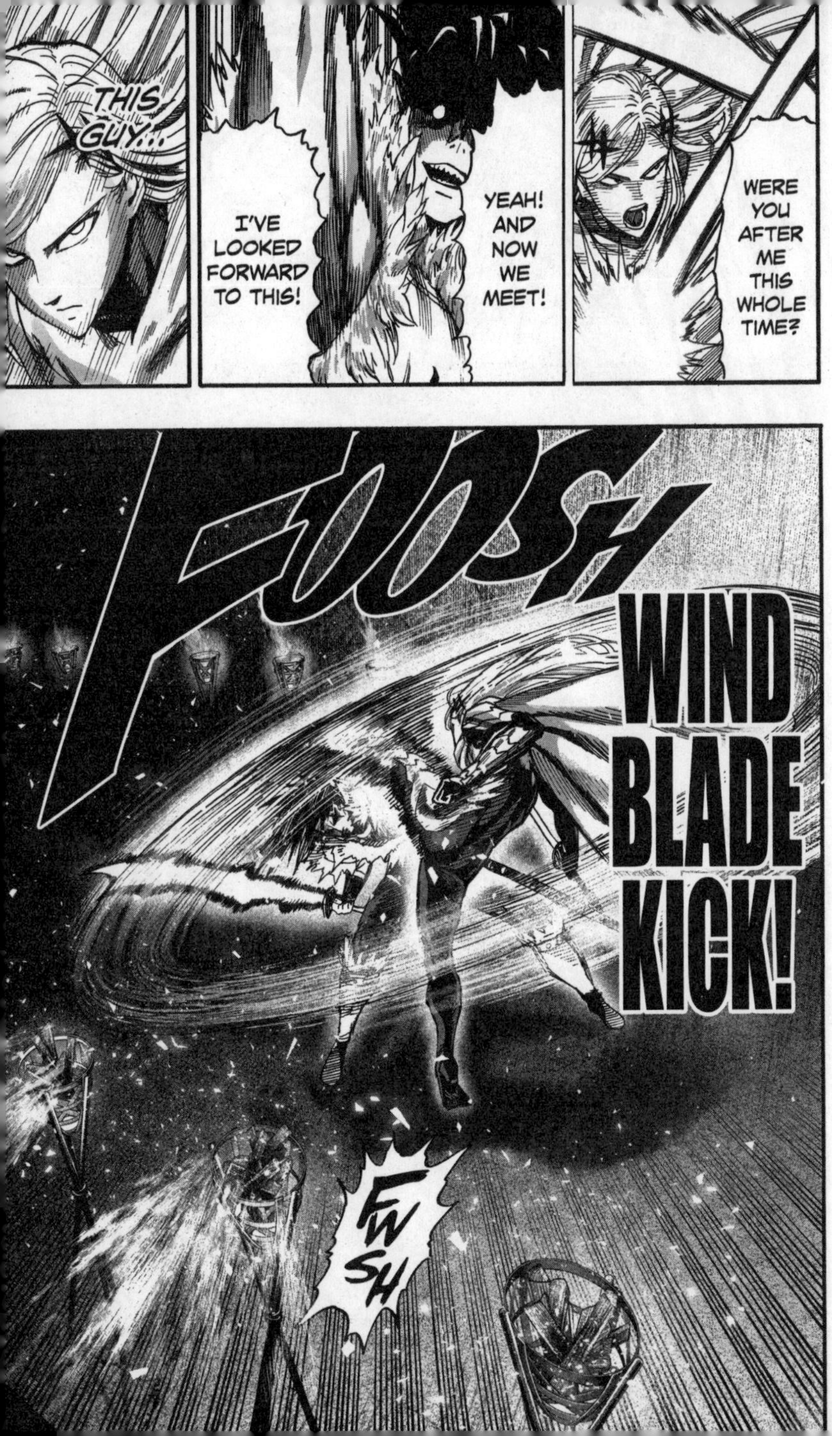
WERE YOU AFTER ME THIS WHOLE TIME?
YEAH! AND NOW WE MEET!
I'VE LOOKED FORWARD TO THIS!
THIS GUY...
FOOSH
WIND BLADE KICK!
FWSH

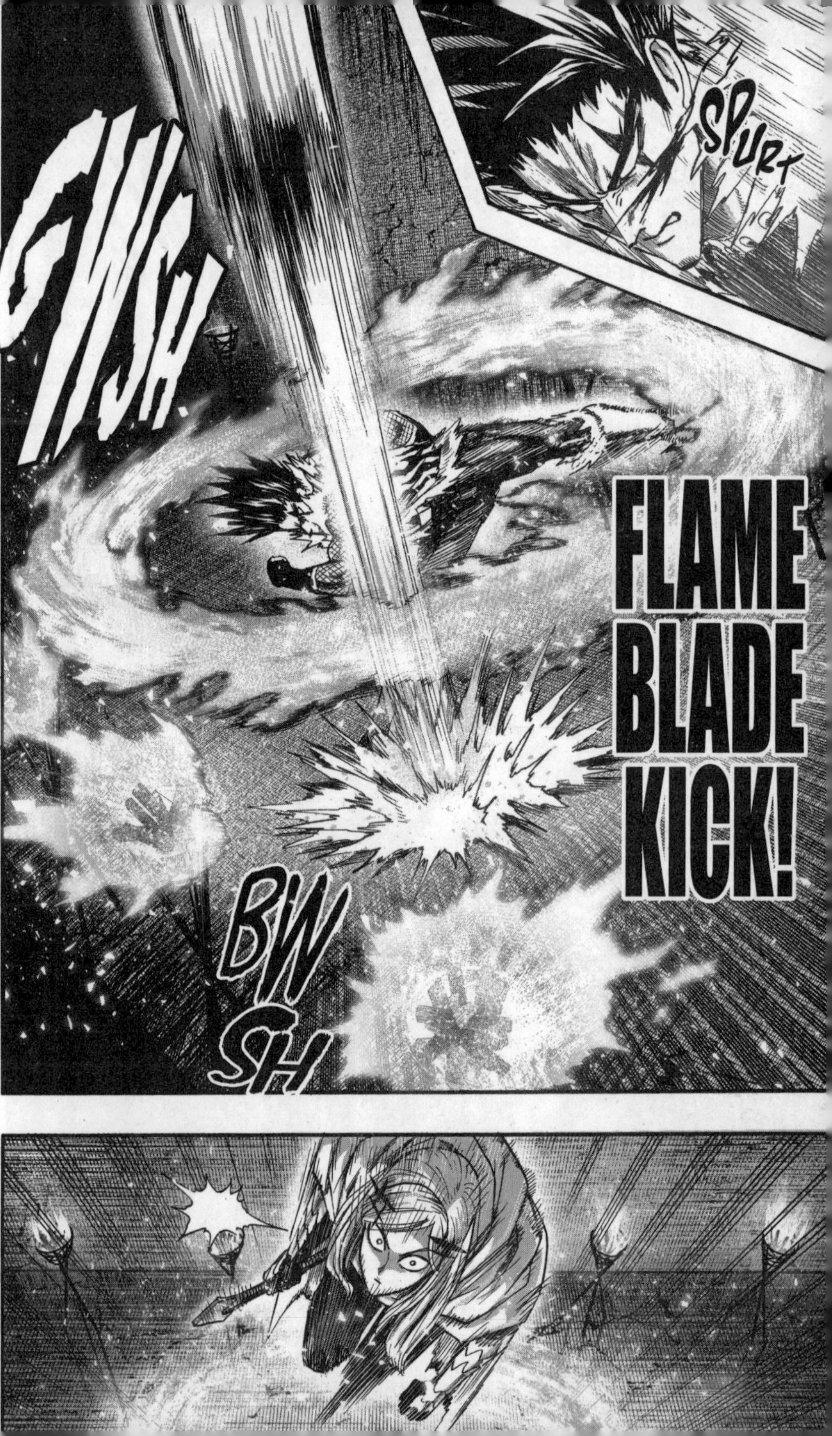
SPURT
GWSH
FLAME BLADE KICK!
BWSH

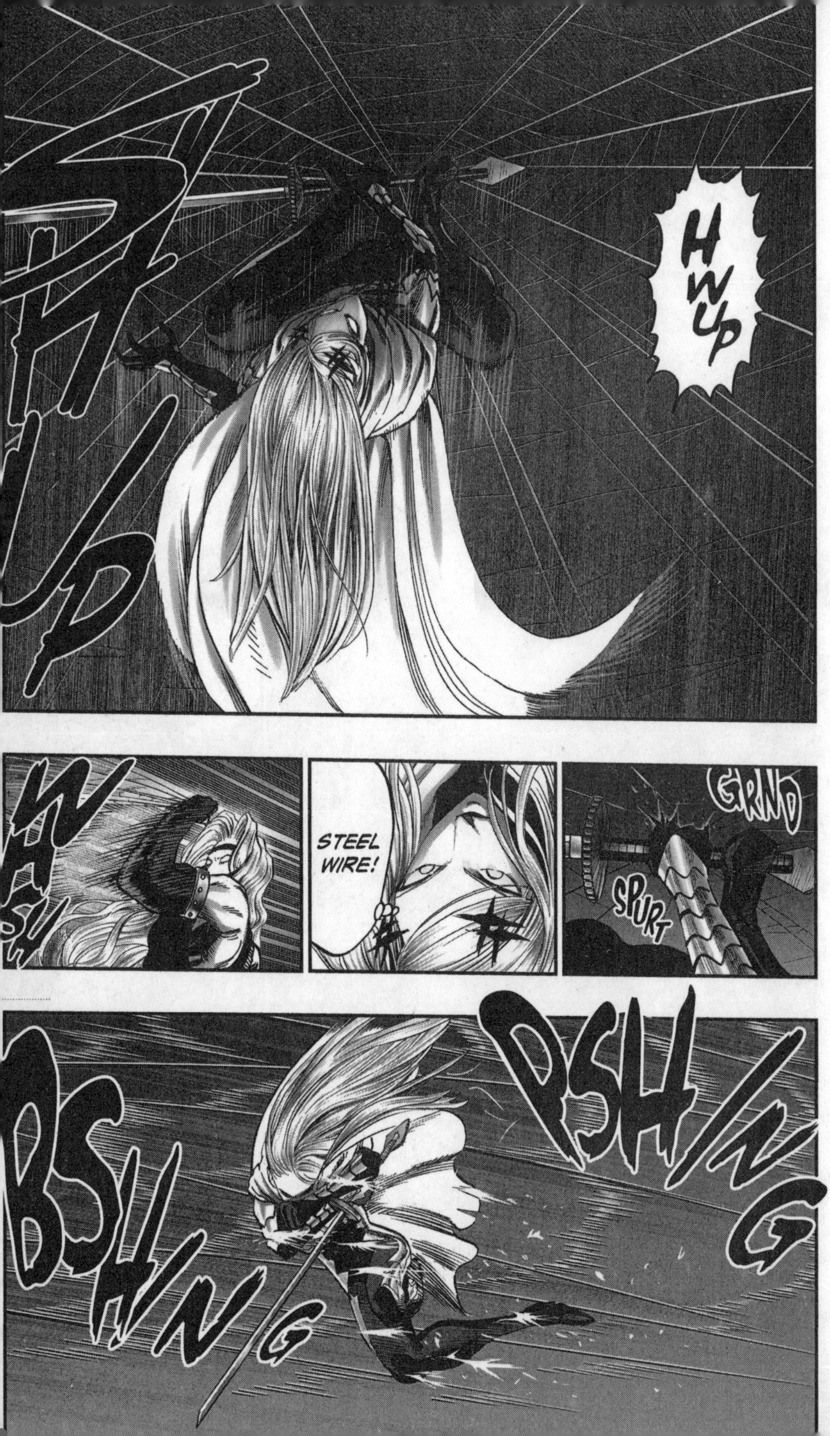
HWUP
GRND
SPURT
STEEL WIRE!
DSHING
BSHING

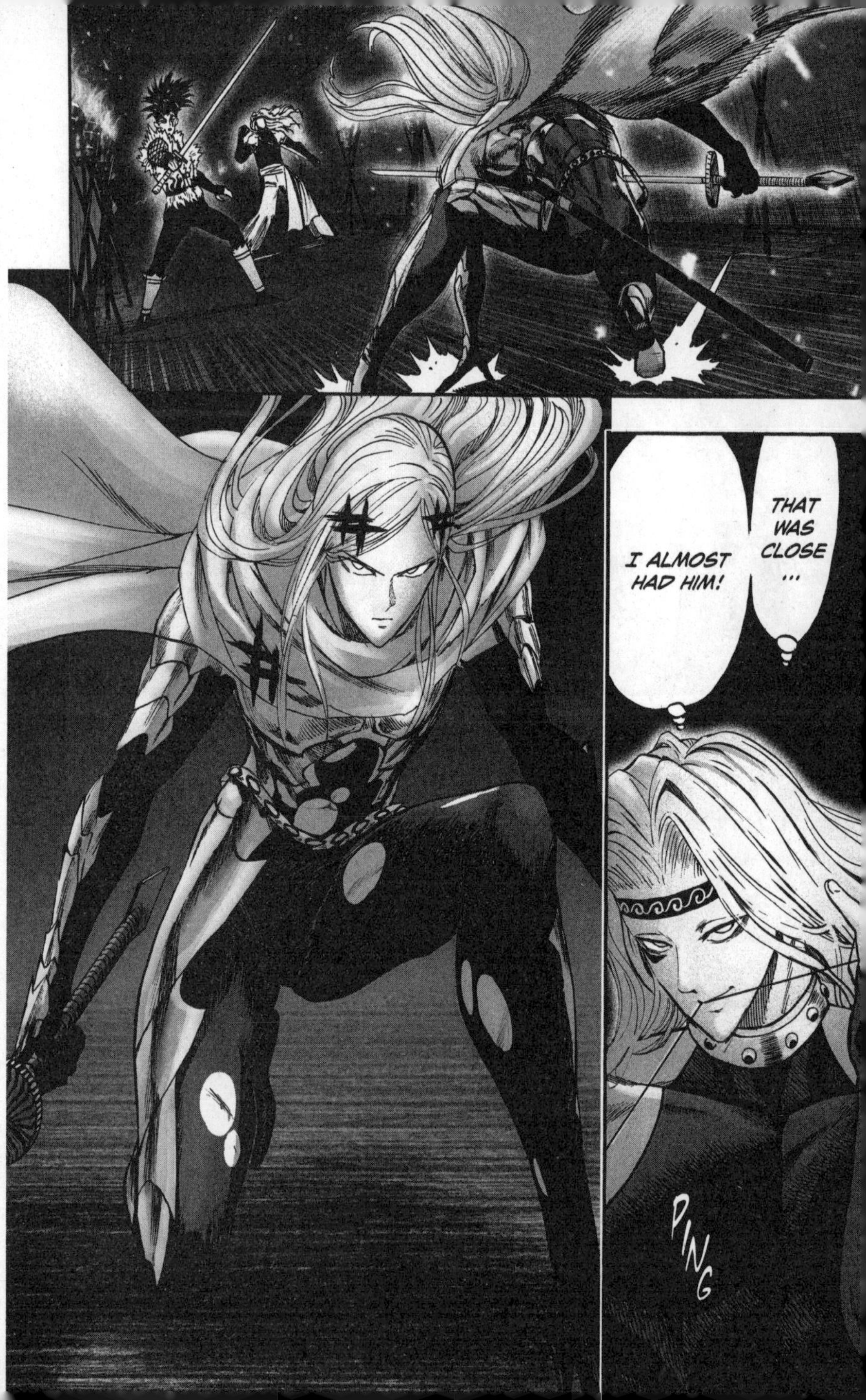
THAT WAS CLOSE ...
I ALMOST HAD HIM!
PING

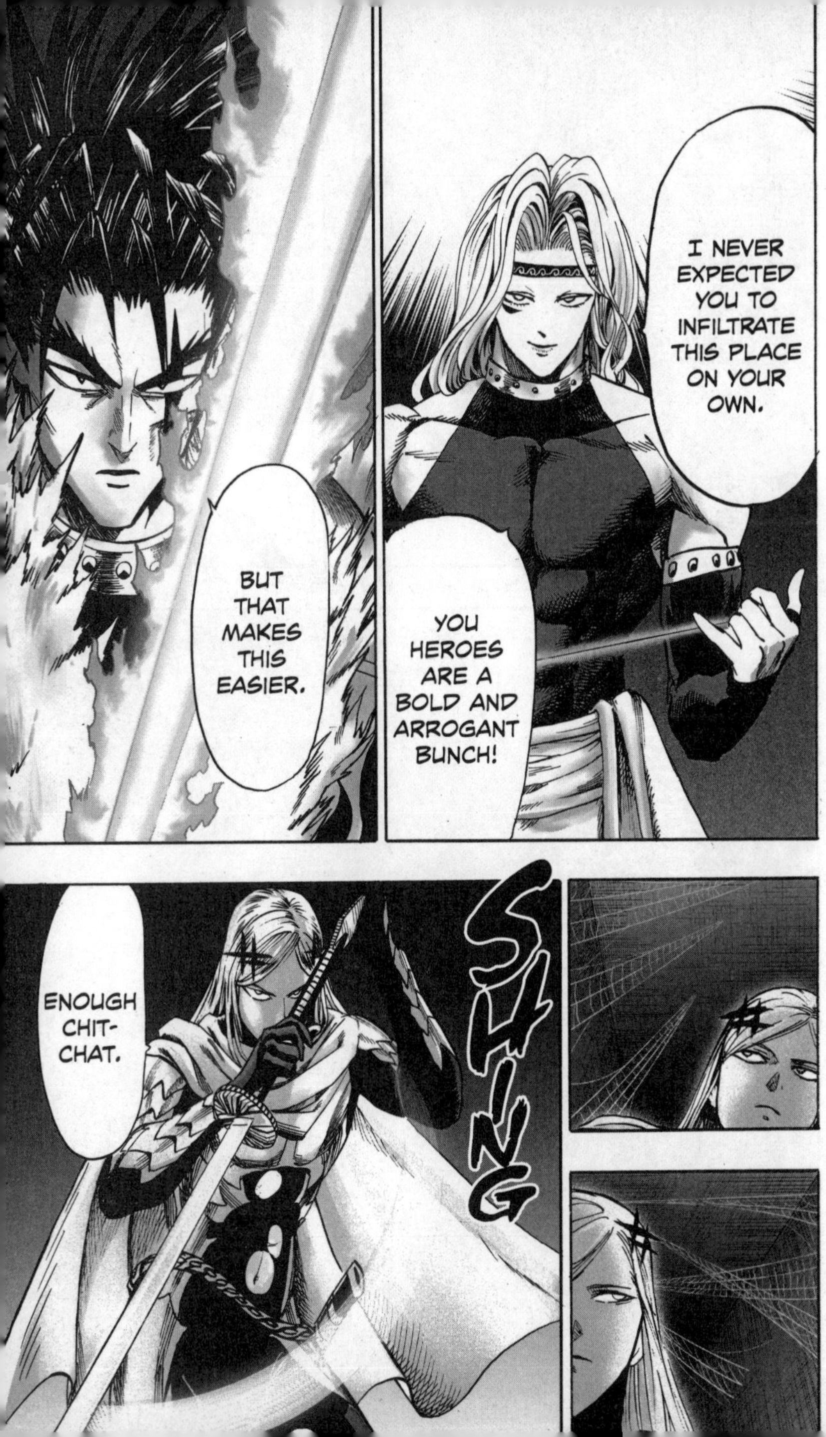
I NEVER EXPECTED YOU TO INFILTRATE THIS PLACE ON YOUR OWN.
YOU HEROES ARE A BOLD AND ARROGANT BUNCH!
BUT THAT MAKES THIS EASIER.
SHING
ENOUGH CHIT-CHAT.

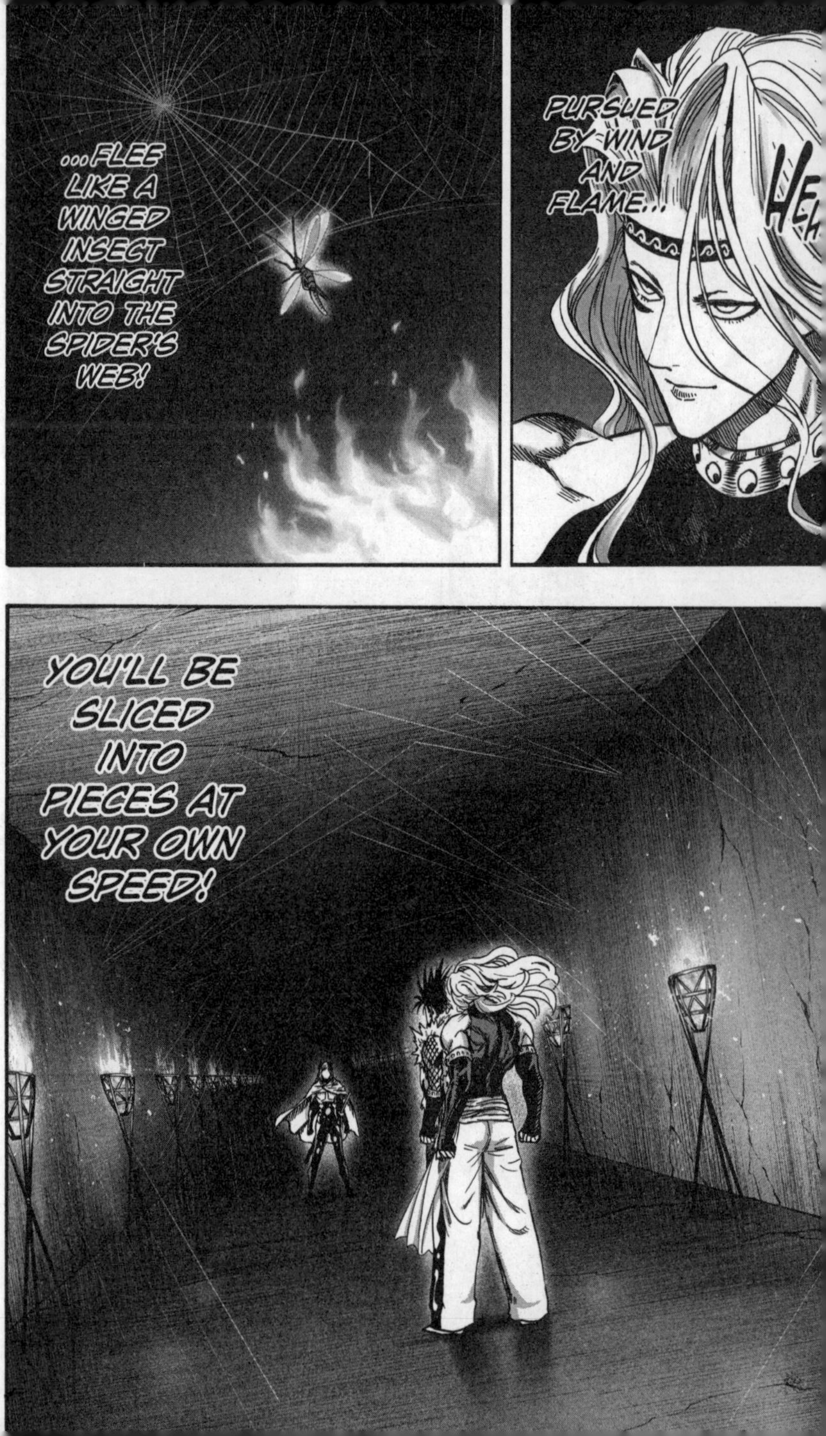
PURSUED BY WIND AND FLAME...
HE
...FLEE LIKE A WINGED INSECT STRAIGHT INTO THE SPIDER'S WEB!
YOU'LL BE SLICED INTO PIECES AT YOUR OWN SPEED!

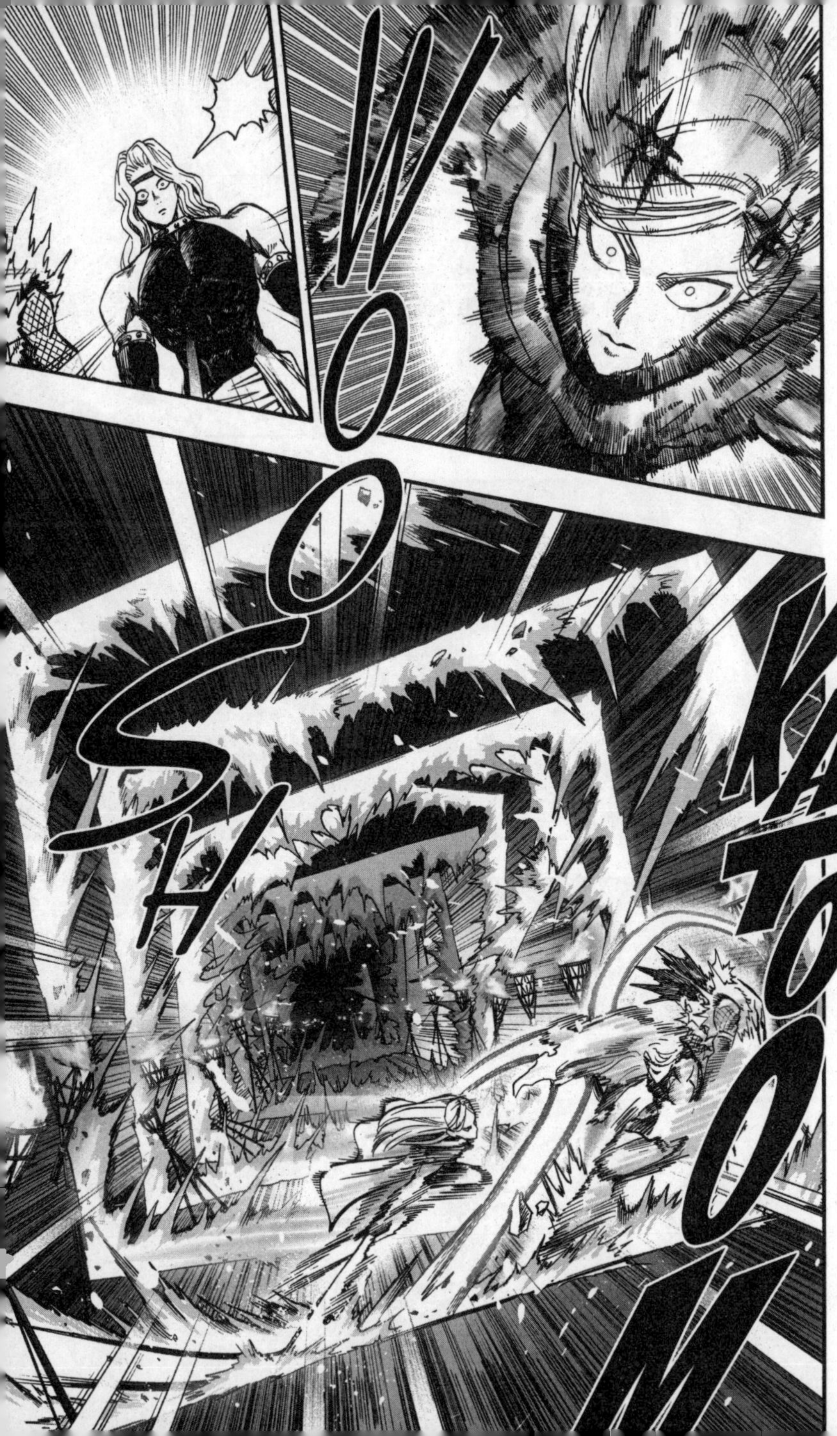
KATOOM
WOOOSH

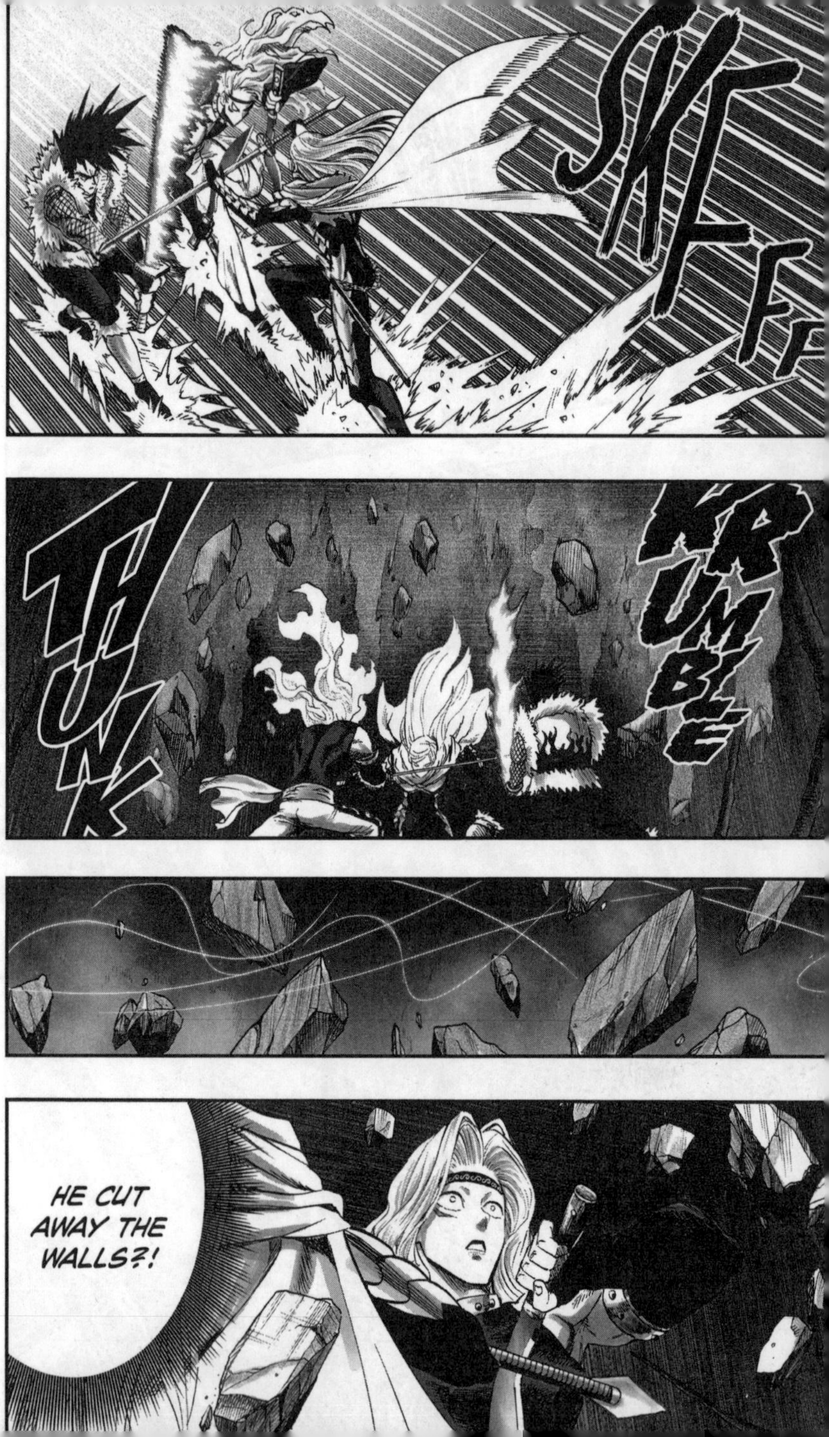
SKAFF
KRUMBLE
THUNK
HE CUT AWAY THE WALLS?!

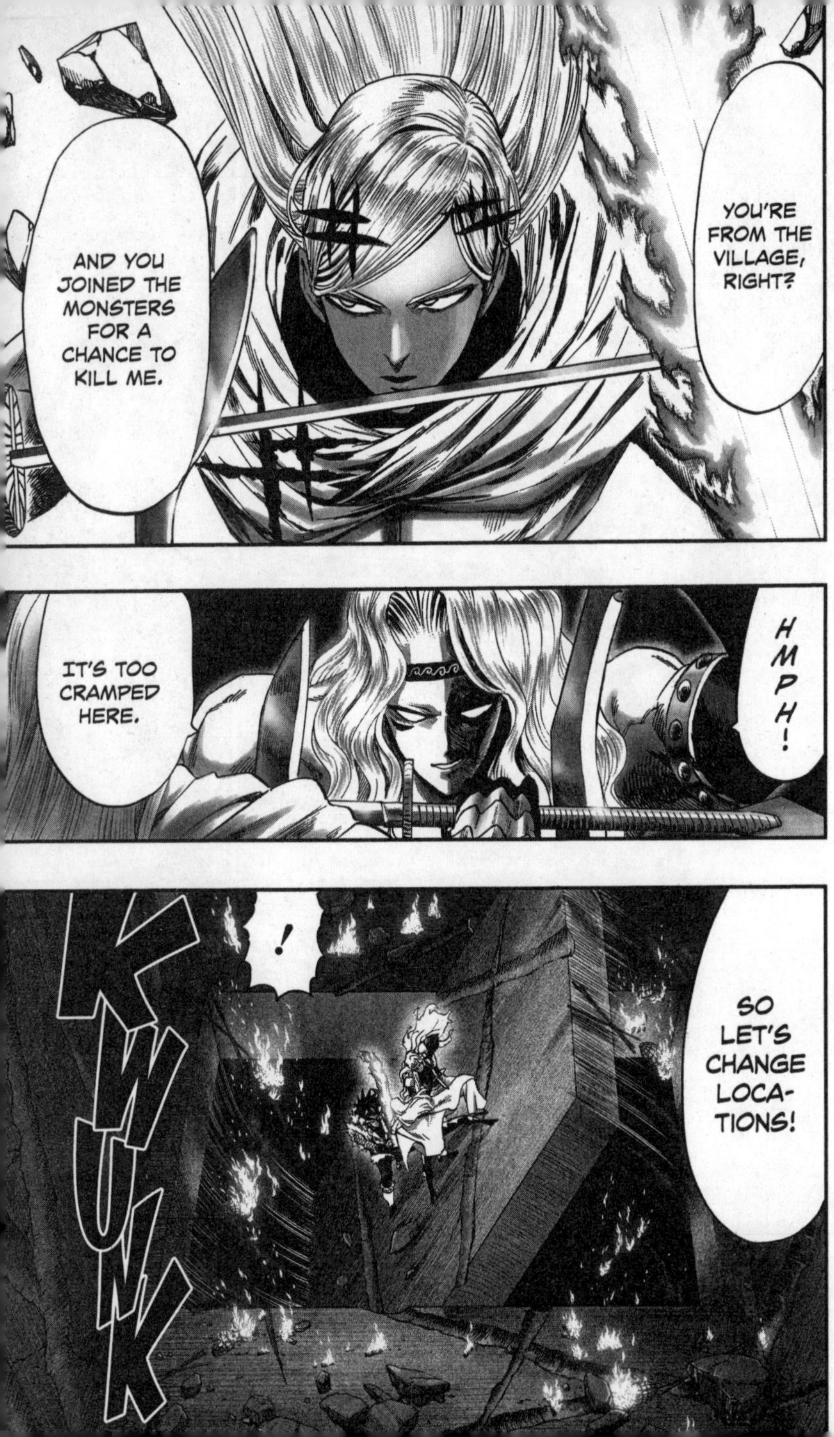
YOU'RE FROM THE VILLAGE, RIGHT?
AND YOU JOINED THE MONSTERS FOR A CHANCE TO KILL ME.
HMPH!
IT'S TOO CRAMPED HERE.
SO LET'S CHANGE LOCA-TIONS!
!
KWUNK

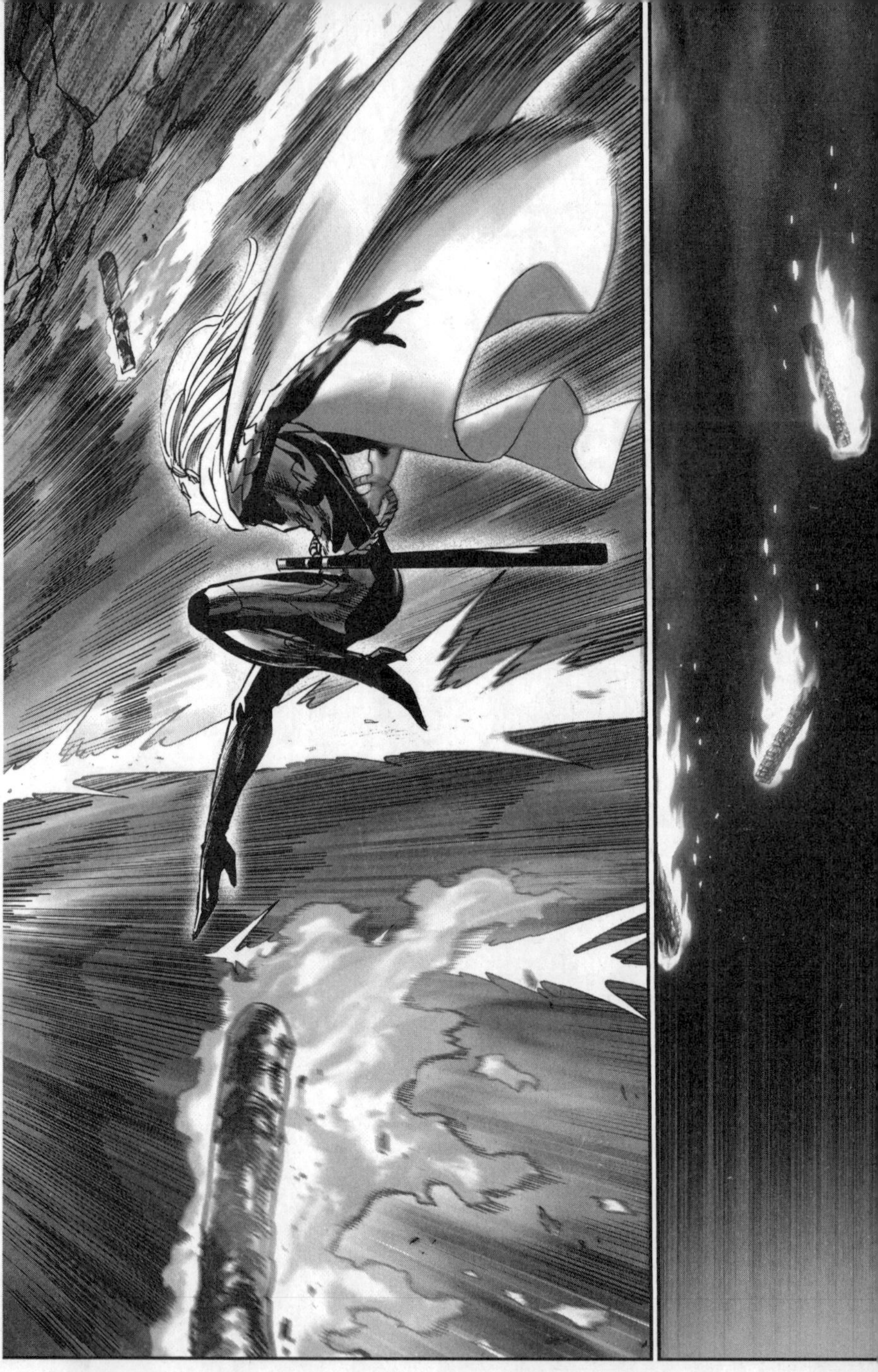

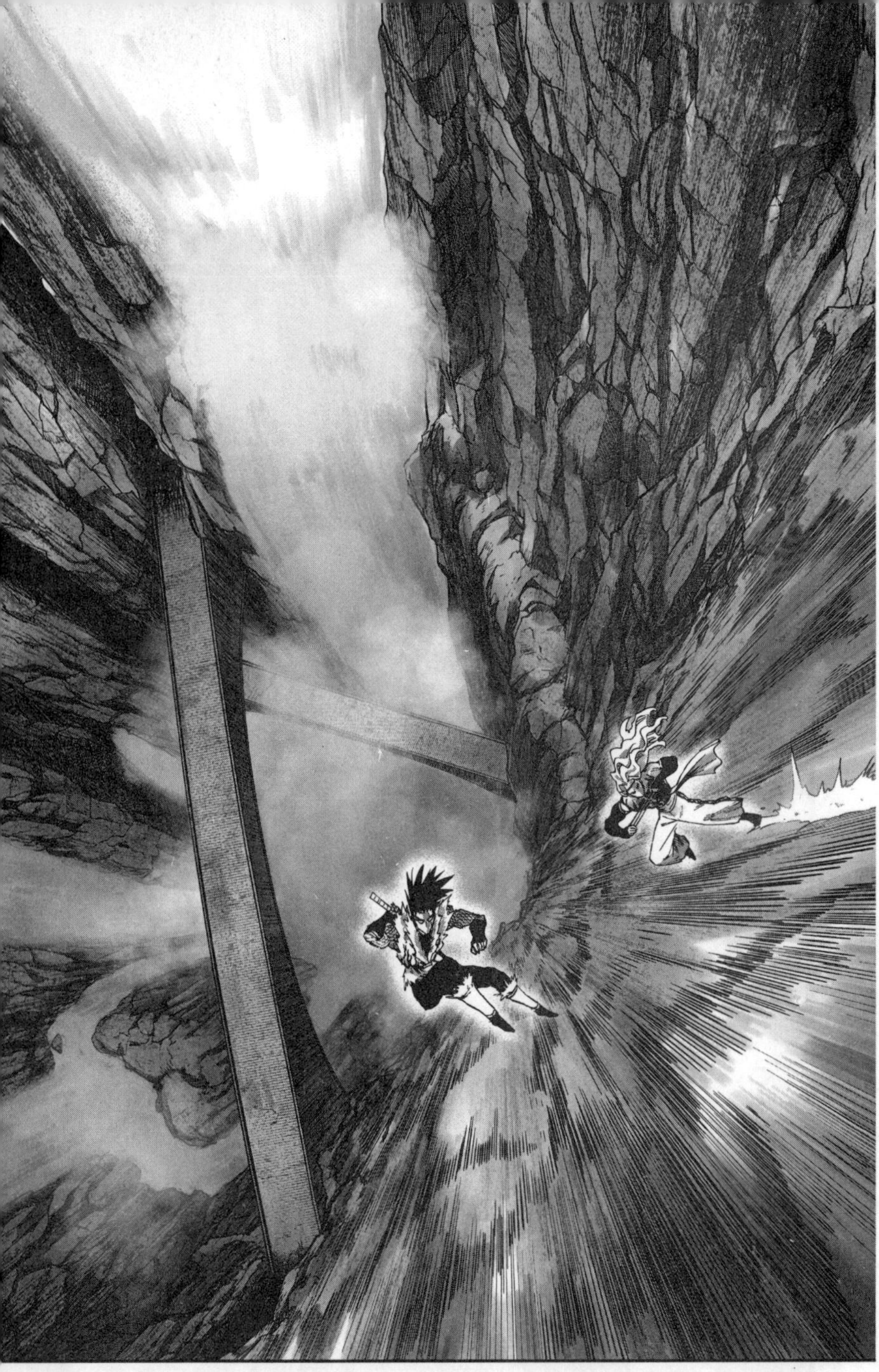

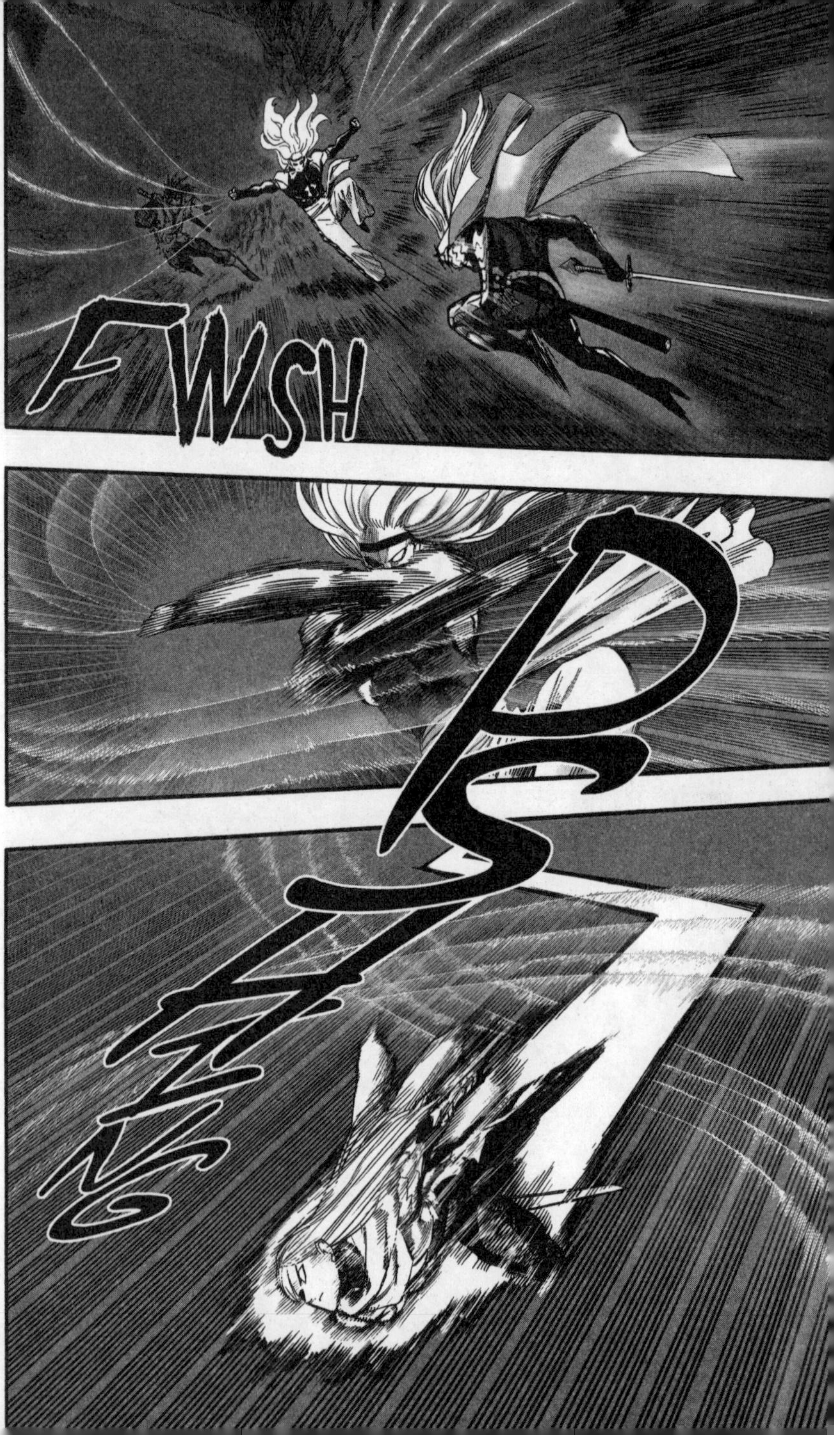
FWSH
DSHING

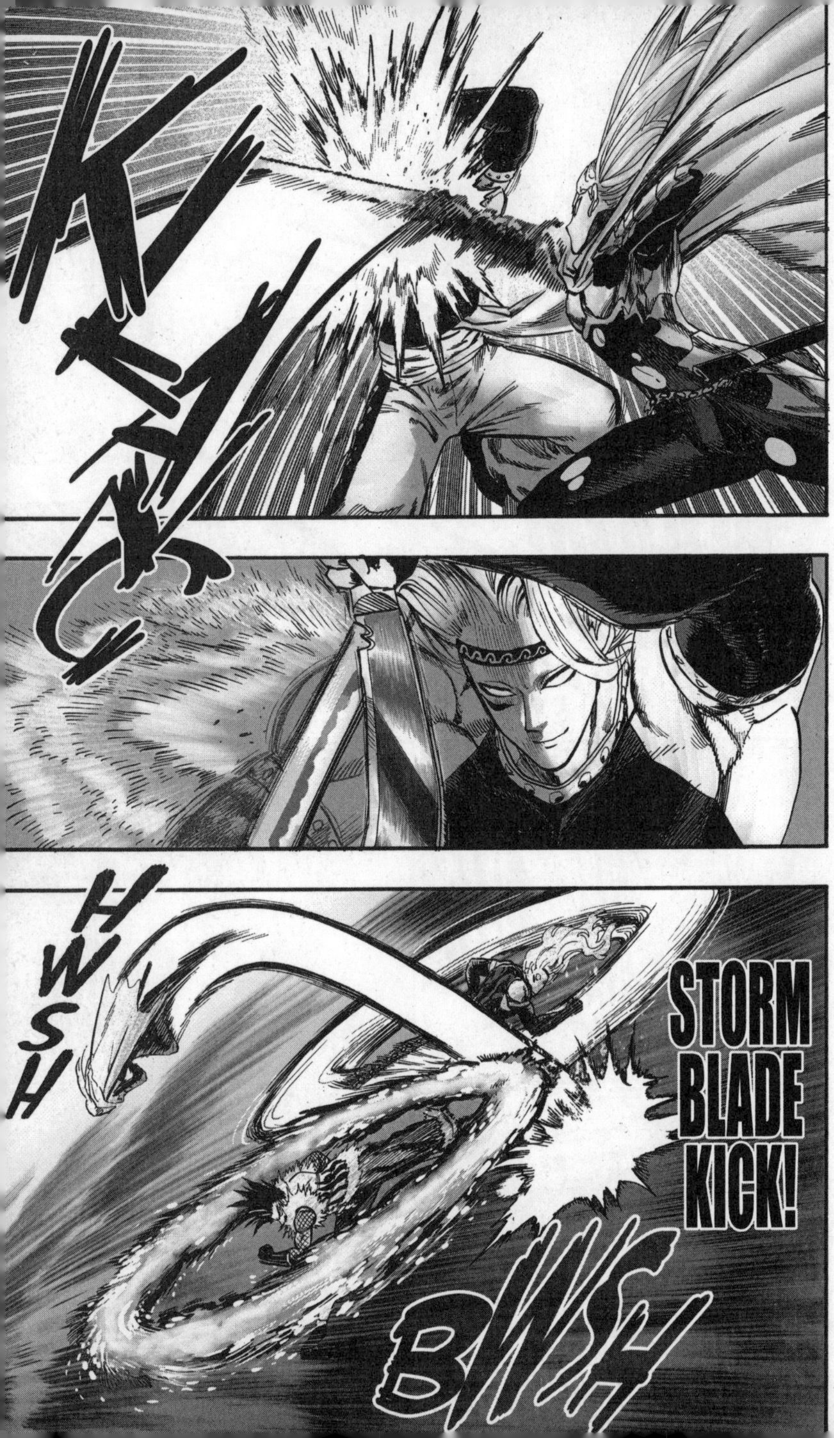
STORM BLADE KICK!
HWSH
BWSH

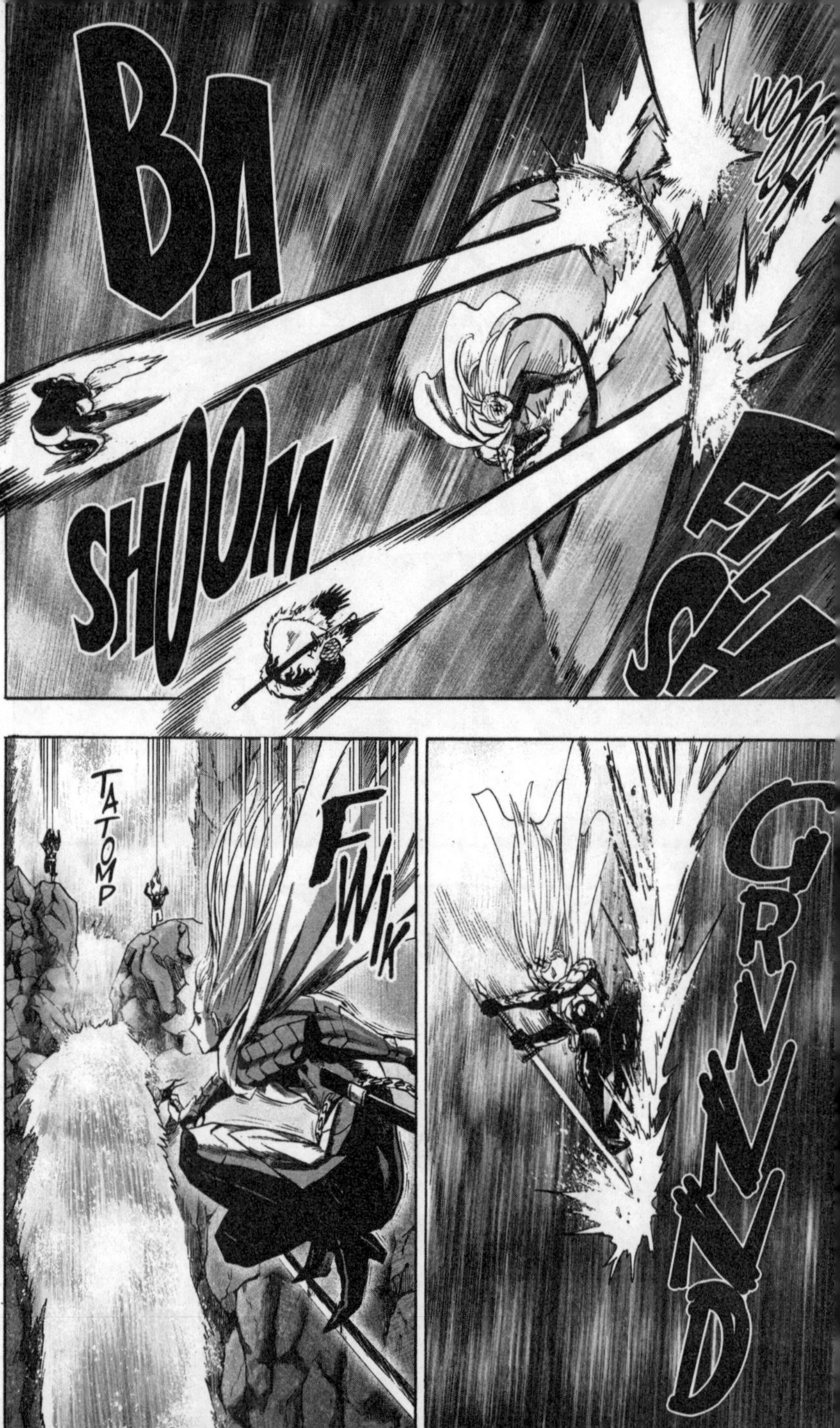
WOOSH
BA
SHOOM
GRNNND
FWIK
TATOMP

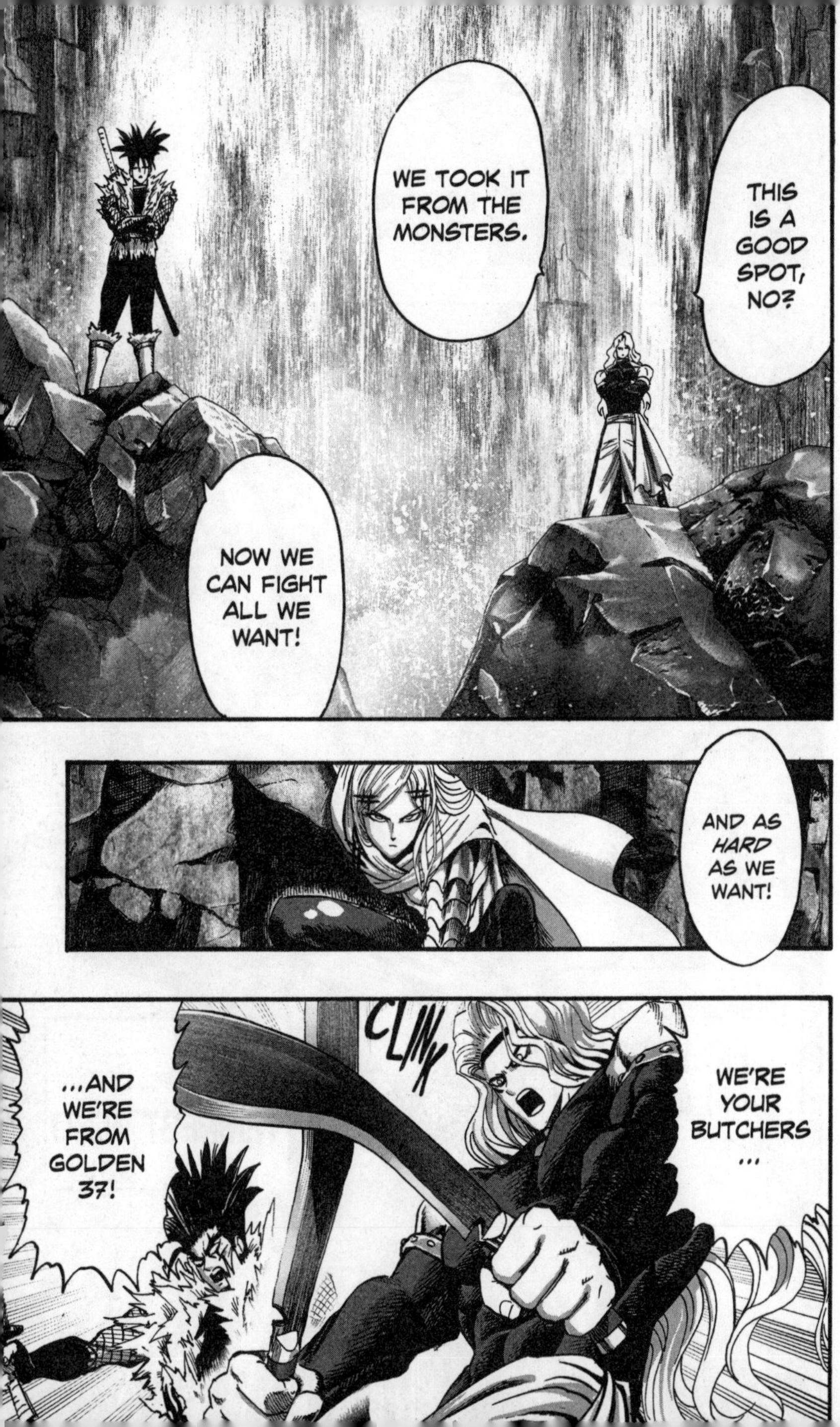
THIS IS A GOOD SPOT, NO?
WE TOOK IT FROM THE MONSTERS.
NOW WE CAN FIGHT ALL WE WANT!
AND AS *HARD* AS WE WANT!
WE'RE YOUR BUTCHERS ...
CLINK
...AND WE'RE FROM GOLDEN 37!

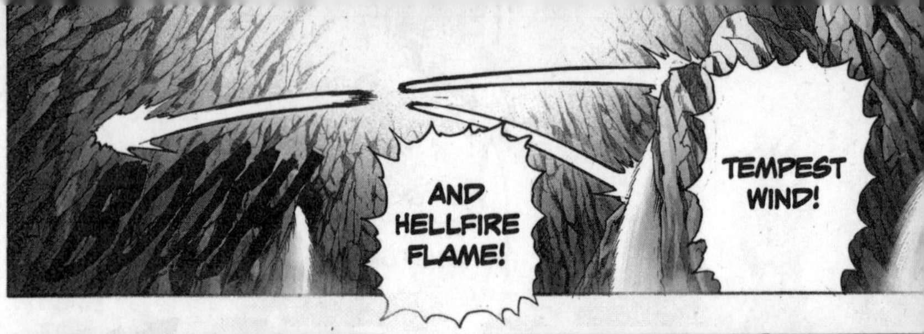
TEMPEST WIND!
AND HELLFIRE FLAME!

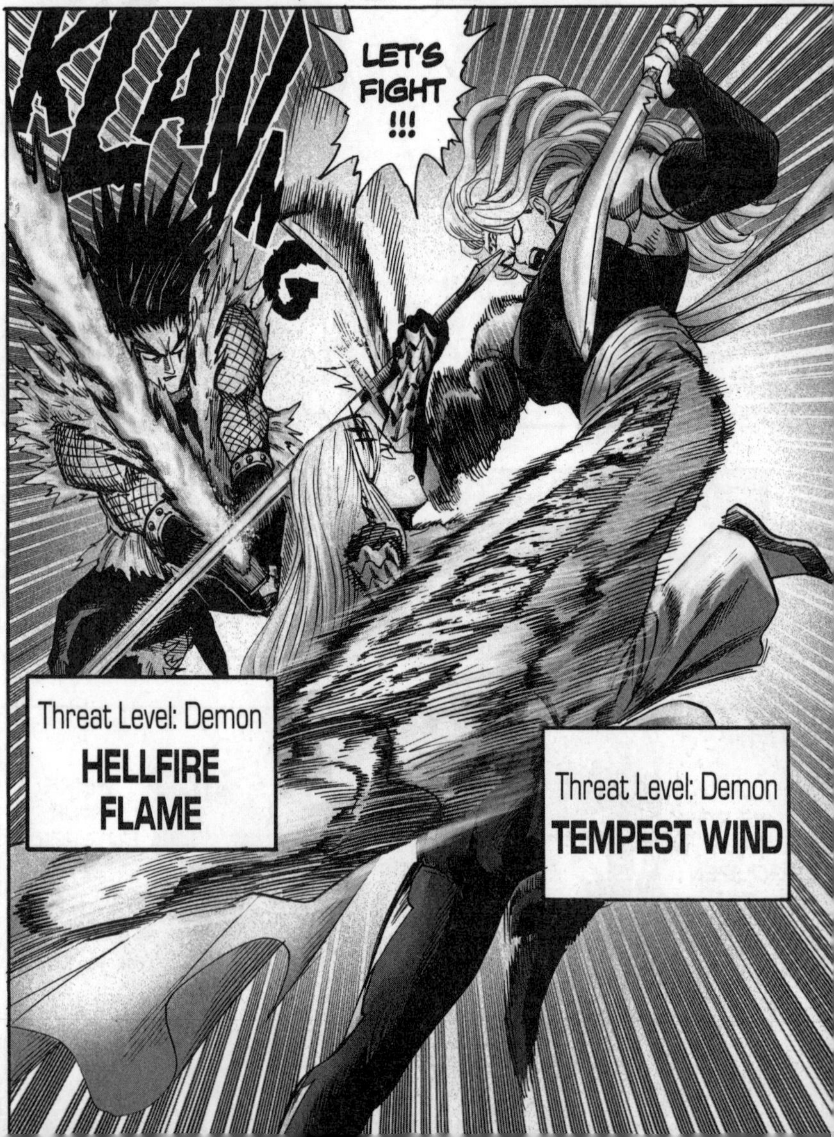
LET'S FIGHT !!!
Threat Level: Demon
TEMPEST WIND
Threat Level: Demon
HELLFIRE FLAME

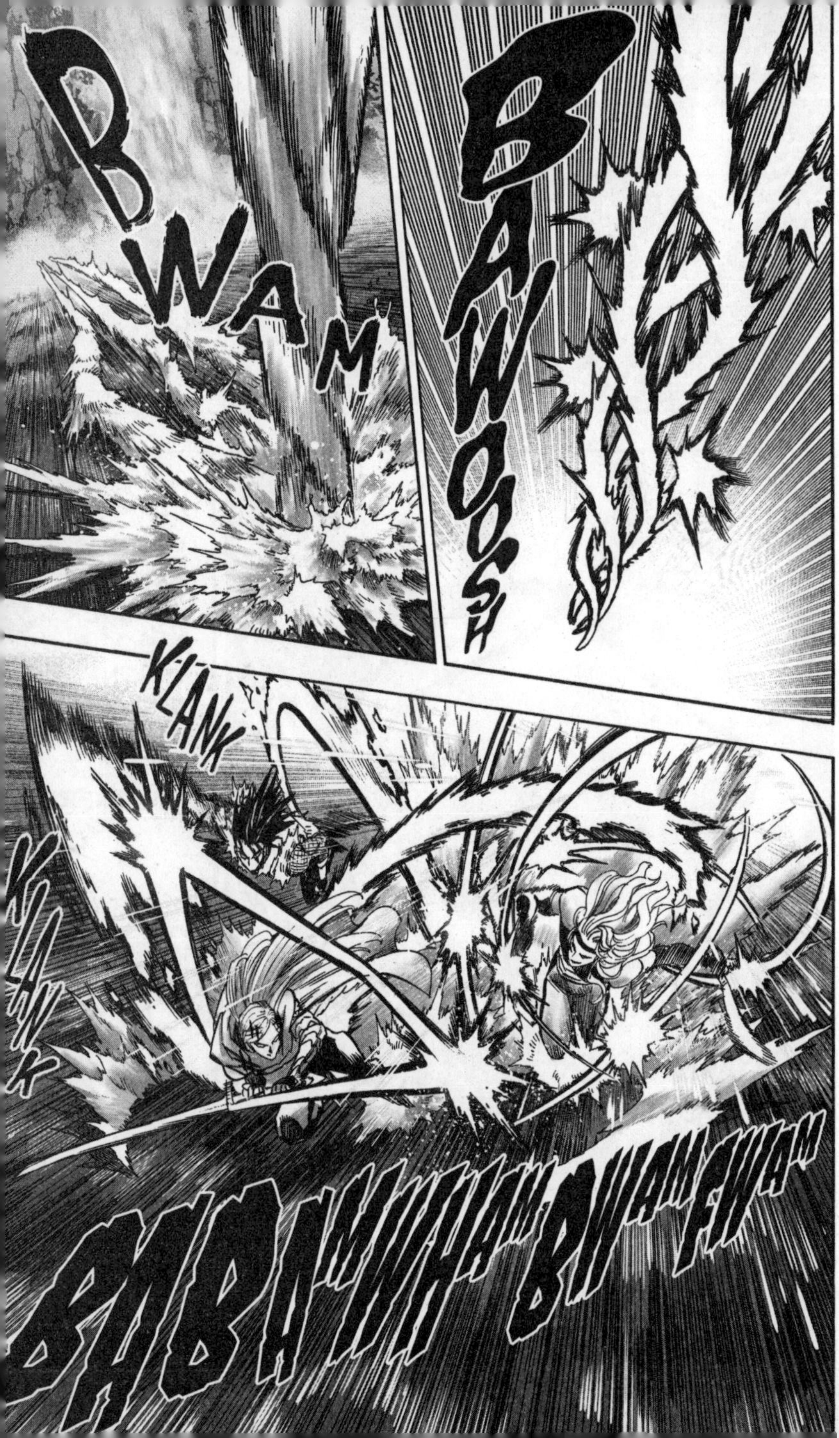
BAWOOSH
BWAM
KLANK
KLANK

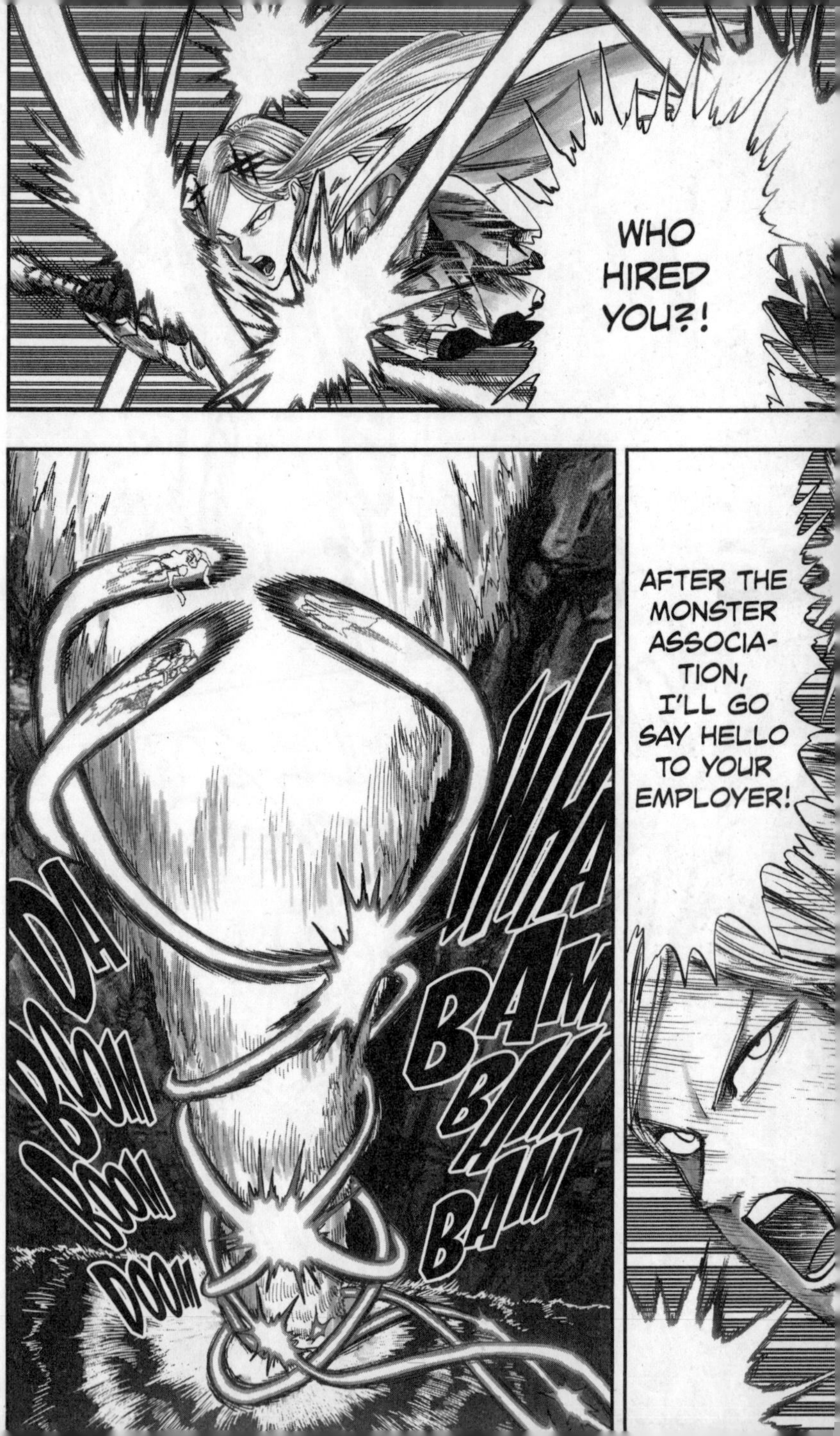
WHO HIRED YOU?!
AFTER THE MONSTER ASSOCIA-TION, I'LL GO SAY HELLO TO YOUR EMPLOYER!
BAM BAM BAM BAM
BOOM BOOM DOOM

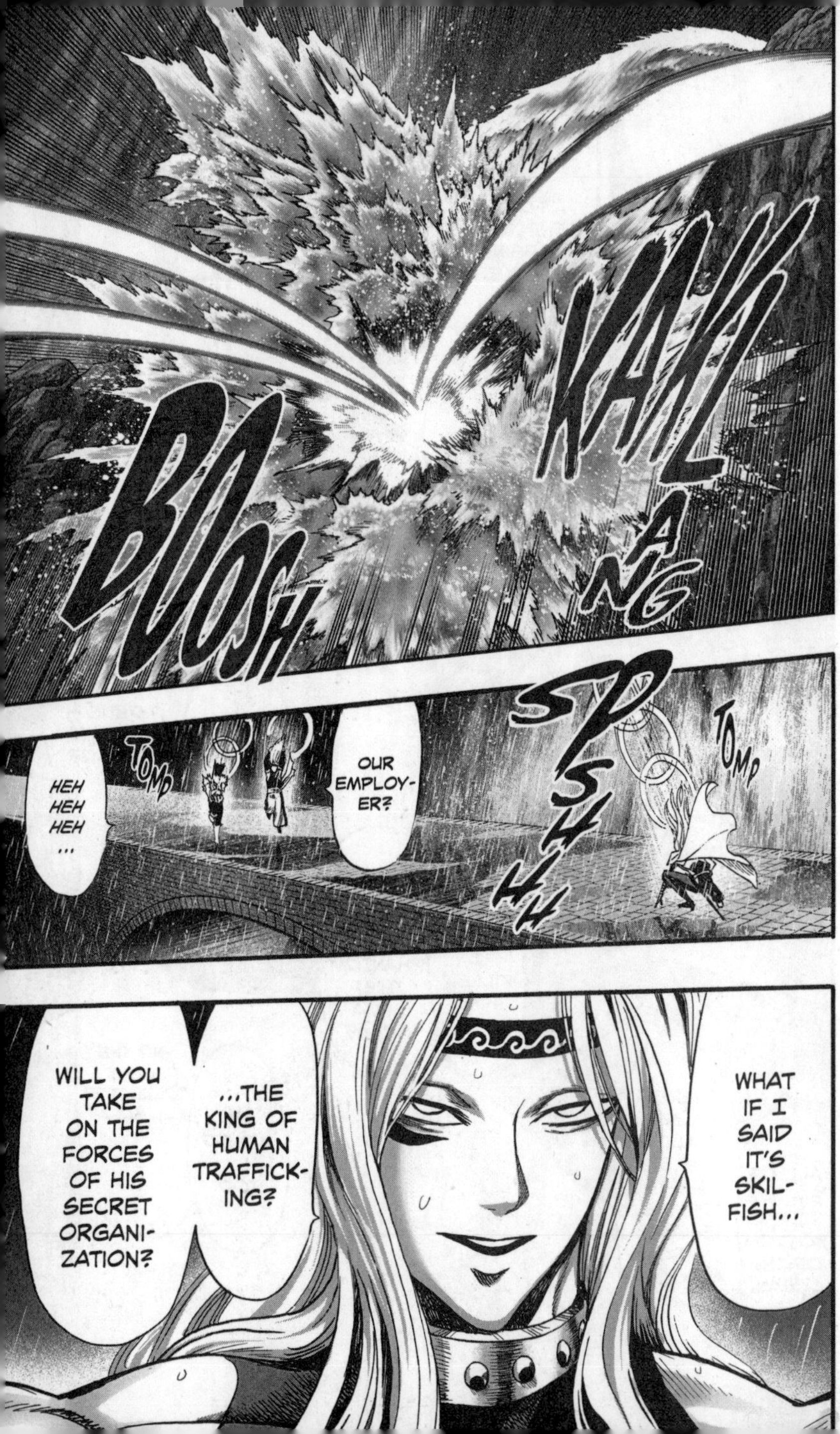
KANANG
BLOSH
TOMP
SPSHHH
OUR EMPLOYER?
TOMP
HEH HEH HEH...
WHAT IF I SAID IT'S SKILFISH...
...THE KING OF HUMAN TRAFFICKING?
WILL YOU TAKE ON THE FORCES OF HIS SECRET ORGANIZATION?

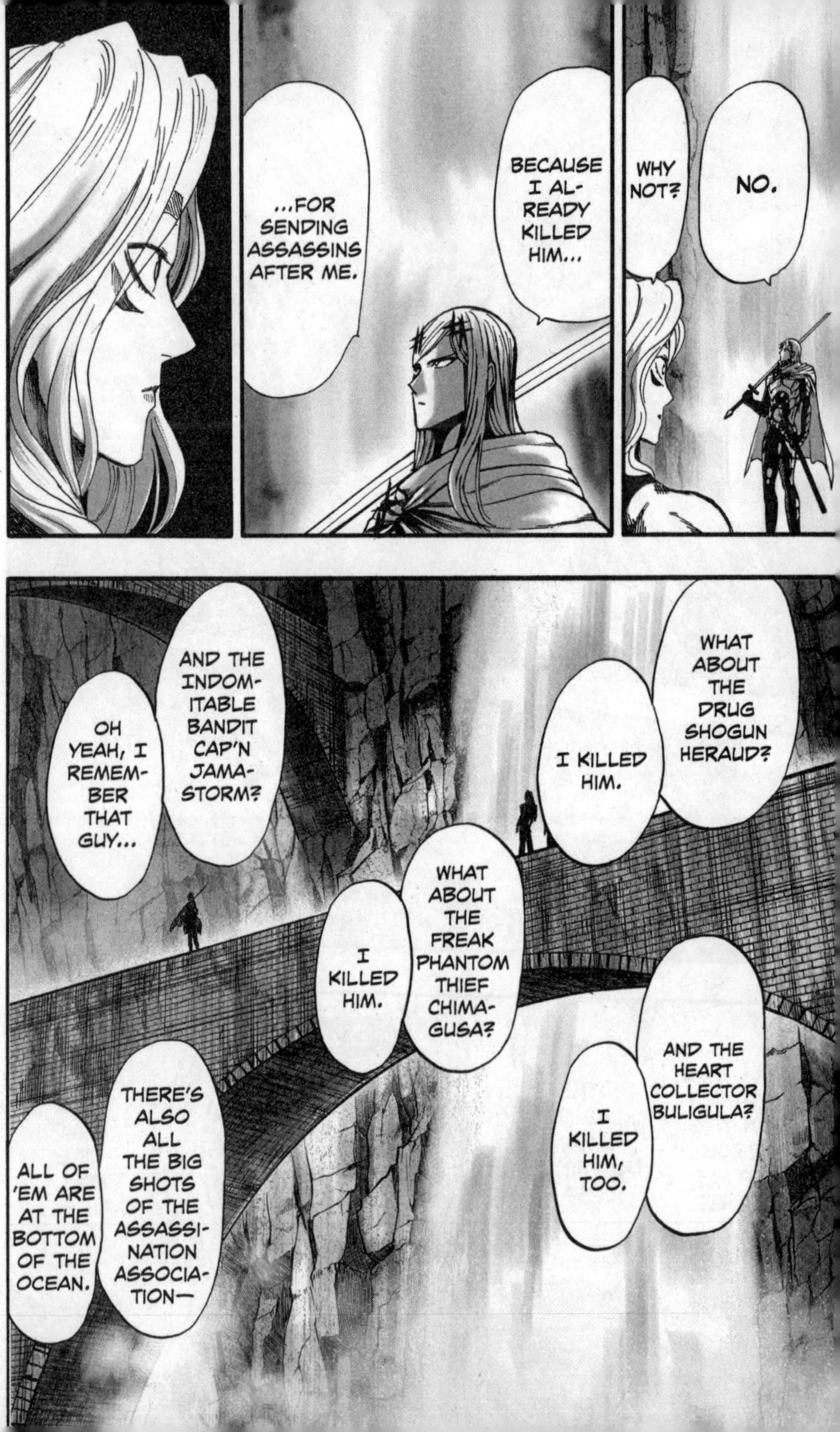
NO.
WHY NOT?
BECAUSE I ALREADY KILLED HIM...
...FOR SENDING ASSASSINS AFTER ME.
WHAT ABOUT THE DRUG SHOGUN HERAUD?
I KILLED HIM.
AND THE INDOMITABLE BANDIT CAP'N JAMASTORM?
OH YEAH, I REMEMBER THAT GUY...
WHAT ABOUT THE FREAK PHANTOM THIEF CHIMAGUSA?
I KILLED HIM.
AND THE HEART COLLECTOR BULIGULA?
I KILLED HIM, TOO.
THERE'S ALSO ALL THE BIG SHOTS OF THE ASSASSINATION ASSOCIATION—
ALL OF 'EM ARE AT THE BOTTOM OF THE OCEAN.

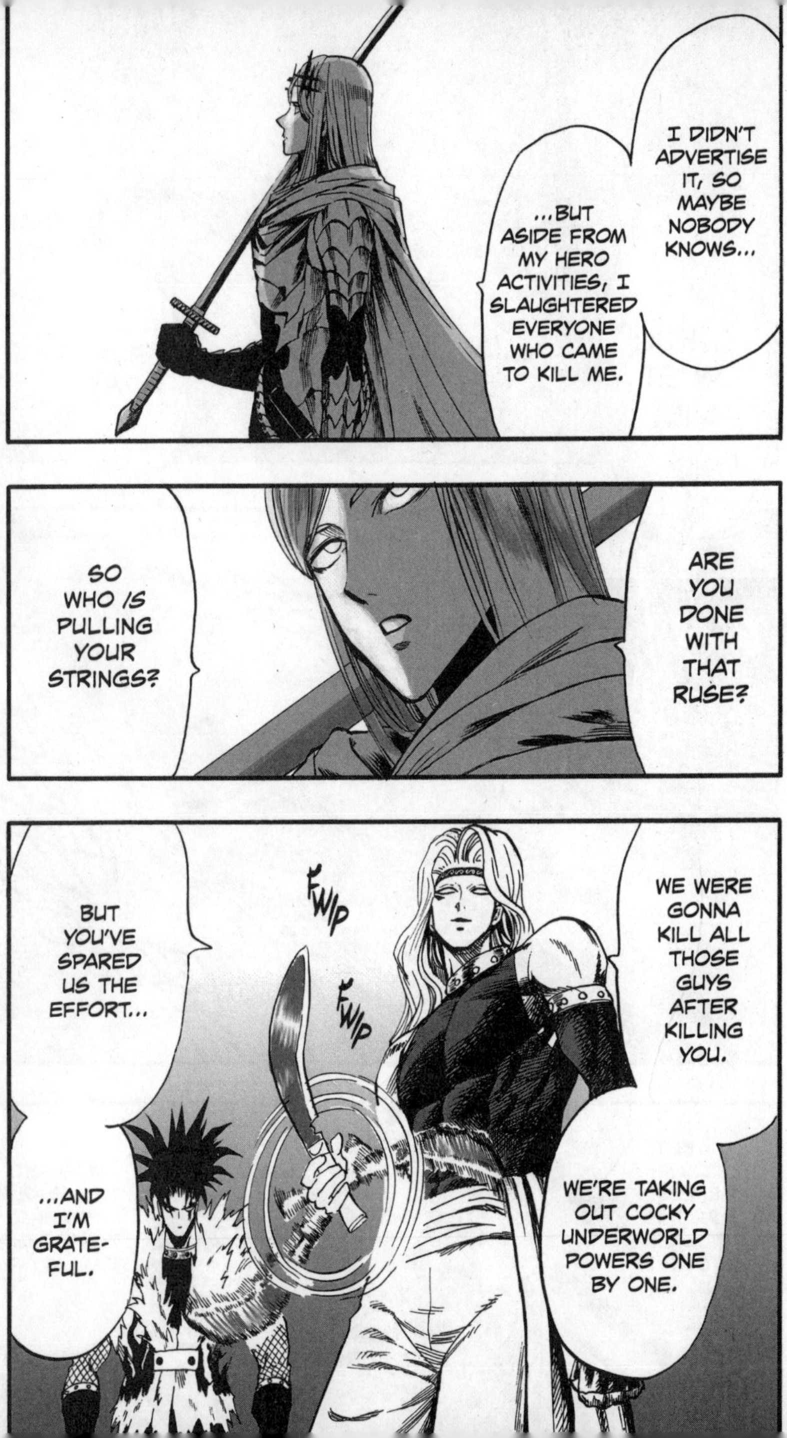
I DIDN'T ADVERTISE IT, SO MAYBE NOBODY KNOWS...
...BUT ASIDE FROM MY HERO ACTIVITIES, I SLAUGHTERED EVERYONE WHO CAME TO KILL ME.
ARE YOU DONE WITH THAT RUSE?
SO WHO *IS* PULLING YOUR STRINGS?
WE WERE GONNA KILL ALL THOSE GUYS AFTER KILLING YOU.
FWIP
FWIP
BUT YOU'VE SPARED US THE EFFORT...
WE'RE TAKING OUT COCKY UNDERWORLD POWERS ONE BY ONE.
...AND I'M GRATE-FUL.

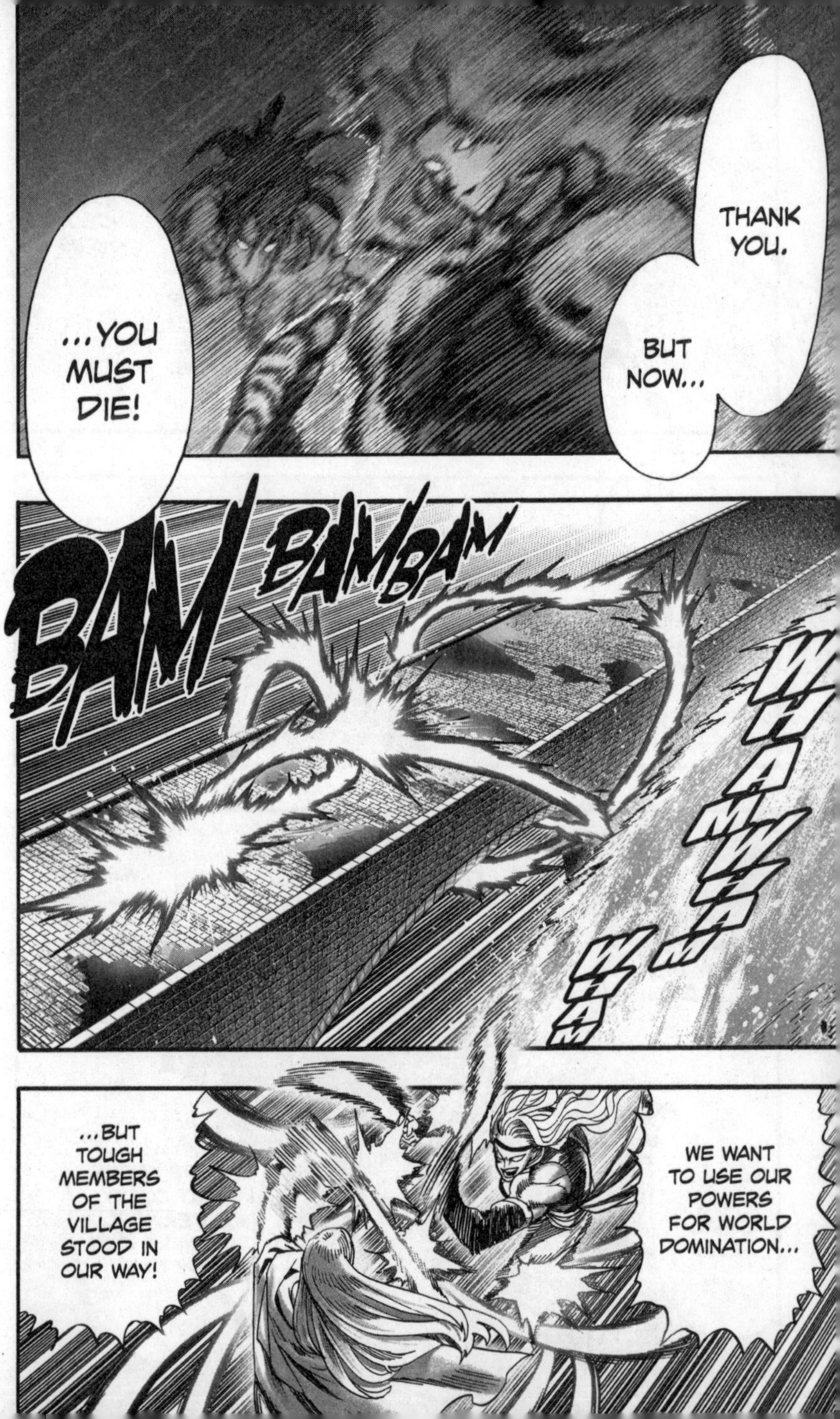
THANK YOU.
BUT NOW...
...YOU MUST DIE!
WHAMWHAMWHAM
WHAM
BAMBAM
BAM
WE WANT TO USE OUR POWERS FOR WORLD DOMINATION...
...BUT TOUGH MEMBERS OF THE VILLAGE STOOD IN OUR WAY!

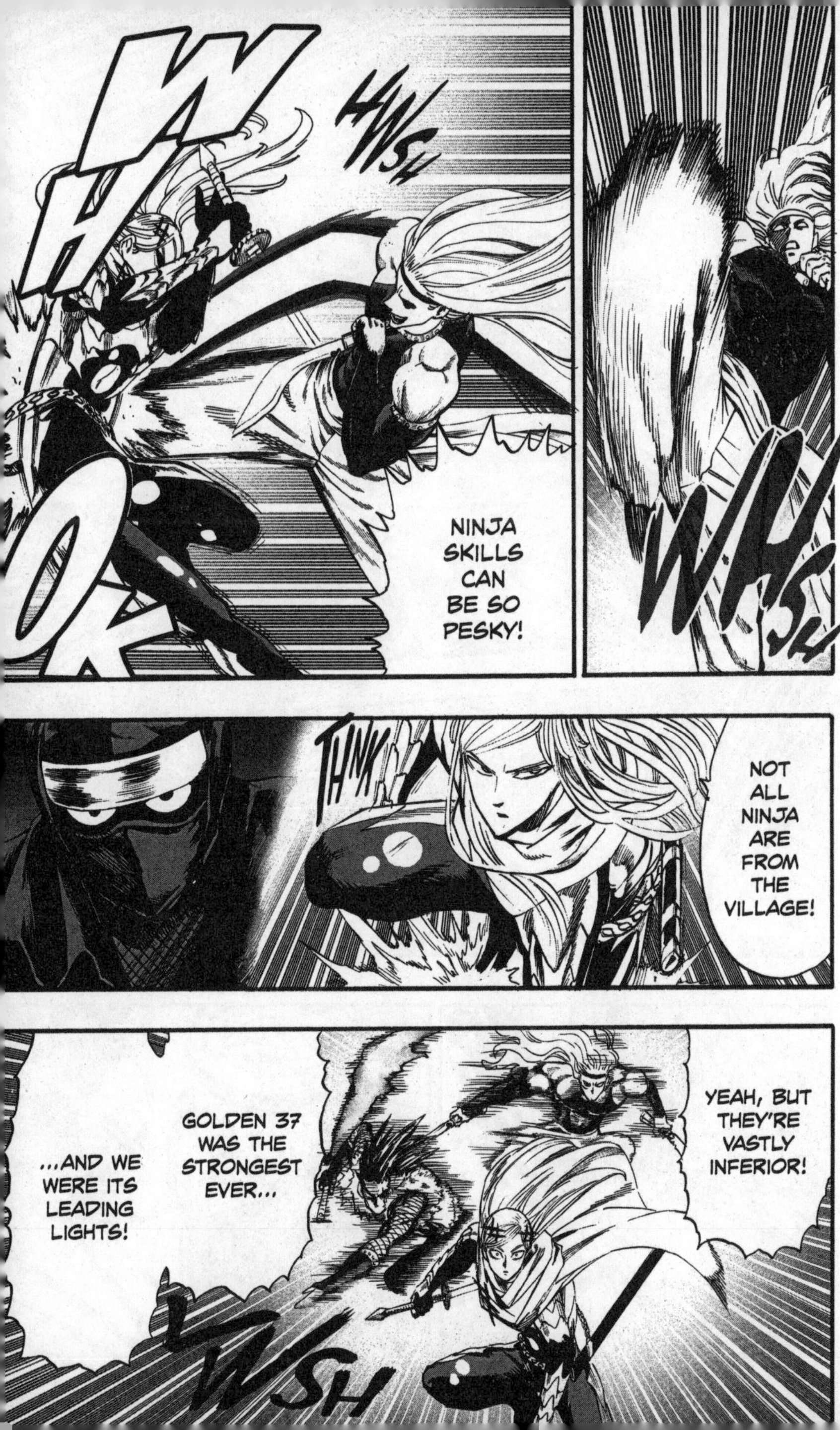
WHSH
WHSH
NINJA SKILLS CAN BE SO PESKY!
NOT ALL NINJA ARE FROM THE VILLAGE!
THNK
YEAH, BUT THEY'RE VASTLY INFERIOR!
GOLDEN 37 WAS THE STRONGEST EVER...
...AND WE WERE ITS LEADING LIGHTS!
WSH

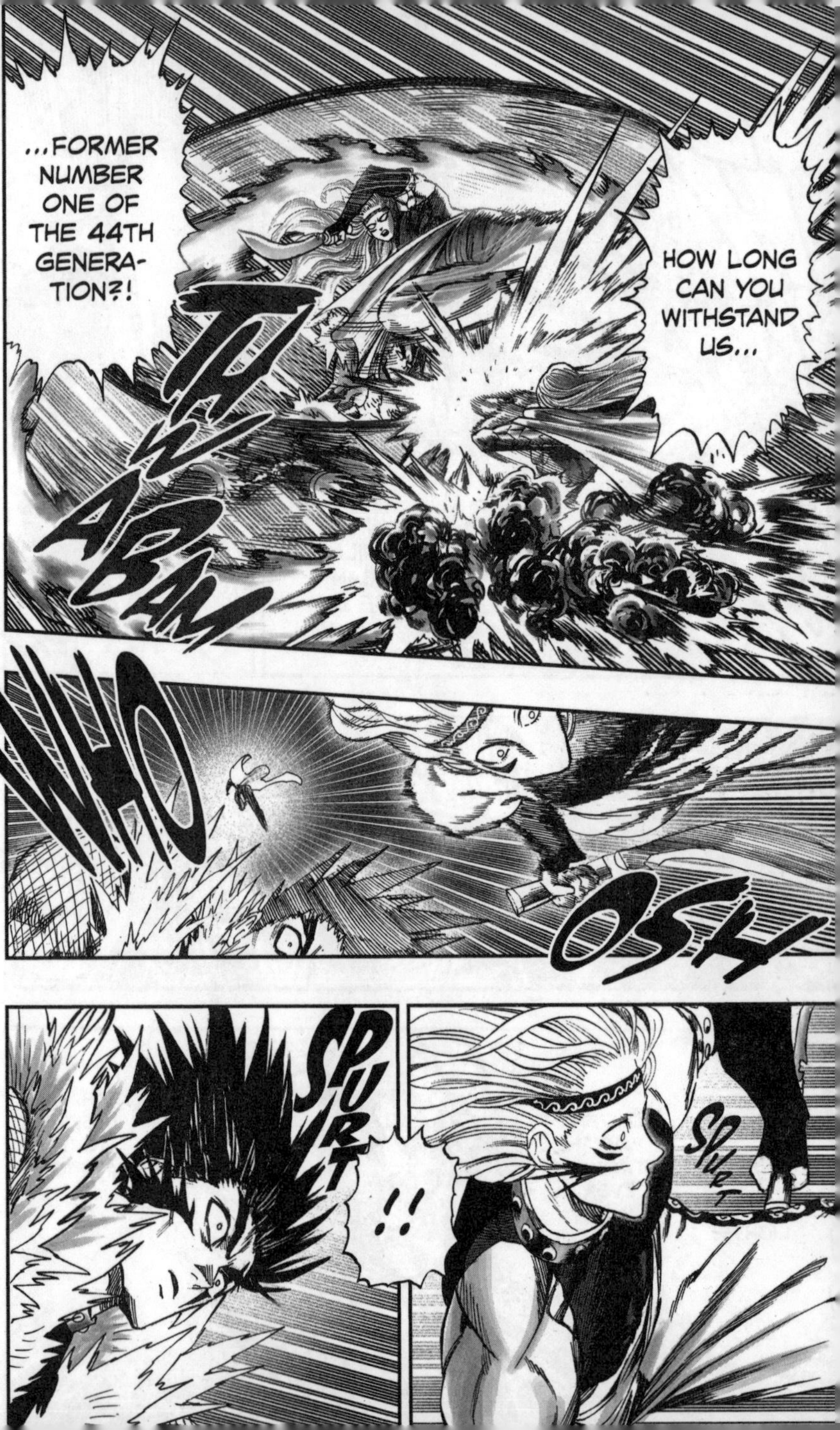
HOW LONG CAN YOU WITHSTAND US...
...FORMER NUMBER ONE OF THE 44TH GENERATION?!
THWABAM
WHO
OSH
SPURT
SPURT
!!

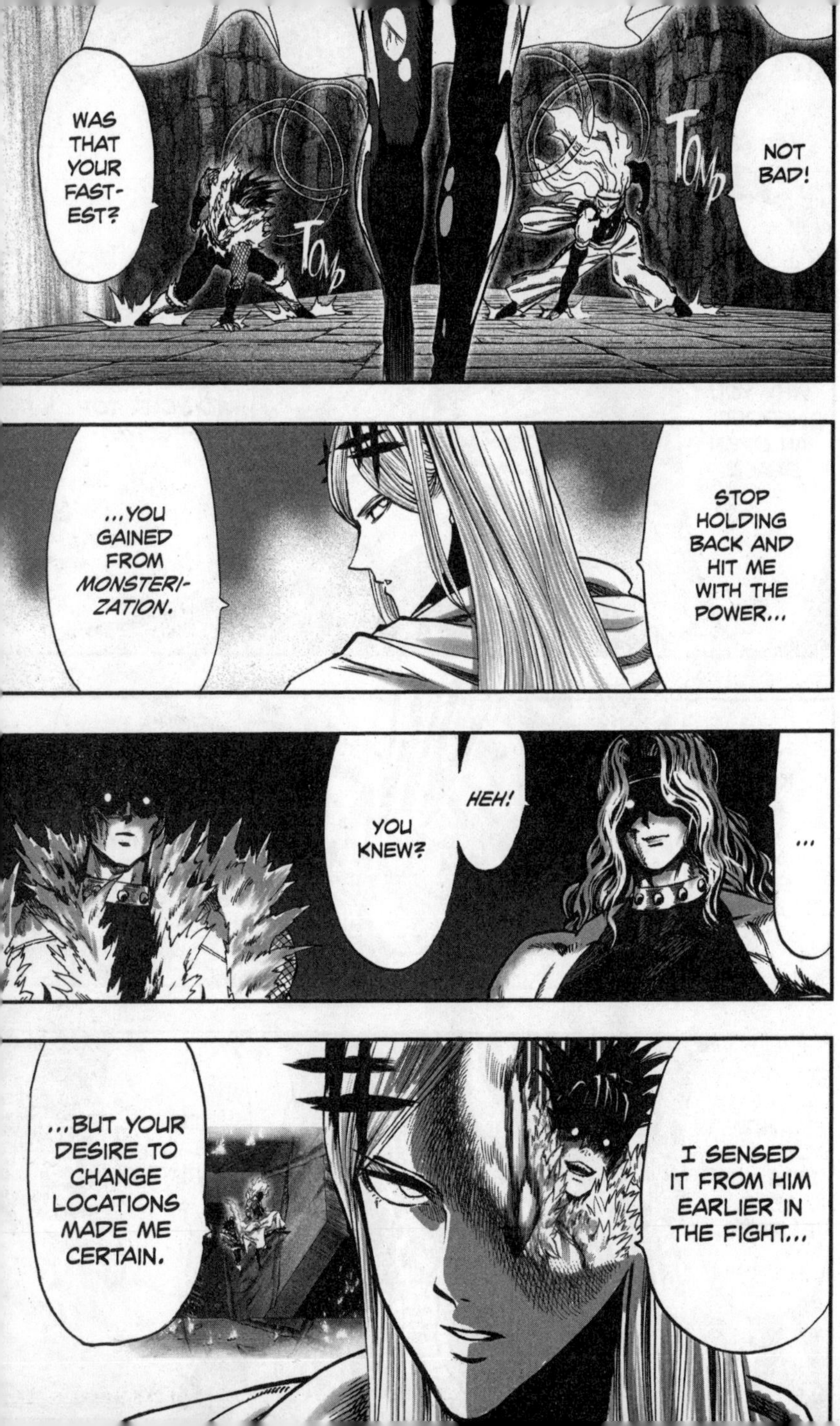
NOT BAD!
TOMP
WAS THAT YOUR FAST-EST?
TOMP
STOP HOLDING BACK AND HIT ME WITH THE POWER...
...YOU GAINED FROM *MONSTERI-ZATION.*
...
HEH!
YOU KNEW?
I SENSED IT FROM HIM EARLIER IN THE FIGHT...
...BUT YOUR DESIRE TO CHANGE LOCATIONS MADE ME CERTAIN.

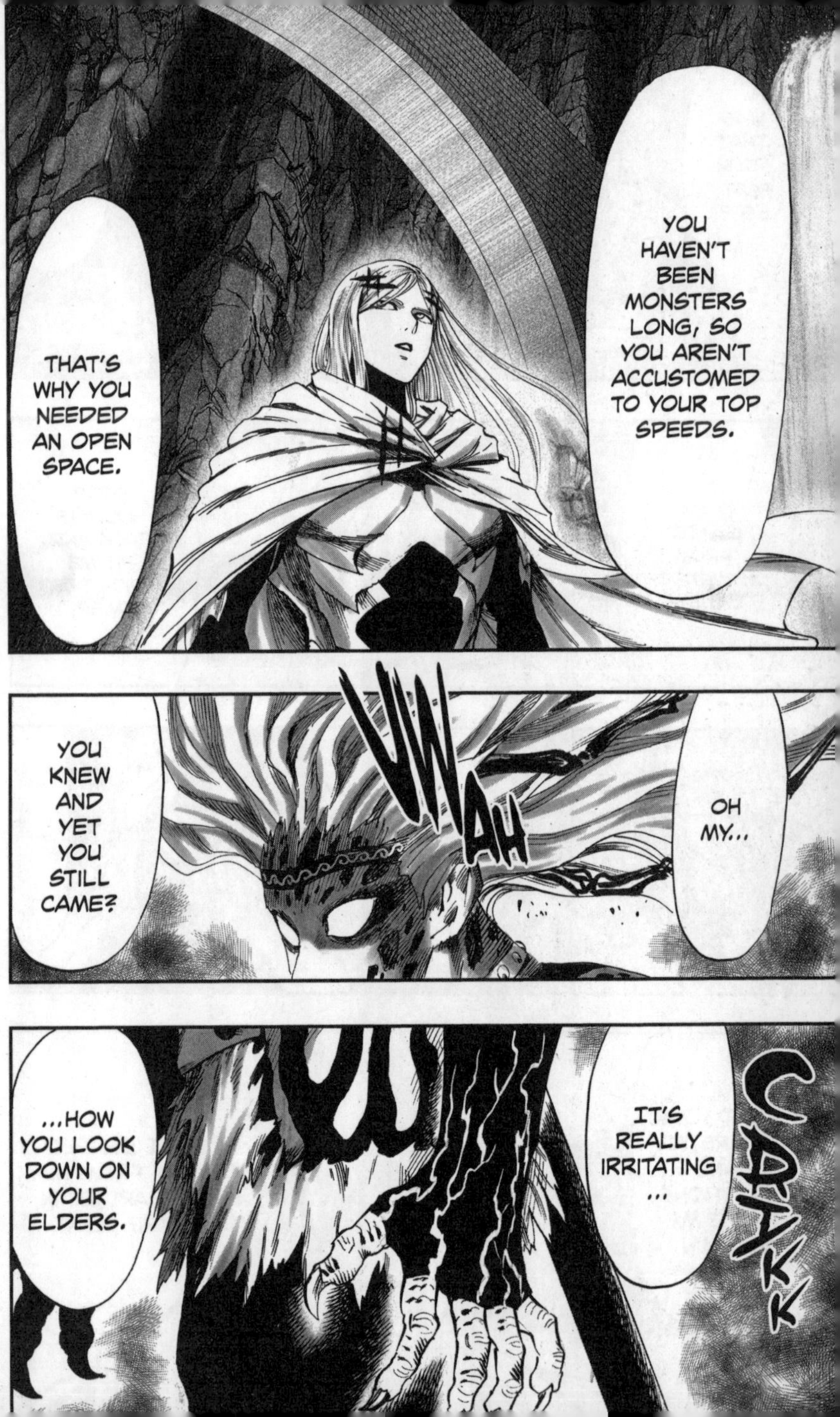
YOU HAVEN'T BEEN MONSTERS LONG, SO YOU AREN'T ACCUSTOMED TO YOUR TOP SPEEDS.
THAT'S WHY YOU NEEDED AN OPEN SPACE.
OH MY...
VWAH
YOU KNEW AND YET YOU STILL CAME?
CRAKK
IT'S REALLY IRRITATING ...
...HOW YOU LOOK DOWN ON YOUR ELDERS.

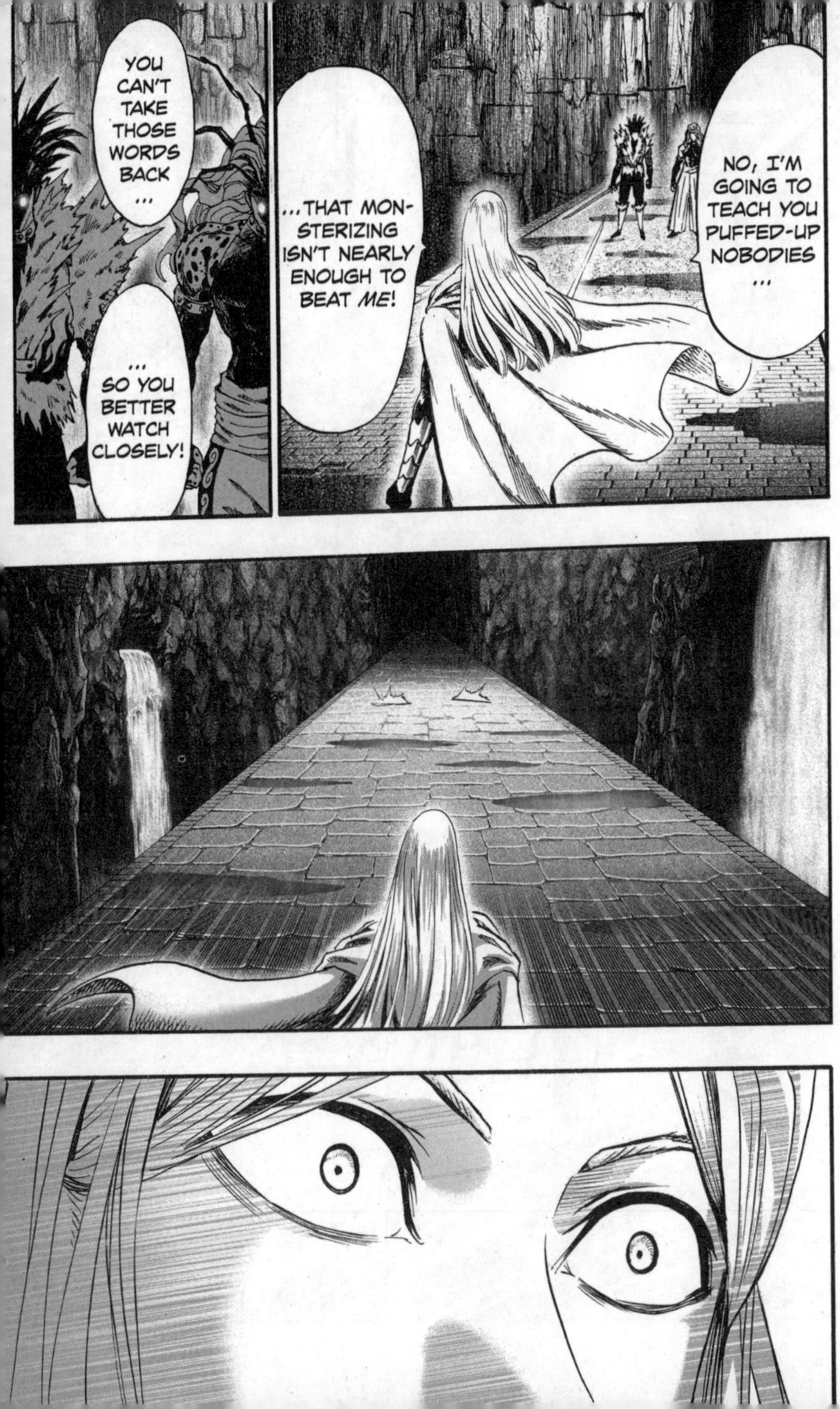
NO, I'M GOING TO TEACH YOU PUFFED-UP NOBODIES...
...THAT MON-STERIZING ISN'T NEARLY ENOUGH TO BEAT *ME*!
YOU CAN'T TAKE THOSE WORDS BACK...
...SO YOU BETTER WATCH CLOSELY!

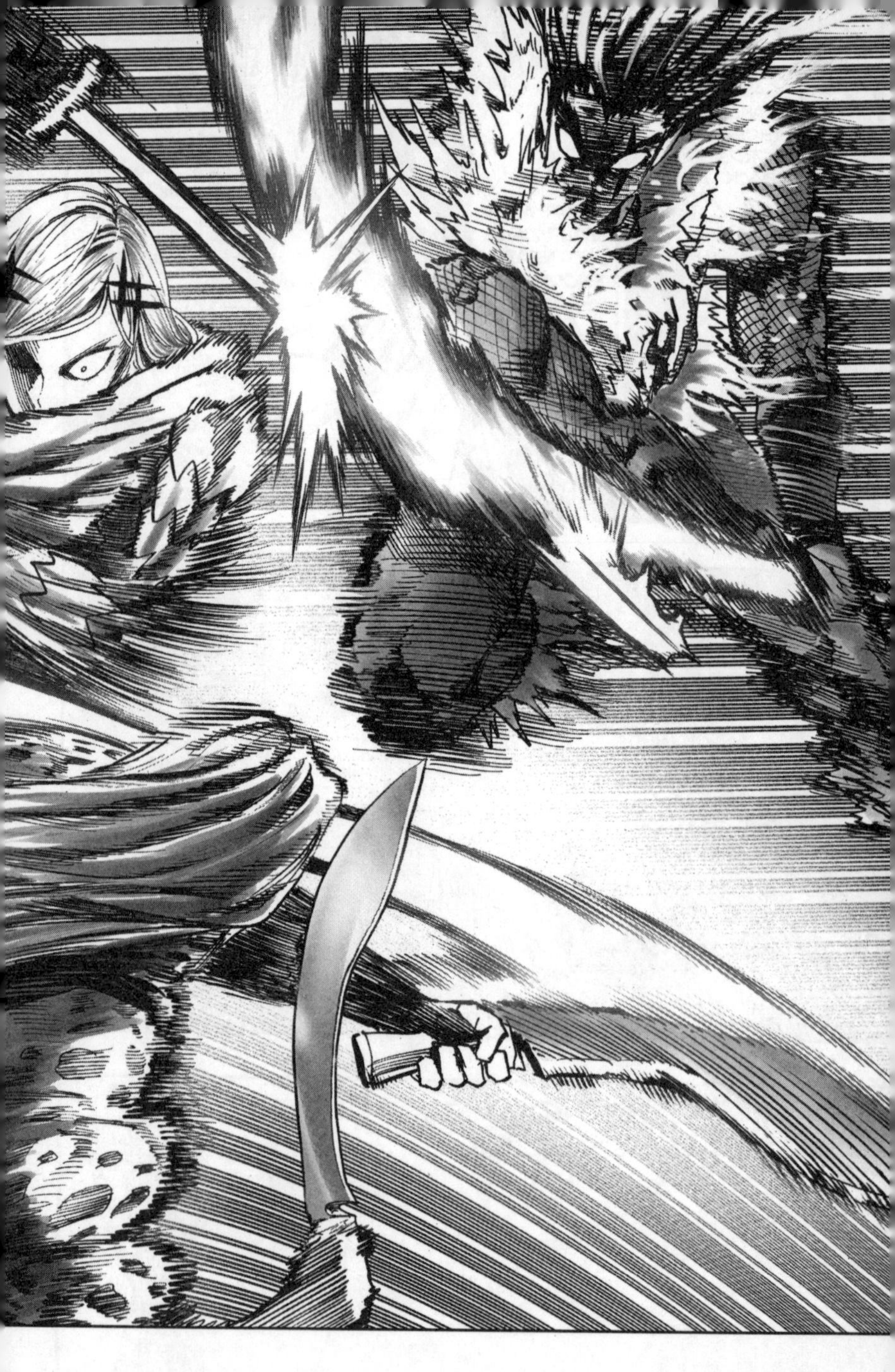

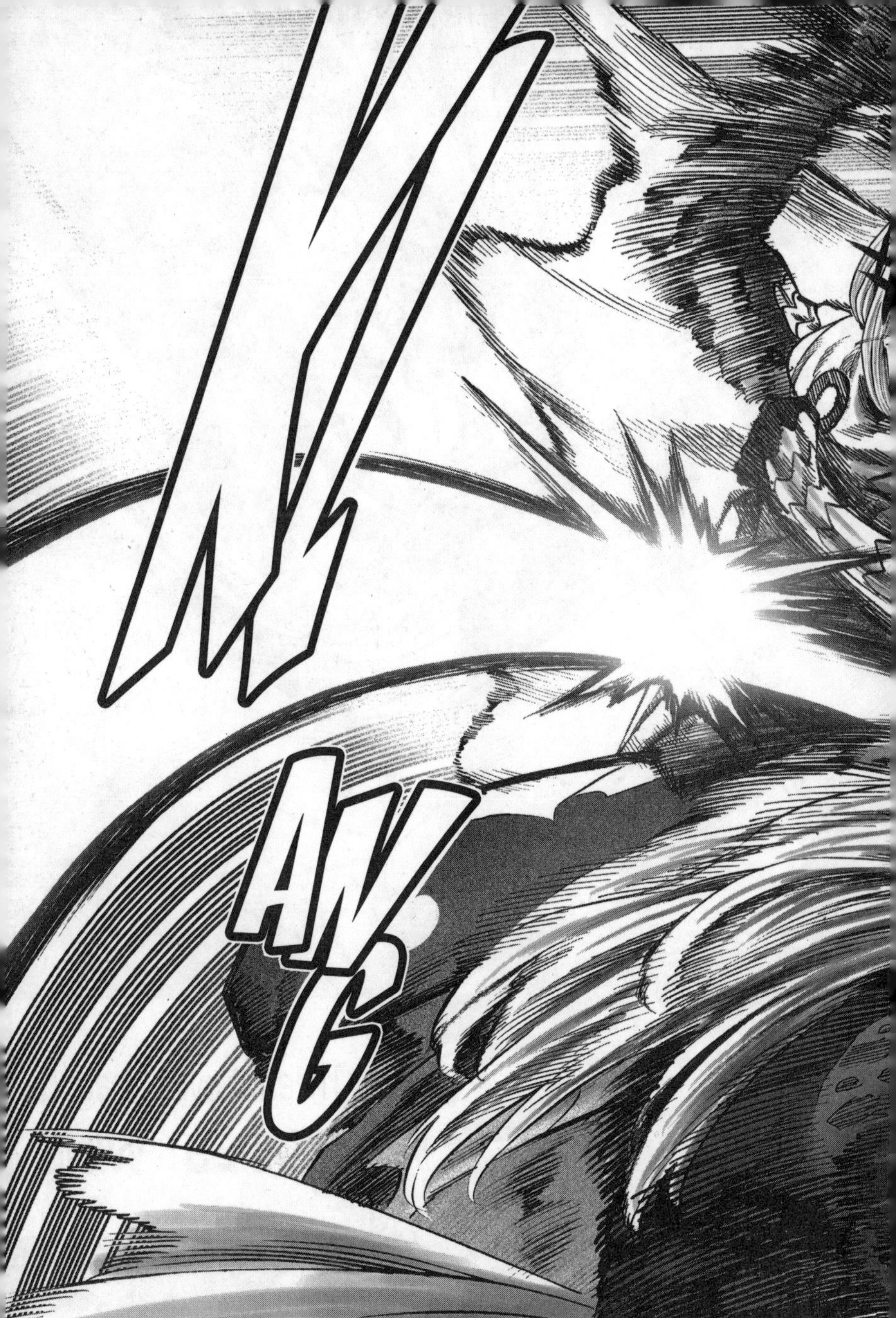
K
ANG

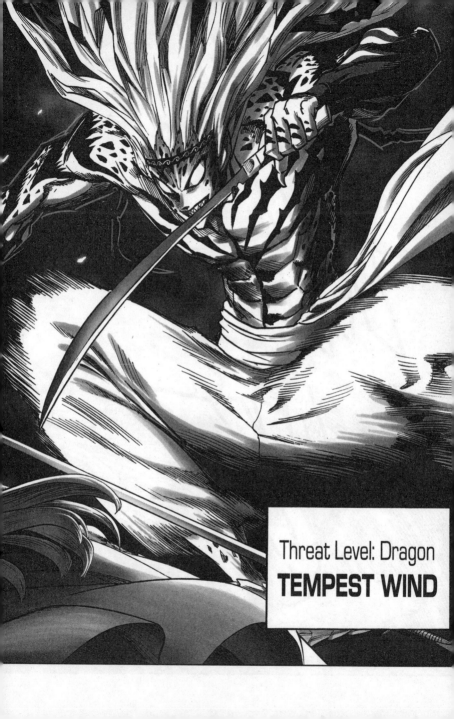

Threat Level: Dragon
TEMPEST WIND

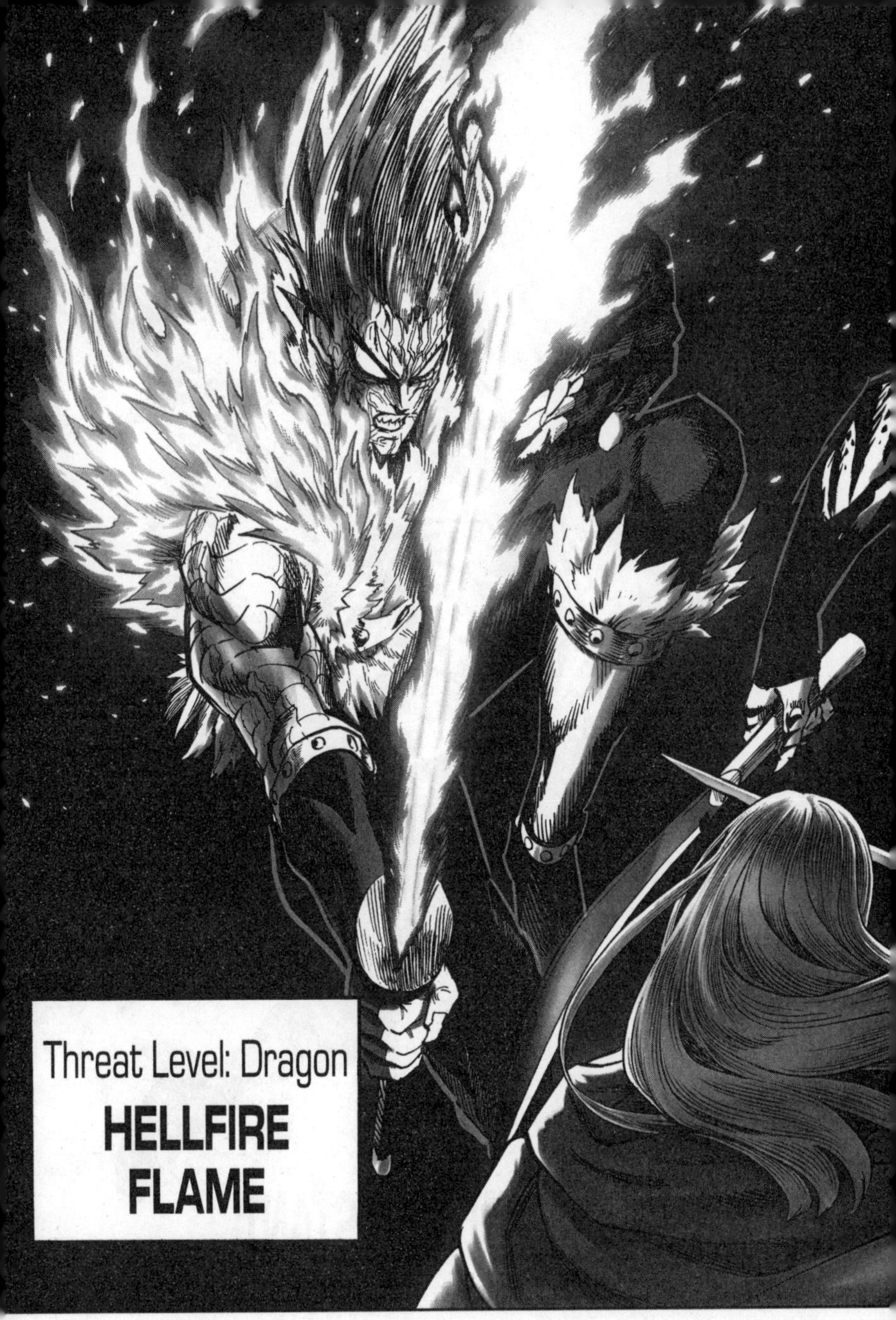
Threat Level: Dragon
HELLFIRE FLAME

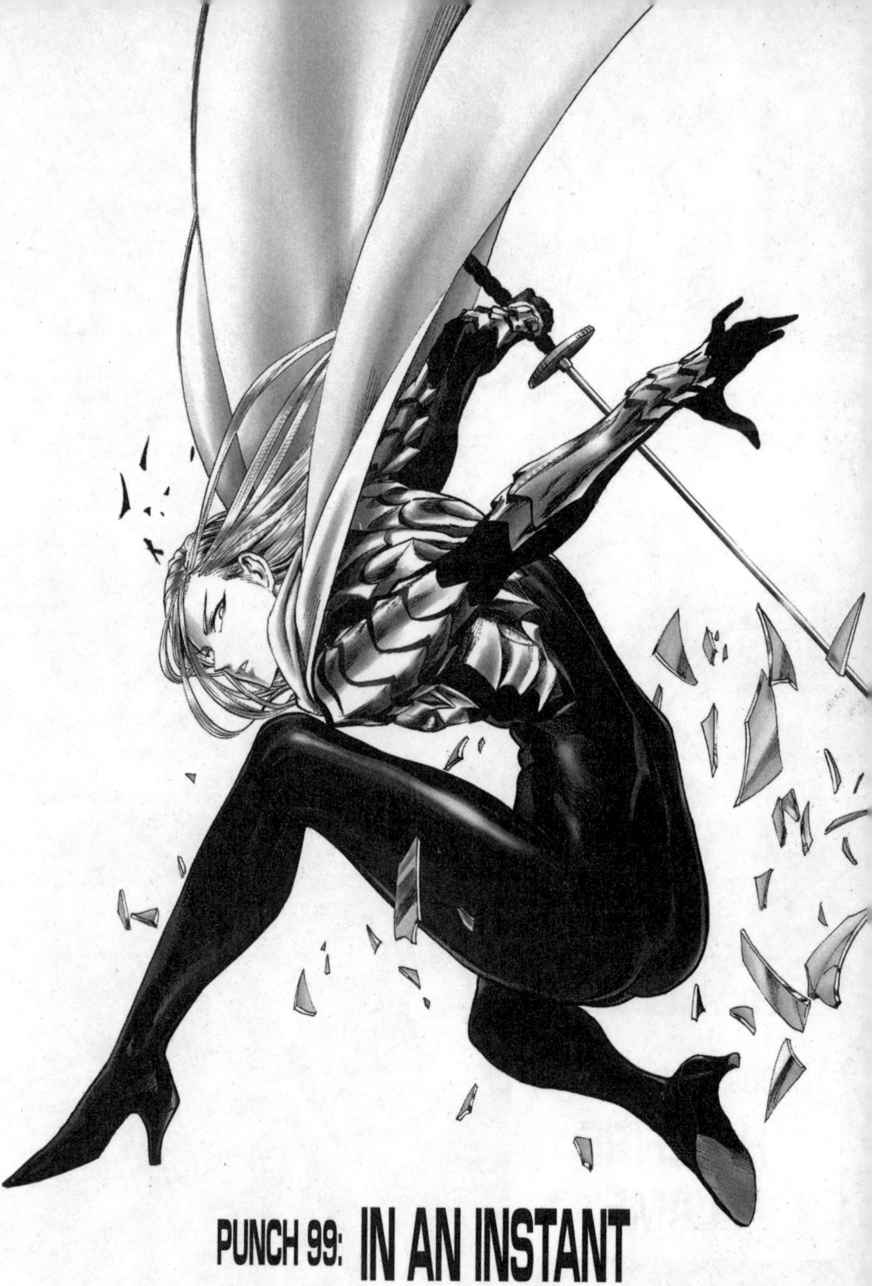

PUNCH 99: IN AN INSTANT

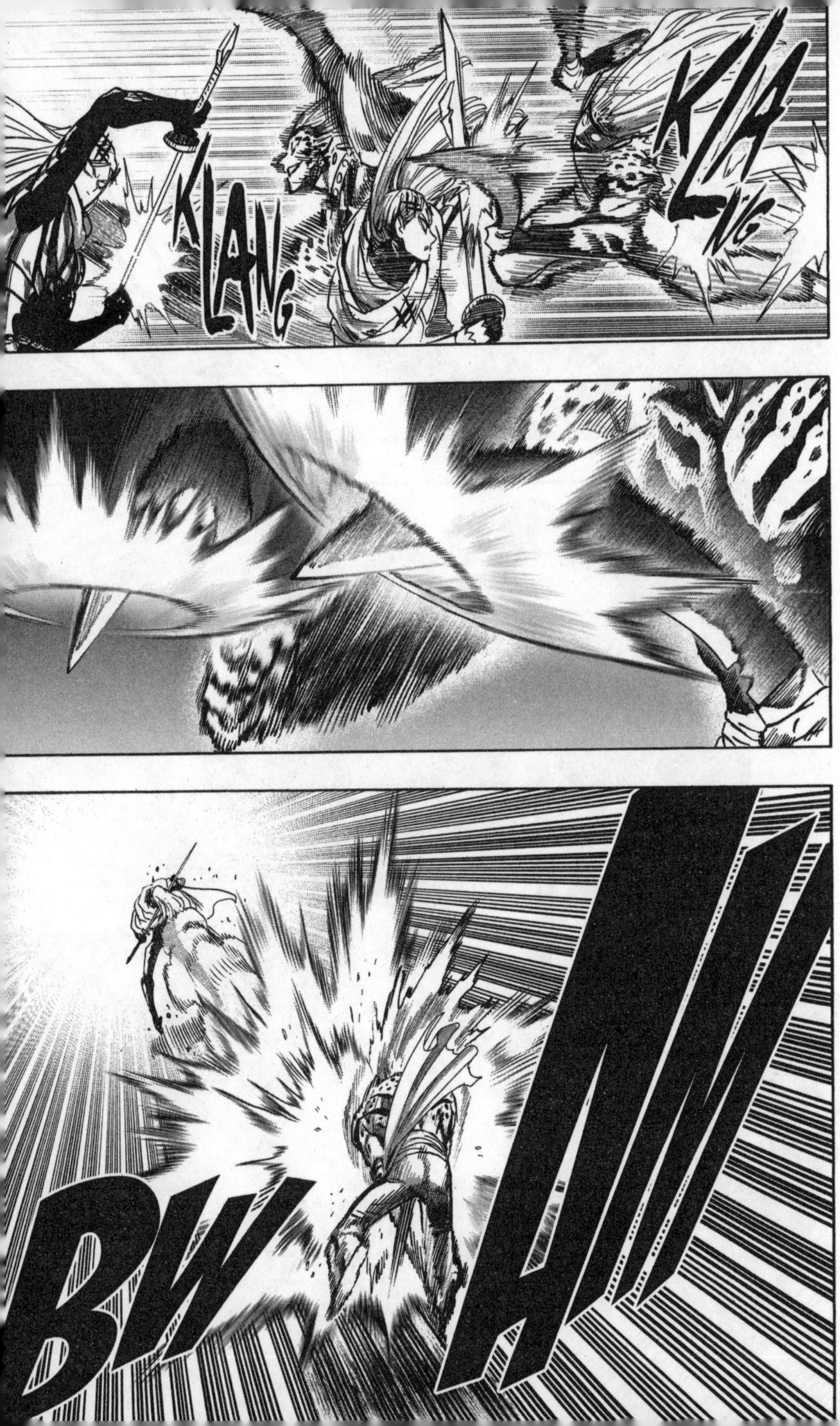
KLANG
KLANG

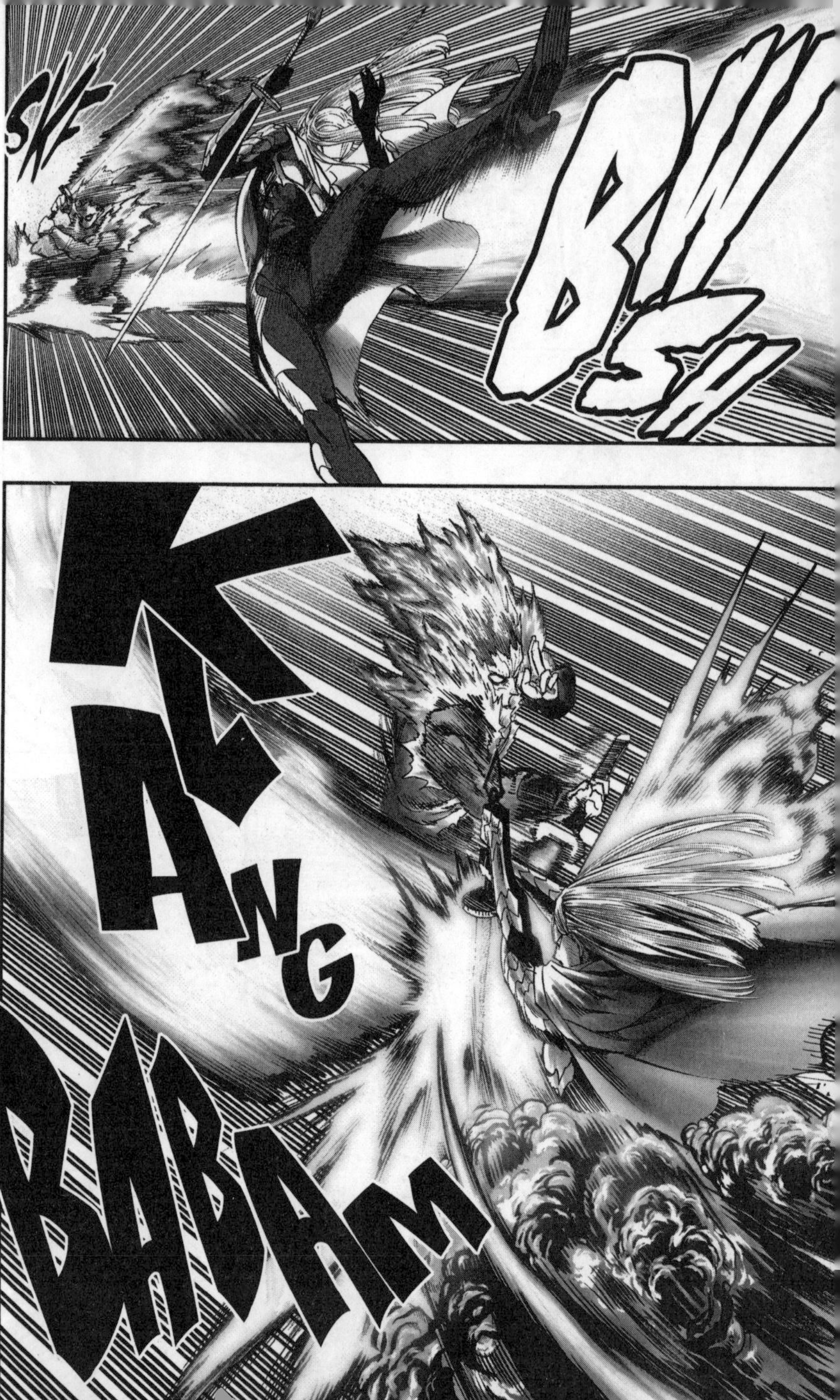
BWSH!!
SHF
KLANG
BABAM

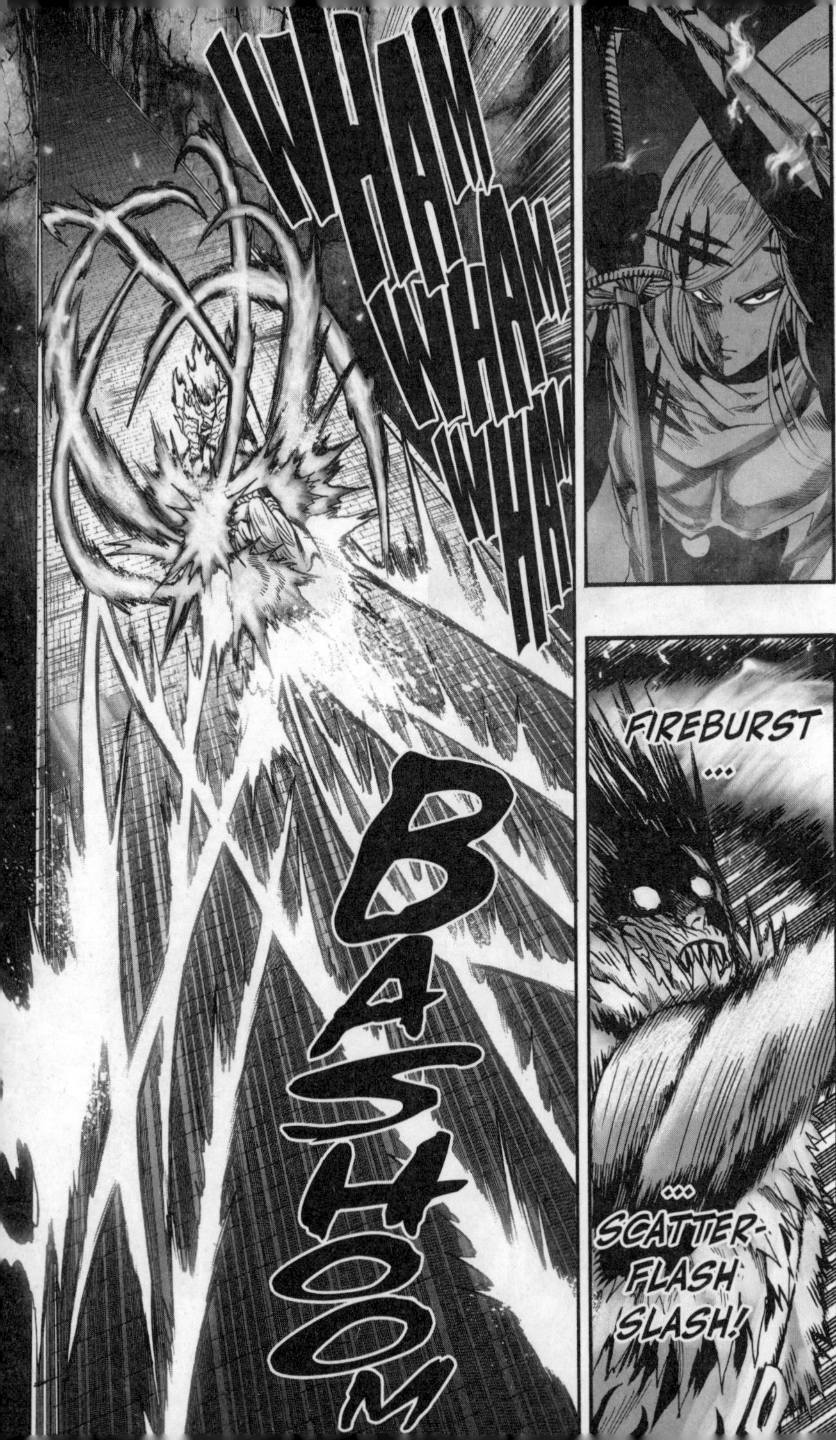
FIREBURST
...
... SCATTER-FLASH SLASH!
WHAM
WHAM
WHAM
BASHOOM

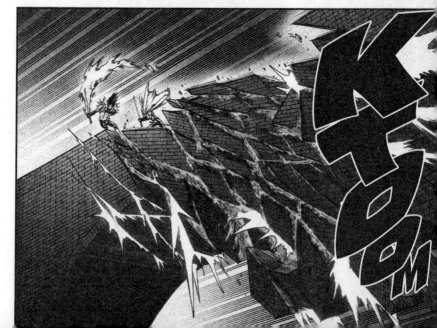

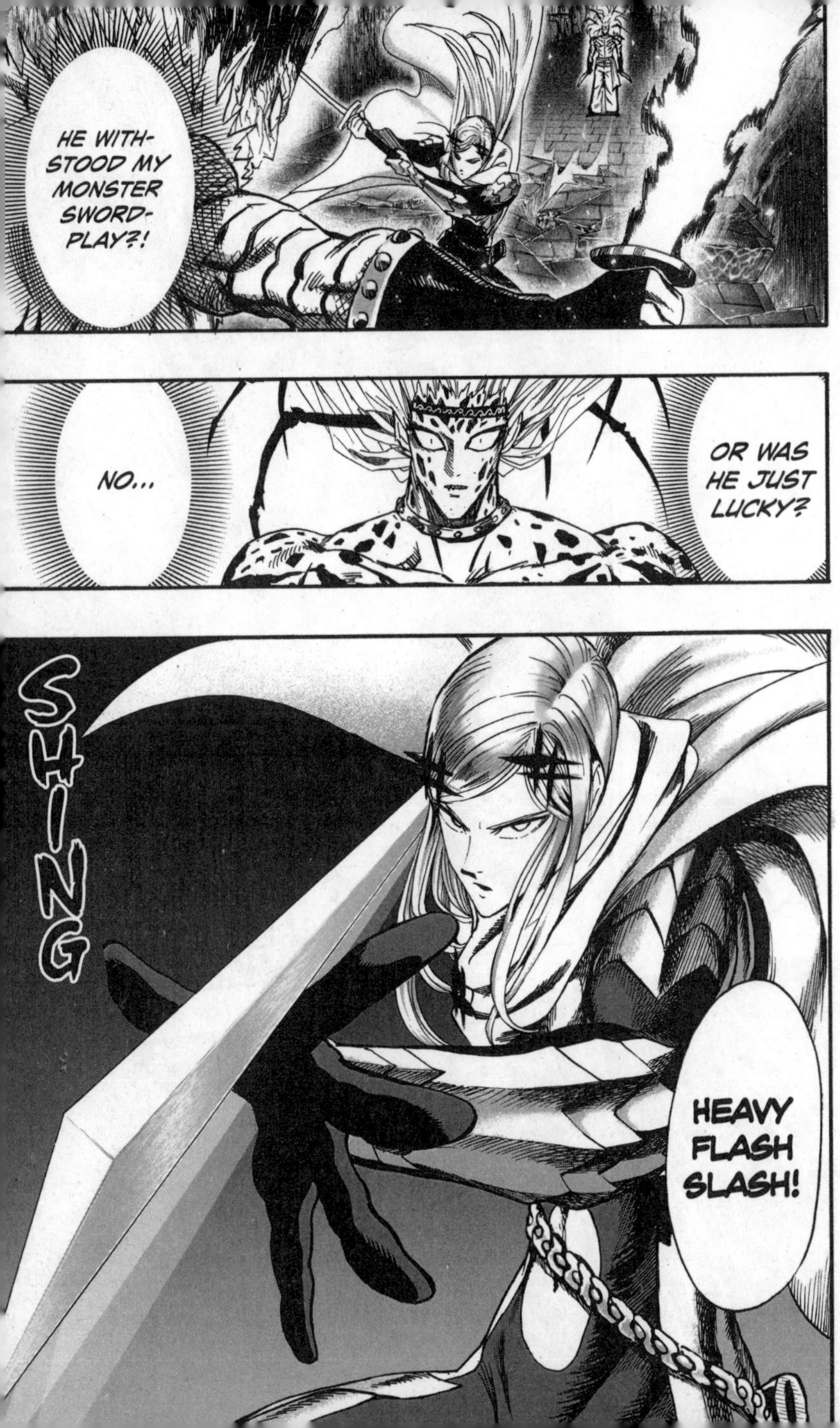
HE WITH-STOOD MY MONSTER SWORD-PLAY?!
OR WAS HE JUST LUCKY?
NO...
HEAVY FLASH SLASH!
SHING

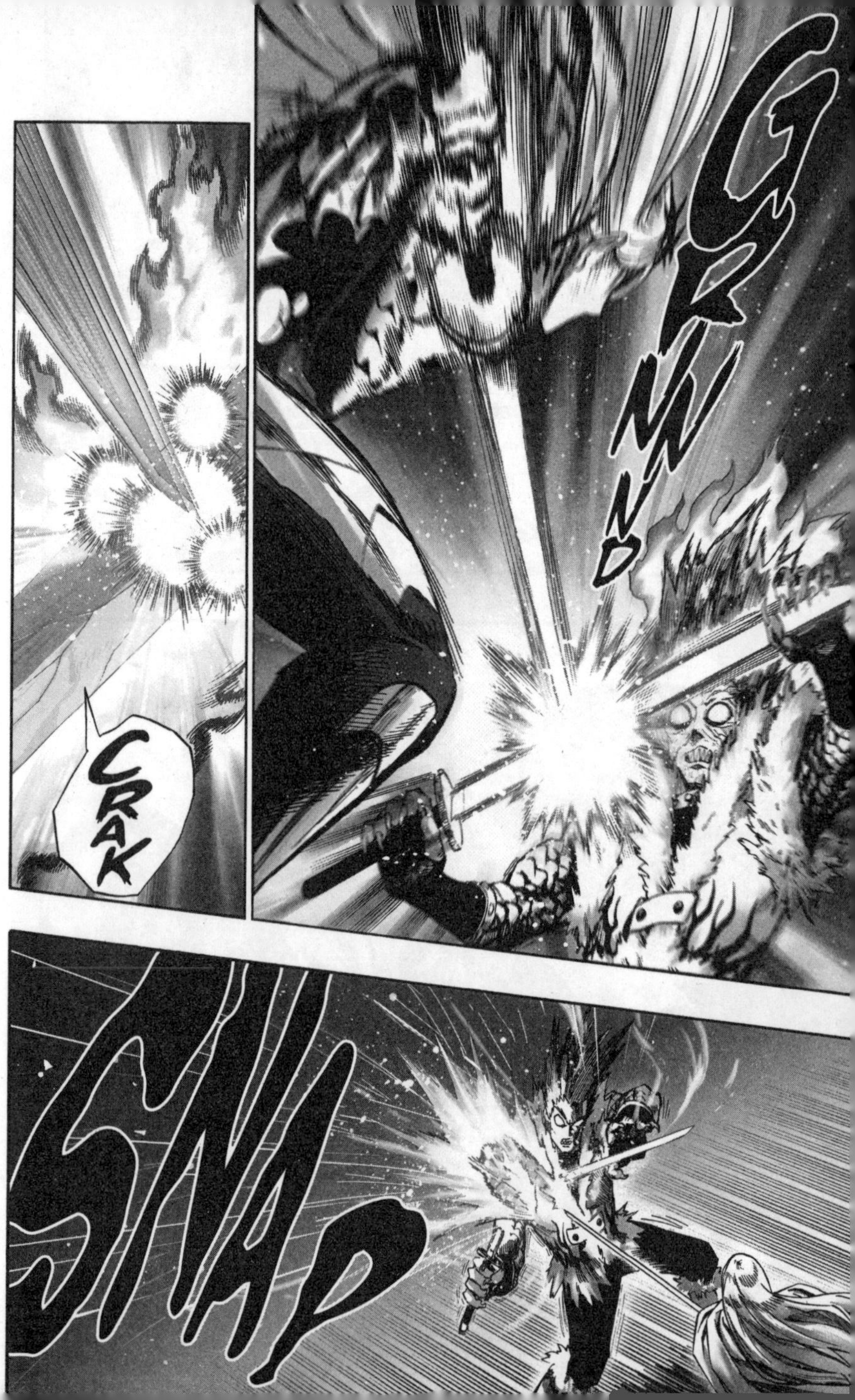
GRIND
CRAK
SNAP

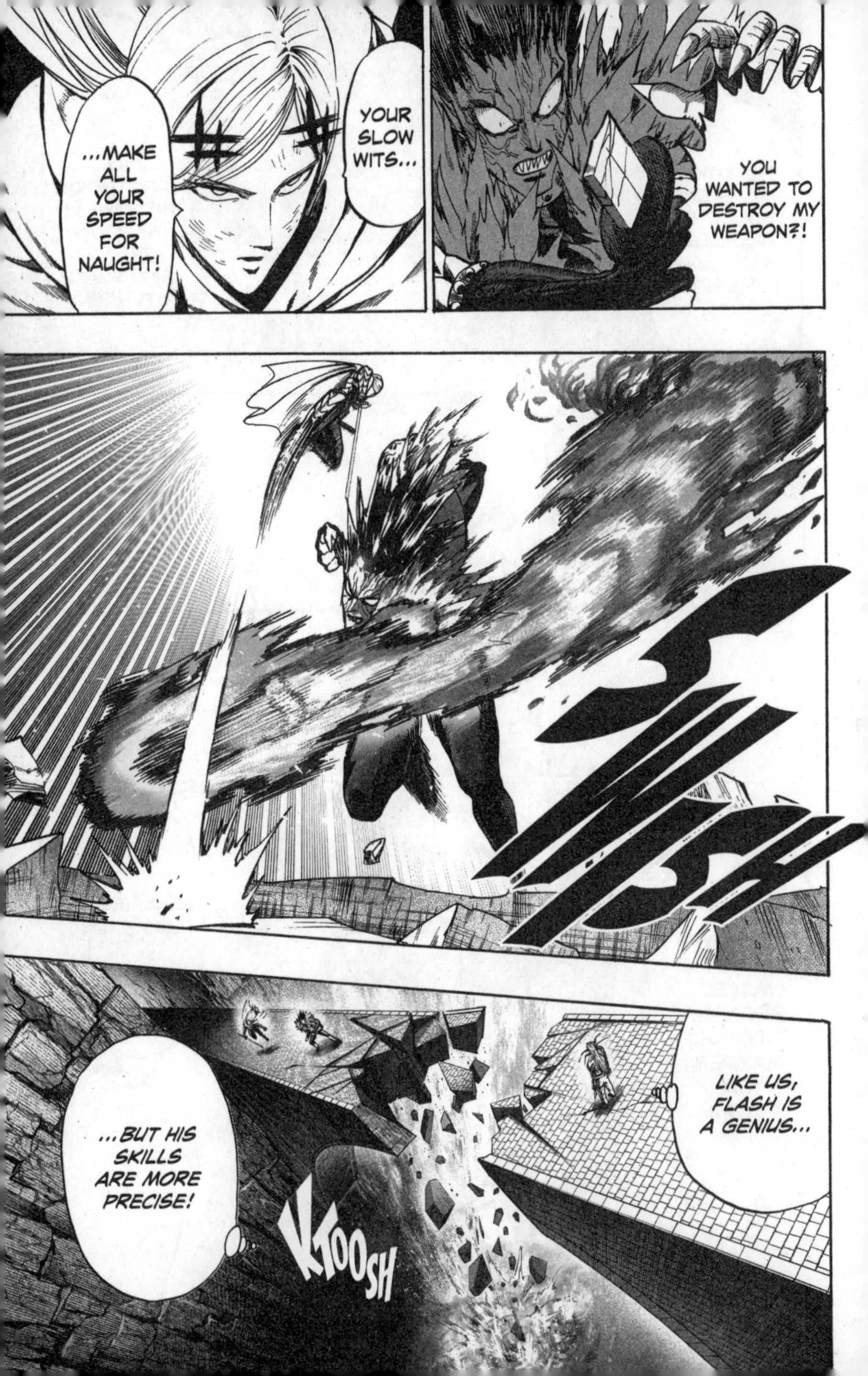
YOU WANTED TO DESTROY MY WEAPON?!
YOUR SLOW WITS...
...MAKE ALL YOUR SPEED FOR NAUGHT!
SWISH
LIKE US, FLASH IS A GENIUS...
...BUT HIS SKILLS ARE MORE PRECISE!
KTOOSH

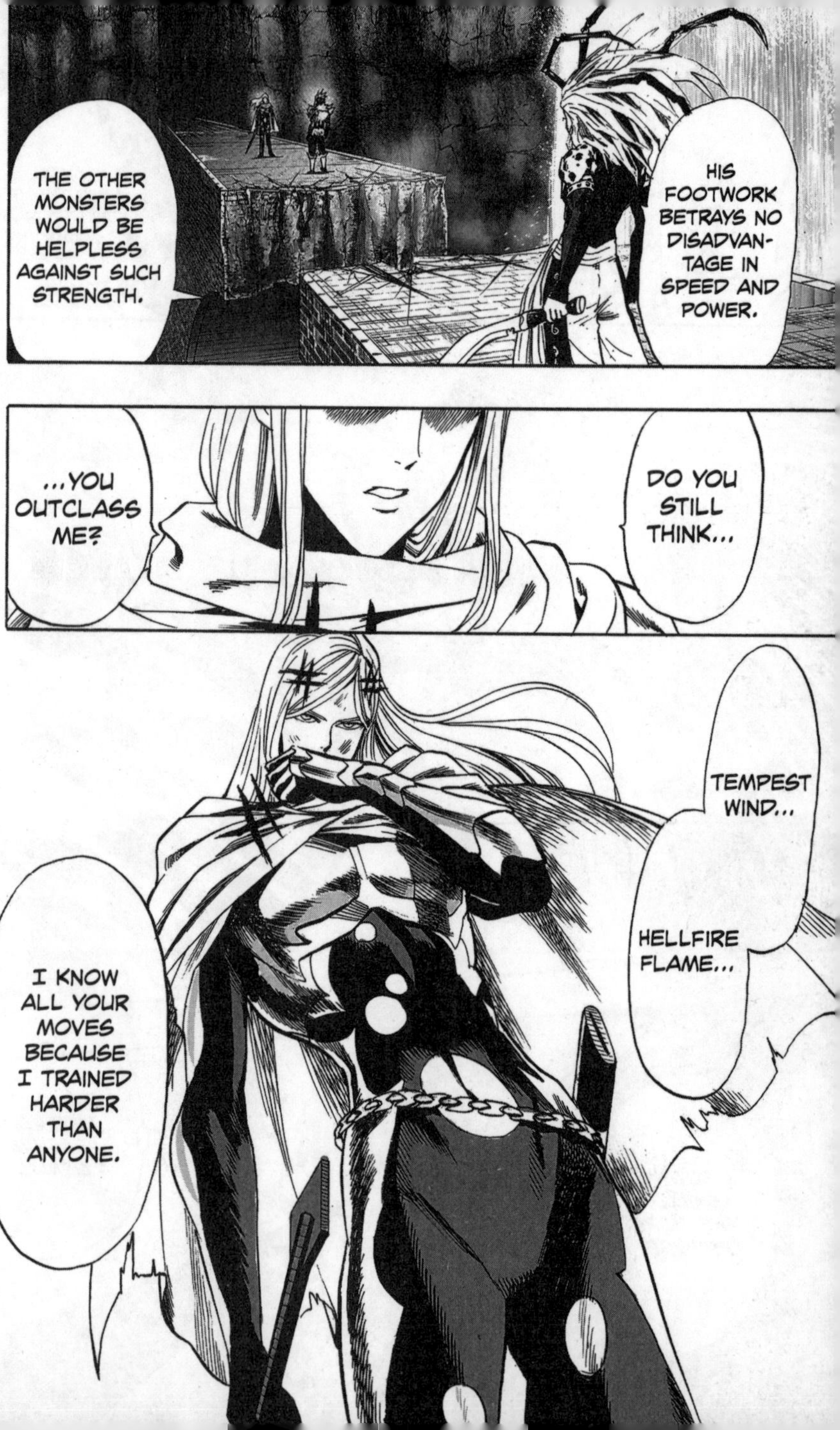
HIS FOOTWORK BETRAYS NO DISADVANTAGE IN SPEED AND POWER.
THE OTHER MONSTERS WOULD BE HELPLESS AGAINST SUCH STRENGTH.
DO YOU STILL THINK...
...YOU OUTCLASS ME?
TEMPEST WIND...
HELLFIRE FLAME...
I KNOW ALL YOUR MOVES BECAUSE I TRAINED HARDER THAN ANYONE.

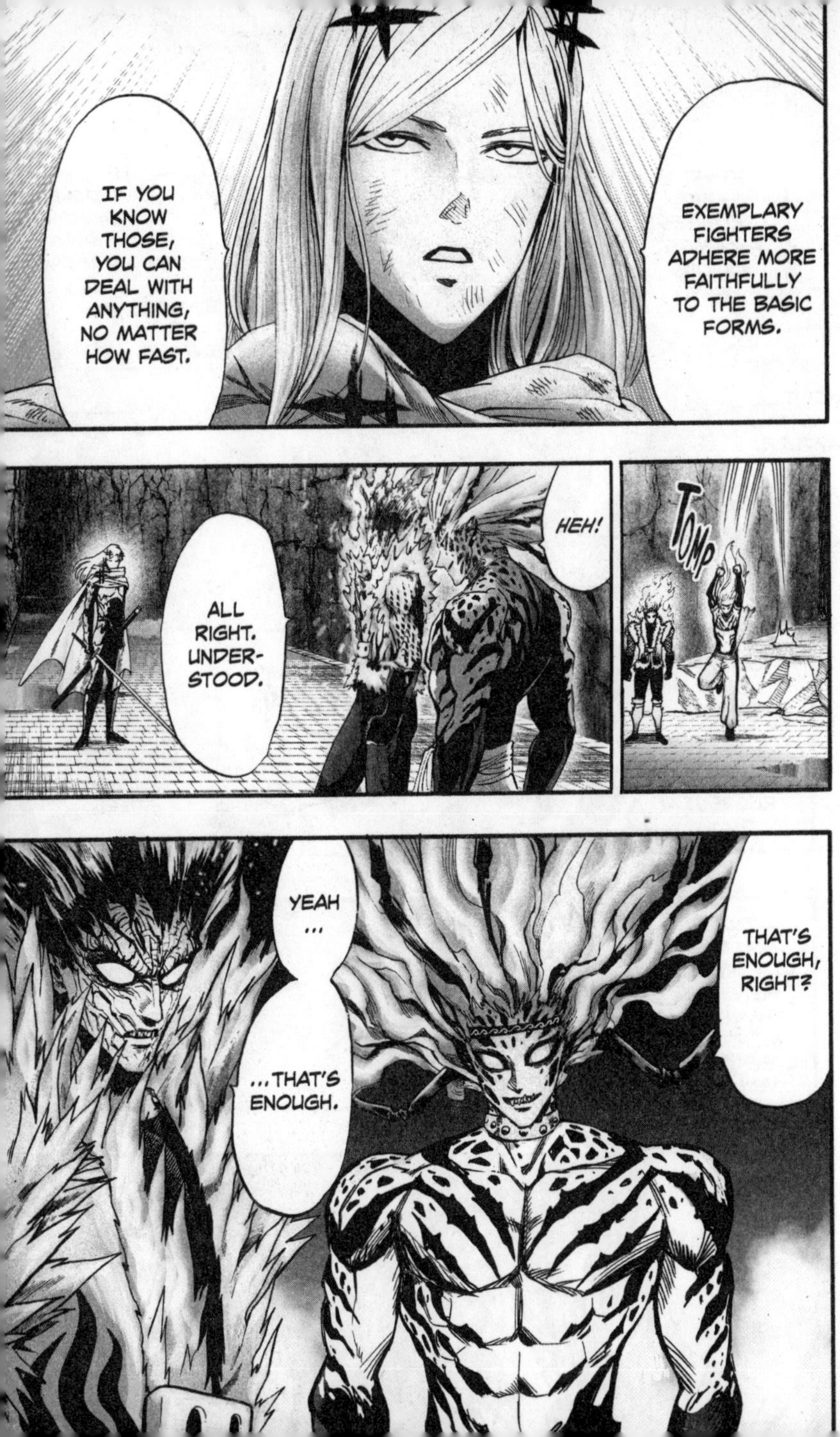
EXEMPLARY FIGHTERS ADHERE MORE FAITHFULLY TO THE BASIC FORMS.
IF YOU KNOW THOSE, YOU CAN DEAL WITH ANYTHING, NO MATTER HOW FAST.
TOMP
HEH!
ALL RIGHT. UNDER-STOOD.
THAT'S ENOUGH, RIGHT?
YEAH ...
...THAT'S ENOUGH.

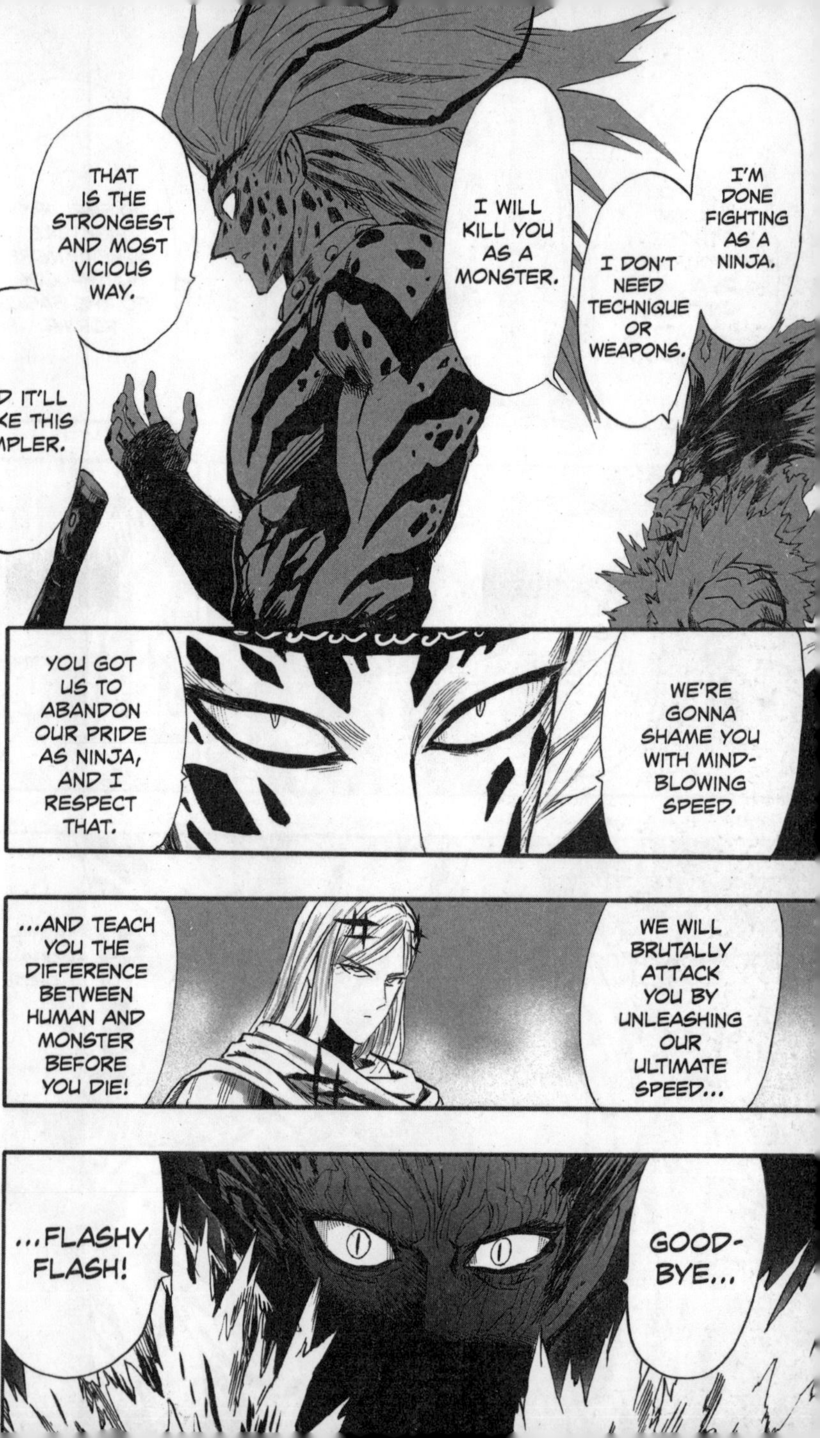
I'M DONE FIGHTING AS A NINJA.
I DON'T NEED TECHNIQUE OR WEAPONS.
I WILL KILL YOU AS A MONSTER.
THAT IS THE STRONGEST AND MOST VICIOUS WAY.
AND IT'LL MAKE THIS SIMPLER.
WE'RE GONNA SHAME YOU WITH MIND-BLOWING SPEED.
YOU GOT US TO ABANDON OUR PRIDE AS NINJA, AND I RESPECT THAT.
WE WILL BRUTALLY ATTACK YOU BY UNLEASHING OUR ULTIMATE SPEED...
...AND TEACH YOU THE DIFFERENCE BETWEEN HUMAN AND MONSTER BEFORE YOU DIE!
GOOD-BYE...
...FLASHY FLASH!

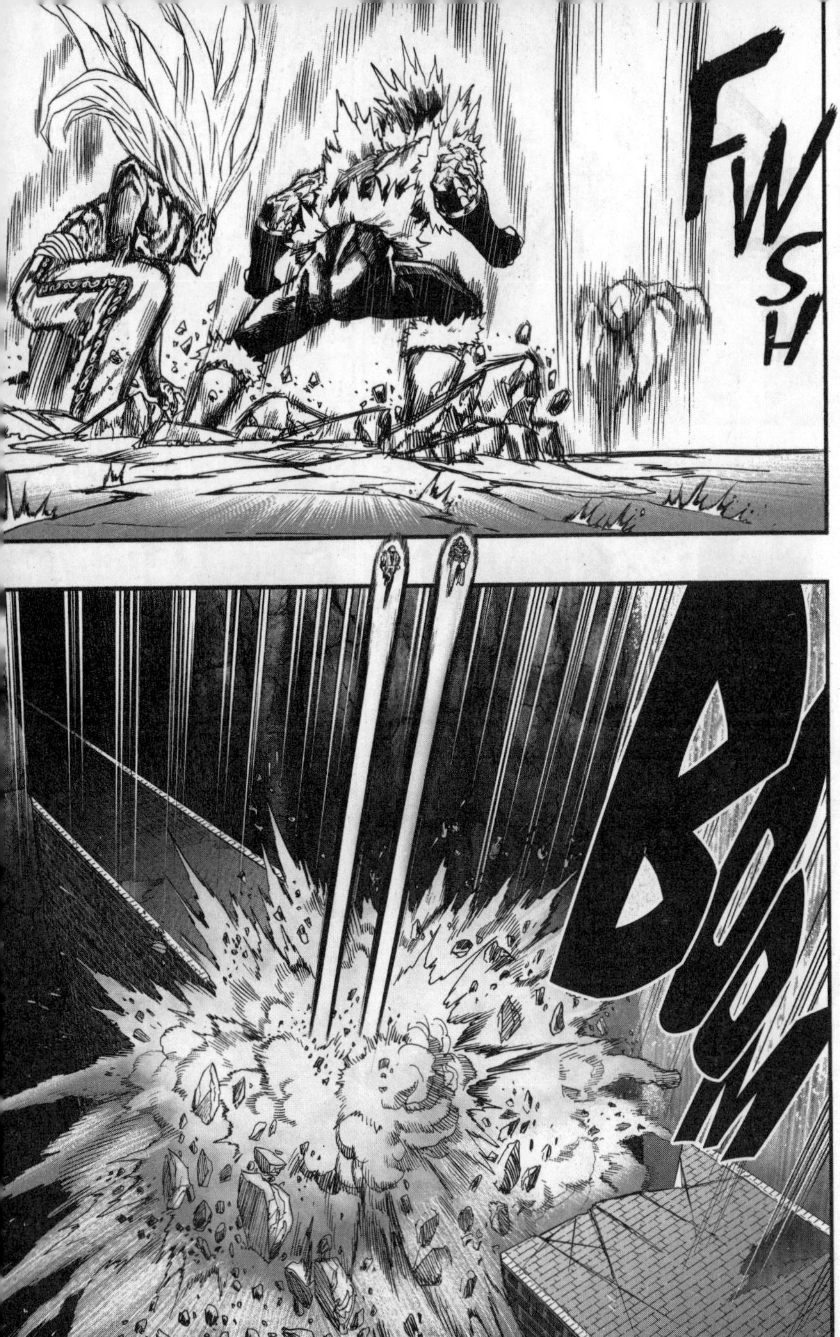
FWSH
BOOM

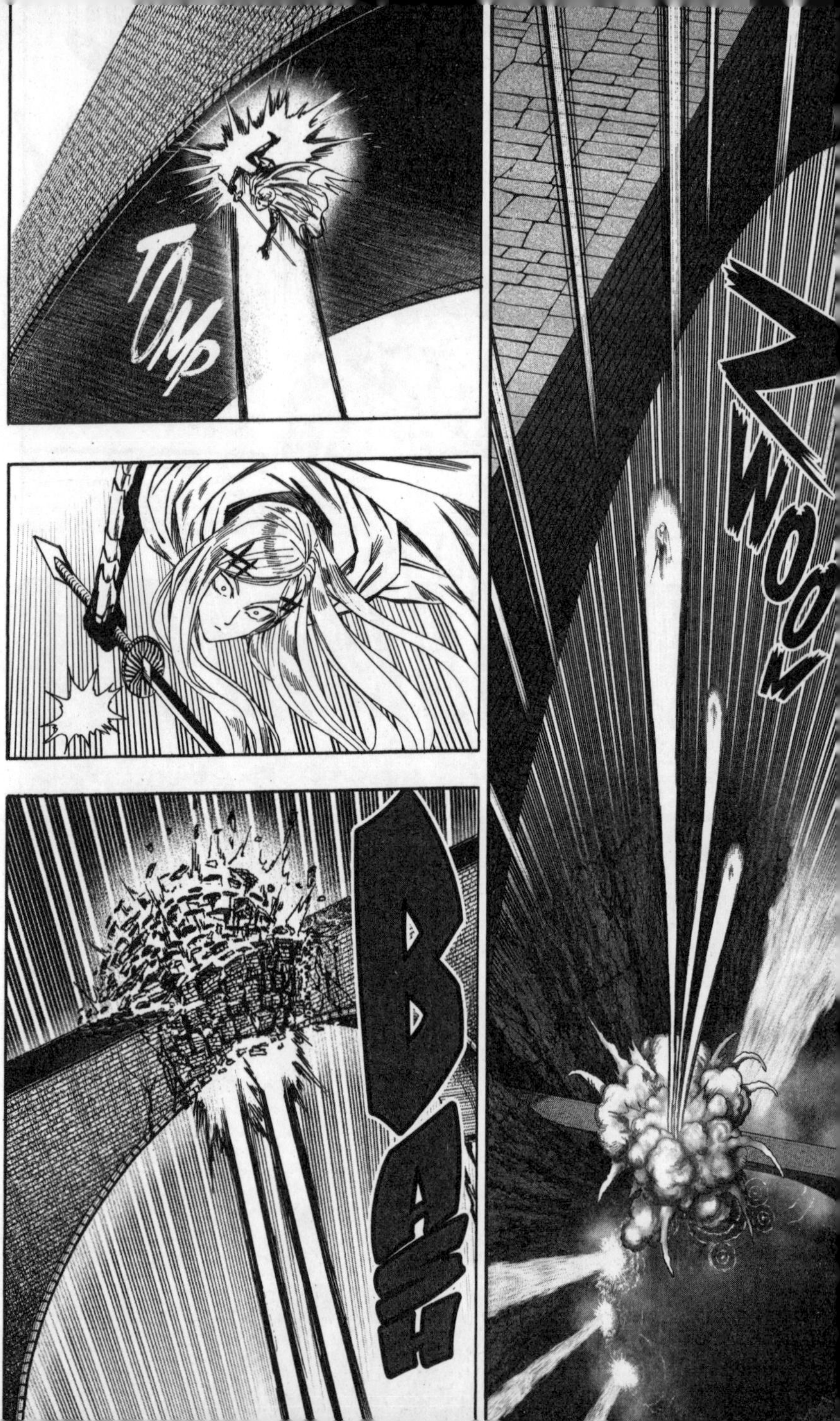
ZWOOM
TOMP
BASH

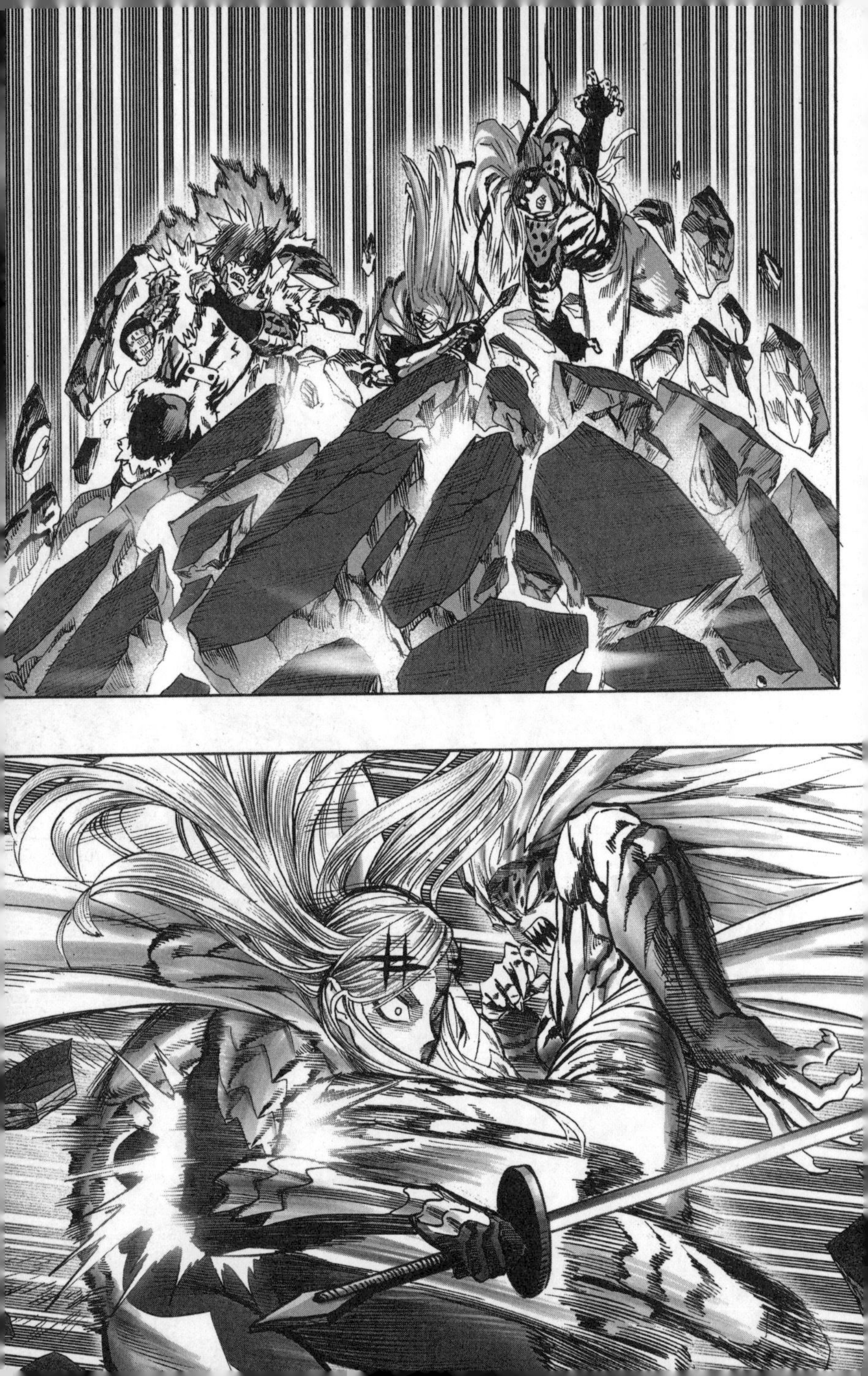

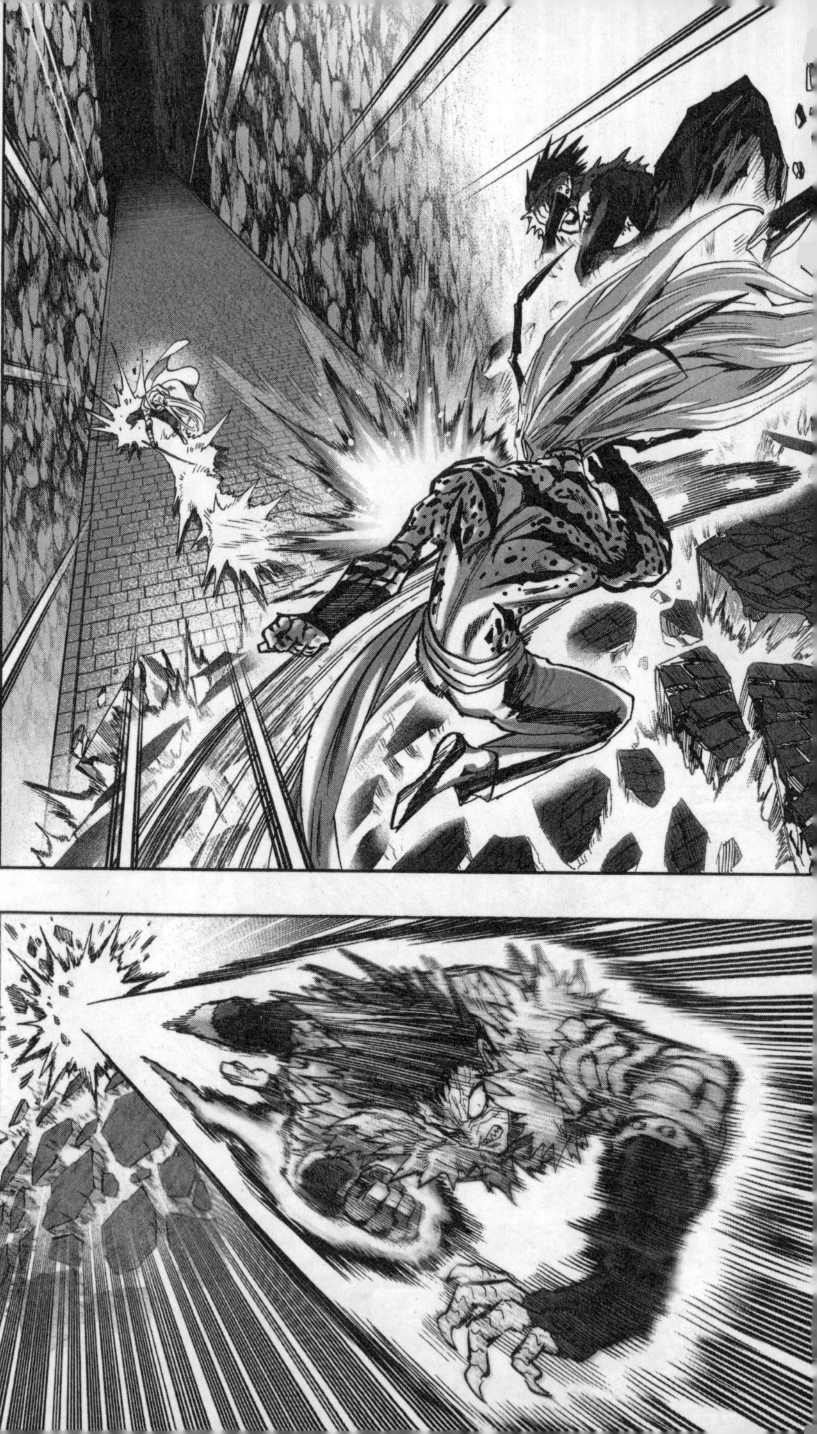

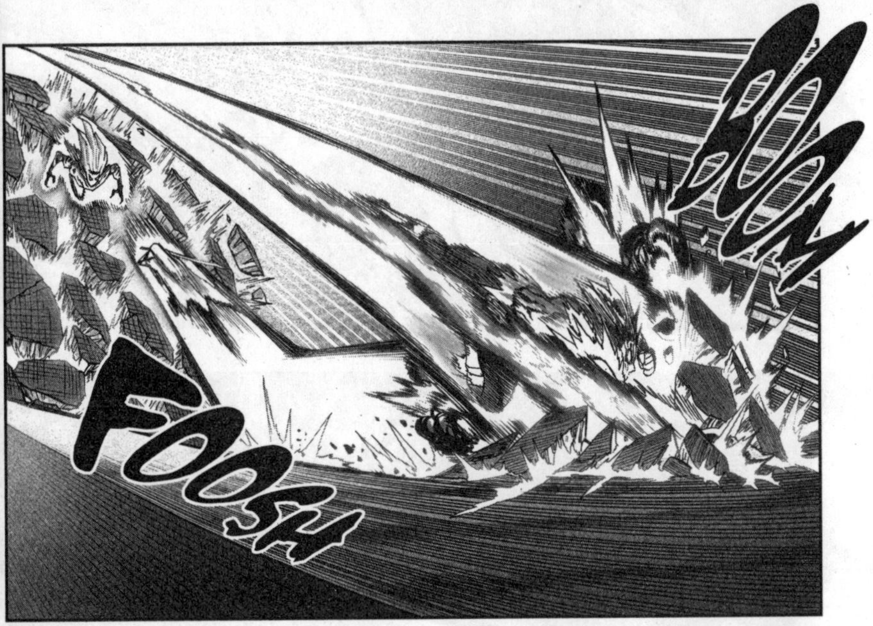
BOOM
FOOSH
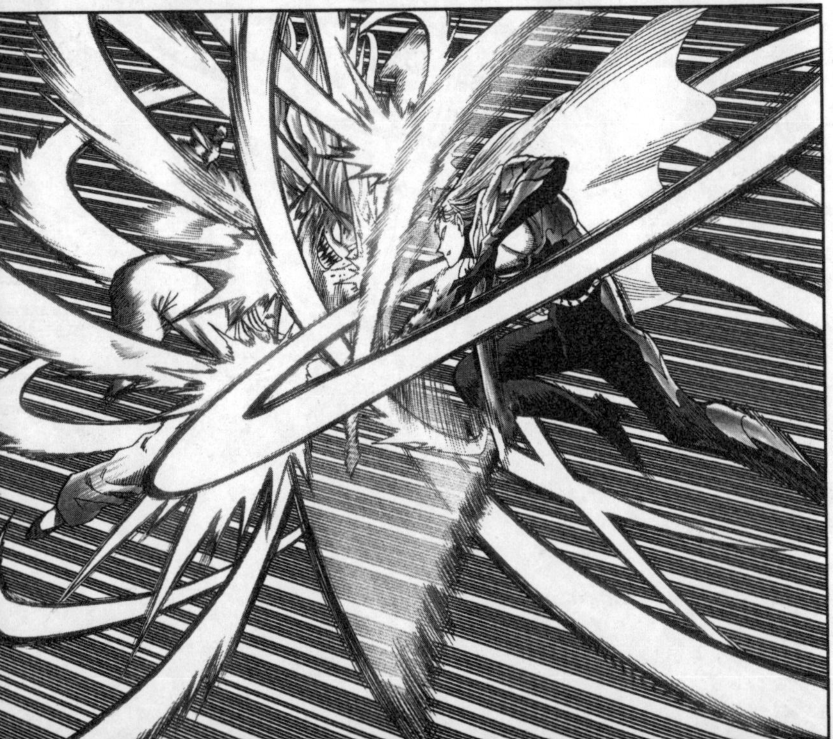

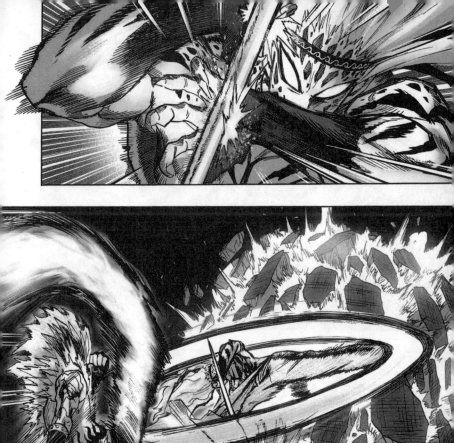

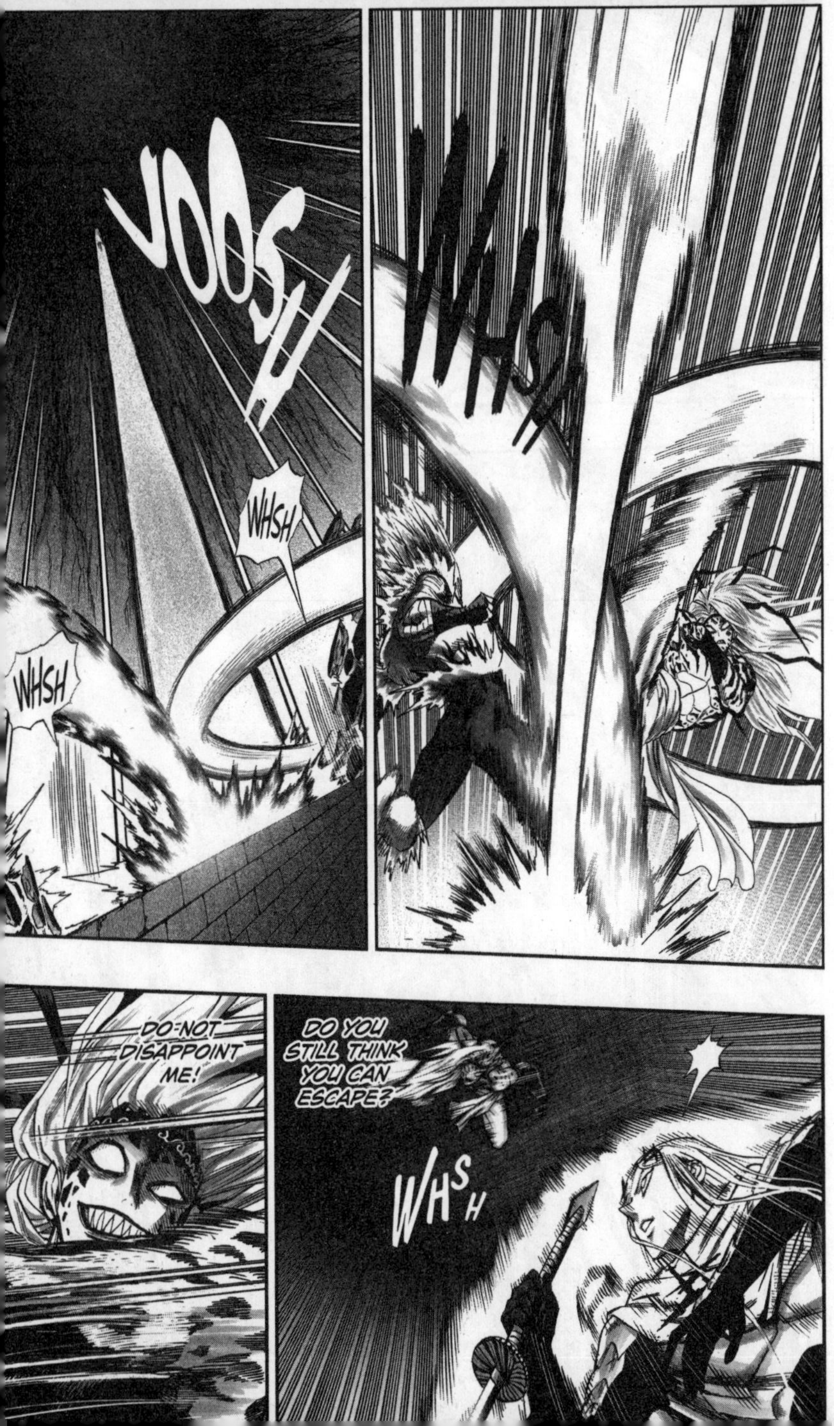
WHSH
VOOSH
WHSH
WHSH
DO YOU STILL THINK YOU CAN ESCAPE?
WHSH
DO NOT DISAPPOINT ME!

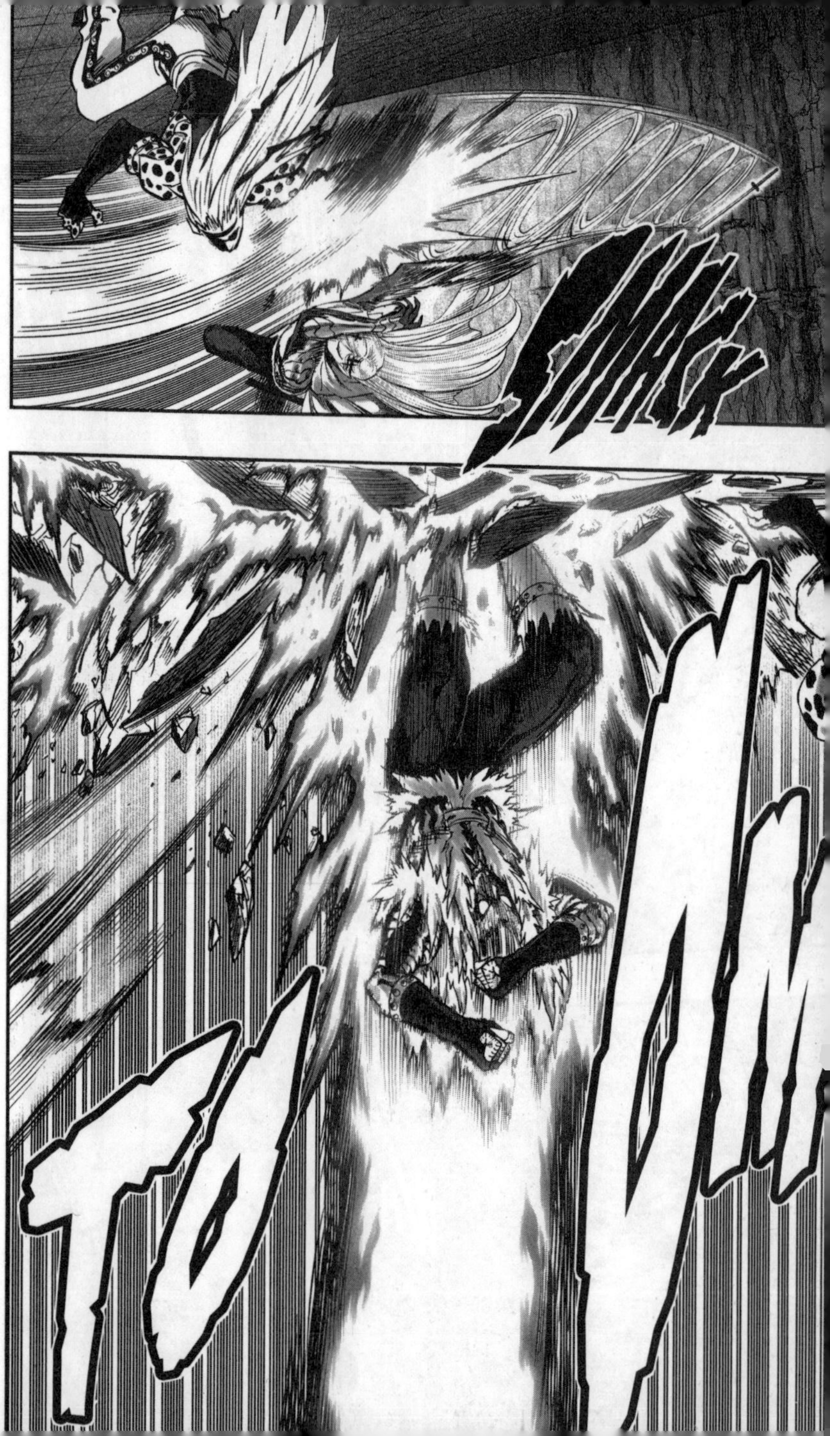

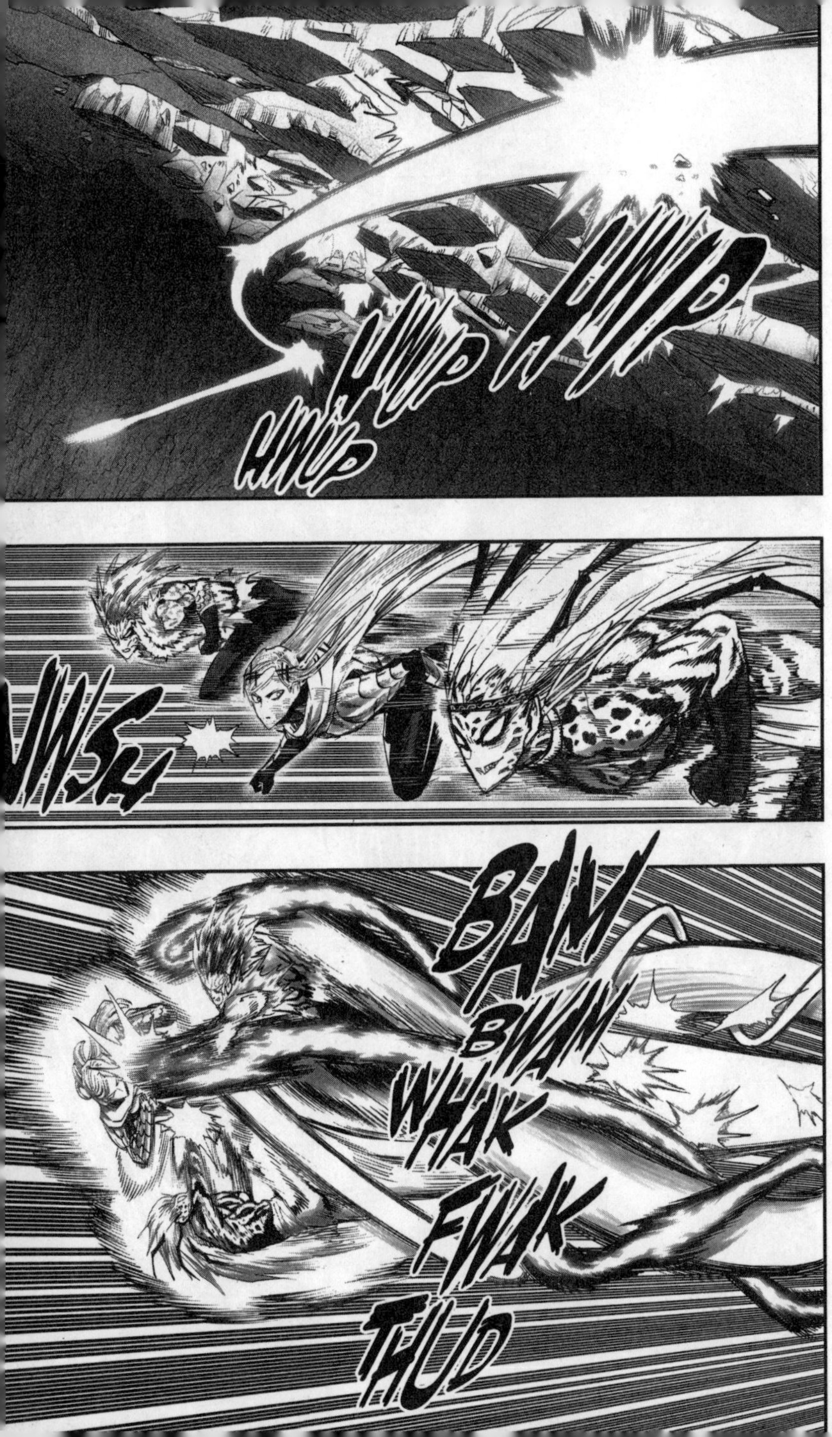
HWIP
HWIP
HWIP
WSH
BAM
BWAM
WHAK
FWAK
THUD

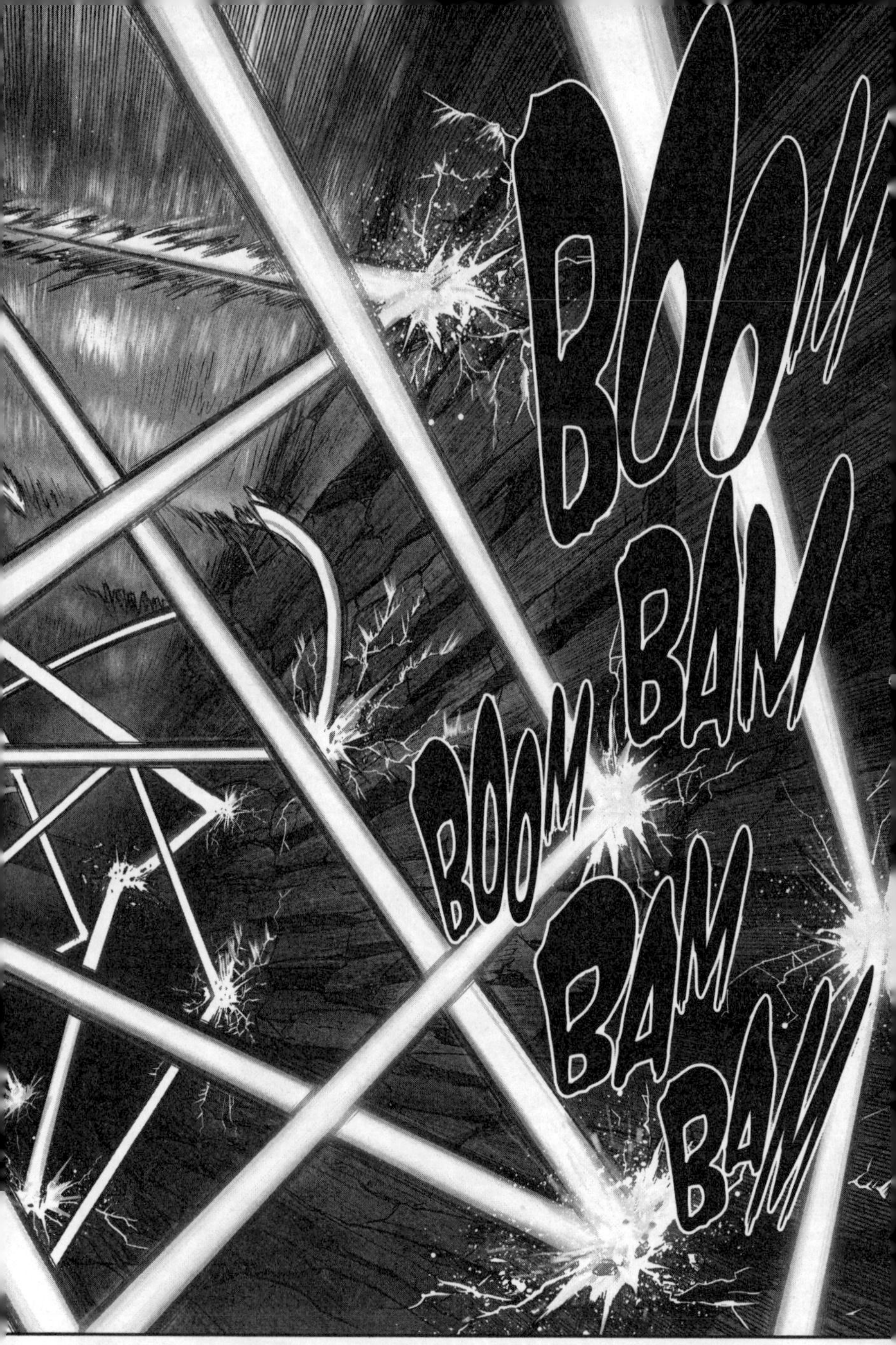
BOOM
BAM
BOOM
BAM
BAM
BAM

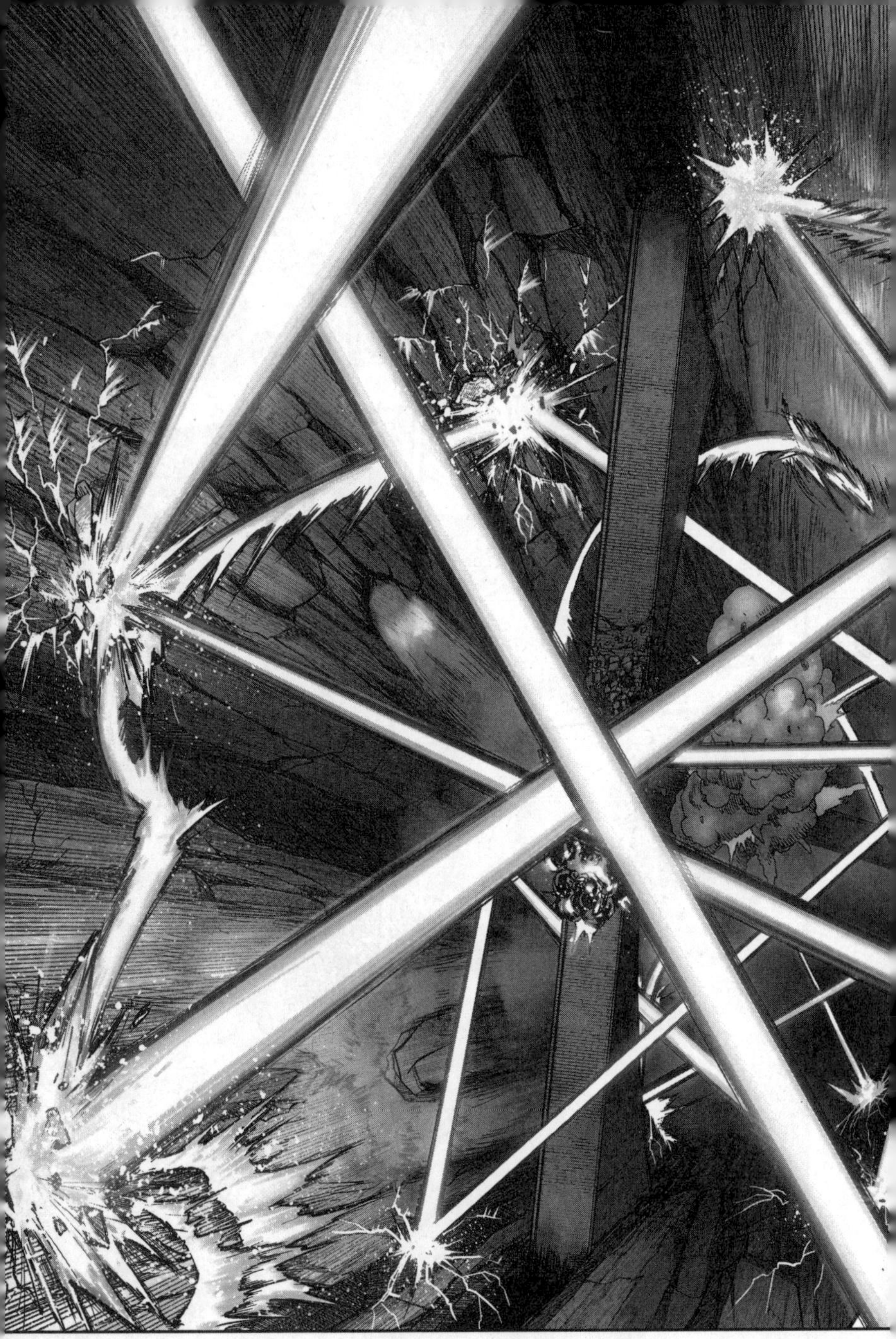

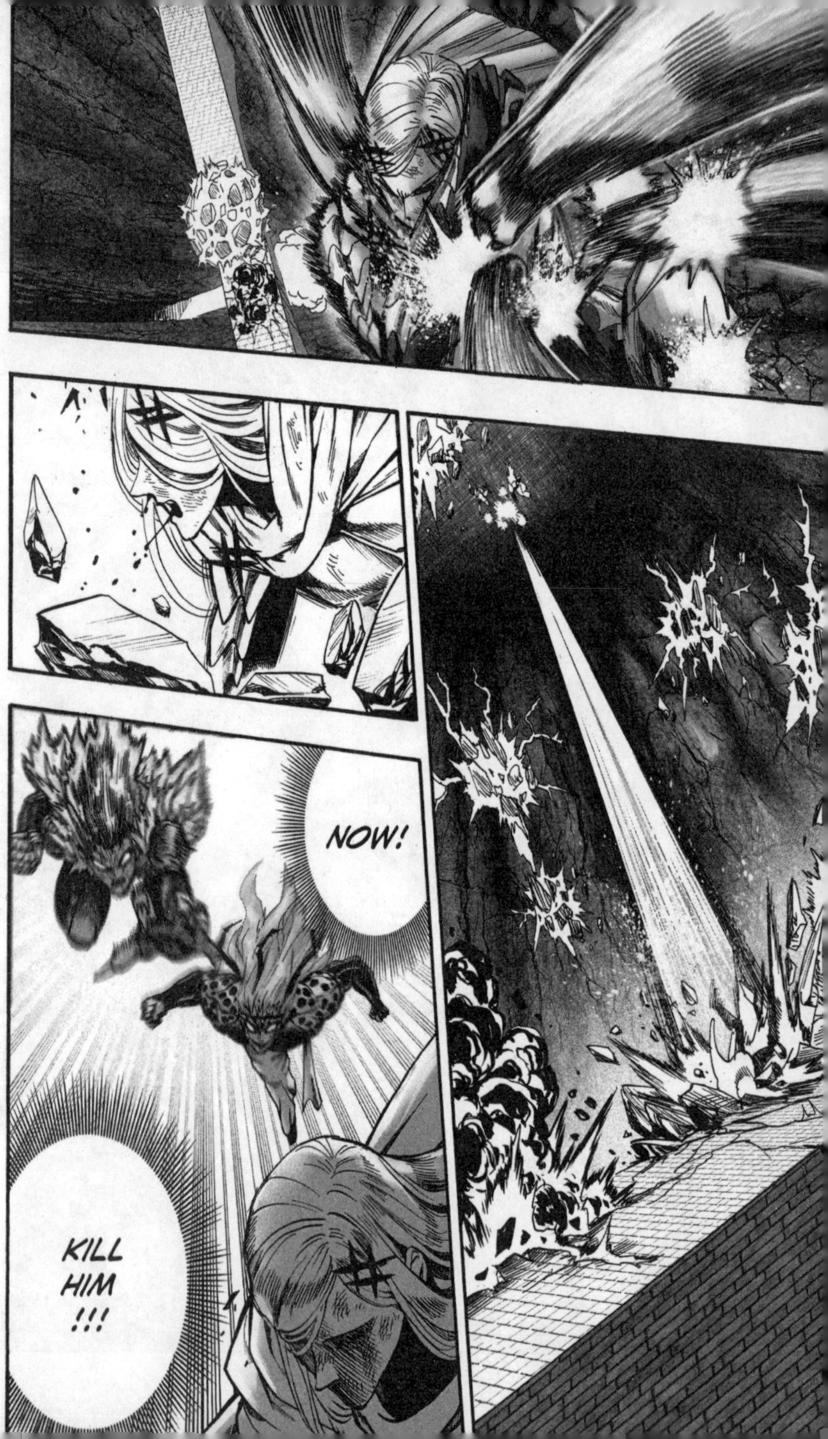
NOW!
KILL HIM !!!

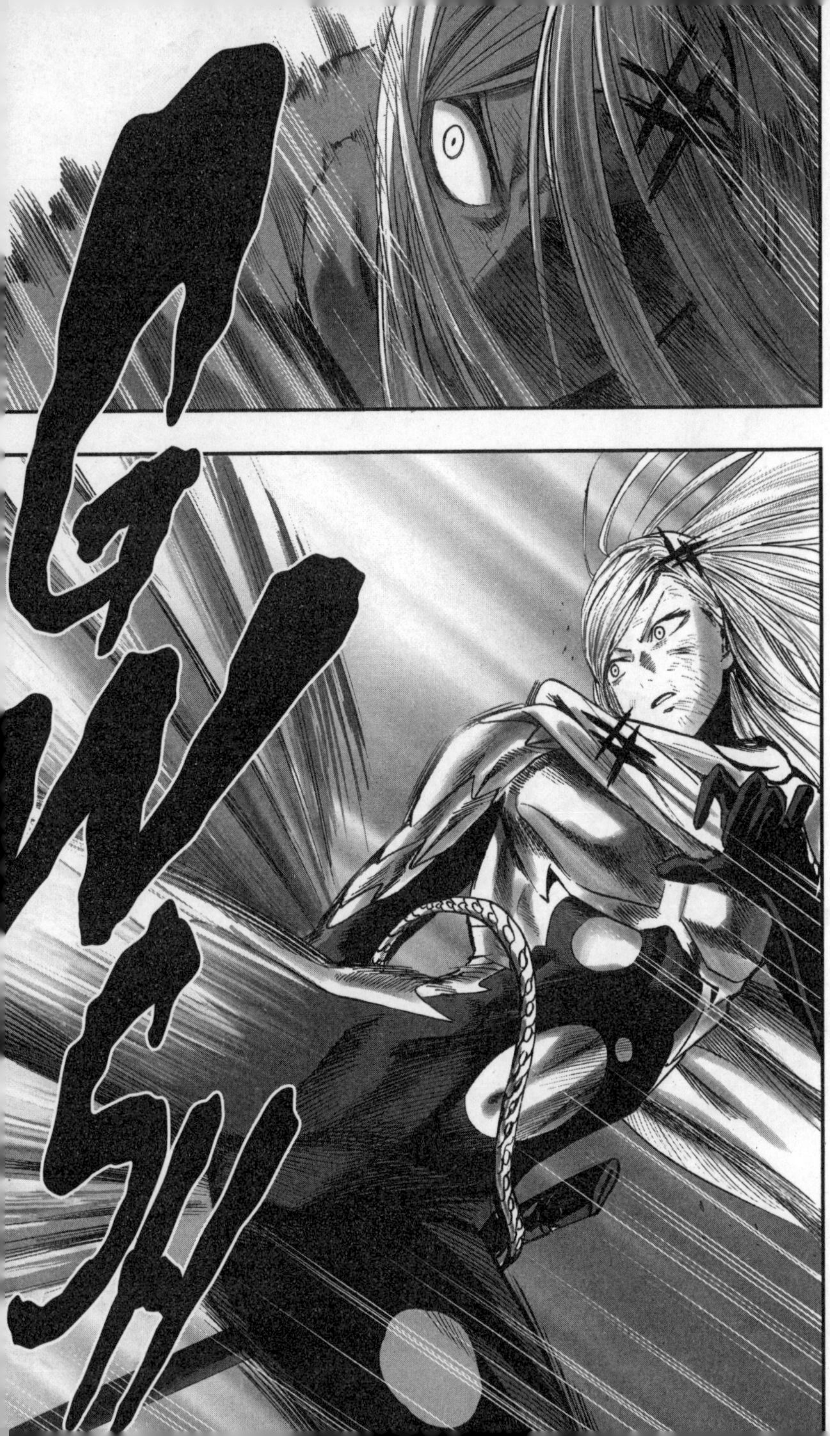

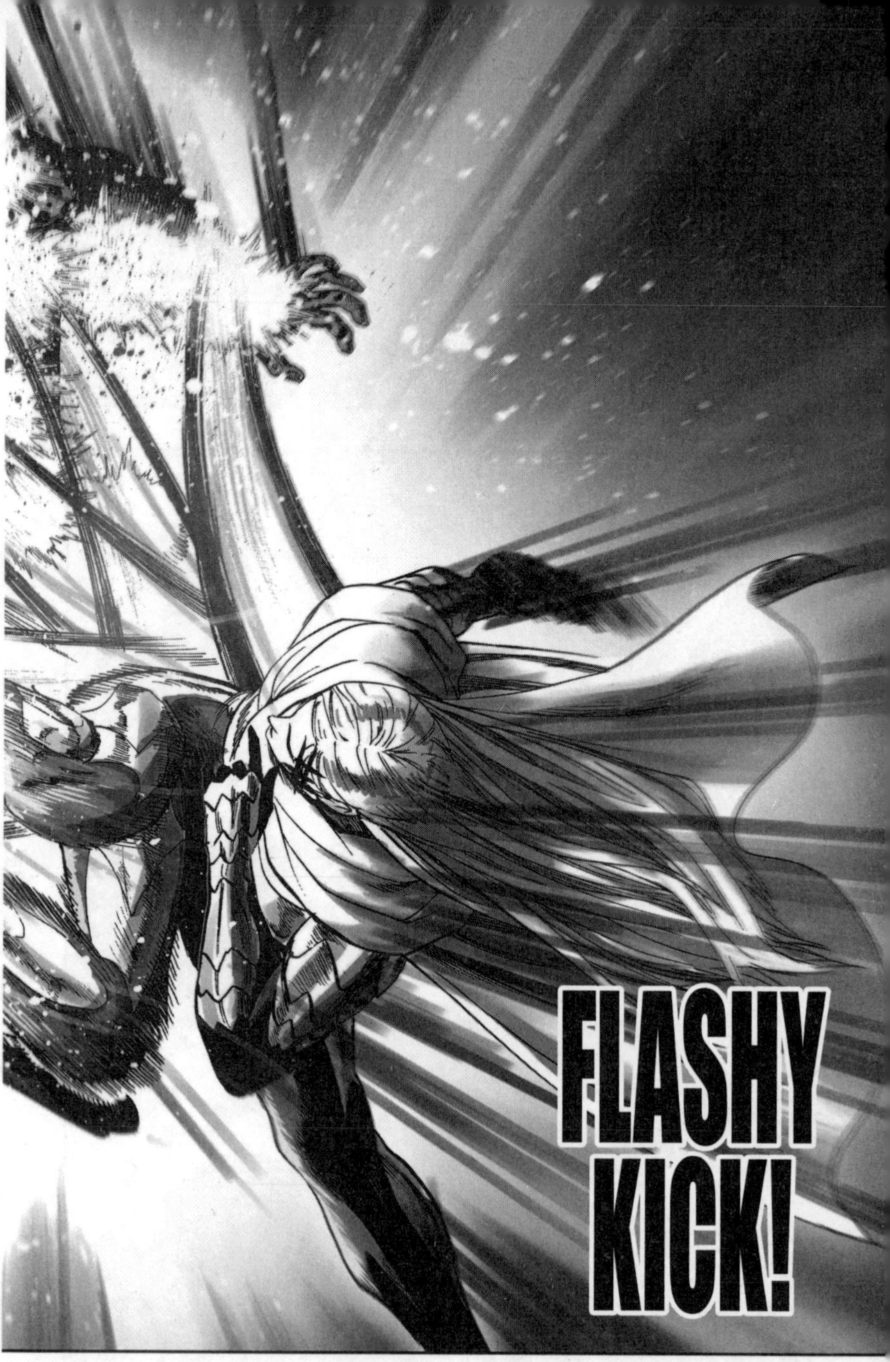
FLASHY KICK!

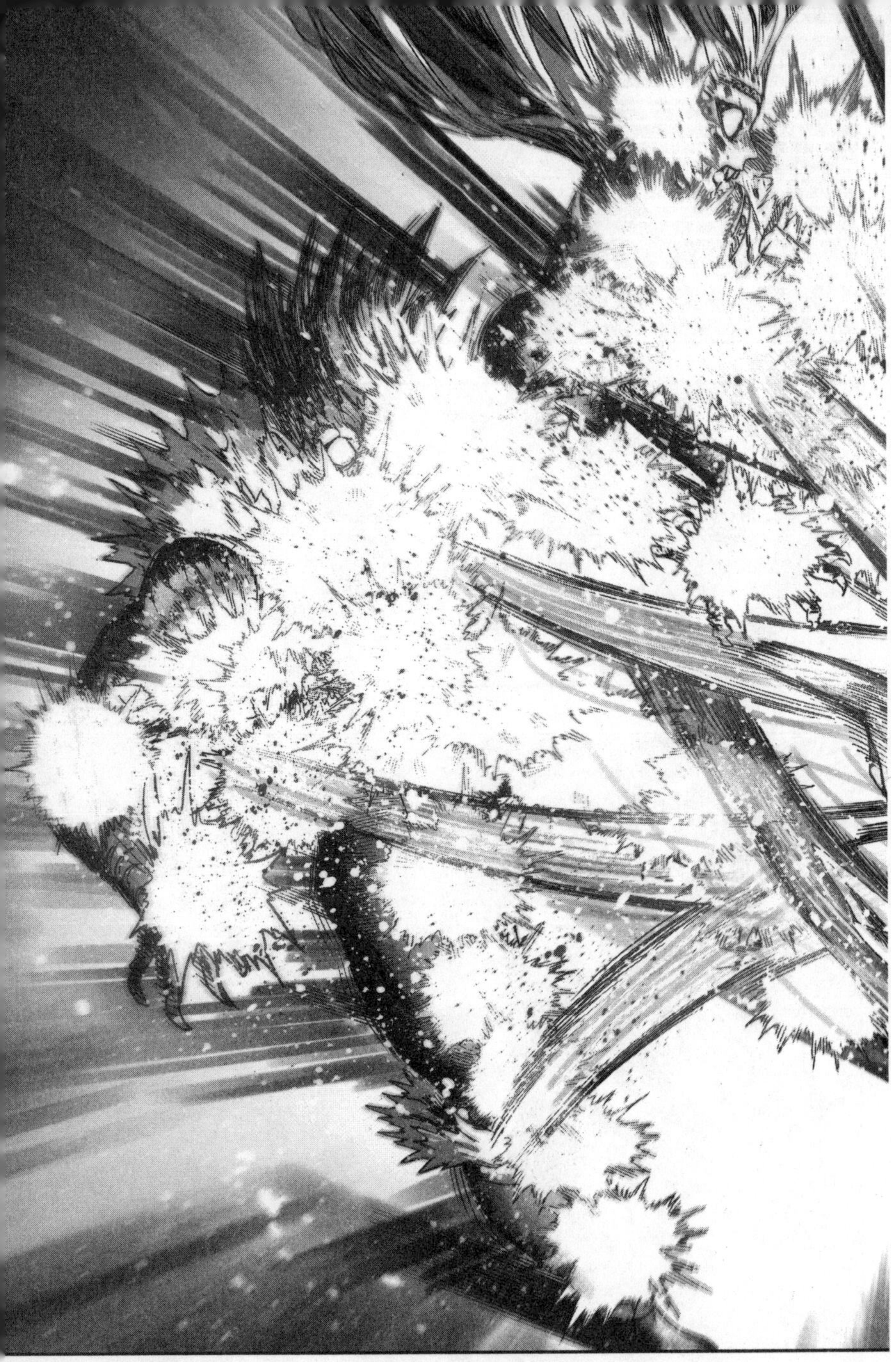

...AND FAST!

UH-OH! HE'S PRESSING US...

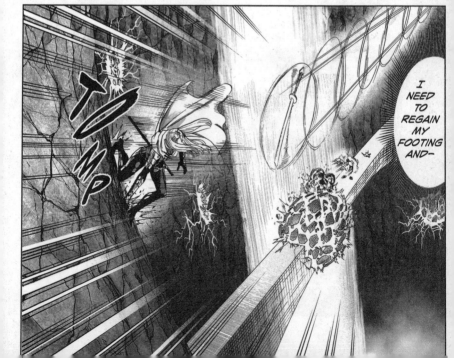

I NEED TO REGAIN MY FOOTING AND—

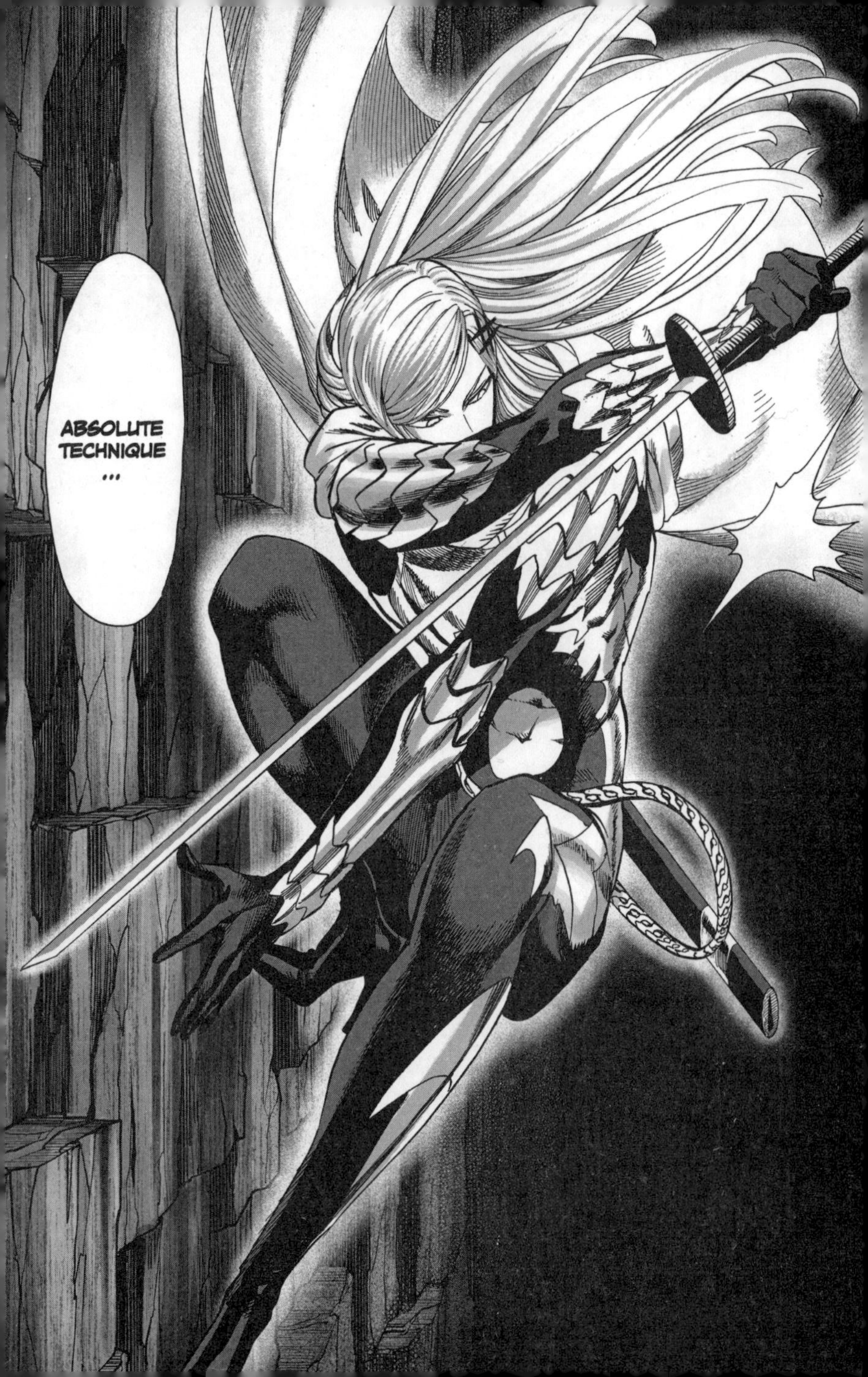
ABSOLUTE TECHNIQUE ...

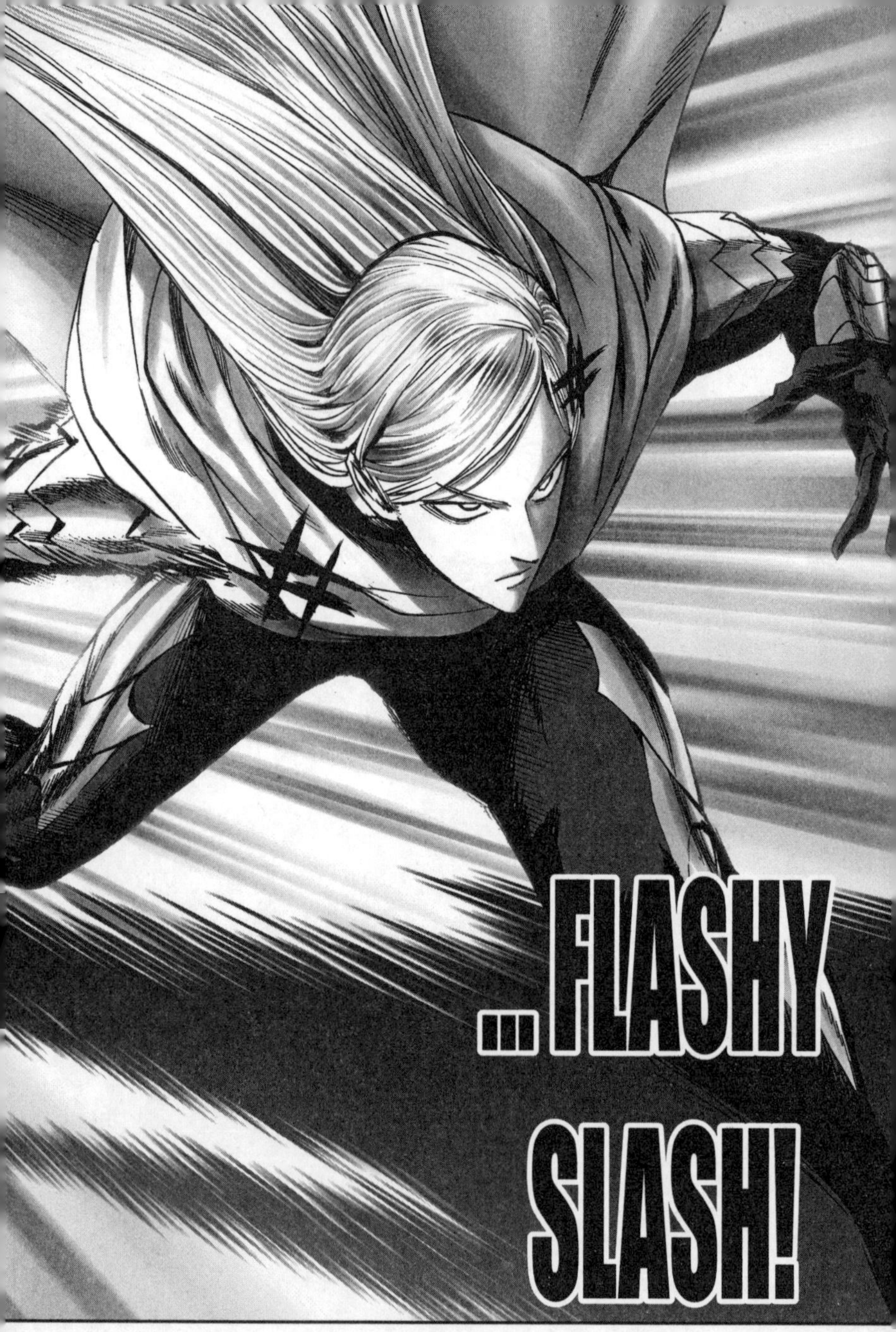
...FLASHY SLASH!

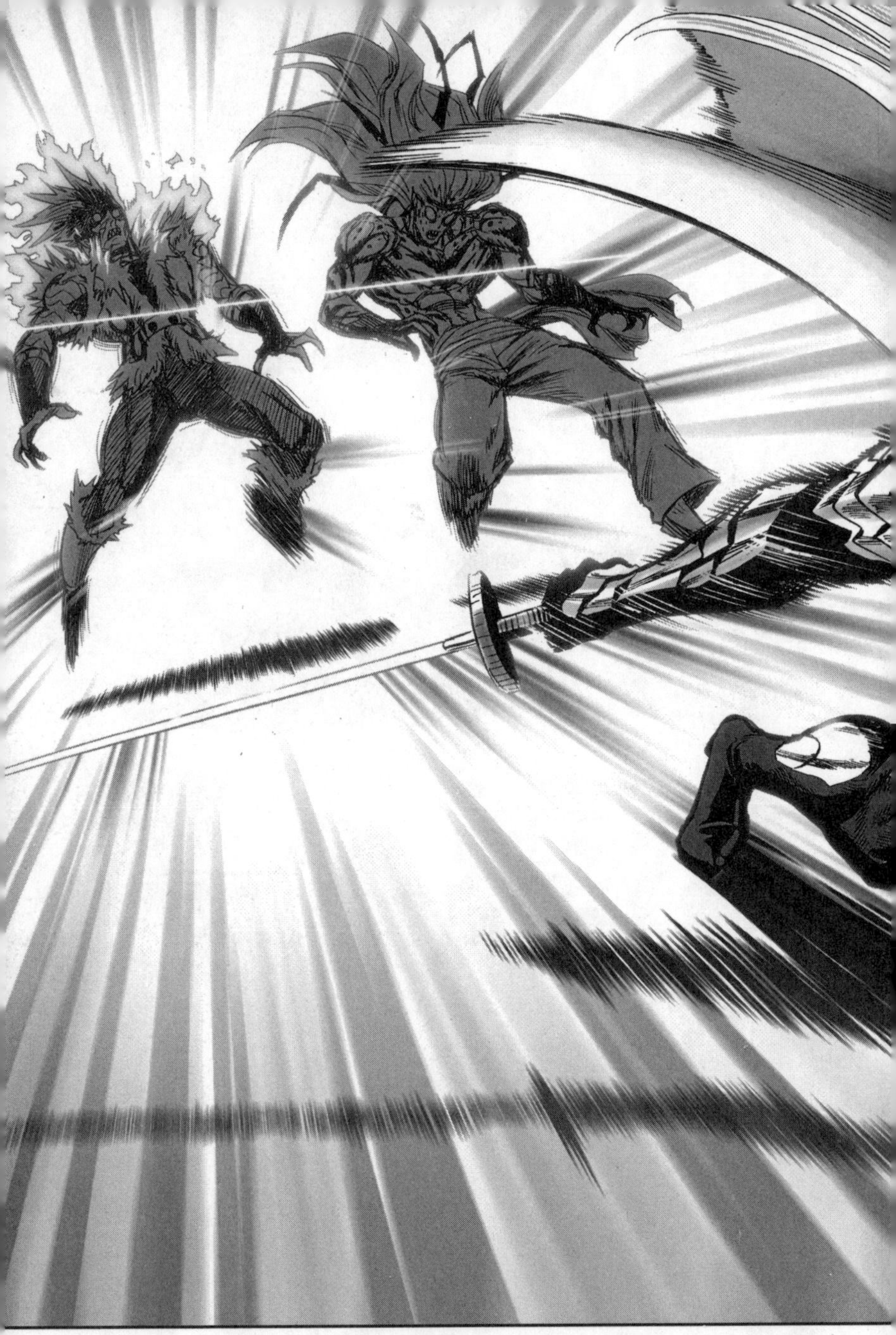

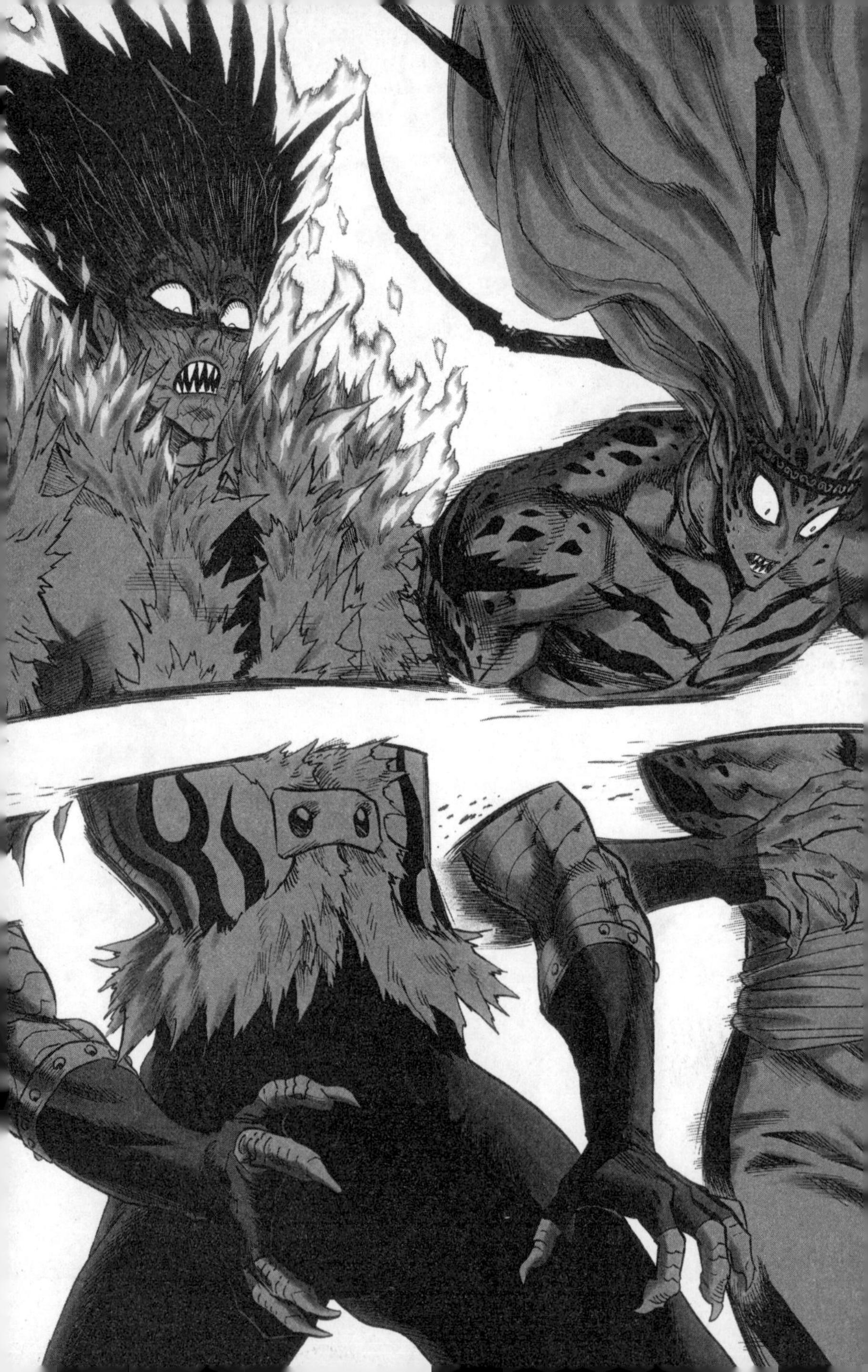

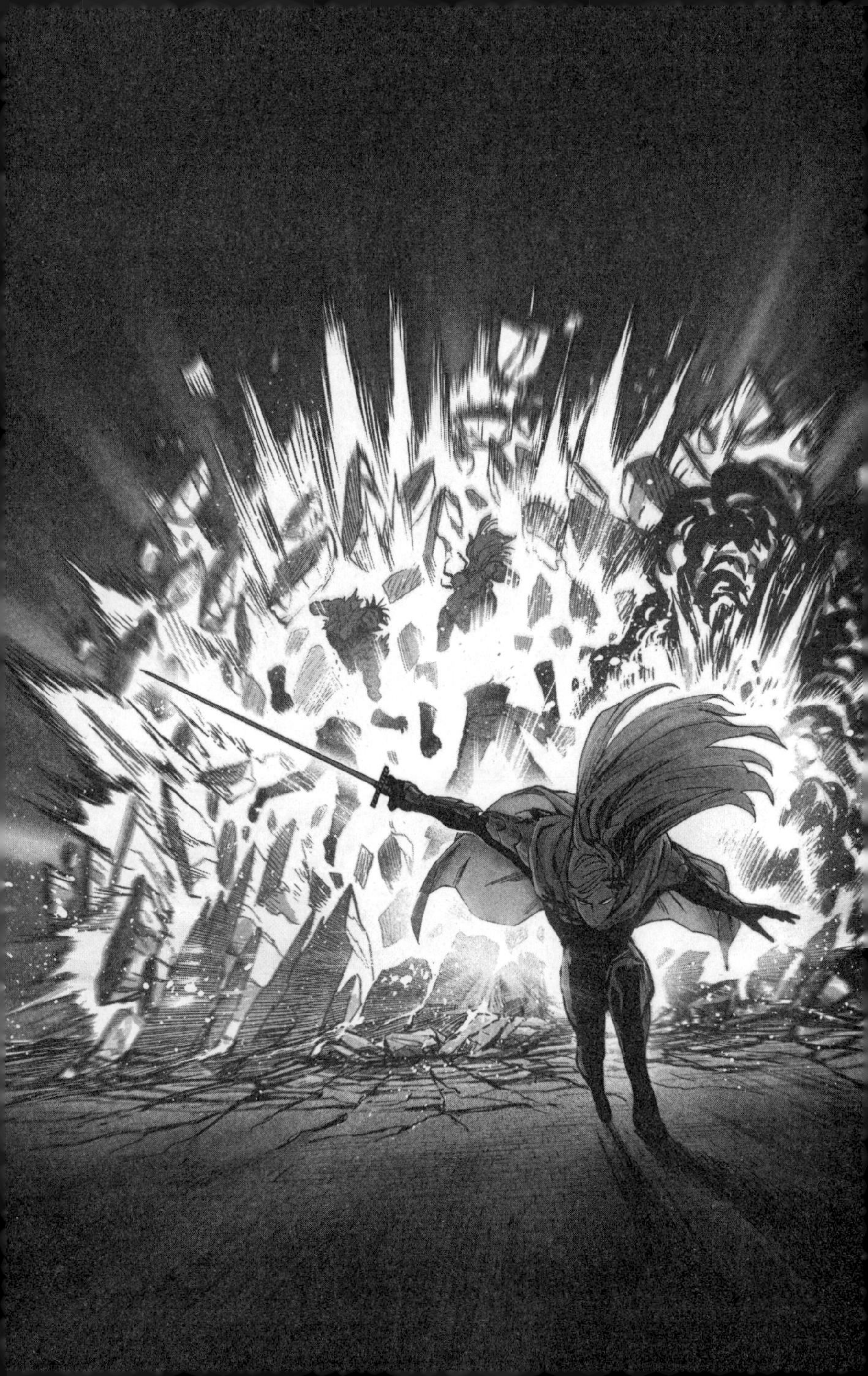

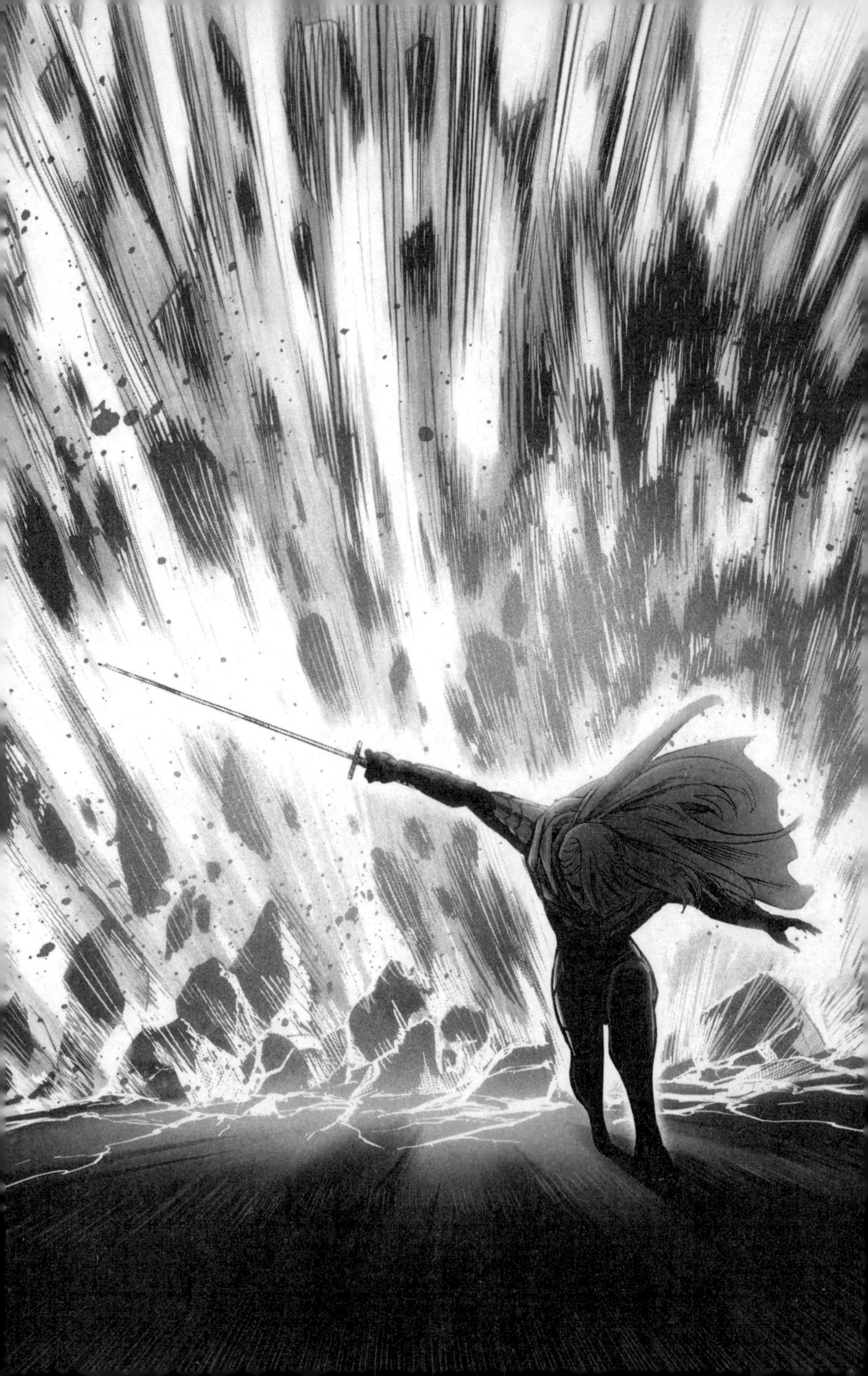

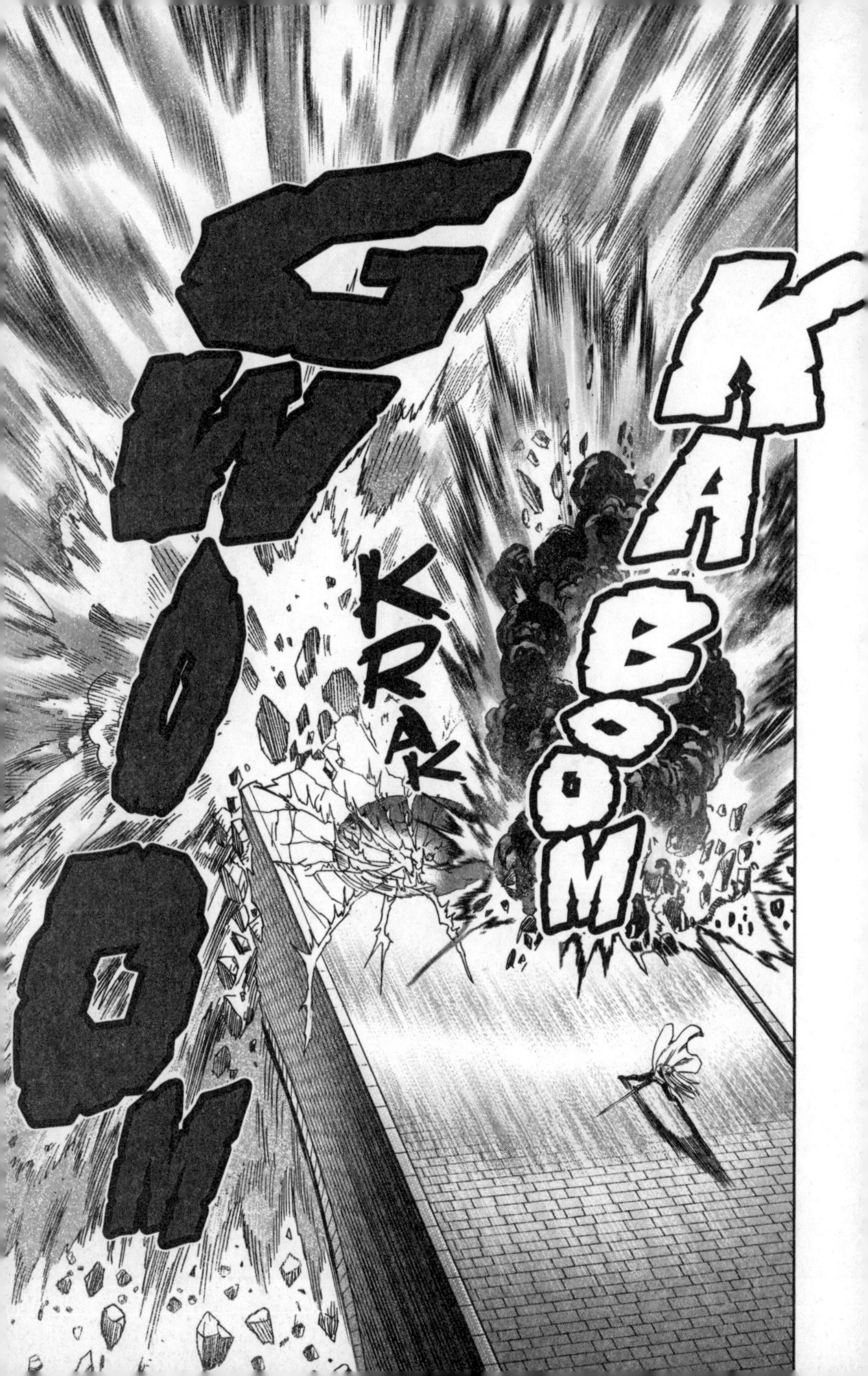
KABOOM
KRAK
GWOOM

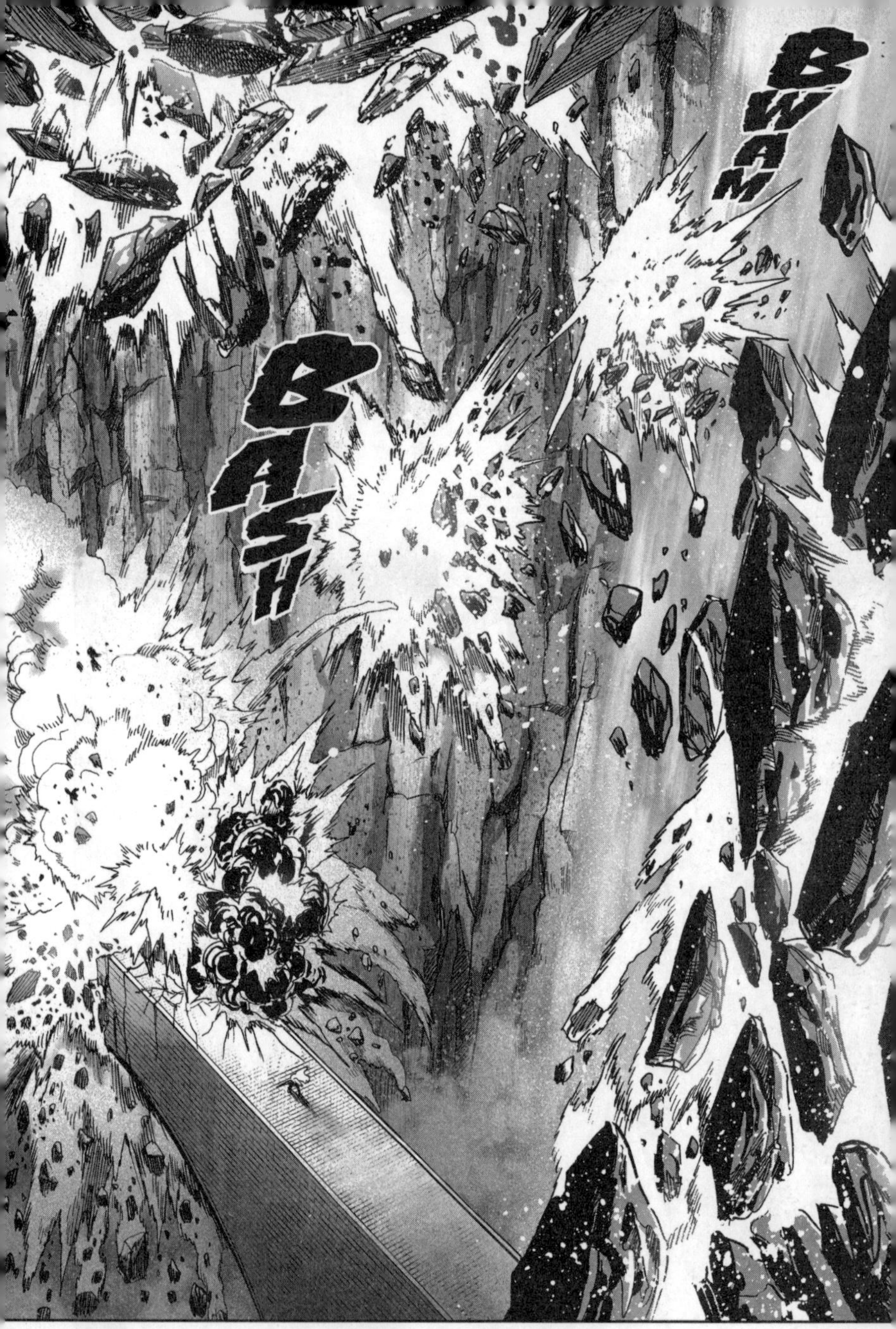
BWAM
BASH

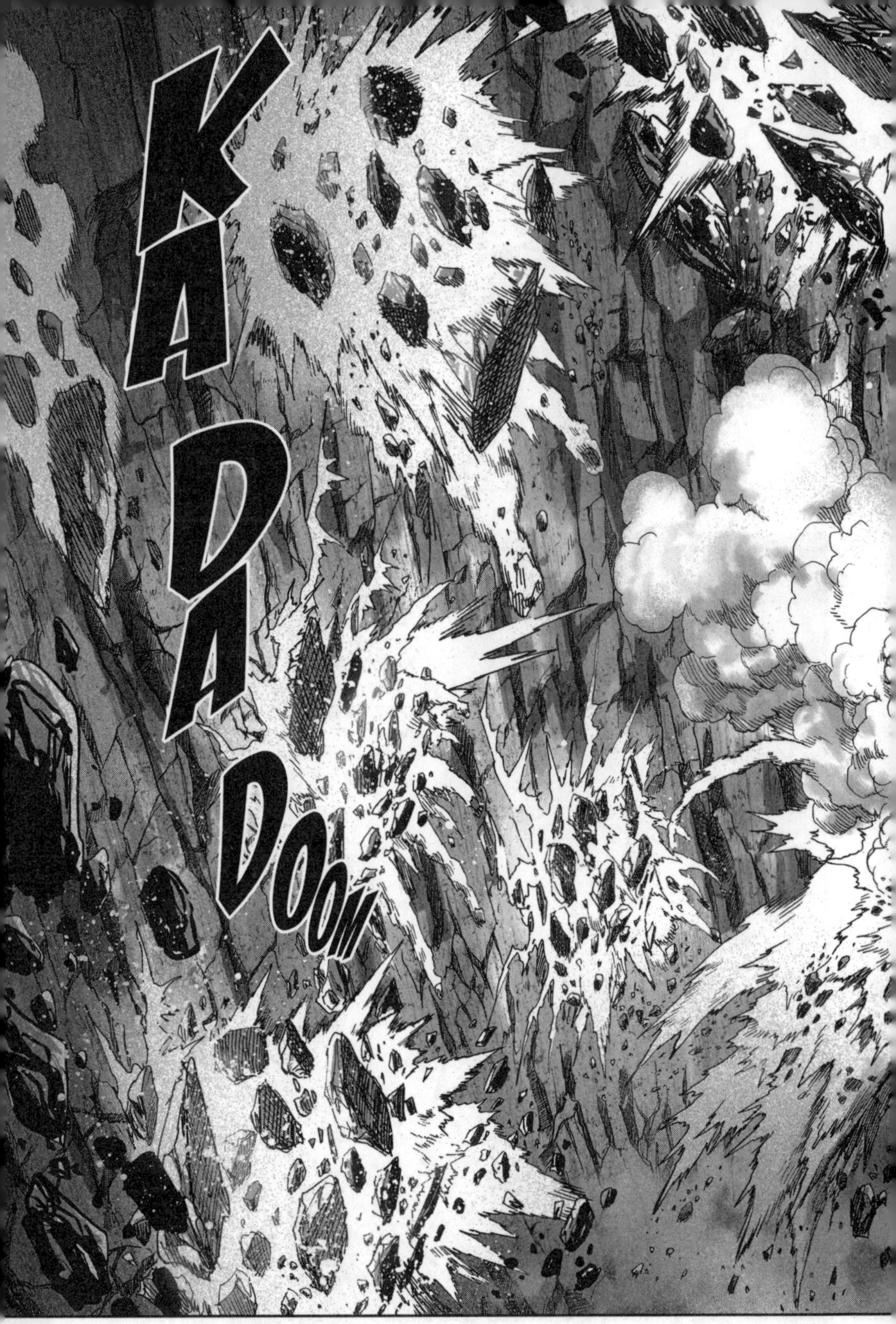
KADADOOM

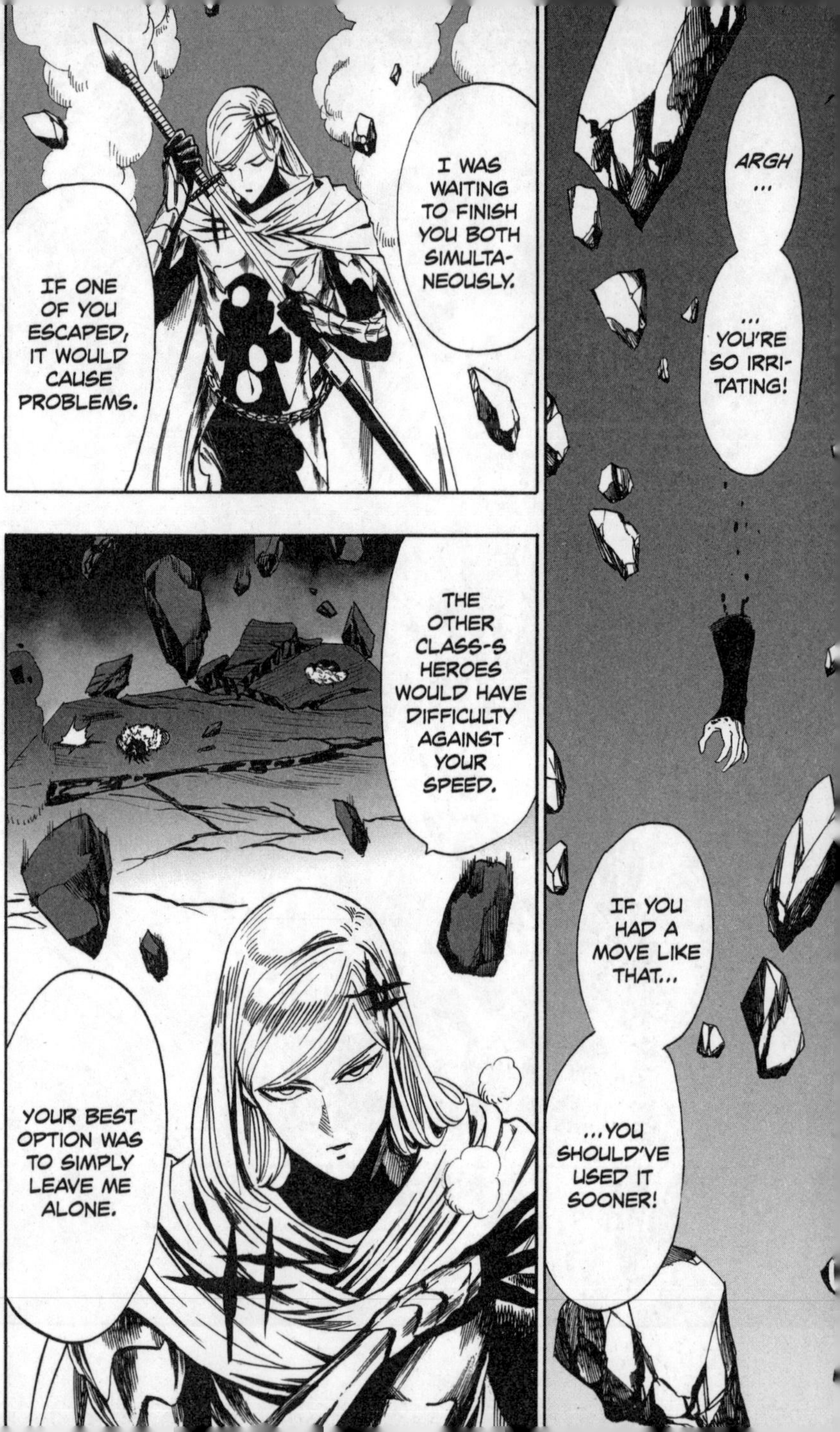
ARGH...
...YOU'RE SO IRRITATING!
IF YOU HAD A MOVE LIKE THAT...
...YOU SHOULD'VE USED IT SOONER!
I WAS WAITING TO FINISH YOU BOTH SIMULTANEOUSLY.
IF ONE OF YOU ESCAPED, IT WOULD CAUSE PROBLEMS.
THE OTHER CLASS-S HEROES WOULD HAVE DIFFICULTY AGAINST YOUR SPEED.
YOUR BEST OPTION WAS TO SIMPLY LEAVE ME ALONE.

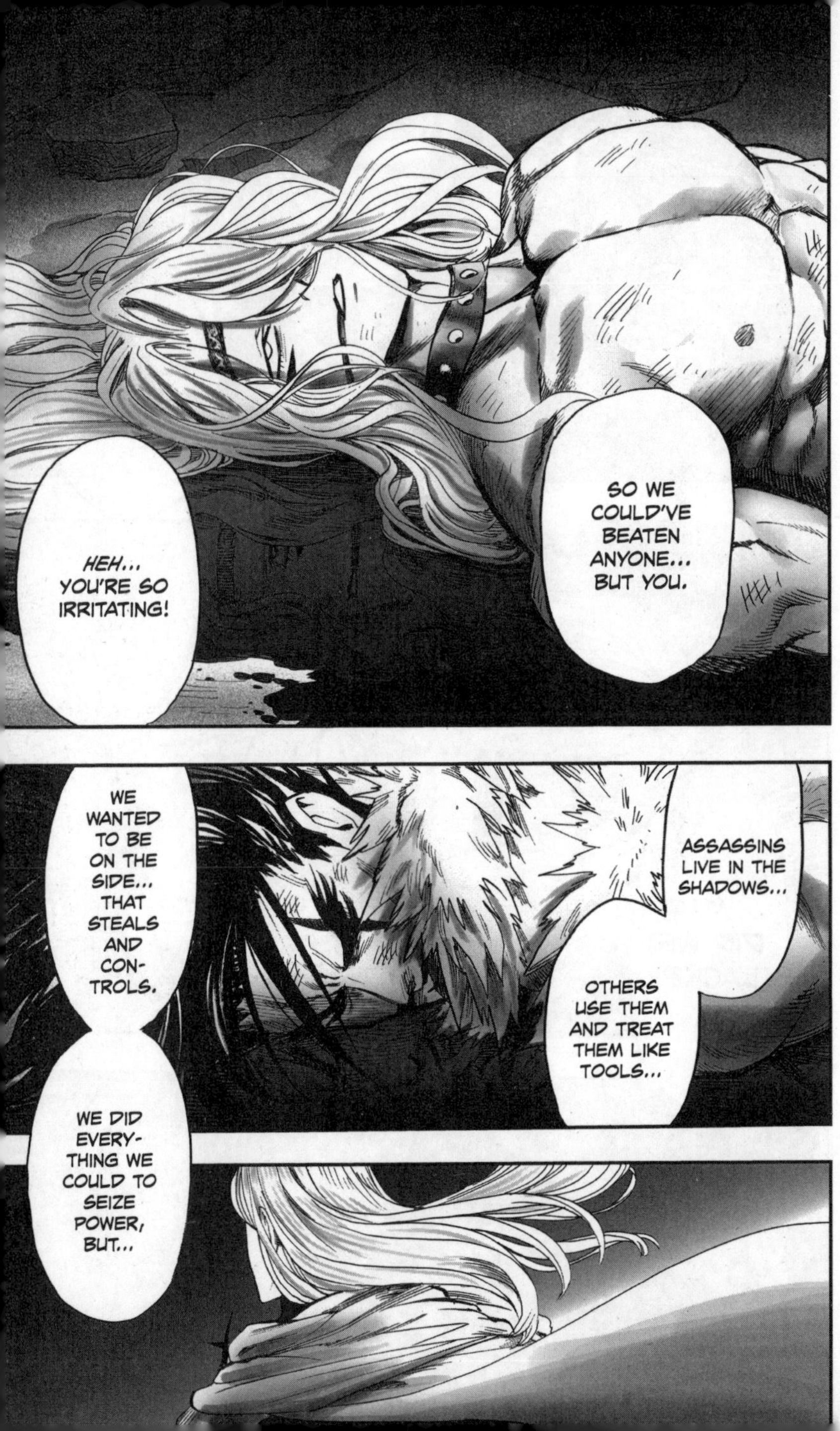
SO WE COULD'VE BEATEN ANYONE... BUT YOU.
HEH... YOU'RE SO IRRITATING!
ASSASSINS LIVE IN THE SHADOWS...
OTHERS USE THEM AND TREAT THEM LIKE TOOLS...
WE WANTED TO BE ON THE SIDE... THAT STEALS AND CON-TROLS.
WE DID EVERY-THING WE COULD TO SEIZE POWER, BUT...

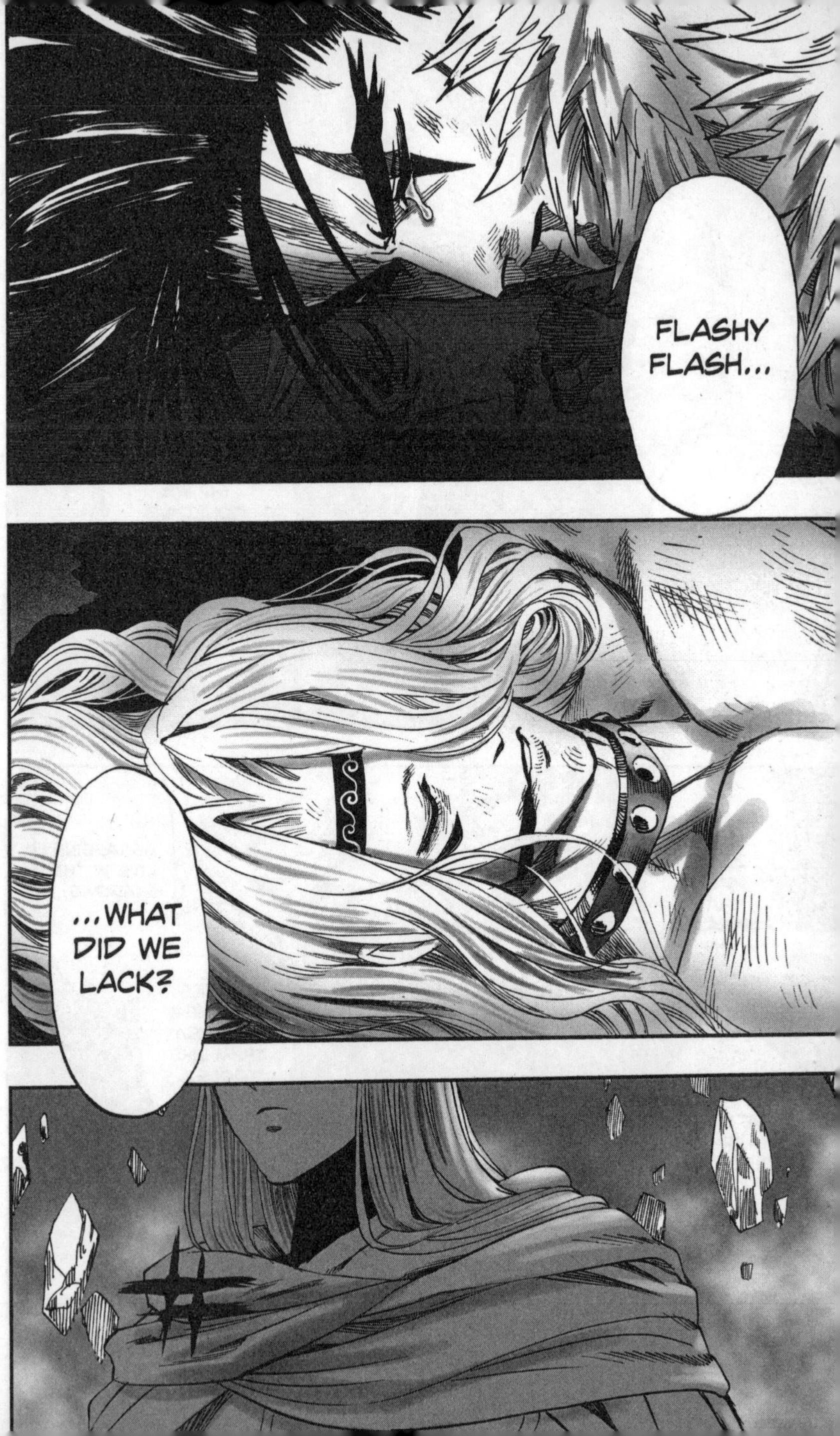
FLASHY FLASH...
...WHAT DID WE LACK?

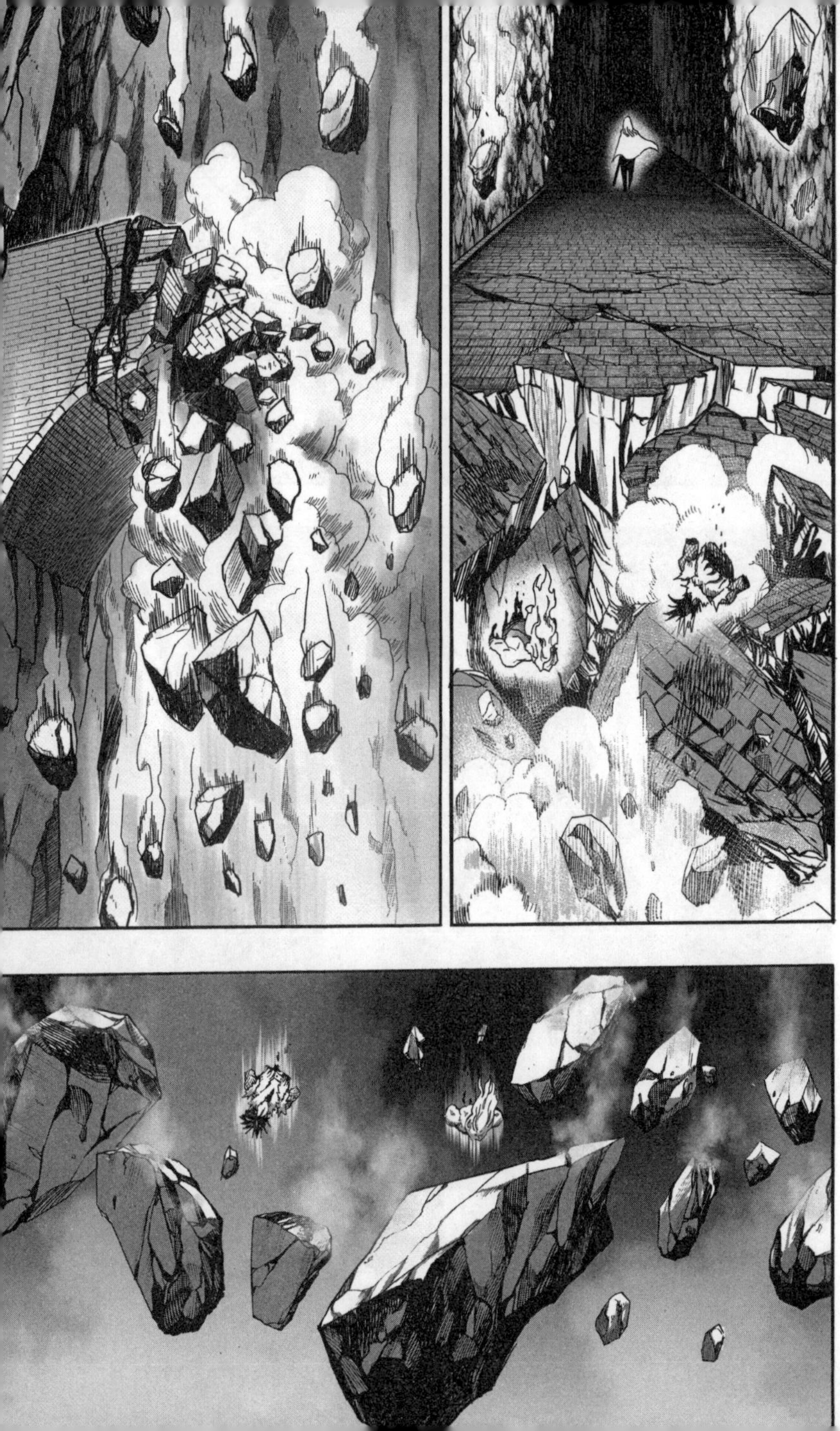

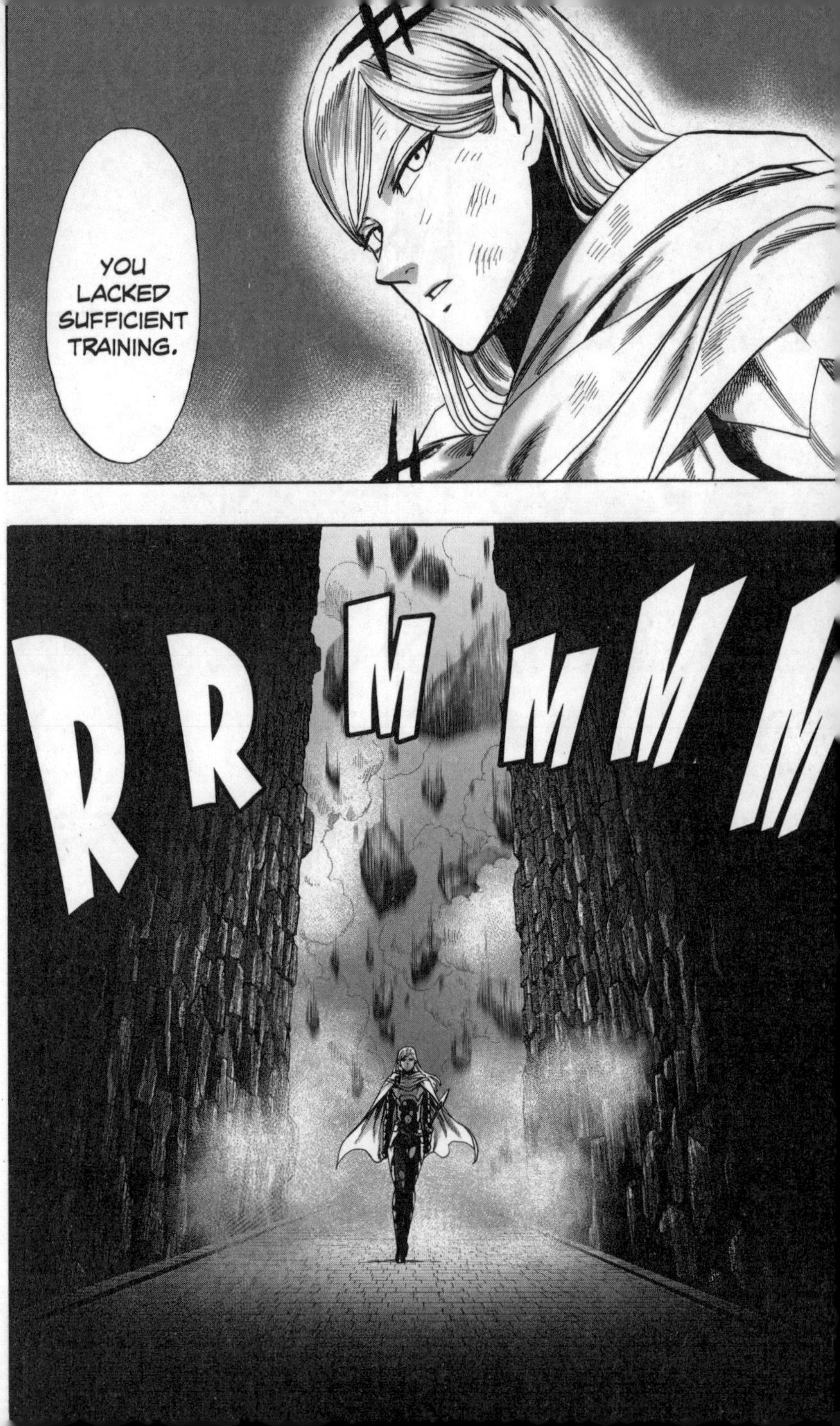
YOU LACKED SUFFICIENT TRAINING.
RRMMMMM

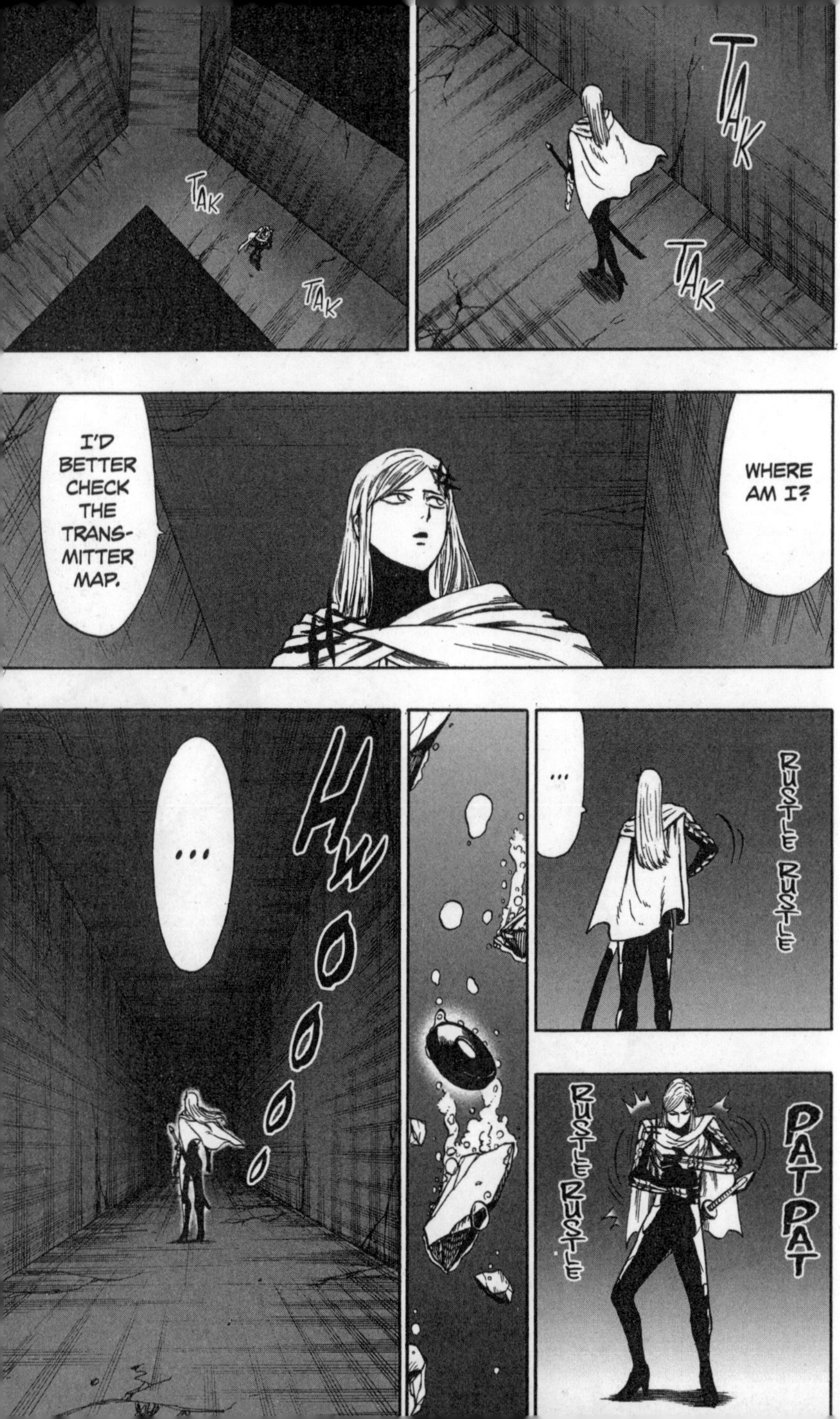
TAK
TAK
TAK
TAK
WHERE AM I?
I'D BETTER CHECK THE TRANS-MITTER MAP.
...
RUSTLE RUSTLE
PAT PAT
RUSTLE RUSTLE
HWOOOOOO
...

PUNCH 100: BACKPACK

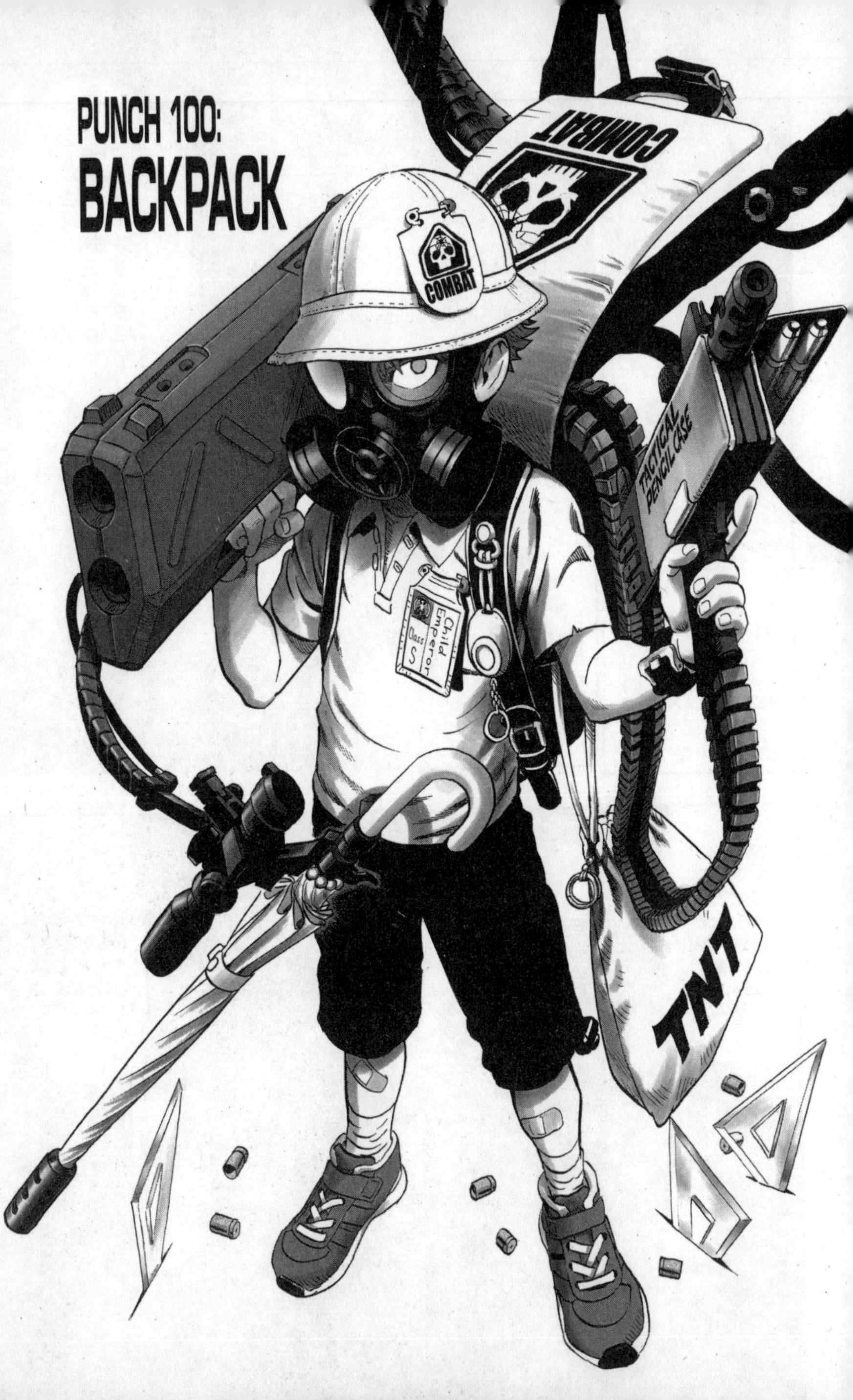
COMBAT
COMBAT
Child Emperor
Class S
TACTICAL PENCIL CASE
TNT

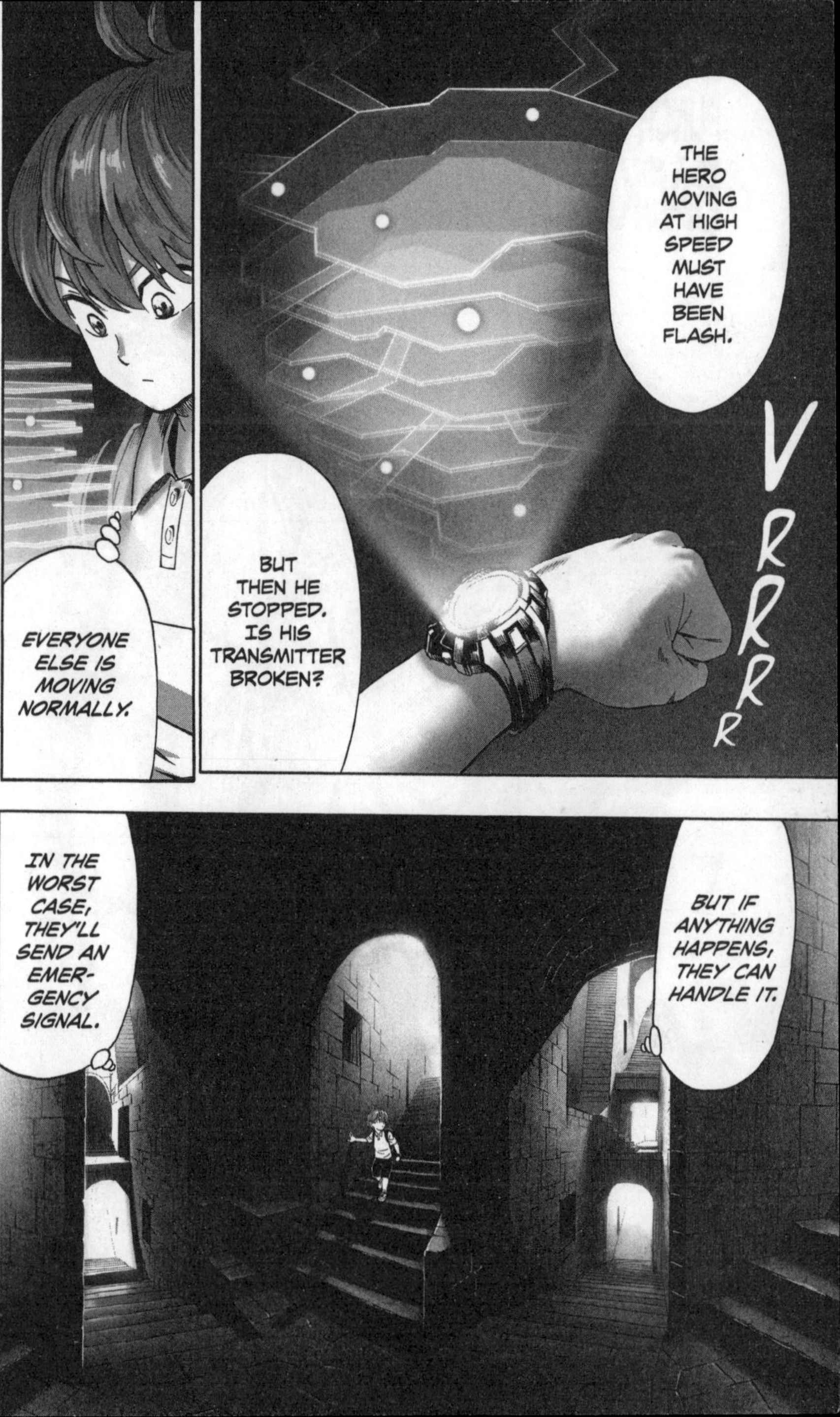
THE HERO MOVING AT HIGH SPEED MUST HAVE BEEN FLASH.
VRRRRR
BUT THEN HE STOPPED. IS HIS TRANSMITTER BROKEN?
EVERYONE ELSE IS MOVING NORMALLY.
BUT IF ANYTHING HAPPENS, THEY CAN HANDLE IT.
IN THE WORST CASE, THEY'LL SEND AN EMERGENCY SIGNAL.

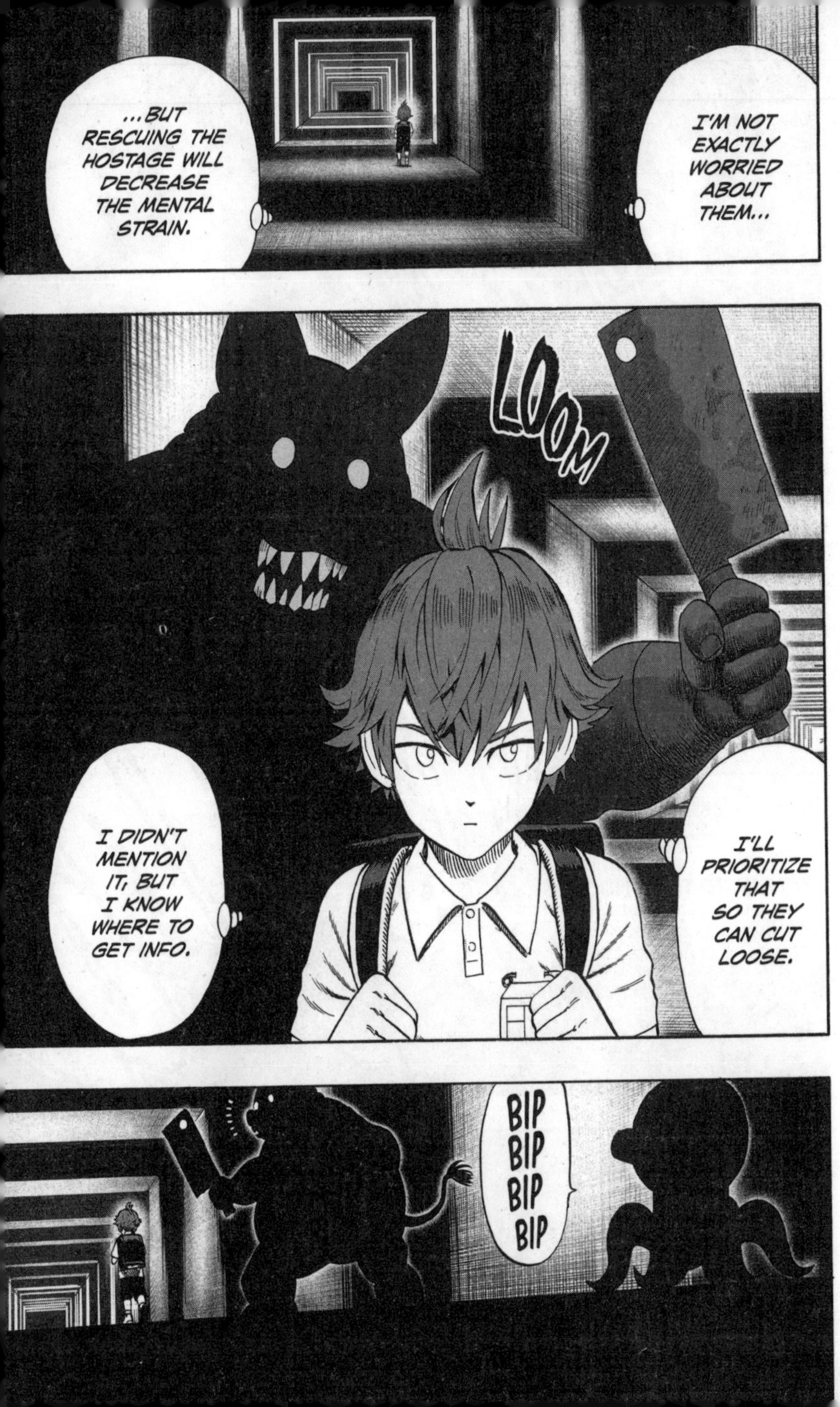
I'M NOT EXACTLY WORRIED ABOUT THEM...
...BUT RESCUING THE HOSTAGE WILL DECREASE THE MENTAL STRAIN.
LOOM
I'LL PRIORITIZE THAT SO THEY CAN CUT LOOSE.
I DIDN'T MENTION IT, BUT I KNOW WHERE TO GET INFO.
BIP BIP BIP BIP

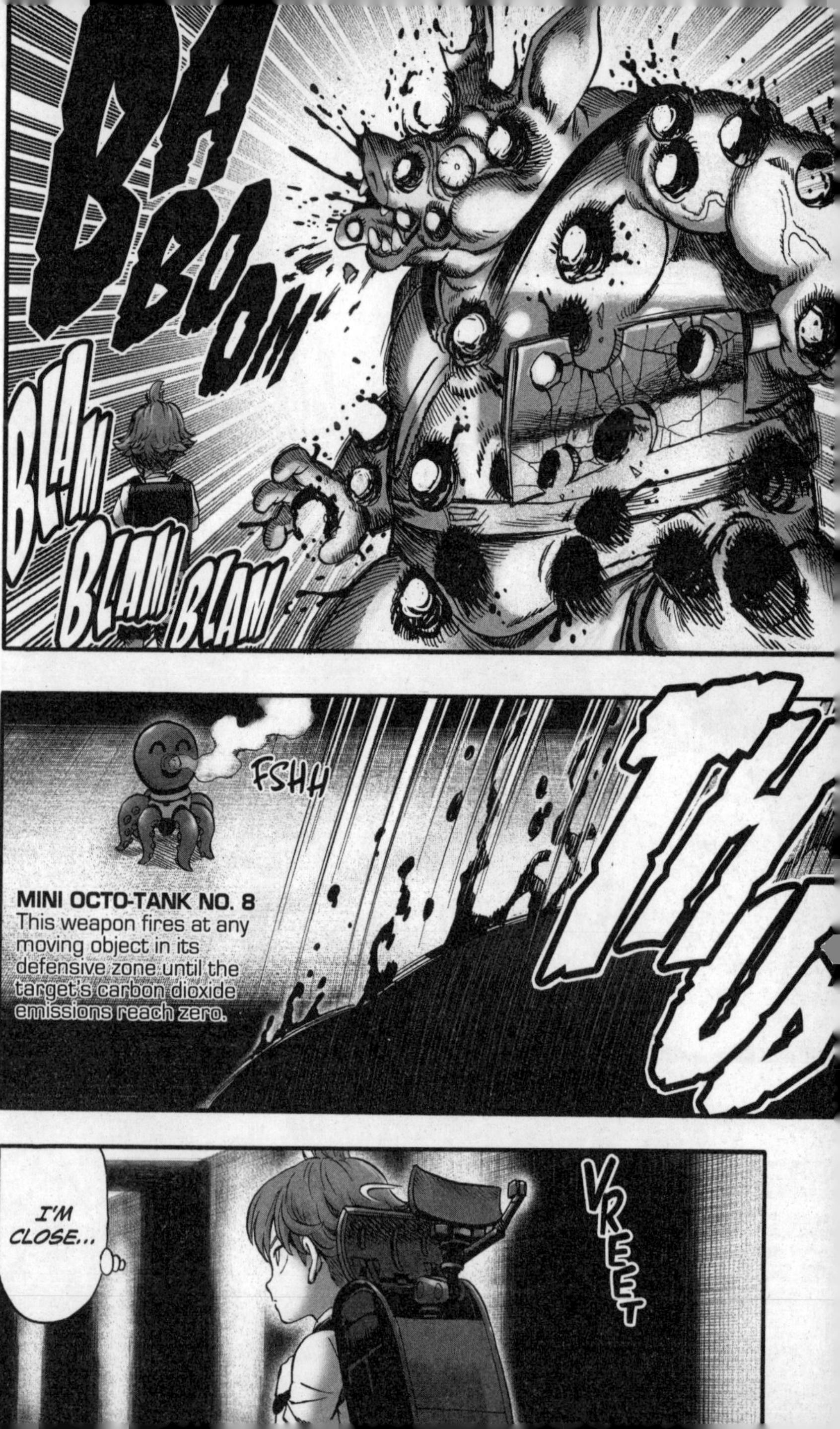
BLAM
BLAM
BLAM
BLAM
FSHH
MINI OCTO-TANK NO. 8
This weapon fires at any moving object in its defensive zone until the target's carbon dioxide emissions reach zero.
VREET
I'M CLOSE...

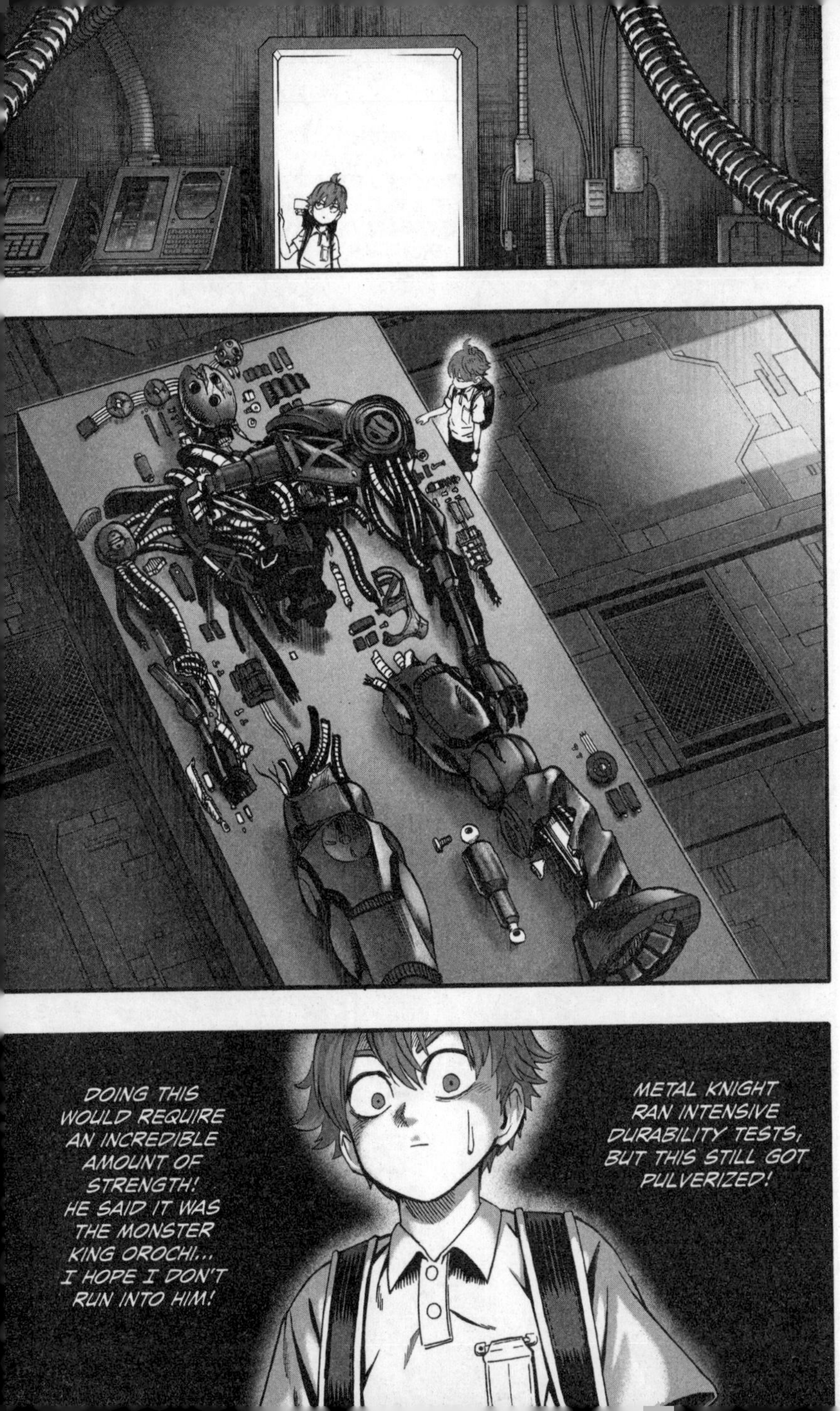
METAL KNIGHT RAN INTENSIVE DURABILITY TESTS, BUT THIS STILL GOT PULVERIZED!
DOING THIS WOULD REQUIRE AN INCREDIBLE AMOUNT OF STRENGTH! HE SAID IT WAS THE MONSTER KING OROCHI... I HOPE I DON'T RUN INTO HIM!

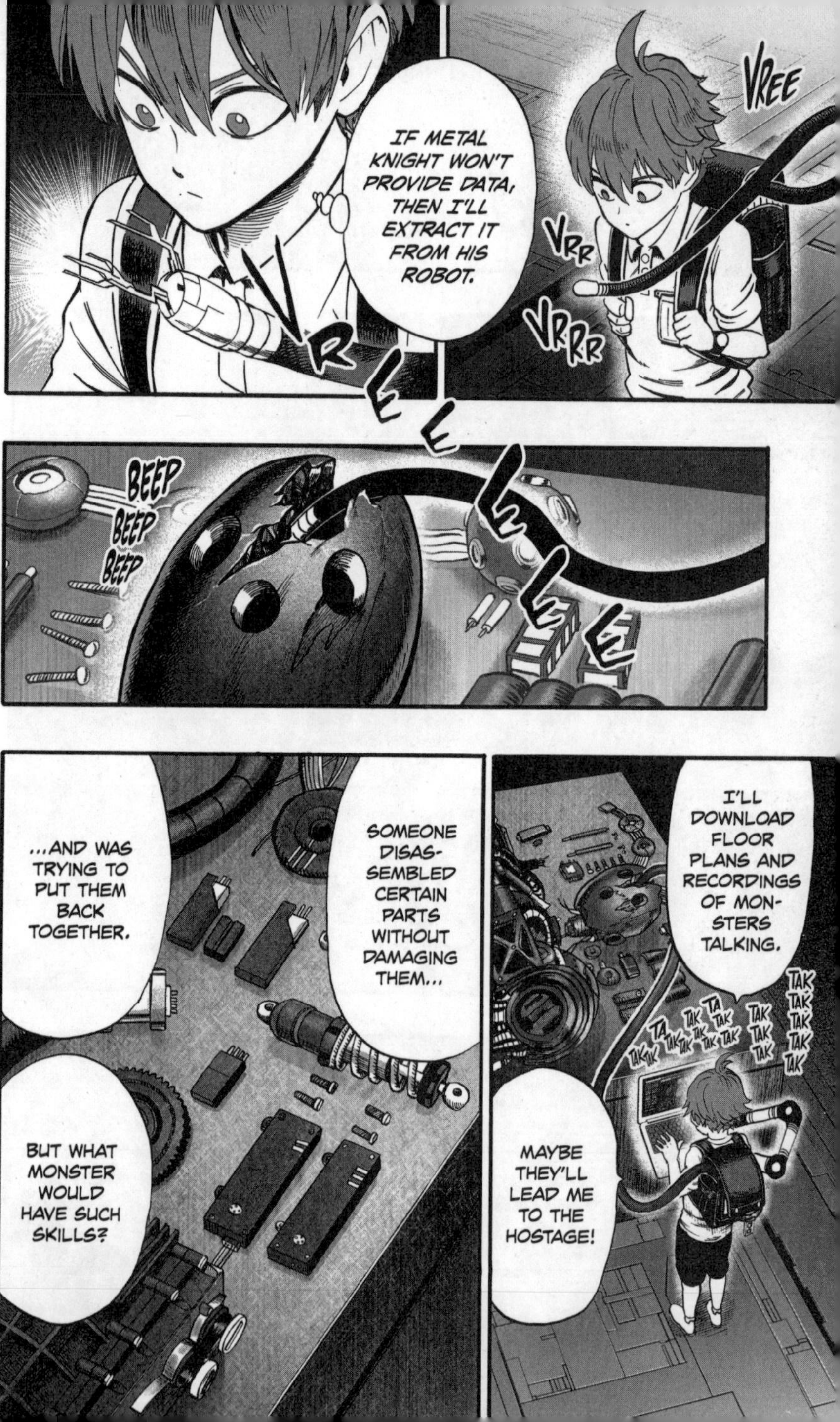
VREE
VRR
VRRR
IF METAL KNIGHT WON'T PROVIDE DATA, THEN I'LL EXTRACT IT FROM HIS ROBOT.
VREEEEEE
BEEP
BEEP
BEEP
I'LL DOWNLOAD FLOOR PLANS AND RECORDINGS OF MON-STERS TALKING.
TAK TAK TAK TAK TAK TA TAK TAK TAK TAK TA TAK TAK TAK TAK TAK TAK TAK TAK
MAYBE THEY'LL LEAD ME TO THE HOSTAGE!
SOMEONE DISAS-SEMBLED CERTAIN PARTS WITHOUT DAMAGING THEM...
...AND WAS TRYING TO PUT THEM BACK TOGETHER.
BUT WHAT MONSTER WOULD HAVE SUCH SKILLS?

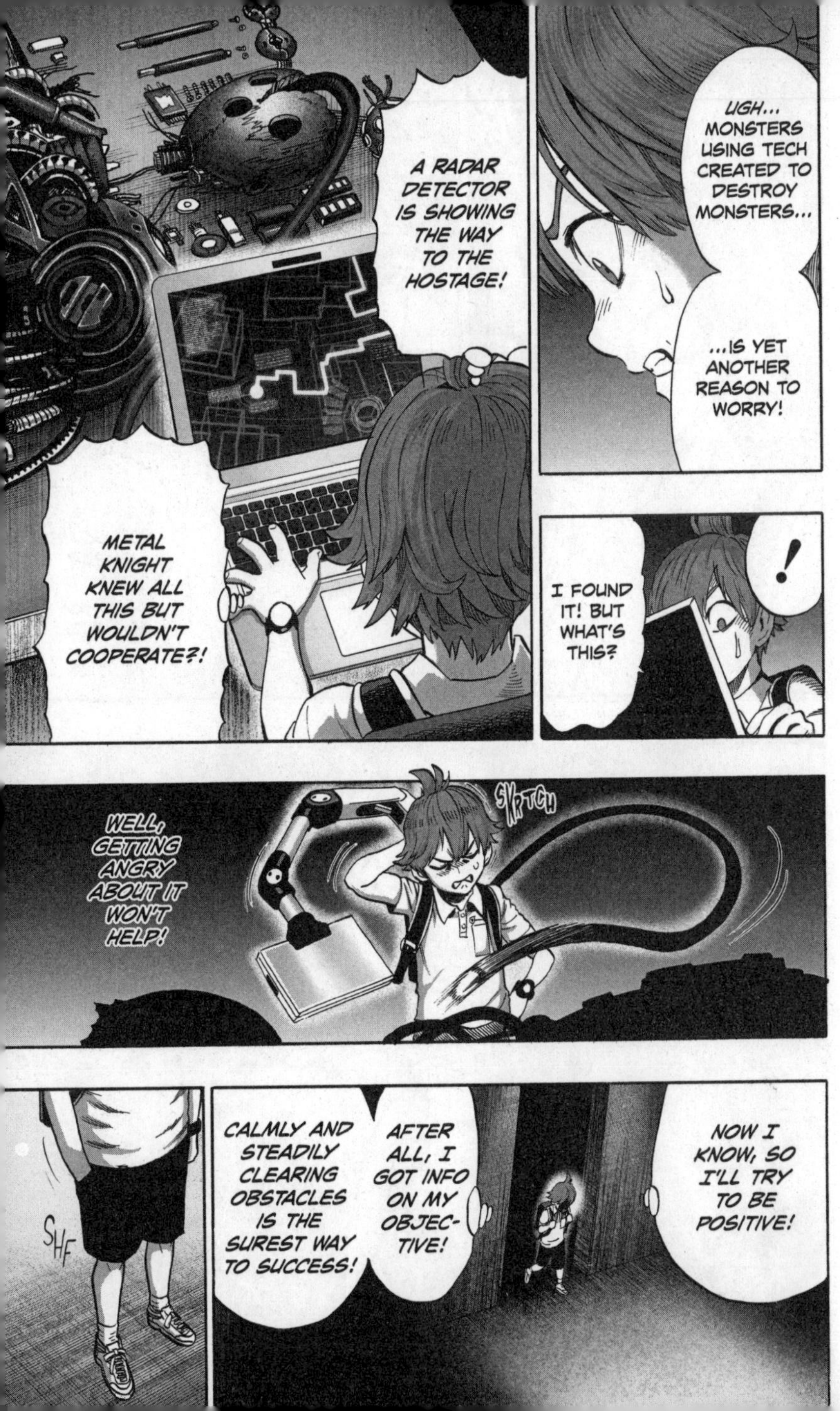
UGH... MONSTERS USING TECH CREATED TO DESTROY MONSTERS...
...IS YET ANOTHER REASON TO WORRY!
!
I FOUND IT! BUT WHAT'S THIS?
A RADAR DETECTOR IS SHOWING THE WAY TO THE HOSTAGE!
METAL KNIGHT KNEW ALL THIS BUT WOULDN'T COOPERATE?!
SKRTCH
WELL, GETTING ANGRY ABOUT IT WON'T HELP!
NOW I KNOW, SO I'LL TRY TO BE POSITIVE!
AFTER ALL, I GOT INFO ON MY OBJEC-TIVE!
CALMLY AND STEADILY CLEARING OBSTACLES IS THE SUREST WAY TO SUCCESS!
SHF

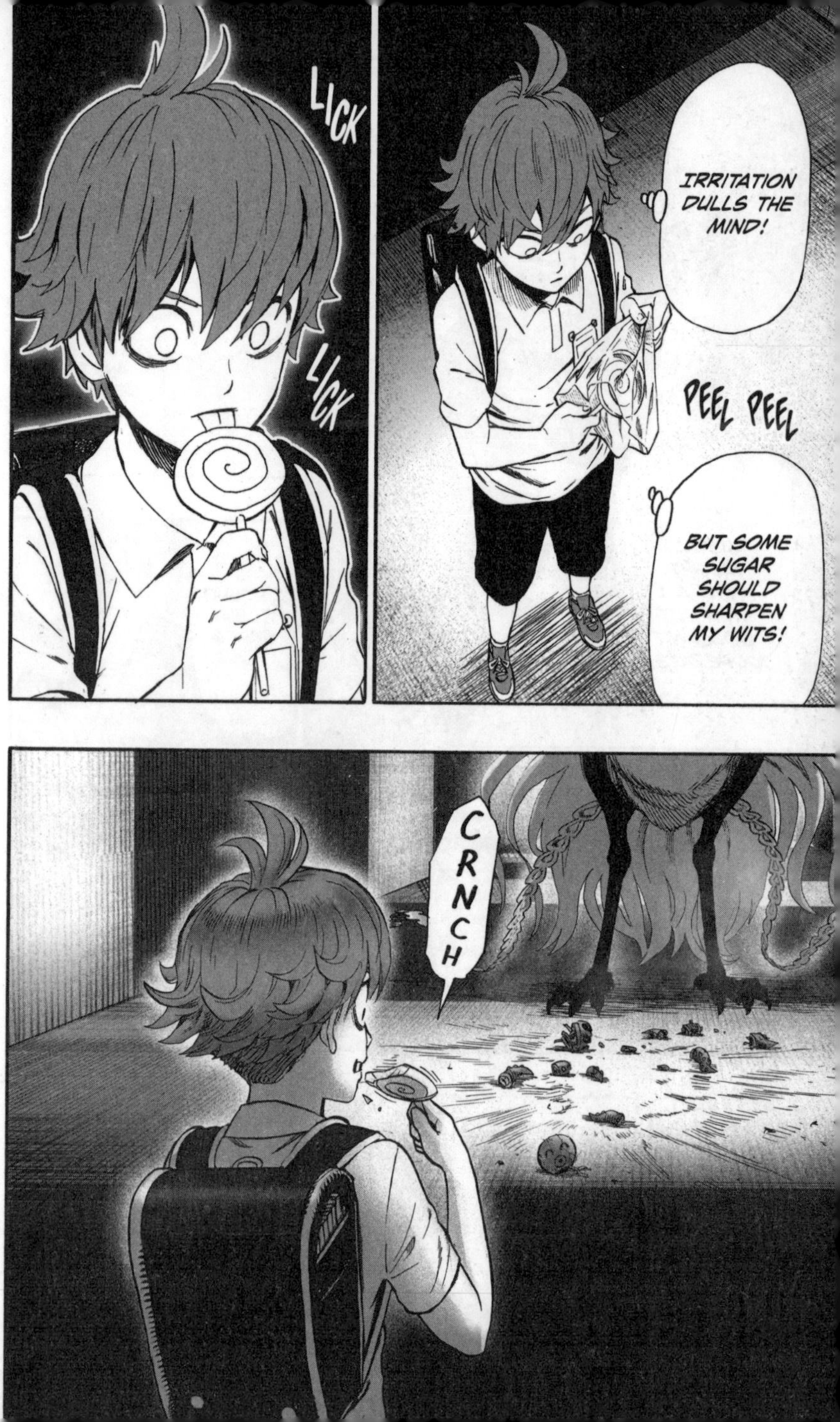
IRRITATION DULLS THE MIND!
PEEL PEEL
BUT SOME SUGAR SHOULD SHARPEN MY WITS!
LICK
LICK
CRNCH

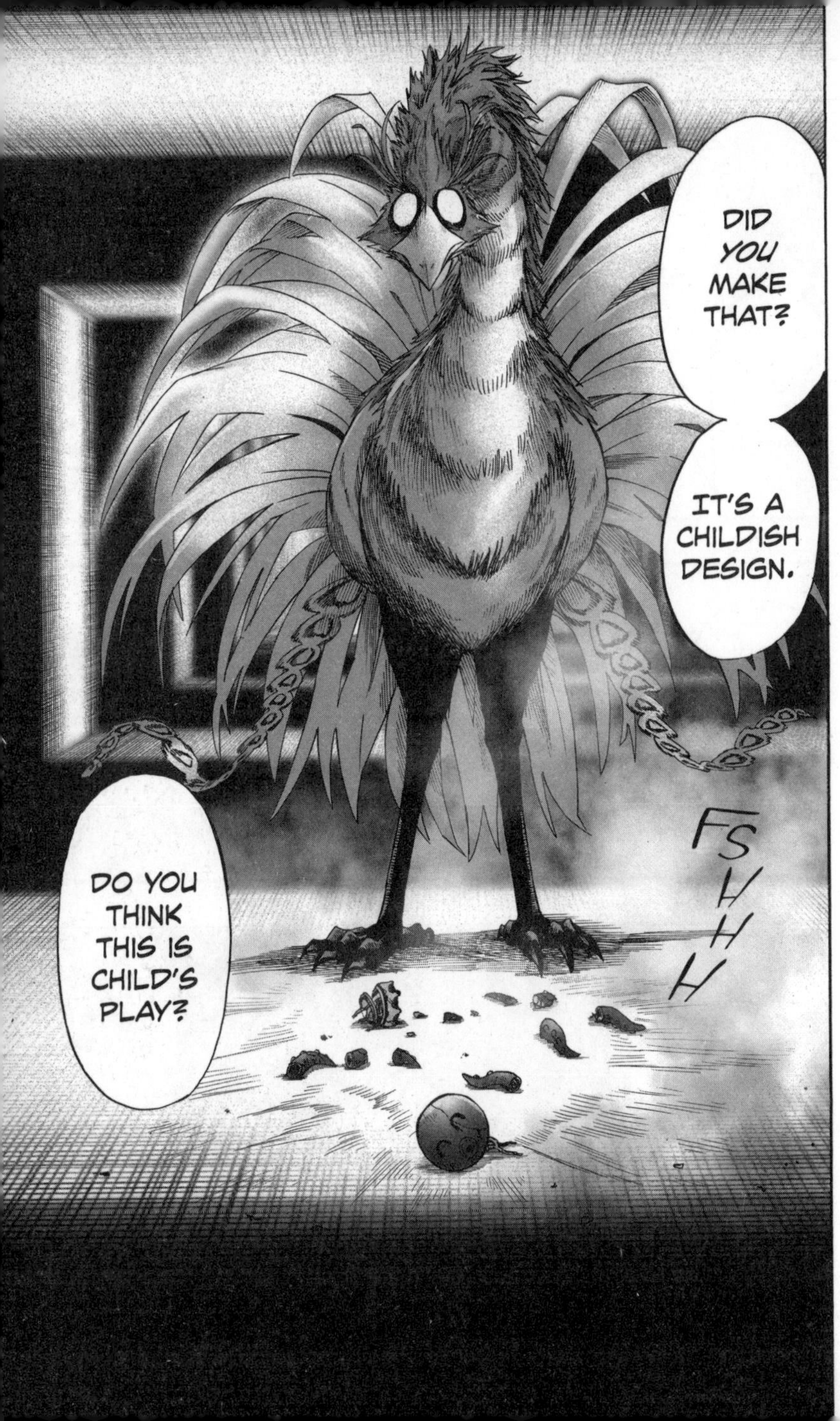
DID YOU MAKE THAT?
IT'S A CHILDISH DESIGN.
FSHHHH
DO YOU THINK THIS IS CHILD'S PLAY?

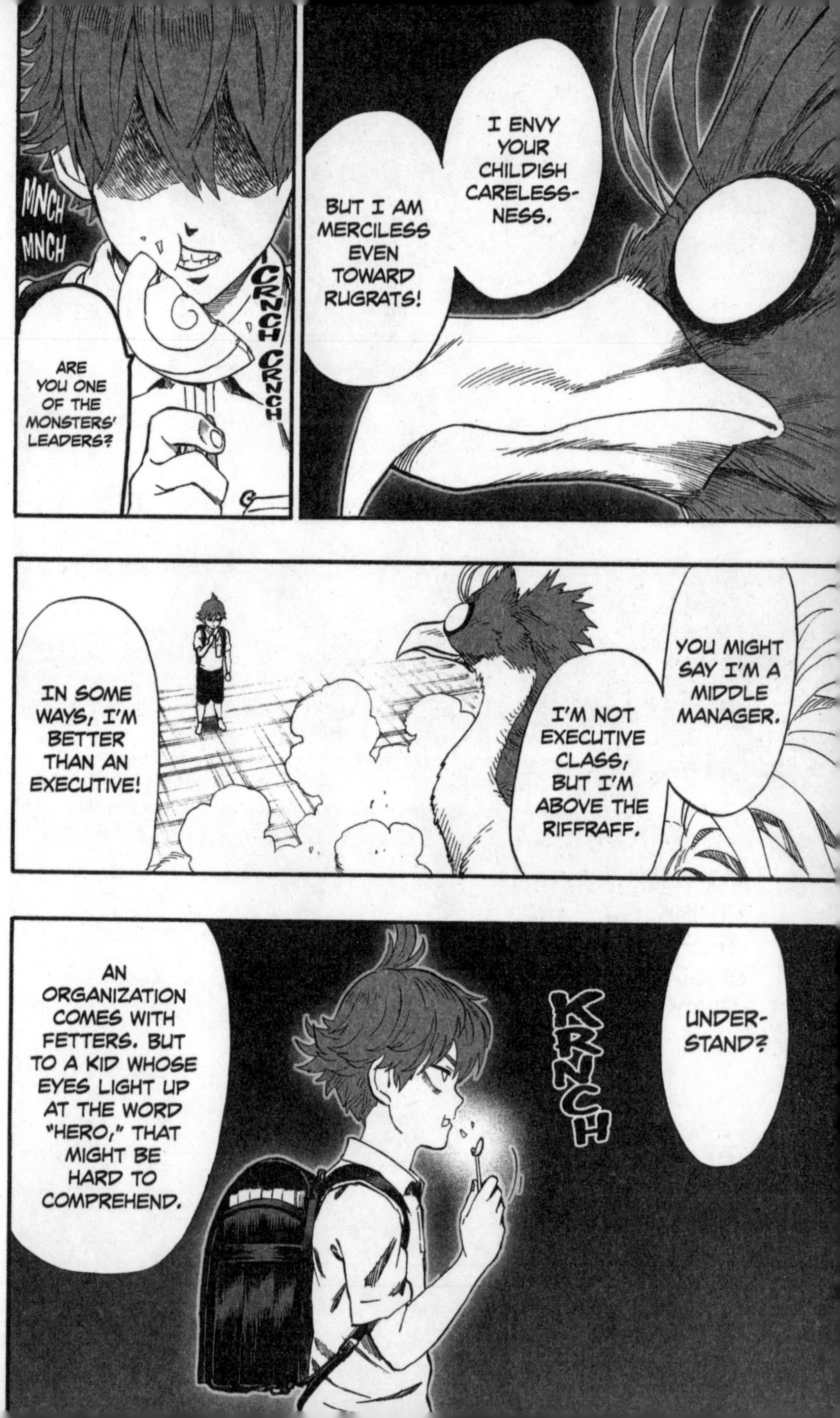
I ENVY YOUR CHILDISH CARELESS-NESS.
BUT I AM MERCILESS EVEN TOWARD RUGRATS!
CRNCH CRNCH
MNCH MNCH
ARE YOU ONE OF THE MONSTERS' LEADERS?
YOU MIGHT SAY I'M A MIDDLE MANAGER.
I'M NOT EXECUTIVE CLASS, BUT I'M ABOVE THE RIFFRAFF.
IN SOME WAYS, I'M BETTER THAN AN EXECUTIVE!
UNDER-STAND?
KRNCH
AN ORGANIZATION COMES WITH FETTERS. BUT TO A KID WHOSE EYES LIGHT UP AT THE WORD "HERO," THAT MIGHT BE HARD TO COMPREHEND.

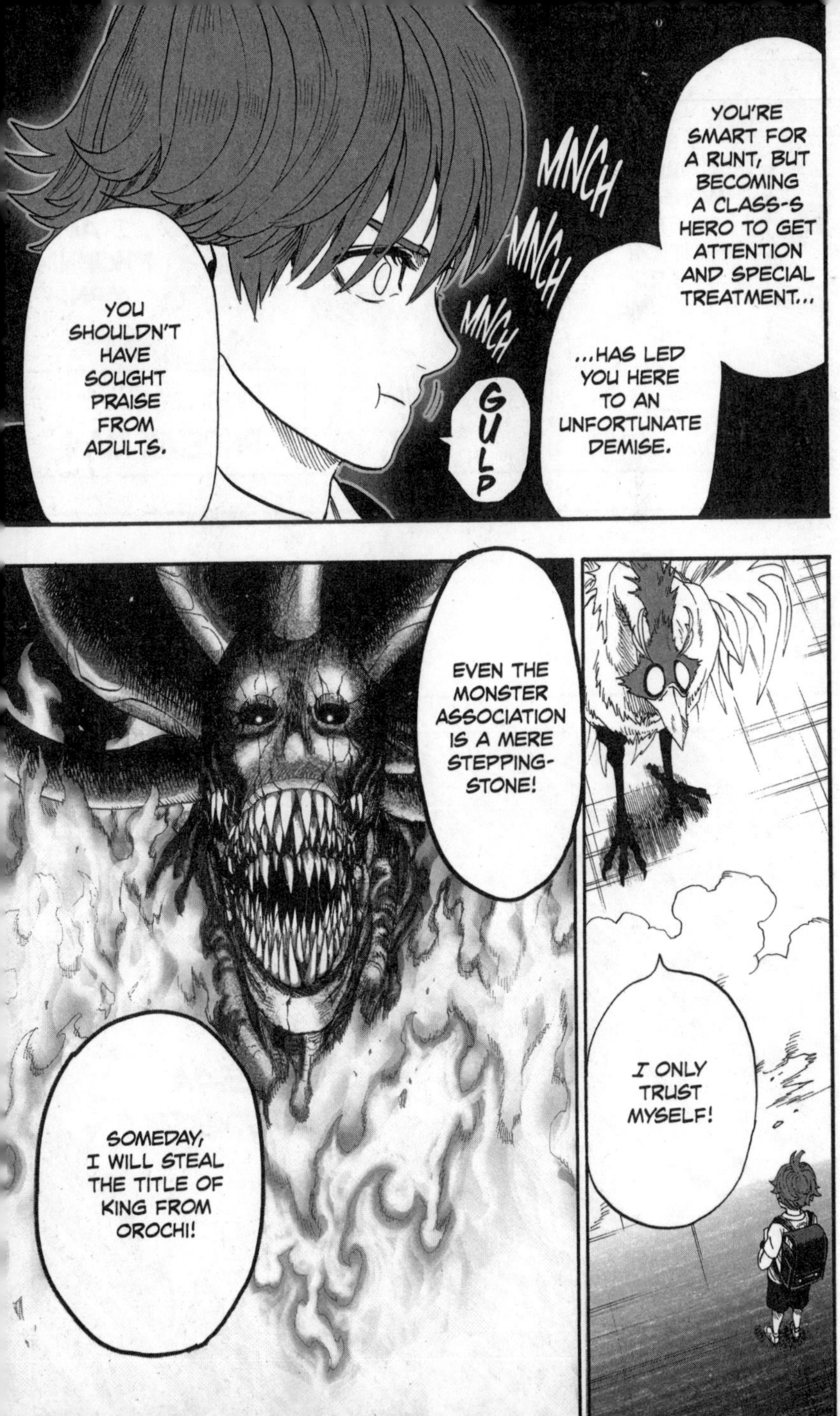
YOU'RE SMART FOR A RUNT, BUT BECOMING A CLASS-S HERO TO GET ATTENTION AND SPECIAL TREATMENT...
MNCH MNCH MNCH
...HAS LED YOU HERE TO AN UNFORTUNATE DEMISE.
GULP
YOU SHOULDN'T HAVE SOUGHT PRAISE FROM ADULTS.
I ONLY TRUST MYSELF!
EVEN THE MONSTER ASSOCIATION IS A MERE STEPPING-STONE!
SOMEDAY, I WILL STEAL THE TITLE OF KING FROM OROCHI!

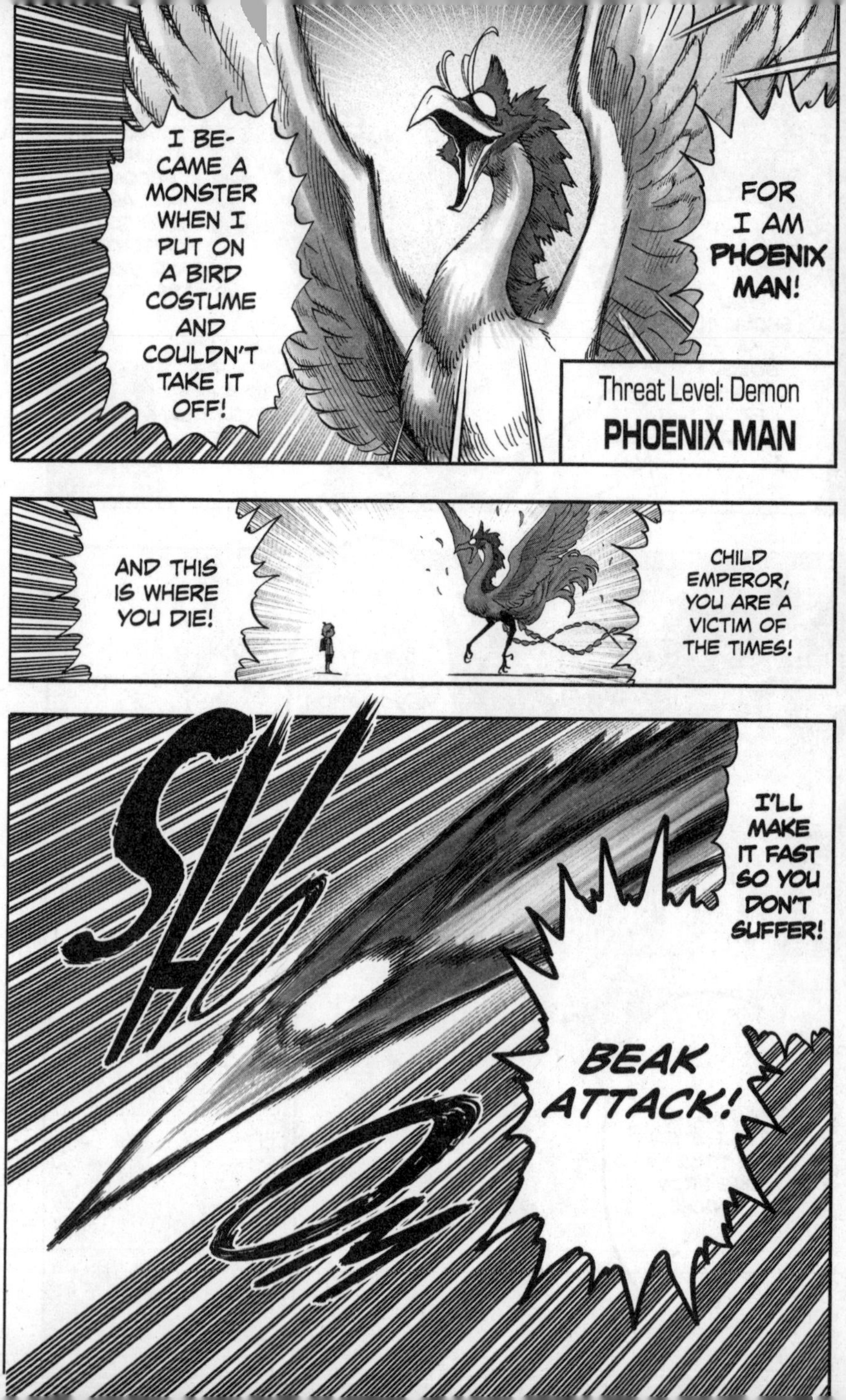
FOR I AM PHOENIX MAN!
I BECAME A MONSTER WHEN I PUT ON A BIRD COSTUME AND COULDN'T TAKE IT OFF!
Threat Level: Demon
PHOENIX MAN
CHILD EMPEROR, YOU ARE A VICTIM OF THE TIMES!
AND THIS IS WHERE YOU DIE!
I'LL MAKE IT FAST SO YOU DON'T SUFFER!
BEAK ATTACK!

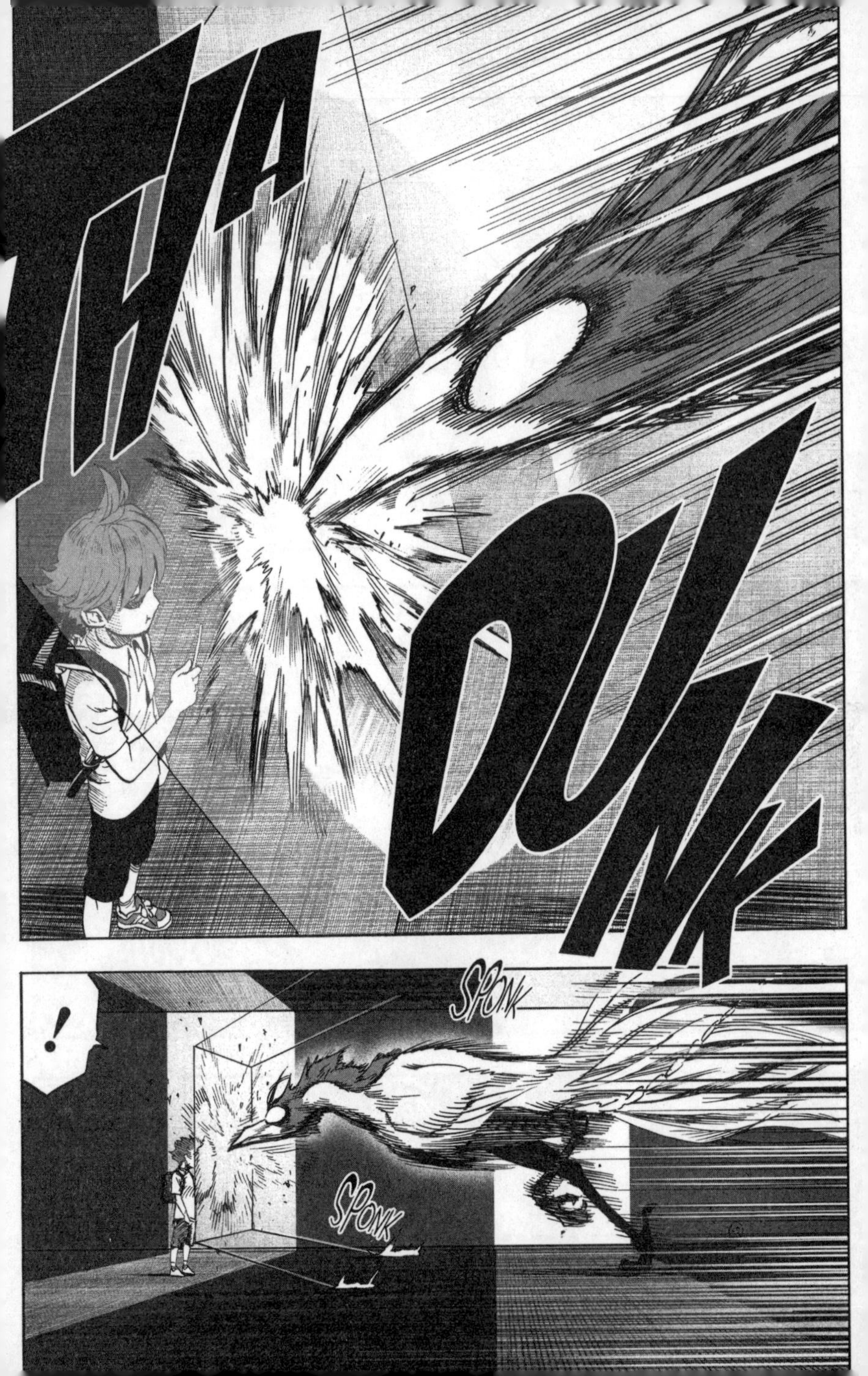
THA
DUNK
SPONK
SPONK
!

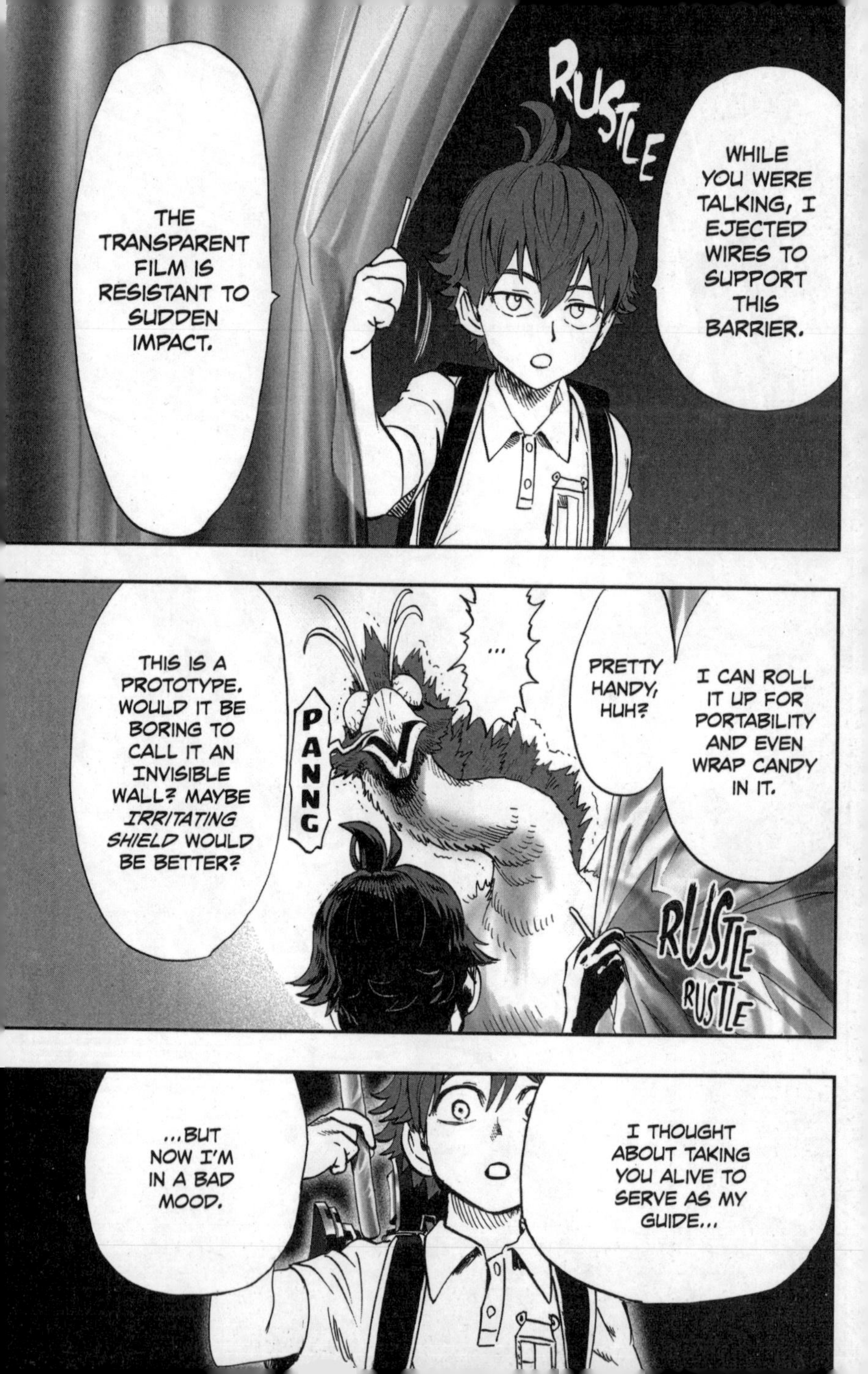
RUSTLE
WHILE YOU WERE TALKING, I EJECTED WIRES TO SUPPORT THIS BARRIER.
THE TRANSPARENT FILM IS RESISTANT TO SUDDEN IMPACT.
I CAN ROLL IT UP FOR PORTABILITY AND EVEN WRAP CANDY IN IT.
PRETTY HANDY, HUH?
RUSTLE RUSTLE
...
PANNG
THIS IS A PROTOTYPE. WOULD IT BE BORING TO CALL IT AN INVISIBLE WALL? MAYBE *IRRITATING SHIELD* WOULD BE BETTER?
I THOUGHT ABOUT TAKING YOU ALIVE TO SERVE AS MY GUIDE...
...BUT NOW I'M IN A BAD MOOD.

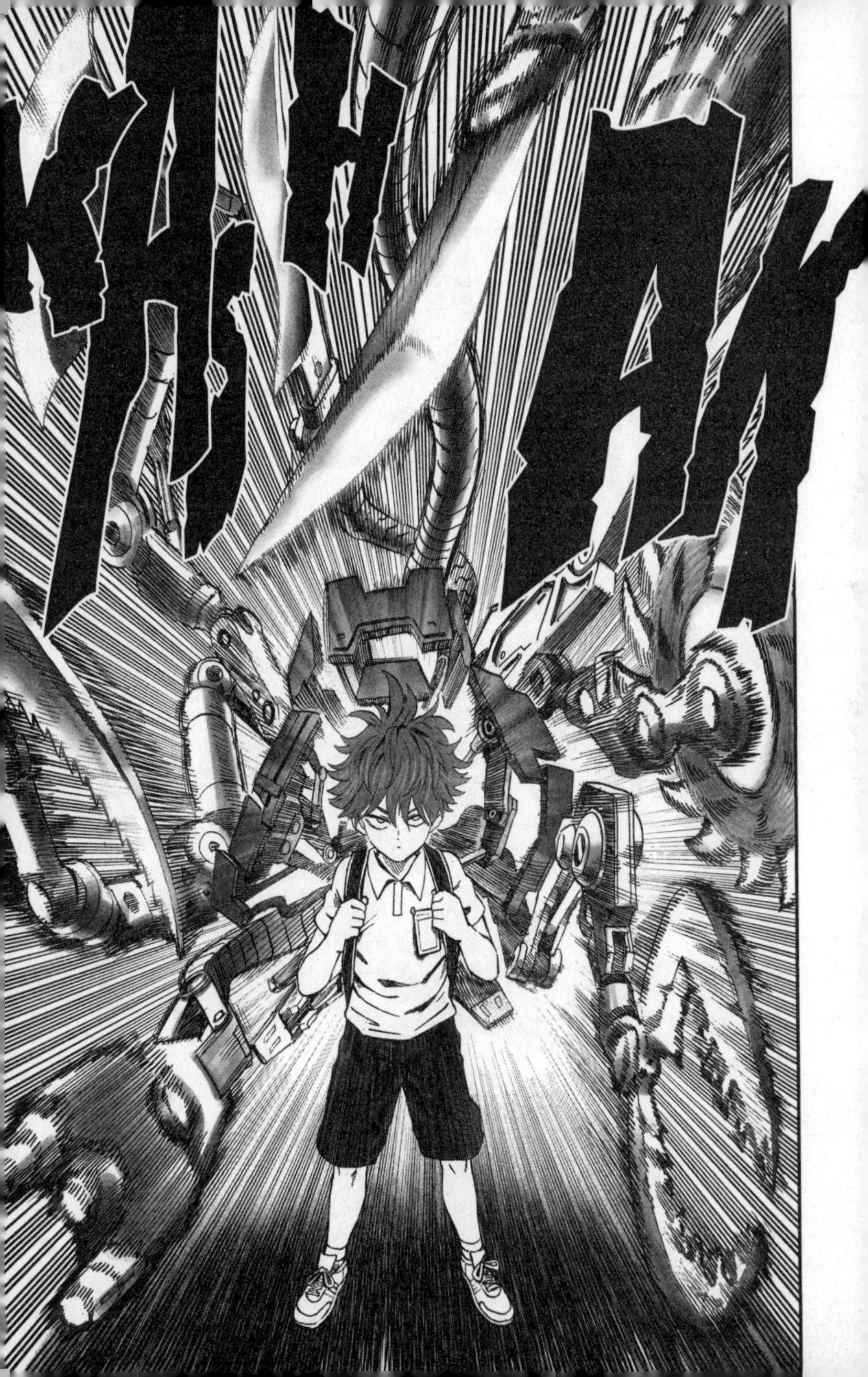

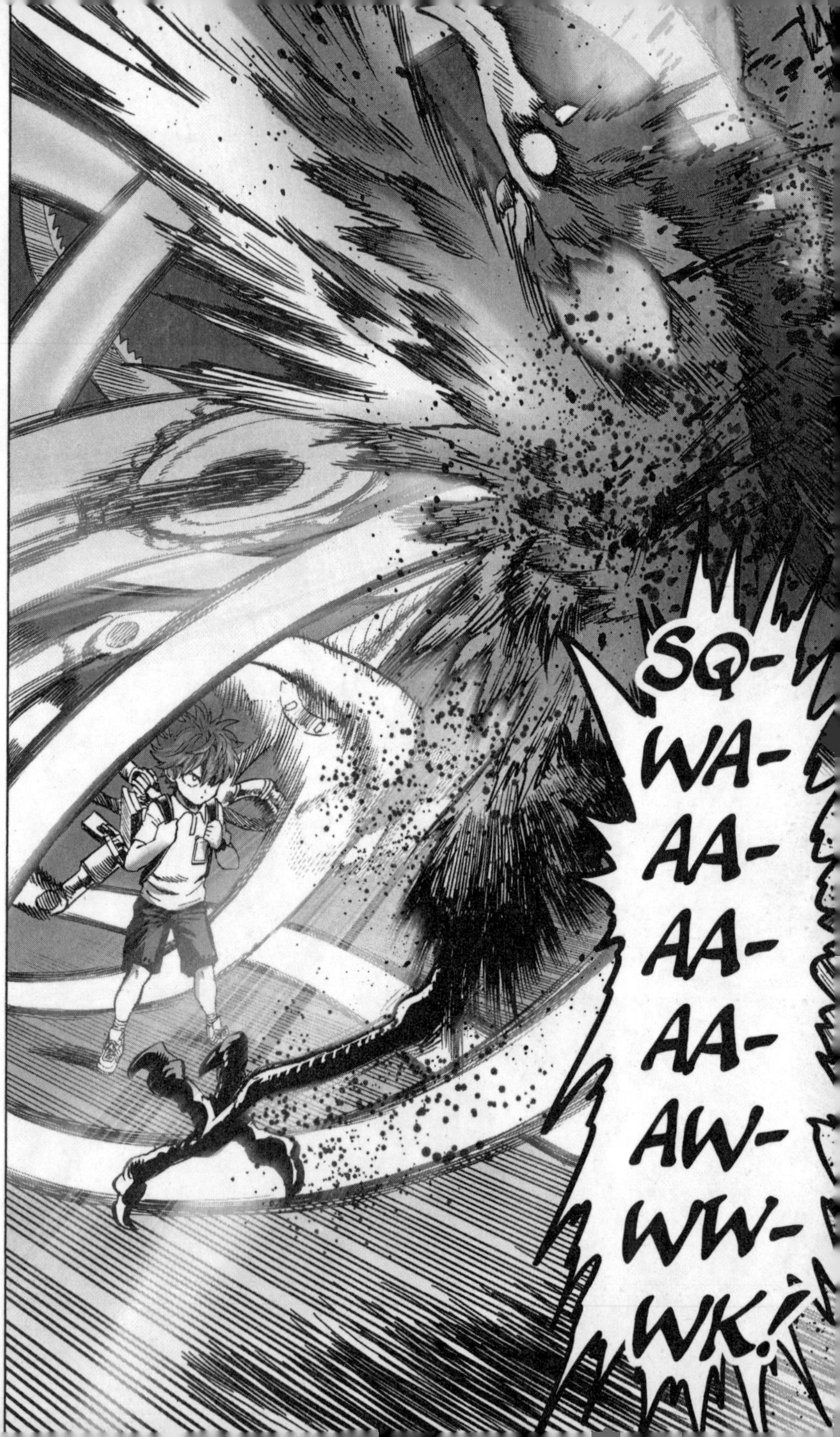
SQ-WA-AA-AA-AA-AW-WW-WK!

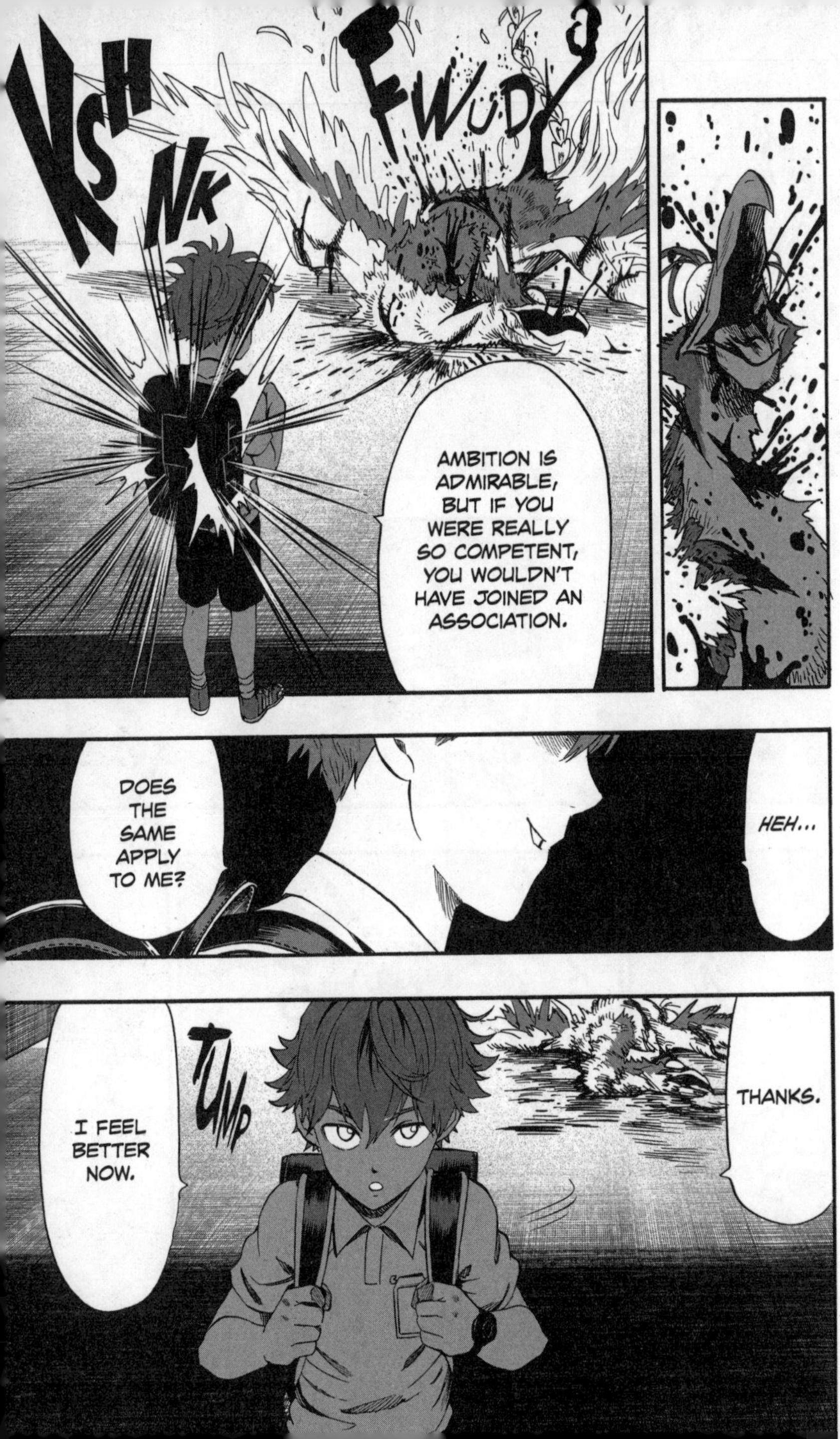
FWUD
KSH NK
AMBITION IS ADMIRABLE, BUT IF YOU WERE REALLY SO COMPETENT, YOU WOULDN'T HAVE JOINED AN ASSOCIATION.
HEH...
DOES THE SAME APPLY TO ME?
THANKS.
TUMP
I FEEL BETTER NOW.

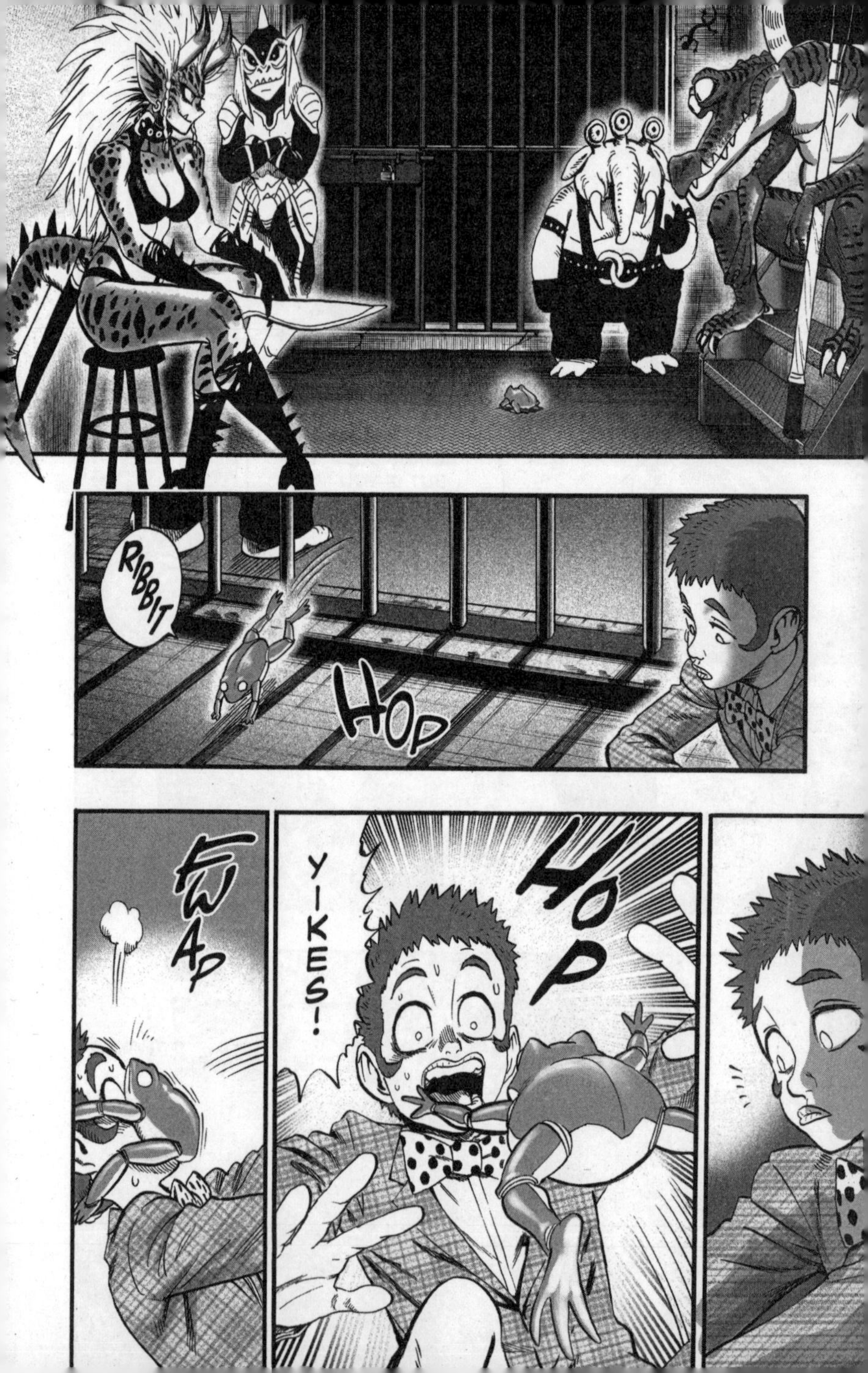
RIBBIT
HOP
HOP
YIKES!
FWAP

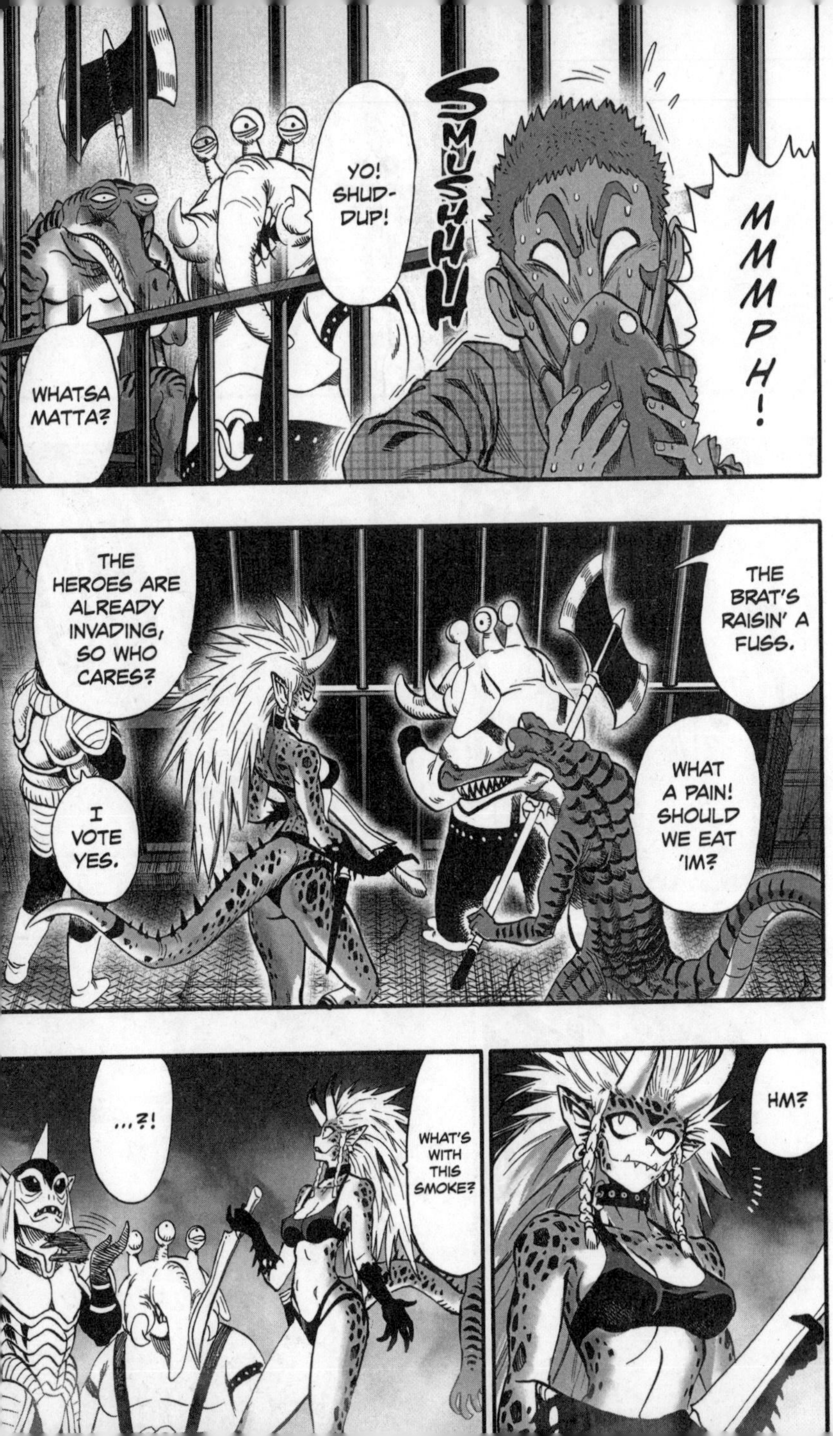
MMMMPH!
SMUSHUHH
YO! SHUD-DUP!
WHATSA MATTA?
THE BRAT'S RAISIN' A FUSS.
WHAT A PAIN! SHOULD WE EAT 'IM?
THE HEROES ARE ALREADY INVADING, SO WHO CARES?
I VOTE YES.
HM?
WHAT'S WITH THIS SMOKE?
...?!

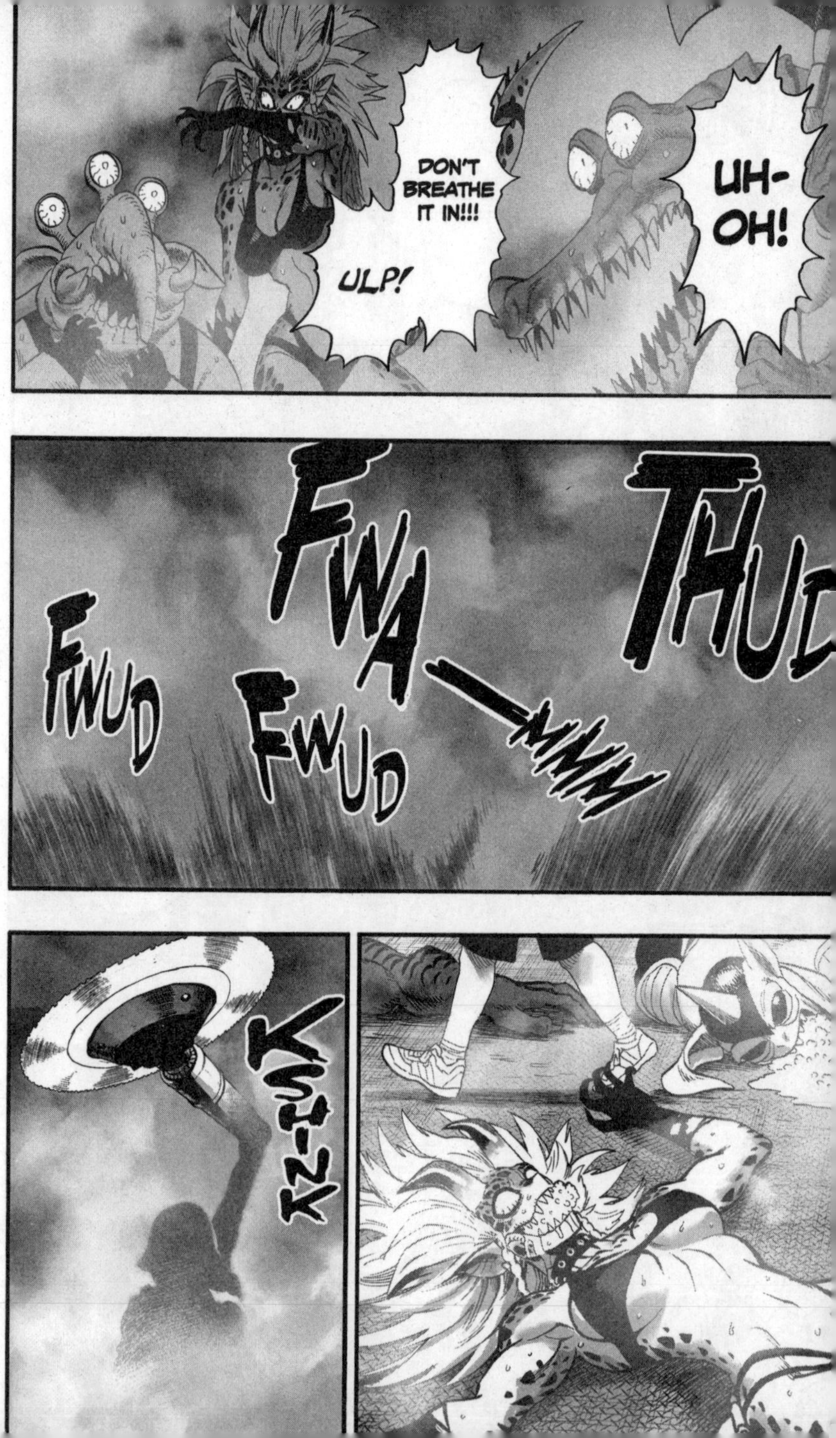
UH-OH!
DON'T BREATHE IT IN!!!
ULP!
THUD
FWA-MMM
FWUD
FWUD
KSHI-INK

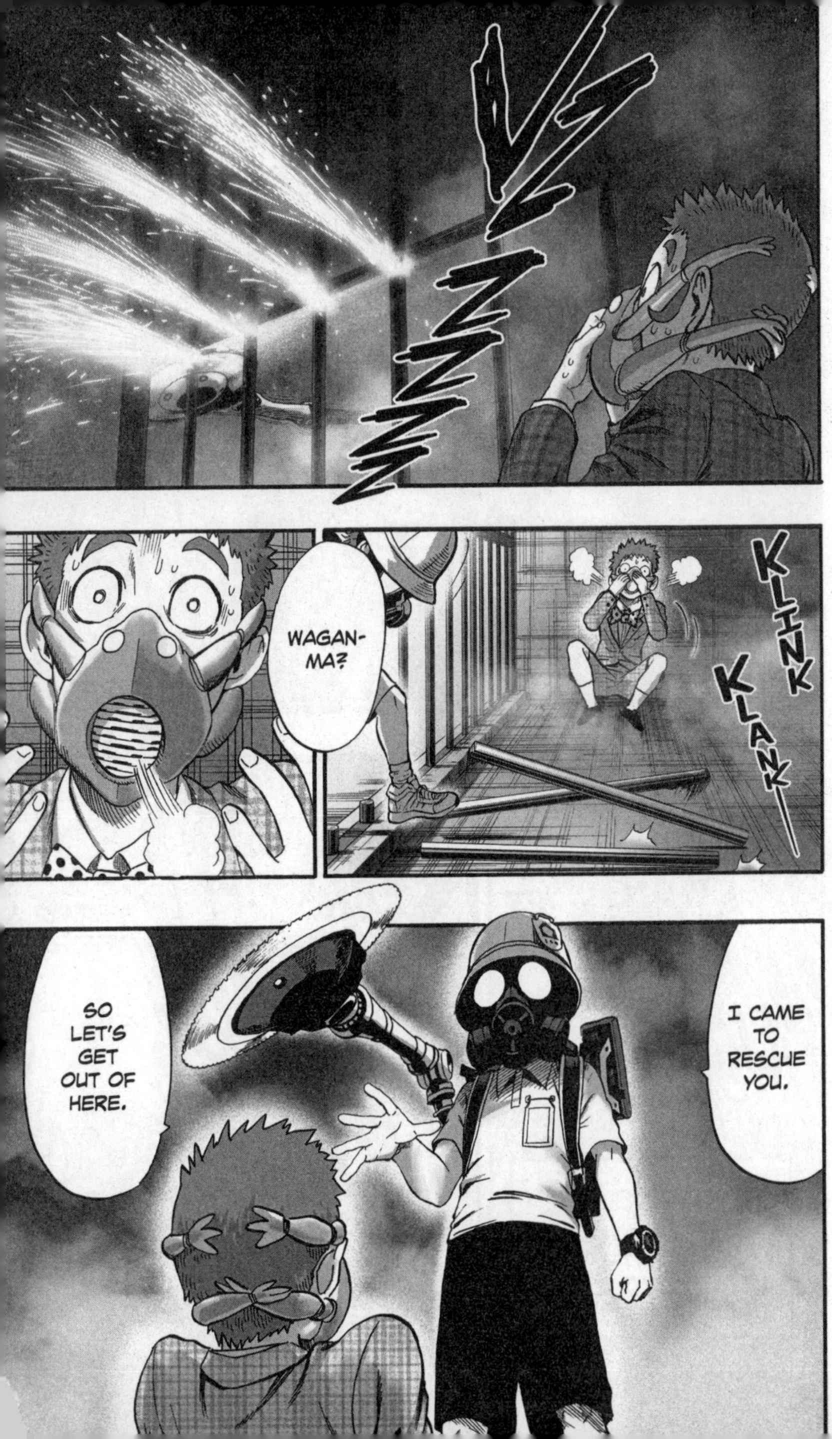
KLINK
KLANK
WAGAN-MA?
I CAME TO RESCUE YOU.
SO LET'S GET OUT OF HERE.

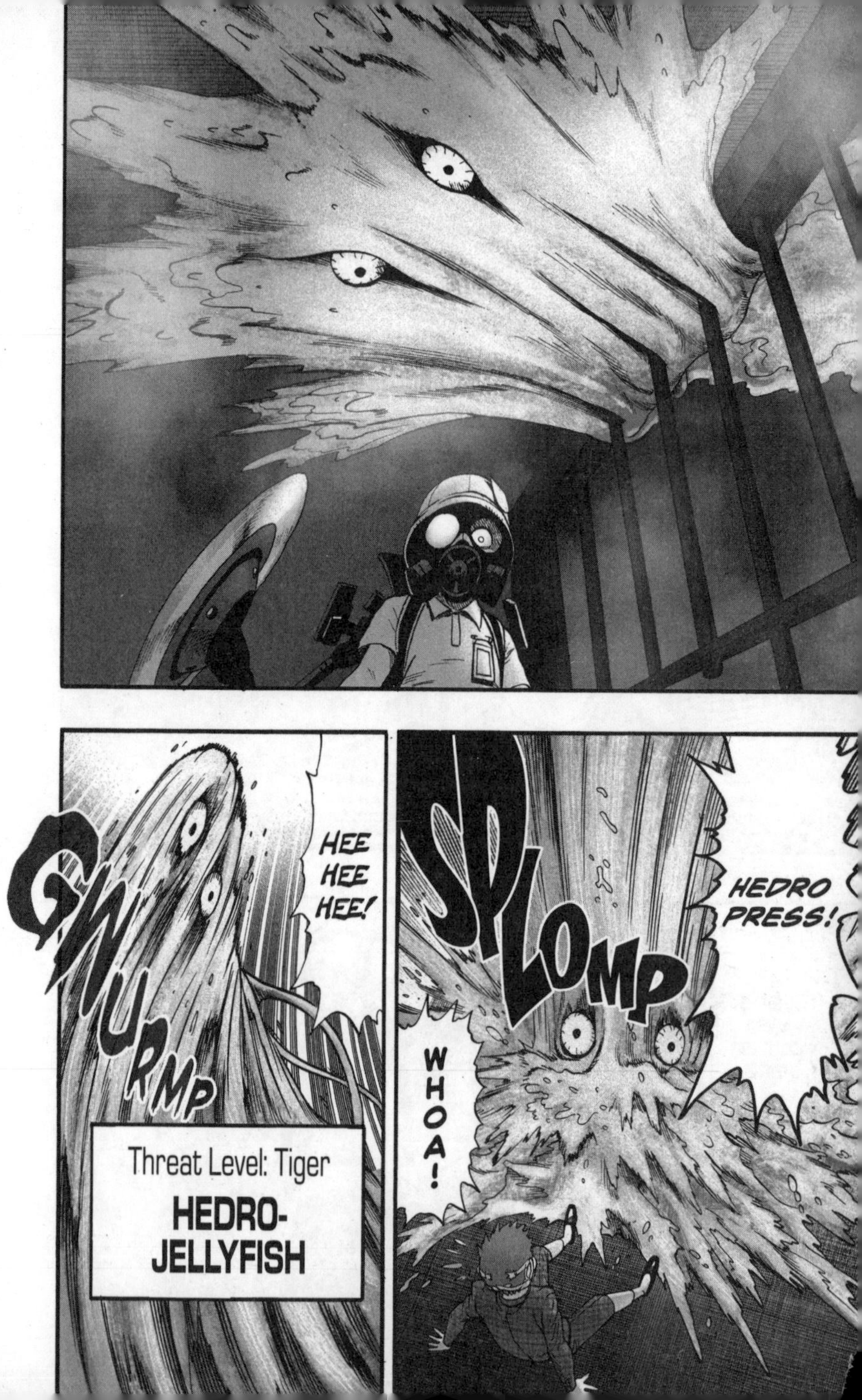
HEDRO PRESS!
SPLOMP
WHOA!
HEE HEE HEE!
GNURMP
Threat Level: Tiger
HEDRO-JELLYFISH

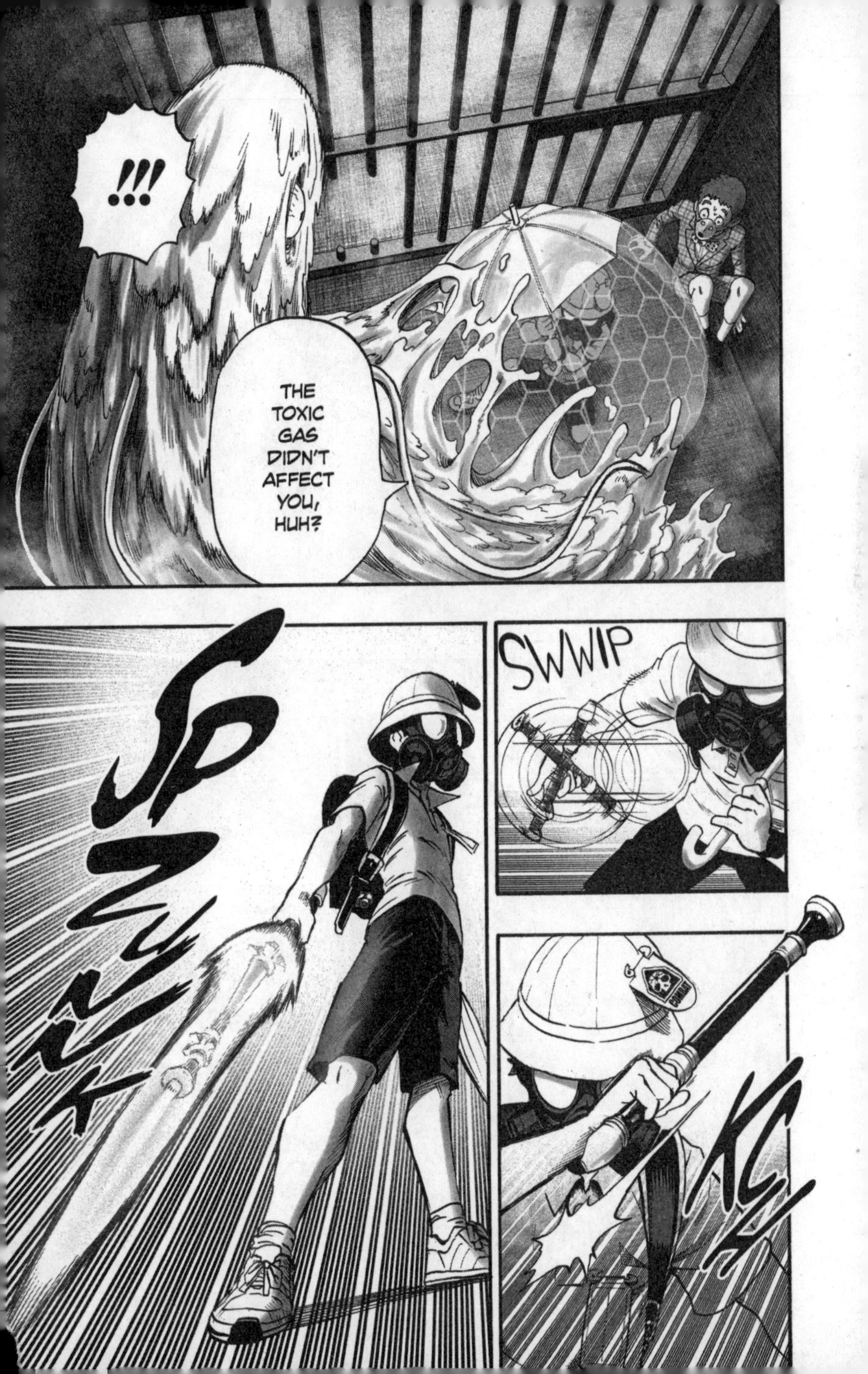
!!!
THE TOXIC GAS DIDN'T AFFECT YOU, HUH?
SWWIP
KC

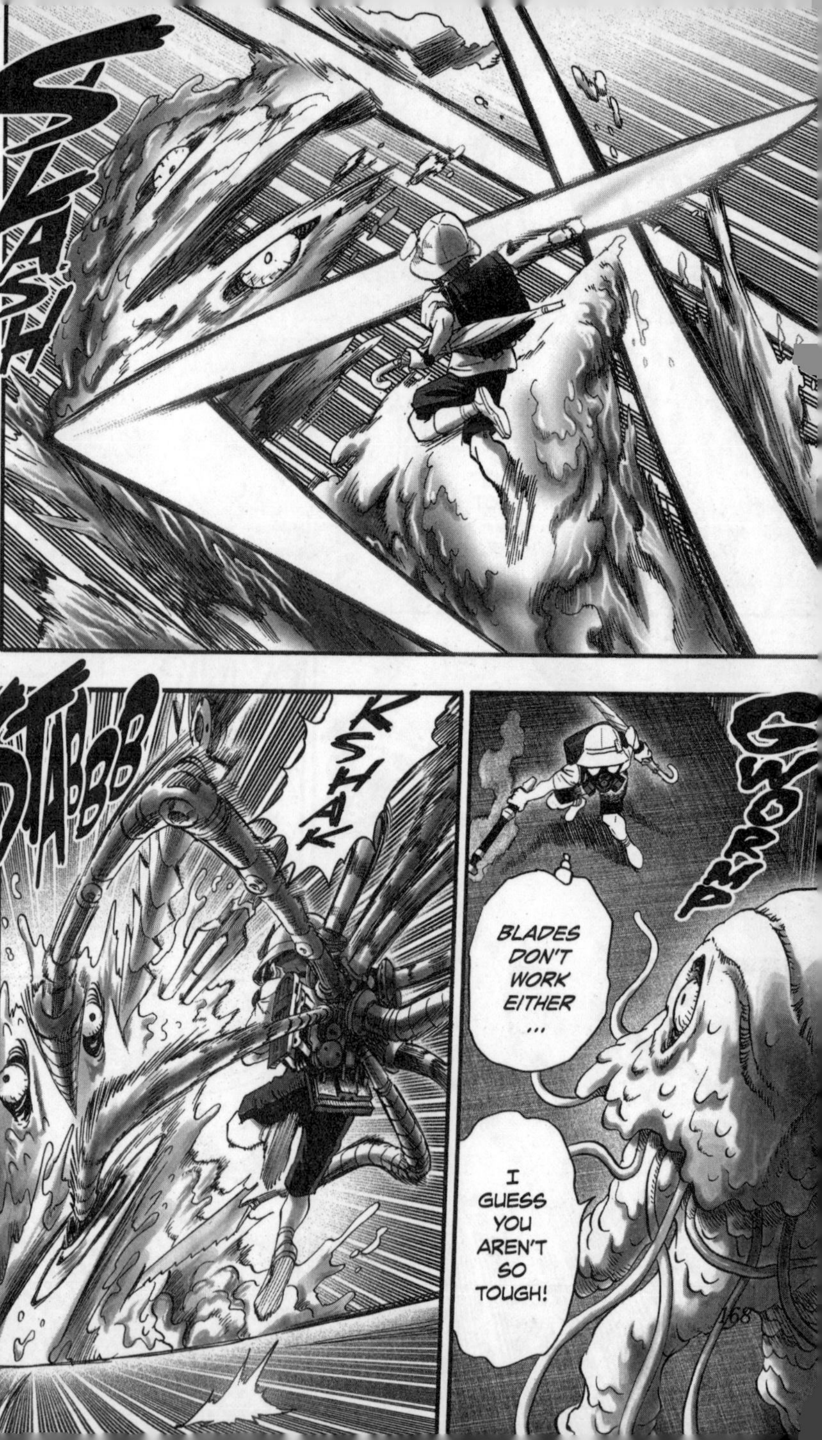
SLASH
GWORBA
BLADES DON'T WORK EITHER ...
I GUESS YOU AREN'T SO TOUGH!
STABBB
KSHAK

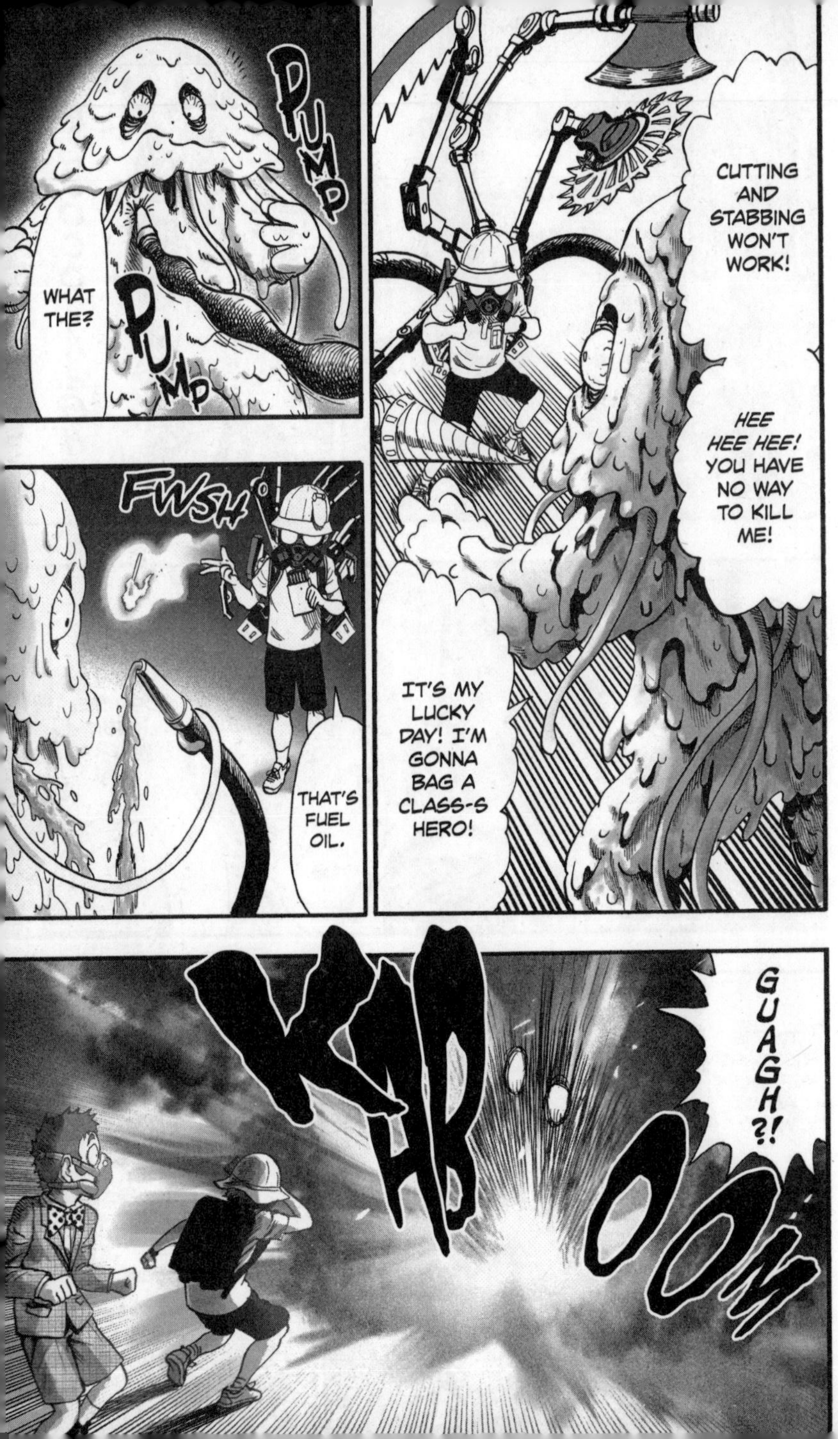
CUTTING AND STABBING WON'T WORK!
HEE HEE HEE! YOU HAVE NO WAY TO KILL ME!
IT'S MY LUCKY DAY! I'M GONNA BAG A CLASS-S HERO!
PUMP
WHAT THE?
PUMP
FWSH
THAT'S FUEL OIL.
GUAGH?!
KABOOM

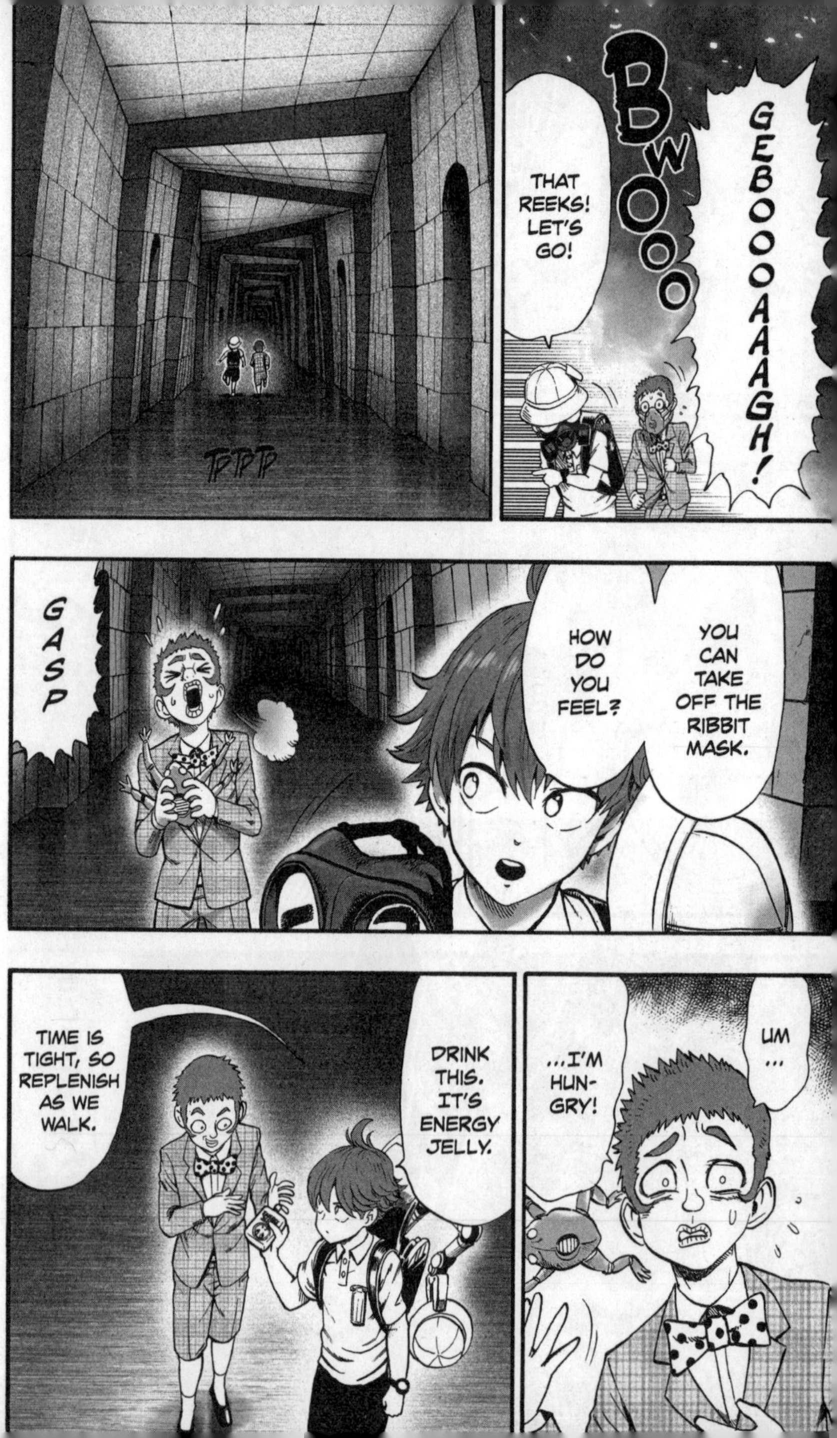
GEBOOOAAAAGH!
BWOOOO
THAT REEKS! LET'S GO!
TPTPTP
YOU CAN TAKE OFF THE RIBBIT MASK.
HOW DO YOU FEEL?
GASP
UM ...
...I'M HUN-GRY!
DRINK THIS. IT'S ENERGY JELLY.
TIME IS TIGHT, SO REPLENISH AS WE WALK.

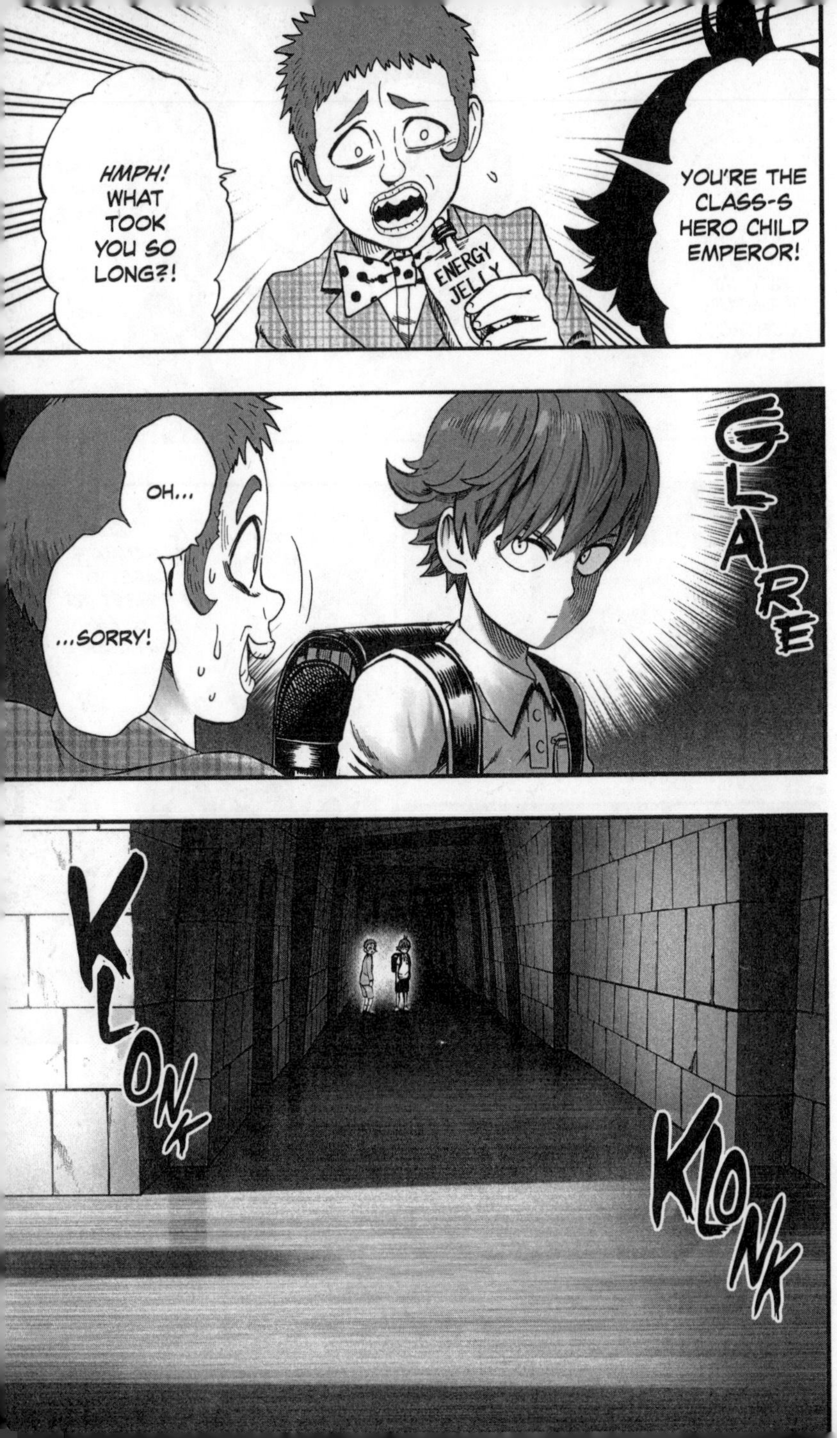
YOU'RE THE CLASS-S HERO CHILD EMPEROR!
ENERGY JELLY
HMPH! WHAT TOOK YOU SO LONG?!
GLARE
OH...
...SORRY!
KLONK
KLONK

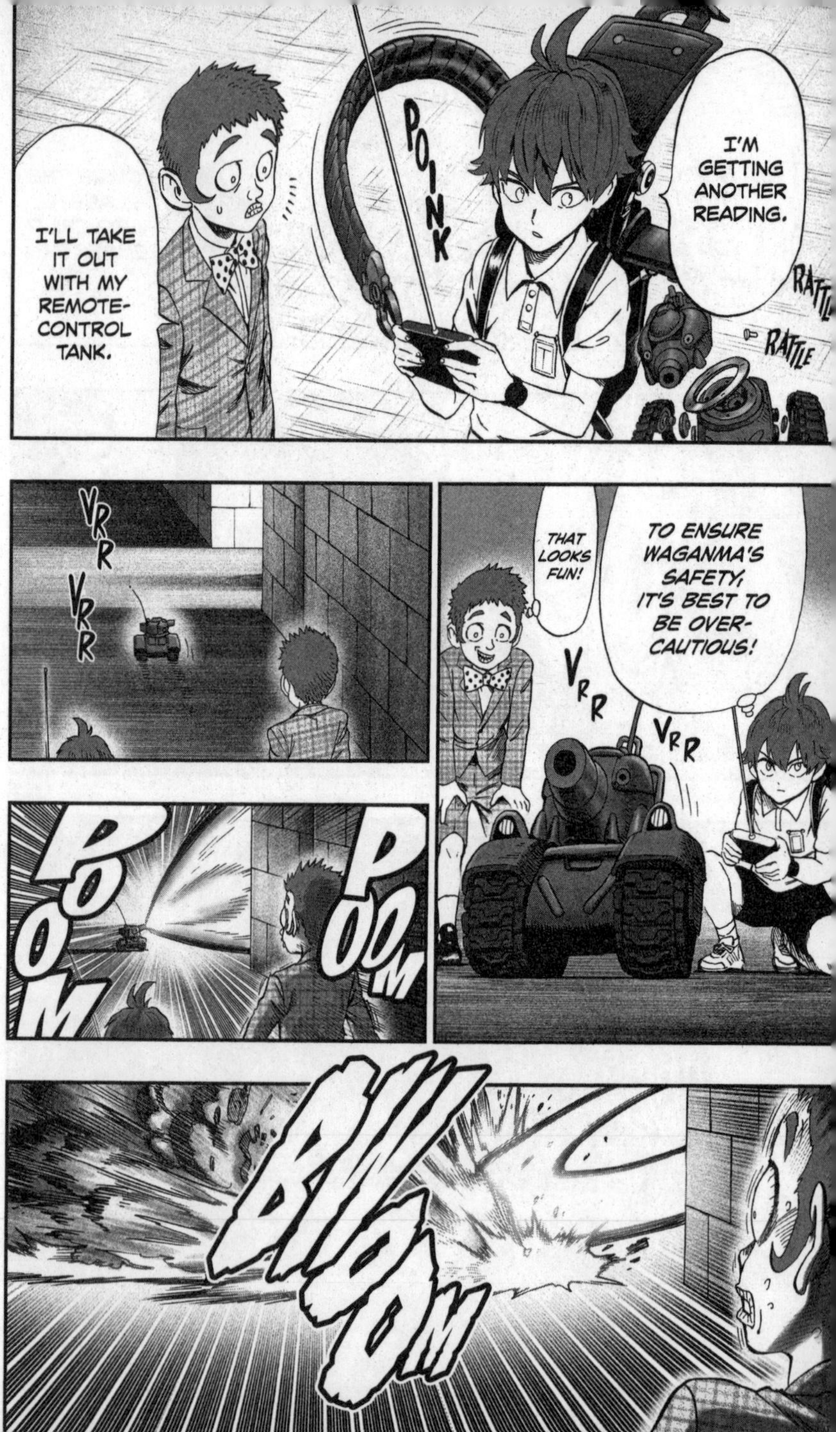
I'M GETTING ANOTHER READING.
RATTLE
RATTLE
POINK
I'LL TAKE IT OUT WITH MY REMOTE-CONTROL TANK.
TO ENSURE WAGANMA'S SAFETY, IT'S BEST TO BE OVER-CAUTIOUS!
THAT LOOKS FUN!
VRR
VRR
VRR
VRR
POOM
POOM
BWOOM

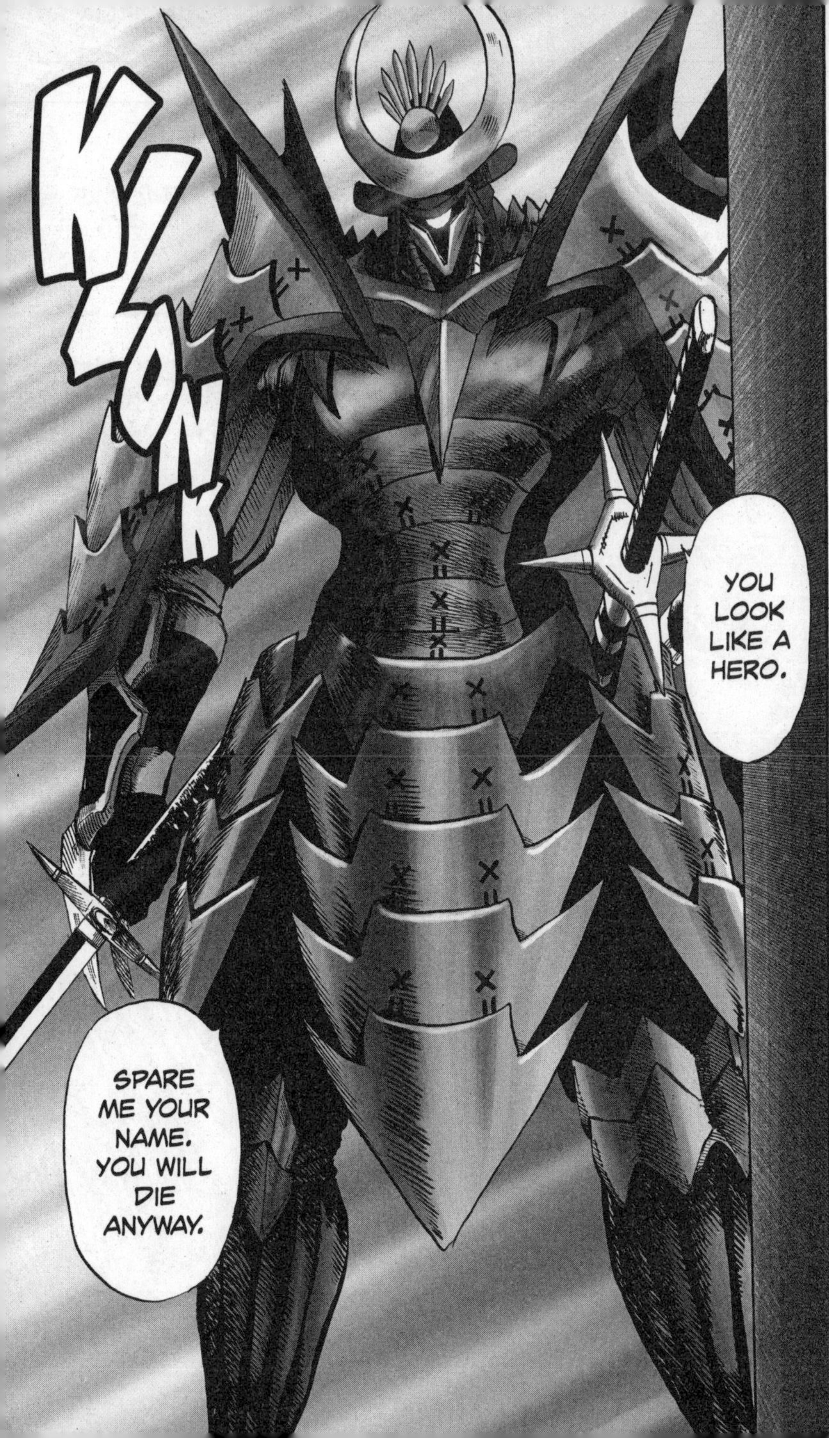
KLONK
YOU LOOK LIKE A HERO.
SPARE ME YOUR NAME. YOU WILL DIE ANYWAY.

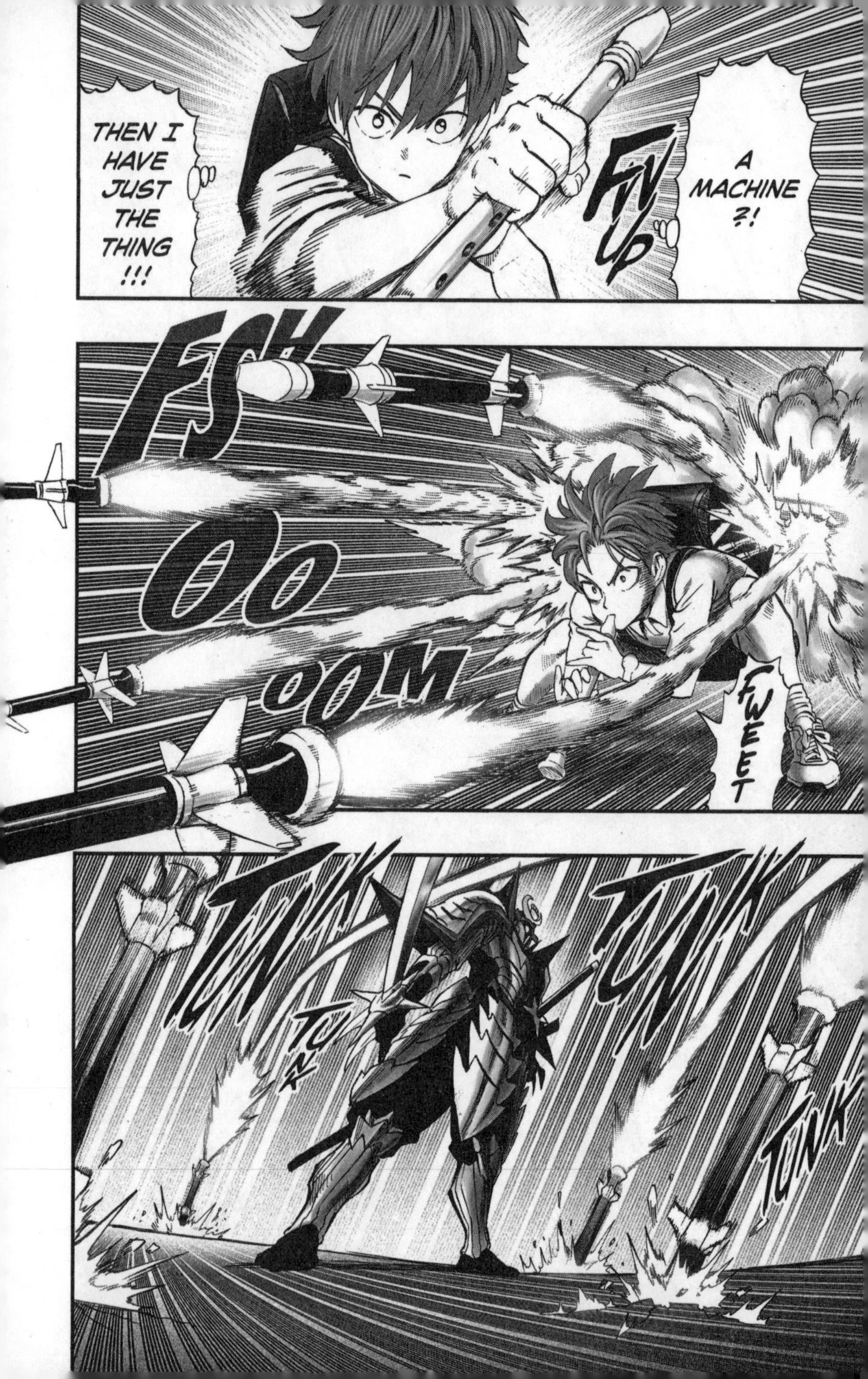
A MACHINE ?!
FWUP
THEN I HAVE JUST THE THING !!!
FWEEET
FSH
OO
OOM
TUNK
TUNK
TUNK
TONK

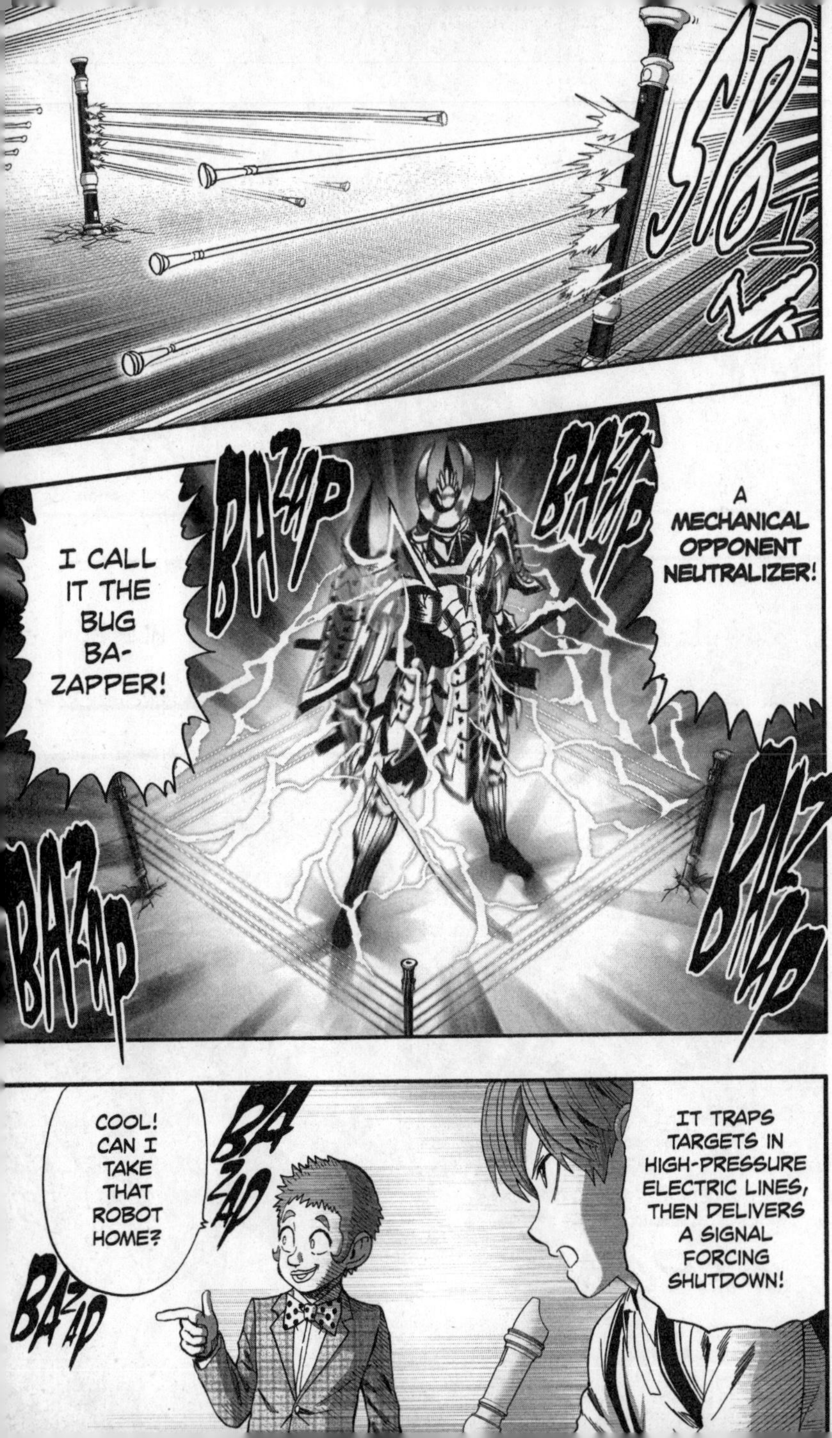
BAZAP
BAZAP
A MECHANICAL OPPONENT NEUTRALIZER!
BAZAP
I CALL IT THE BUG BA-ZAPPER!
BAZAP
IT TRAPS TARGETS IN HIGH-PRESSURE ELECTRIC LINES, THEN DELIVERS A SIGNAL FORCING SHUTDOWN!
BAZAP
COOL! CAN I TAKE THAT ROBOT HOME?
BAZAP

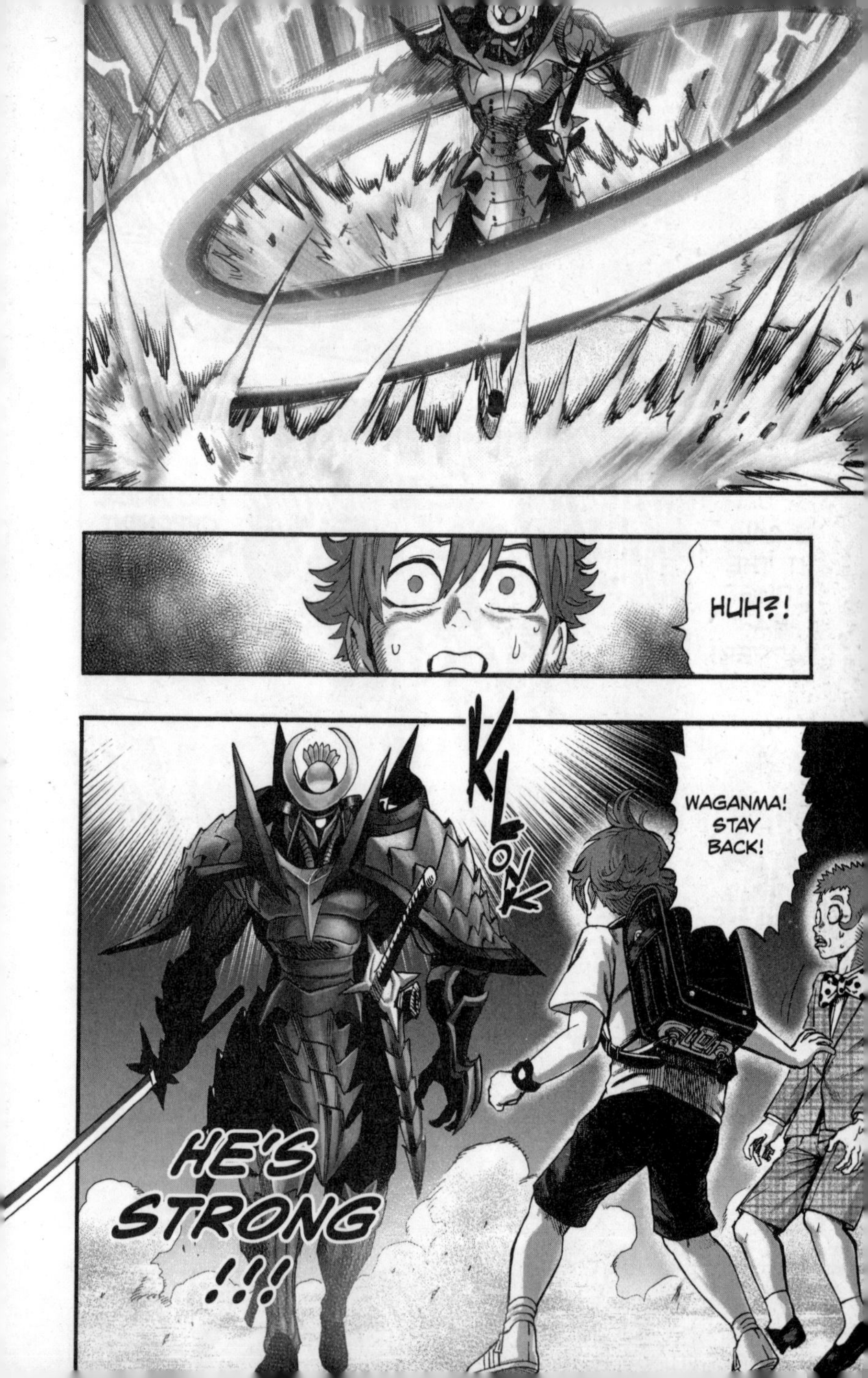
HUH?!
KLONK
WAGANMA! STAY BACK!
HE'S STRONG !!!

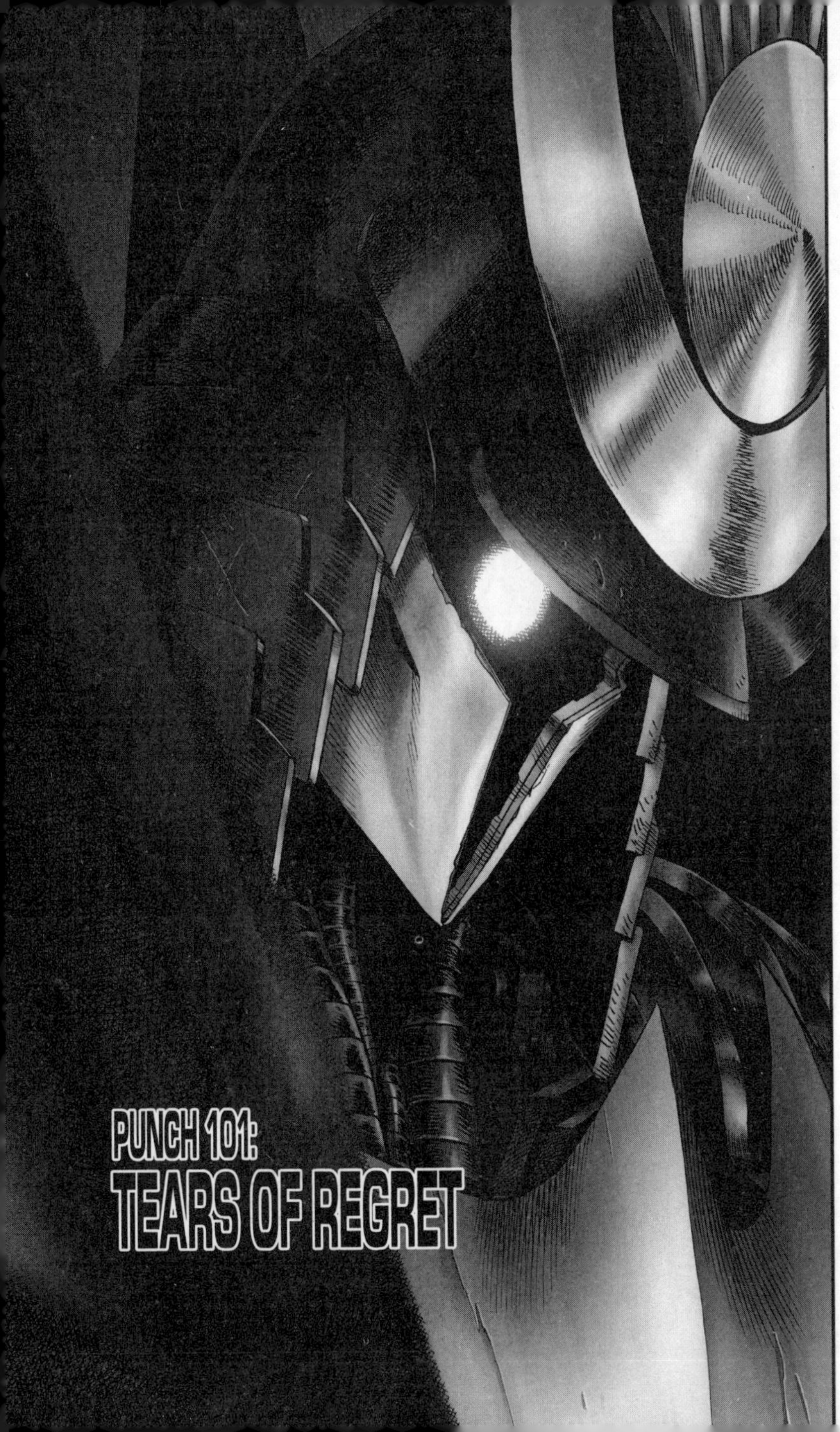
PUNCH 101:
TEARS OF REGRET

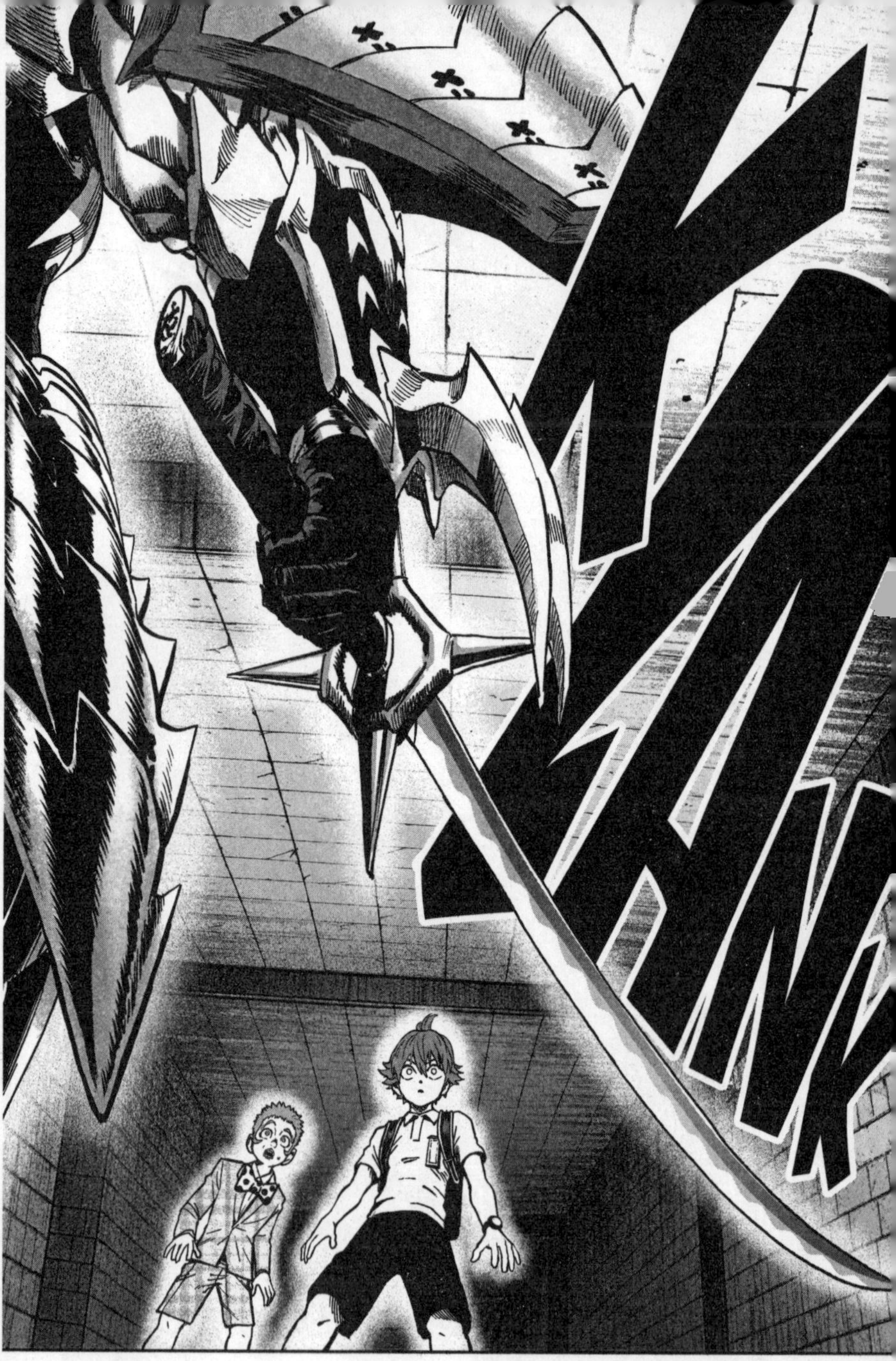

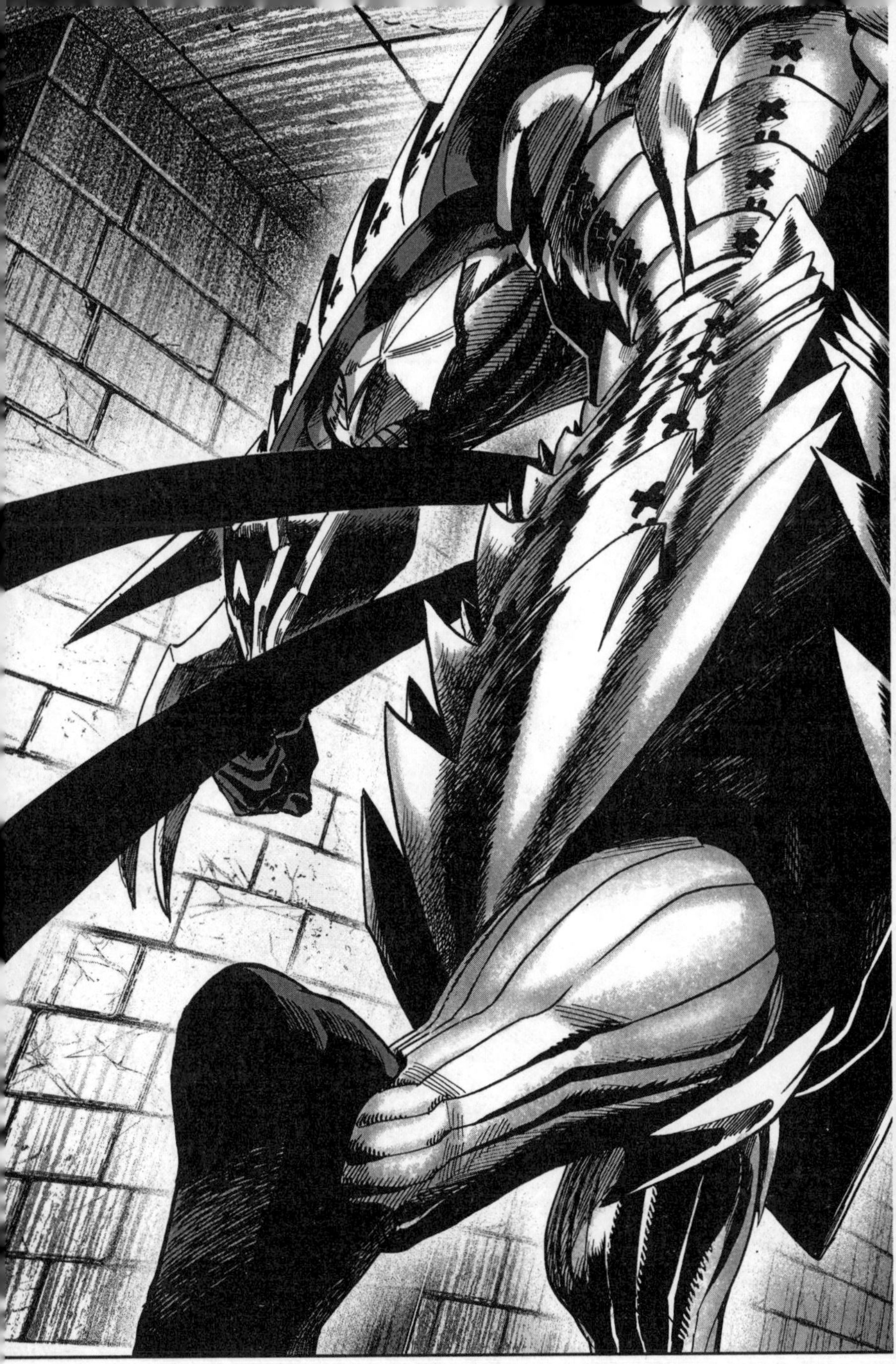

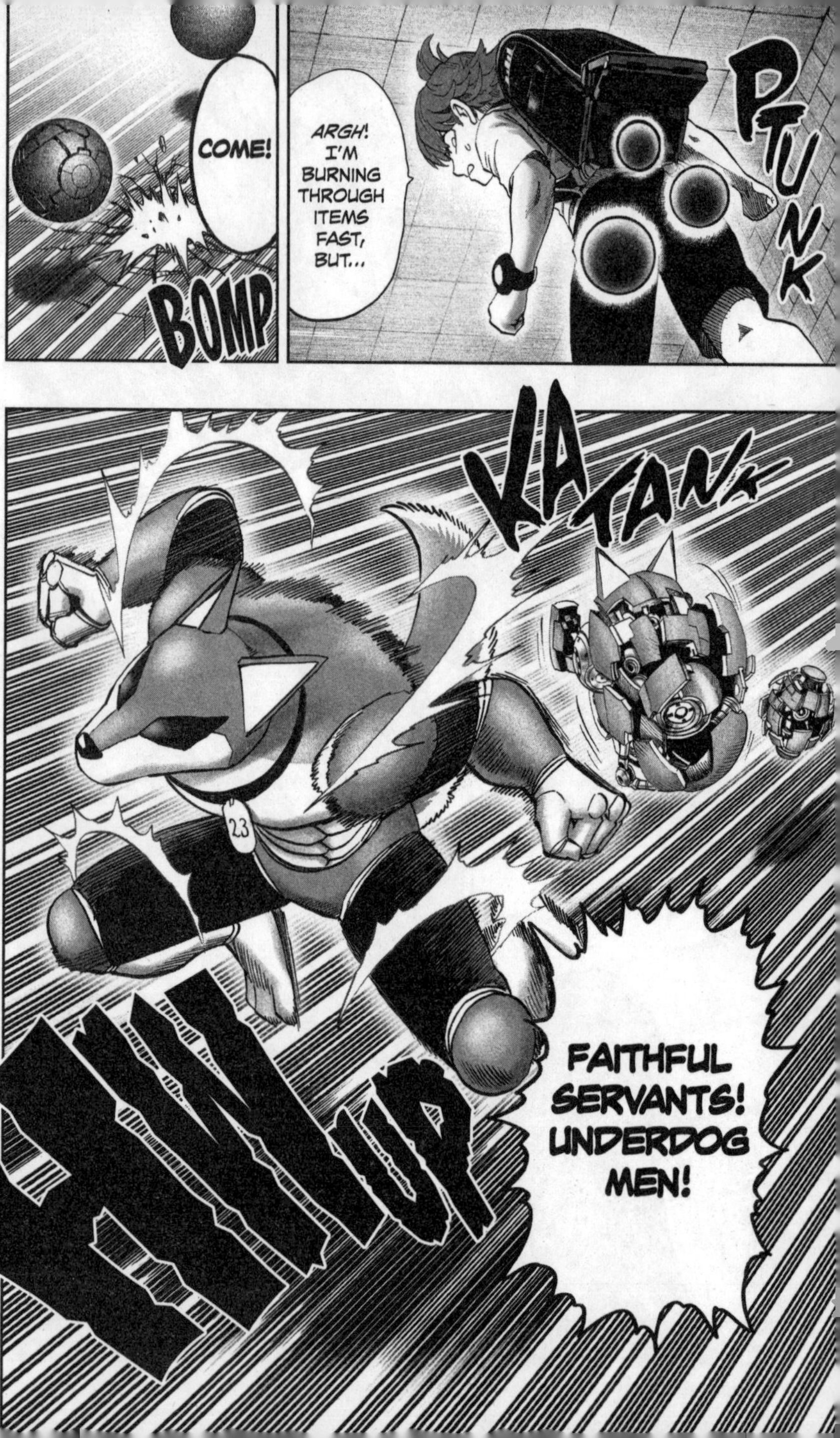
PTUNK
ARGH! I'M BURNING THROUGH ITEMS FAST, BUT...
COME!
BOMP
KATANK
FAITHFUL SERVANTS! UNDERDOG MEN!
HWUP

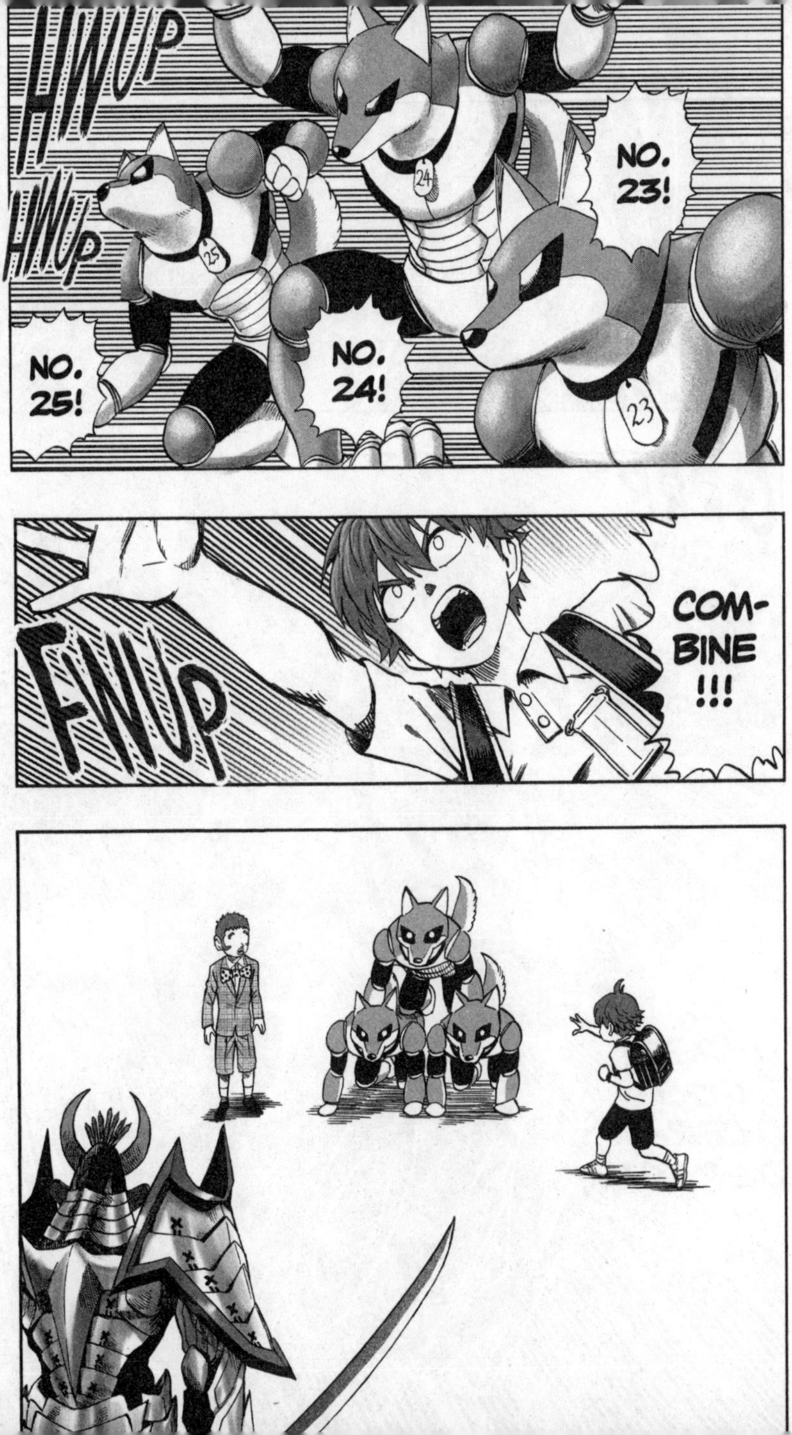
NO. 23!
HWUP HWUP
NO. 24!
NO. 25!
COM-BINE!!!
FWUP

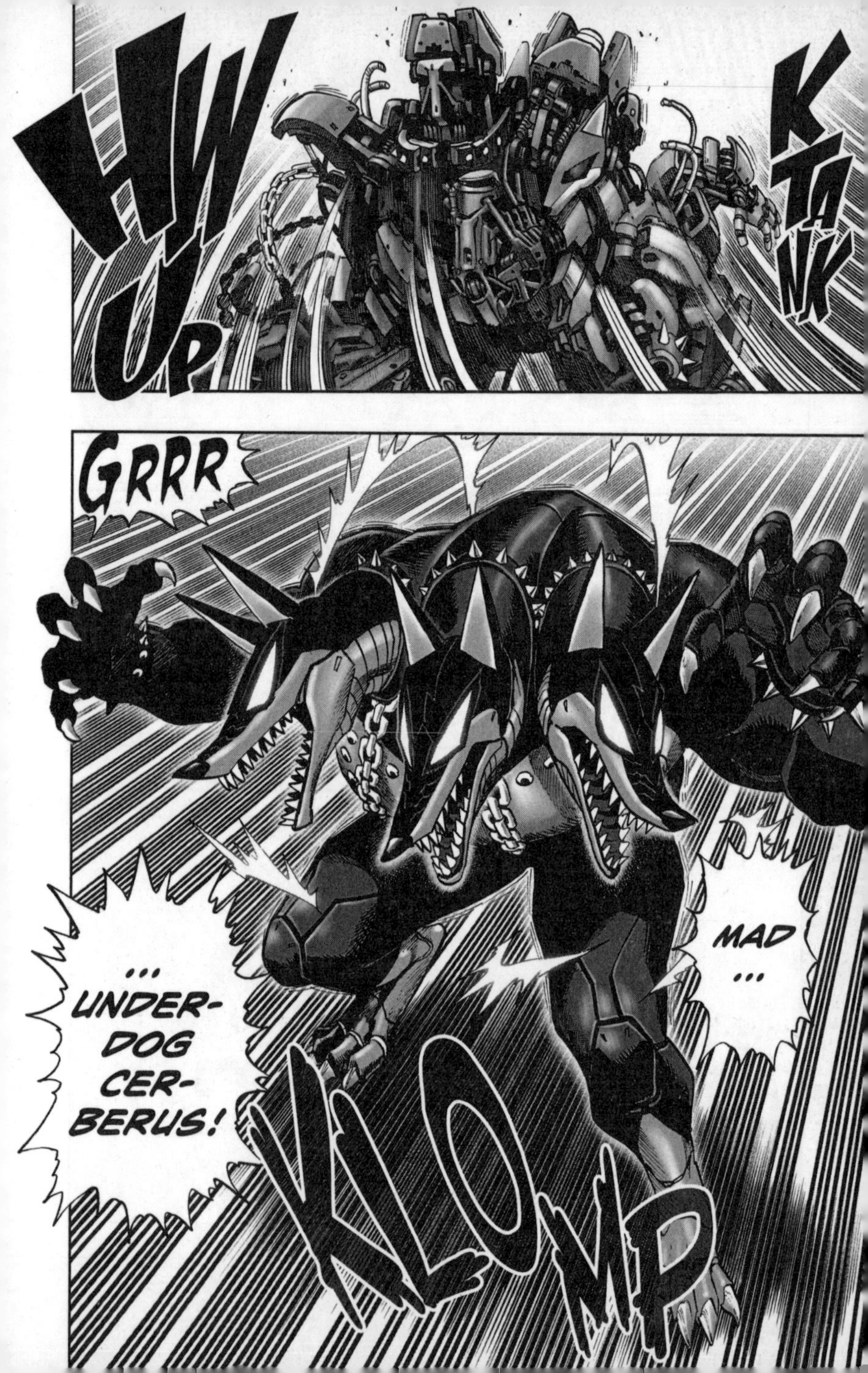
KTANK
WHUP
GRRR
MAD ...
... UNDER-DOG CER-BERUS!
KLOMP

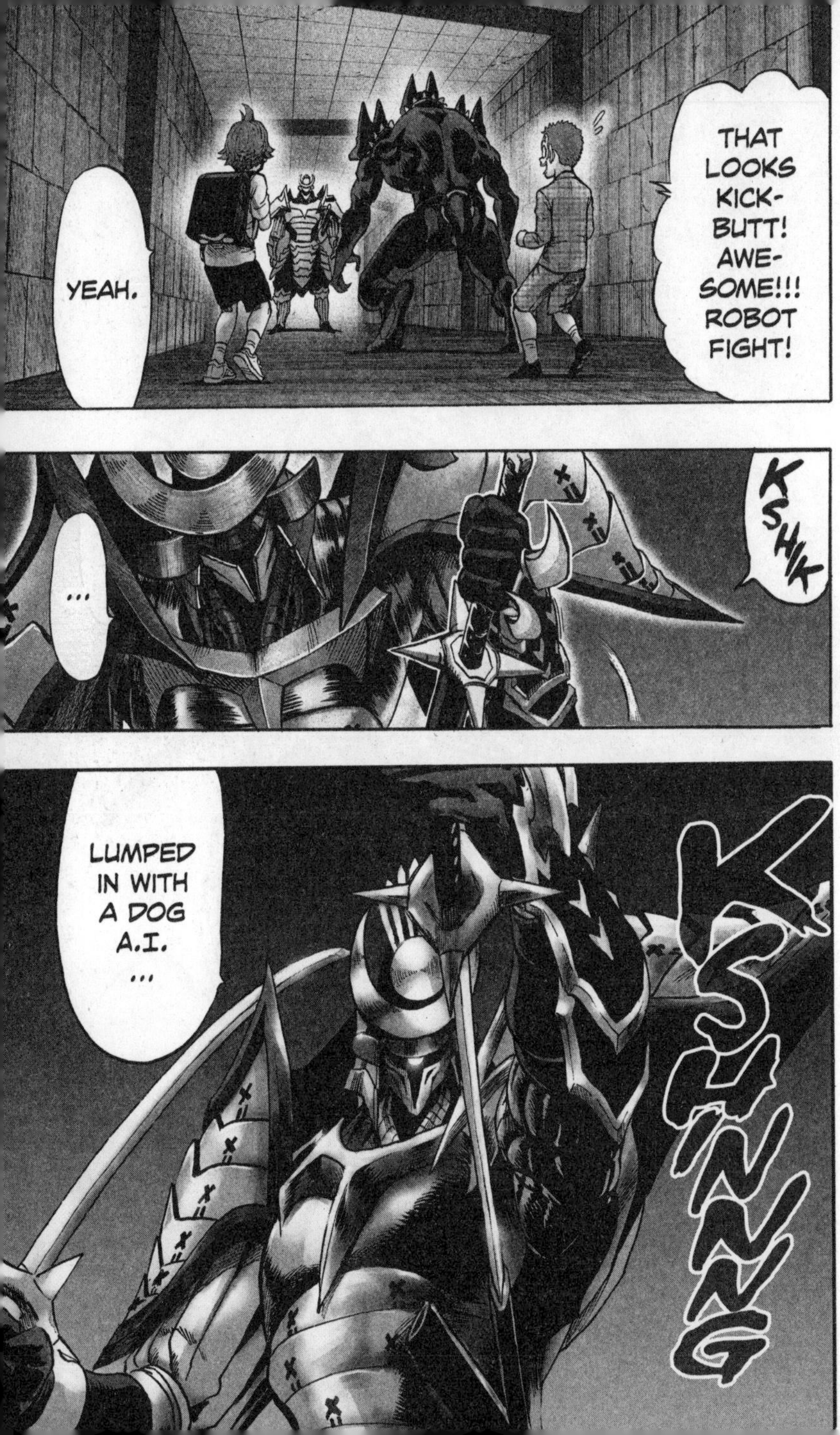
THAT LOOKS KICK-BUTT! AWESOME!!! ROBOT FIGHT!
YEAH.
KSHIK
...
KSHING
LUMPED IN WITH A DOG A.I. ...

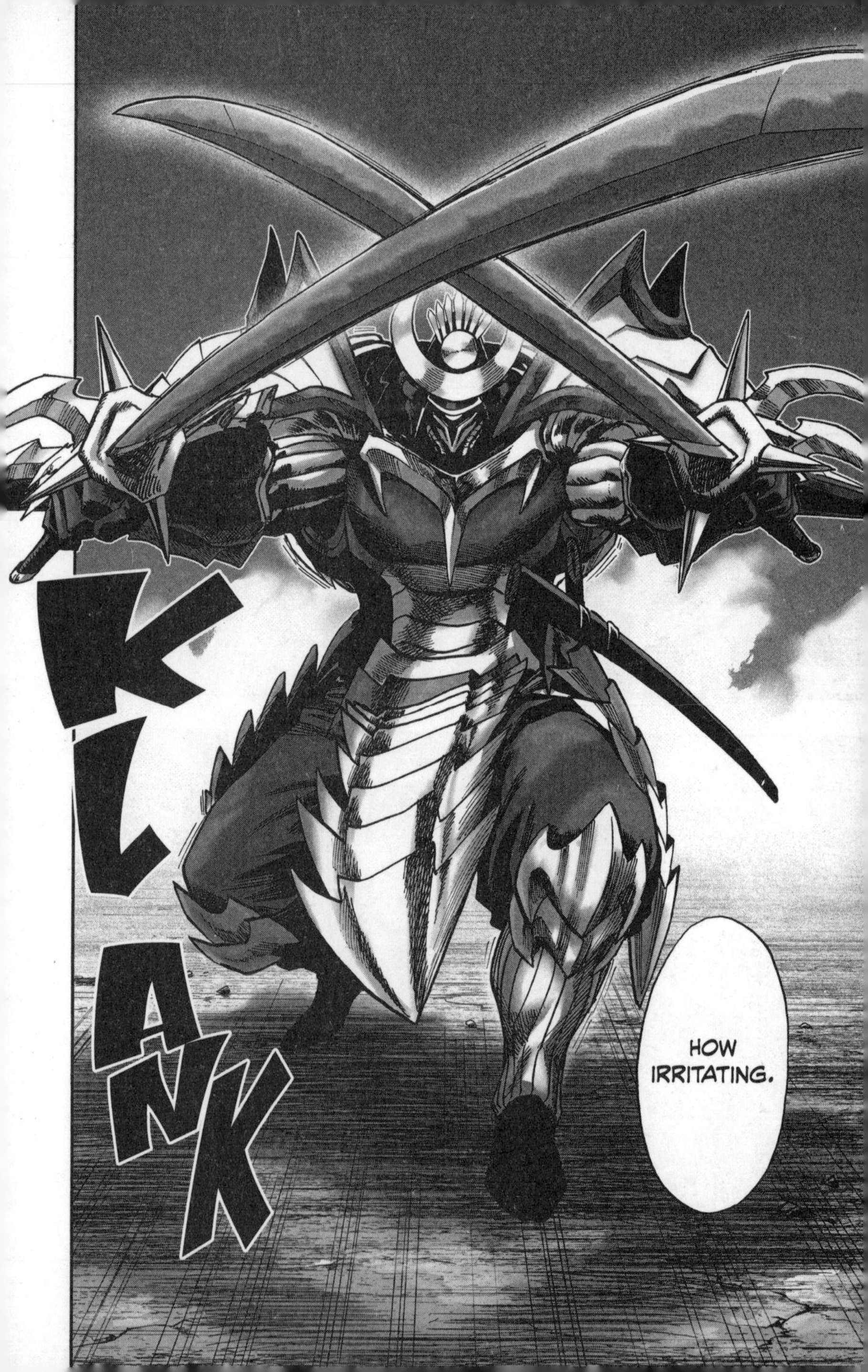
KLANK
HOW IRRITATING.

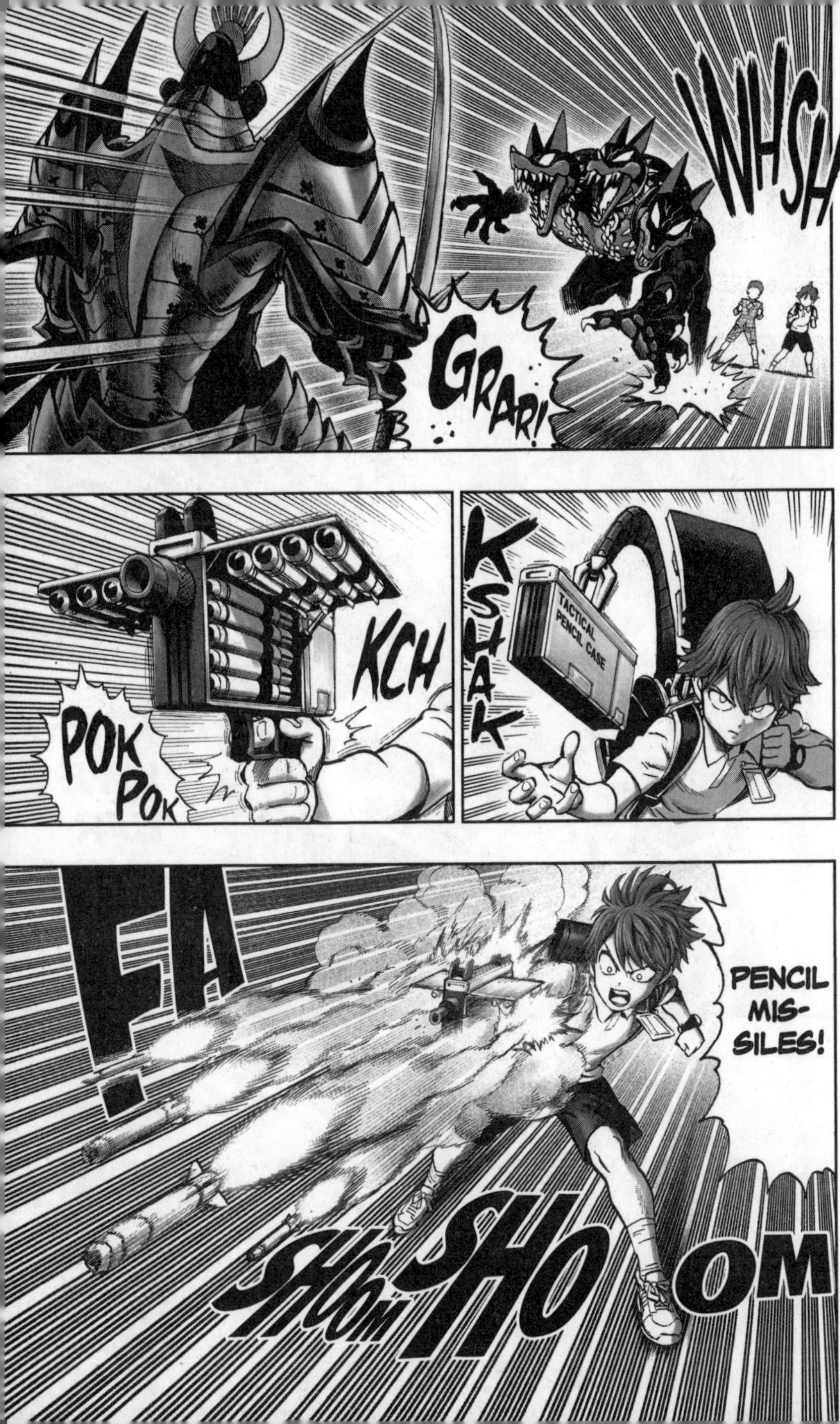
WHSH
GRAR!
KSHAK
TACTICAL PENCIL CASE
KCH
POK POK
PENCIL MIS-SILES!
FA!
SHOOM
SHO OM

SPLAT
SPLAT

BIRD-
LIME
WAR-
HEADS
!!!

CREEEAK
SPWOO

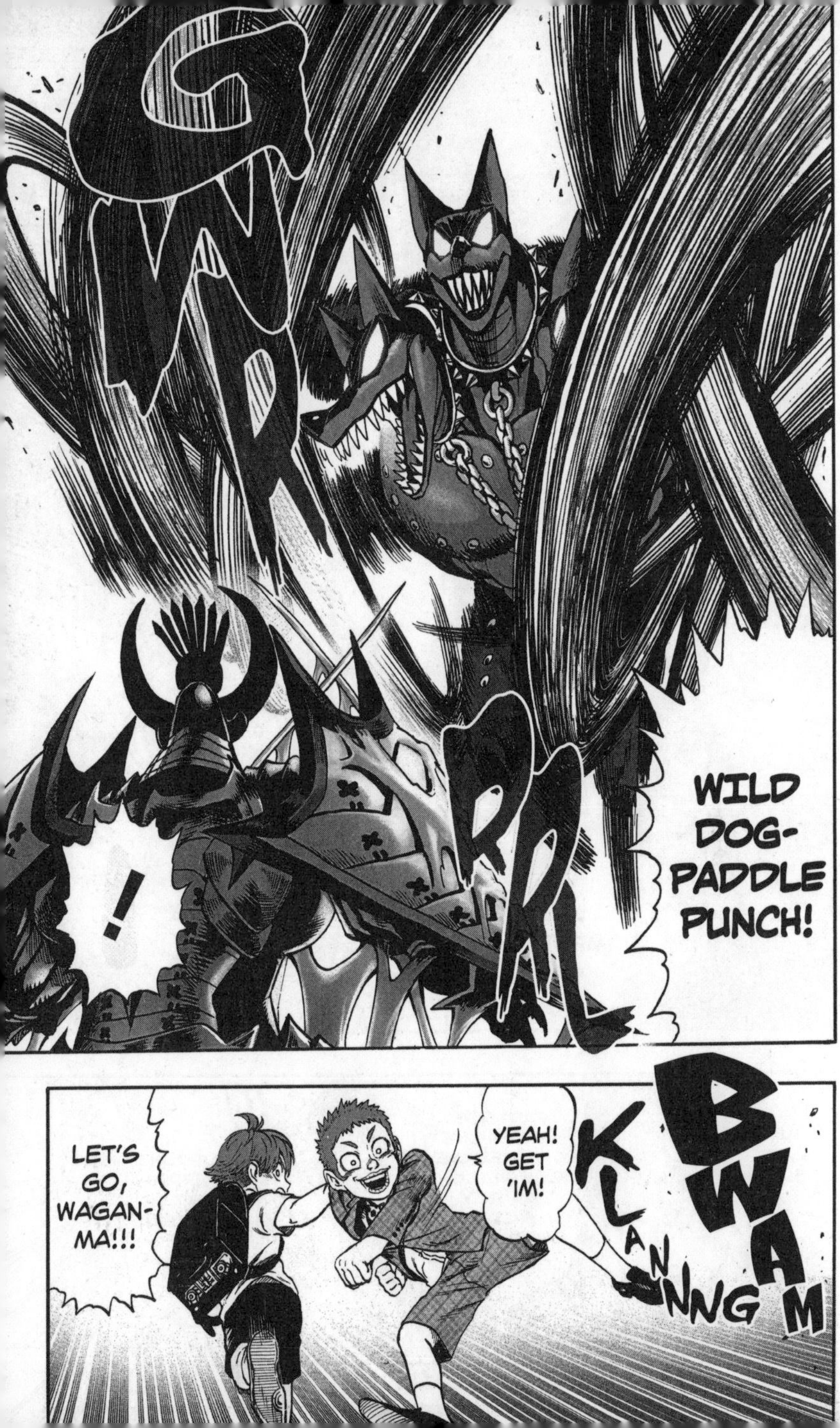
WILD DOG-PADDLE PUNCH!
!
BWAM
KLANNNG
YEAH! GET 'IM!
LET'S GO, WAGAN-MA!!!

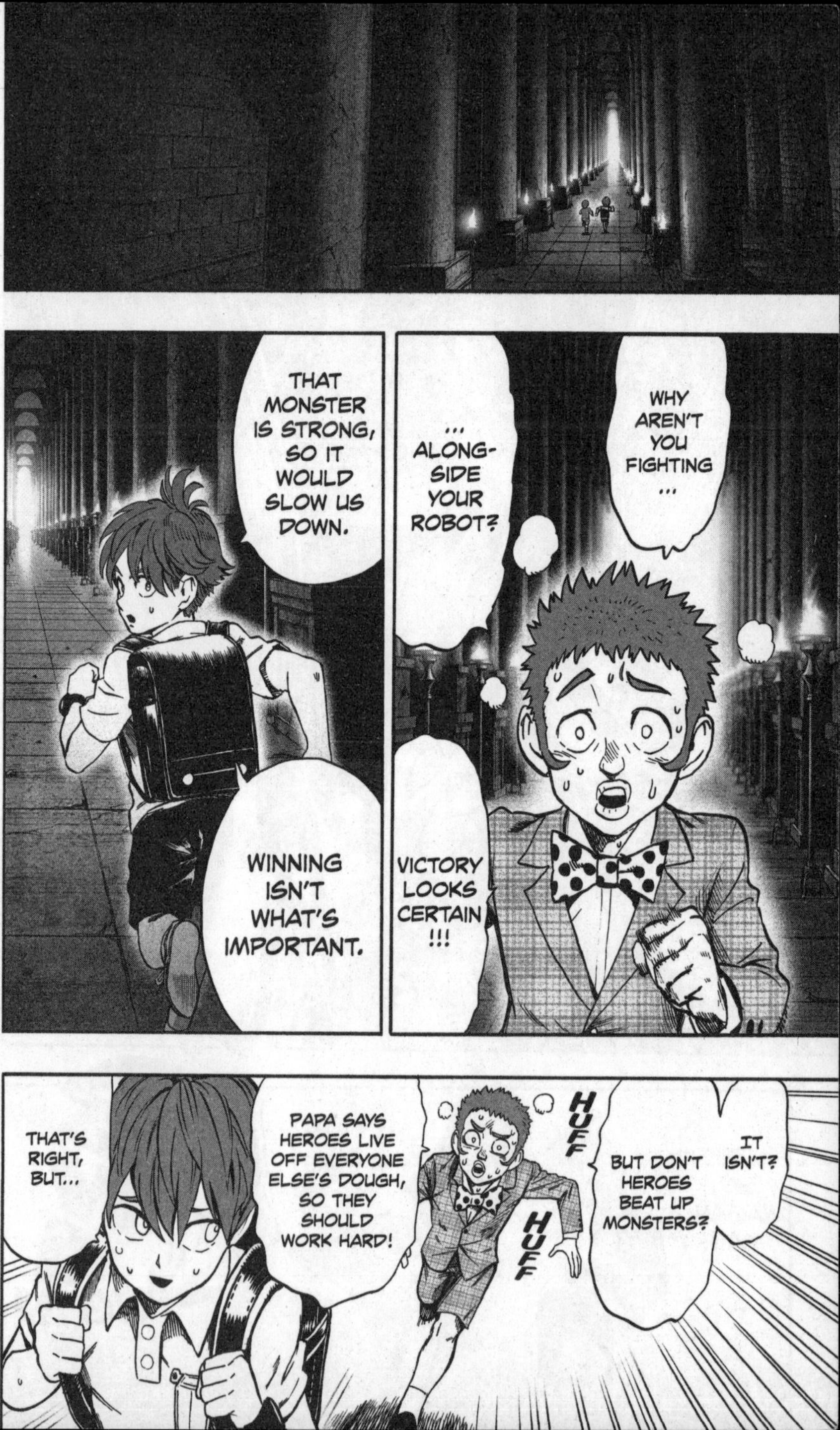
WHY AREN'T YOU FIGHTING ...
... ALONG-SIDE YOUR ROBOT?
VICTORY LOOKS CERTAIN !!!
THAT MONSTER IS STRONG, SO IT WOULD SLOW US DOWN.
WINNING ISN'T WHAT'S IMPORTANT.
IT ISN'T?
BUT DON'T HEROES BEAT UP MONSTERS?
HUFF
HUFF
PAPA SAYS HEROES LIVE OFF EVERYONE ELSE'S DOUGH, SO THEY SHOULD WORK HARD!
THAT'S RIGHT, BUT...

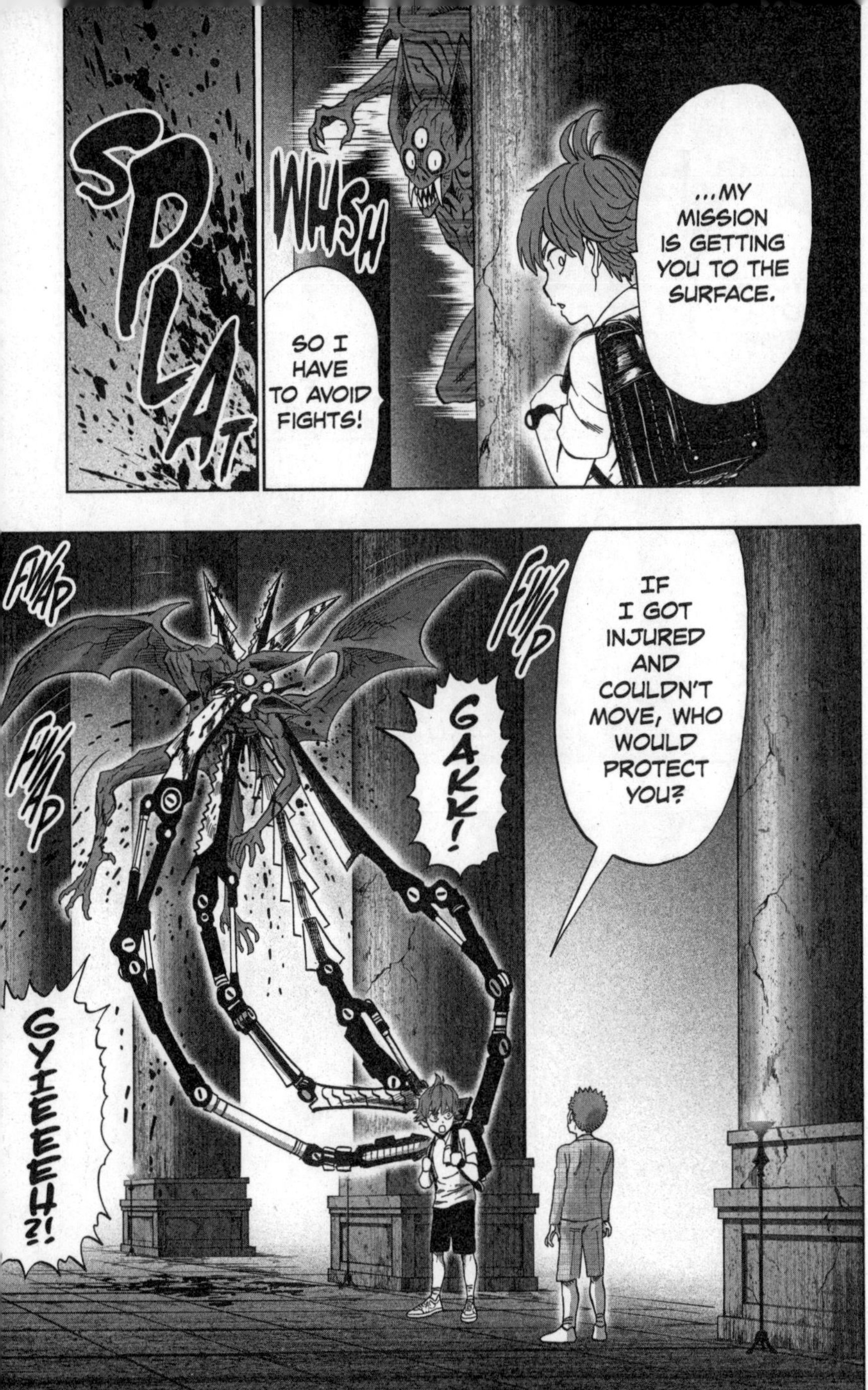
...MY MISSION IS GETTING YOU TO THE SURFACE.
WHSH
SO I HAVE TO AVOID FIGHTS!
SPLAT
IF I GOT INJURED AND COULDN'T MOVE, WHO WOULD PROTECT YOU?
FWP
GAKK!
FWAP
FWAP
GYIEEEEH?!

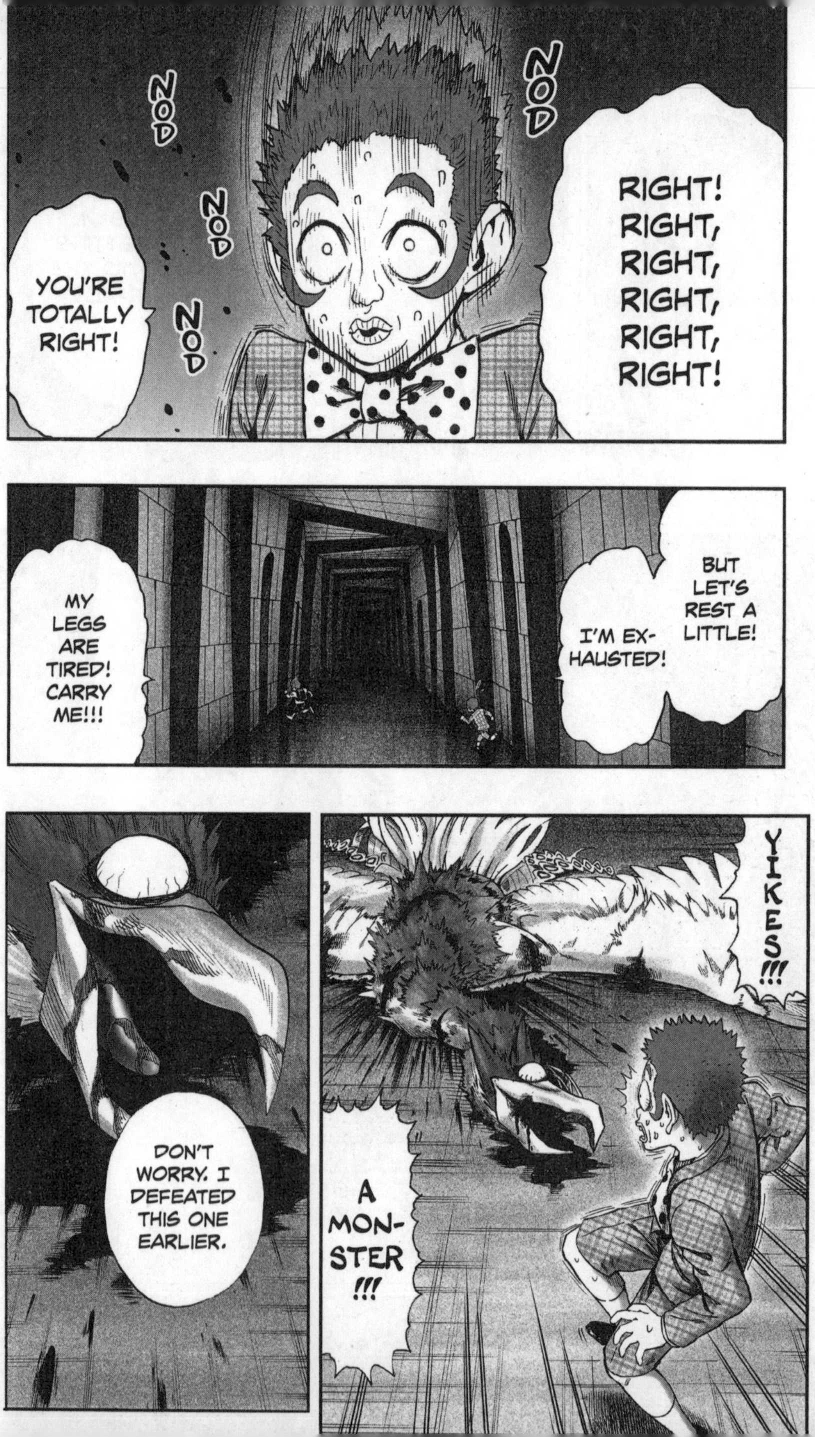
NOD
RIGHT! RIGHT, RIGHT, RIGHT, RIGHT, RIGHT!
NOD
NOD
NOD
YOU'RE TOTALLY RIGHT!
BUT LET'S REST A LITTLE!
I'M EX-HAUSTED!
MY LEGS ARE TIRED! CARRY ME!!!
YIKES!!!
A MON-STER!!!
DON'T WORRY. I DEFEATED THIS ONE EARLIER.

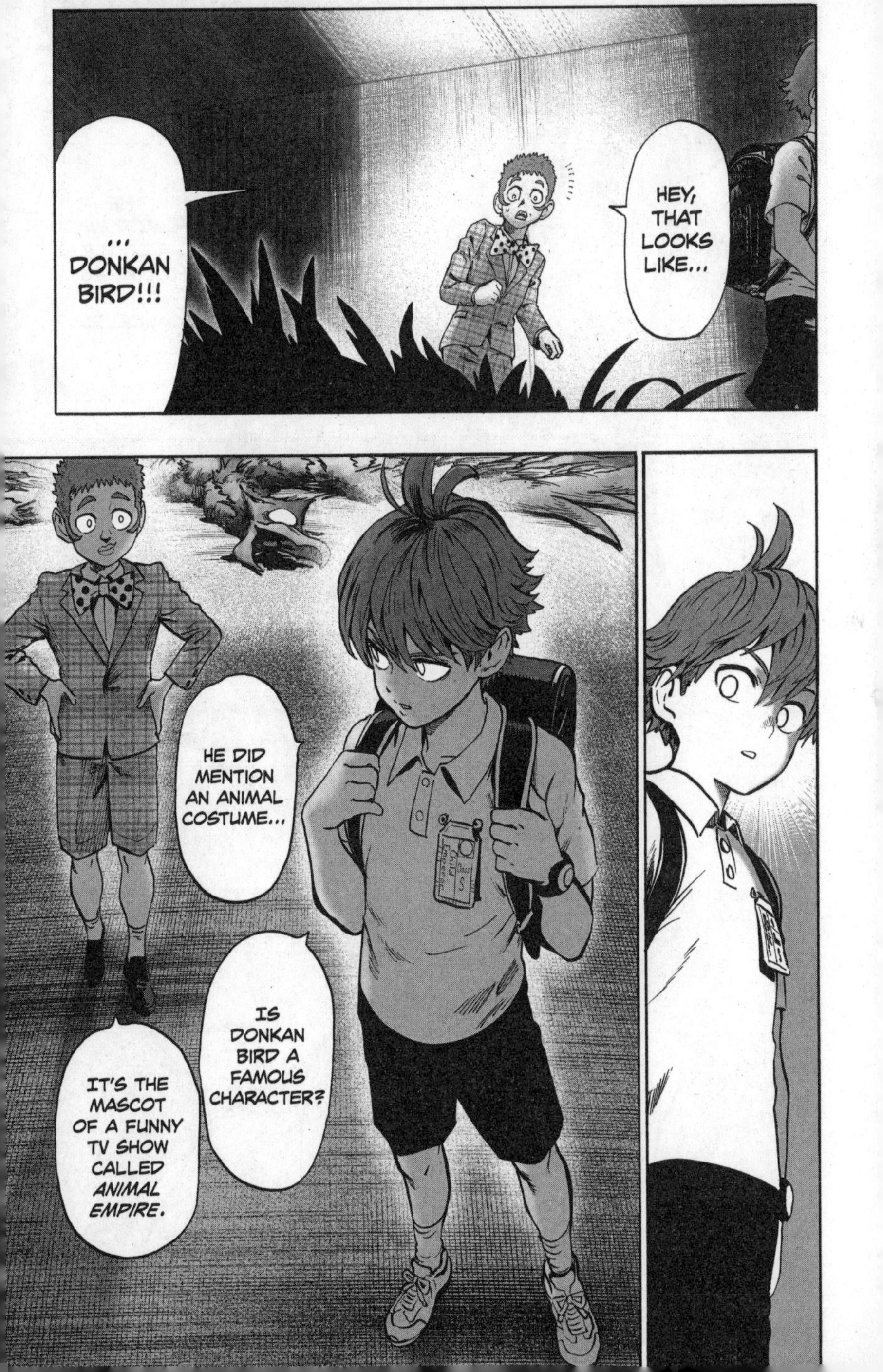
HEY, THAT LOOKS LIKE...
... DONKAN BIRD!!!
HE DID MENTION AN ANIMAL COSTUME...
IS DONKAN BIRD A FAMOUS CHARACTER?
IT'S THE MASCOT OF A FUNNY TV SHOW CALLED *ANIMAL EMPIRE*.

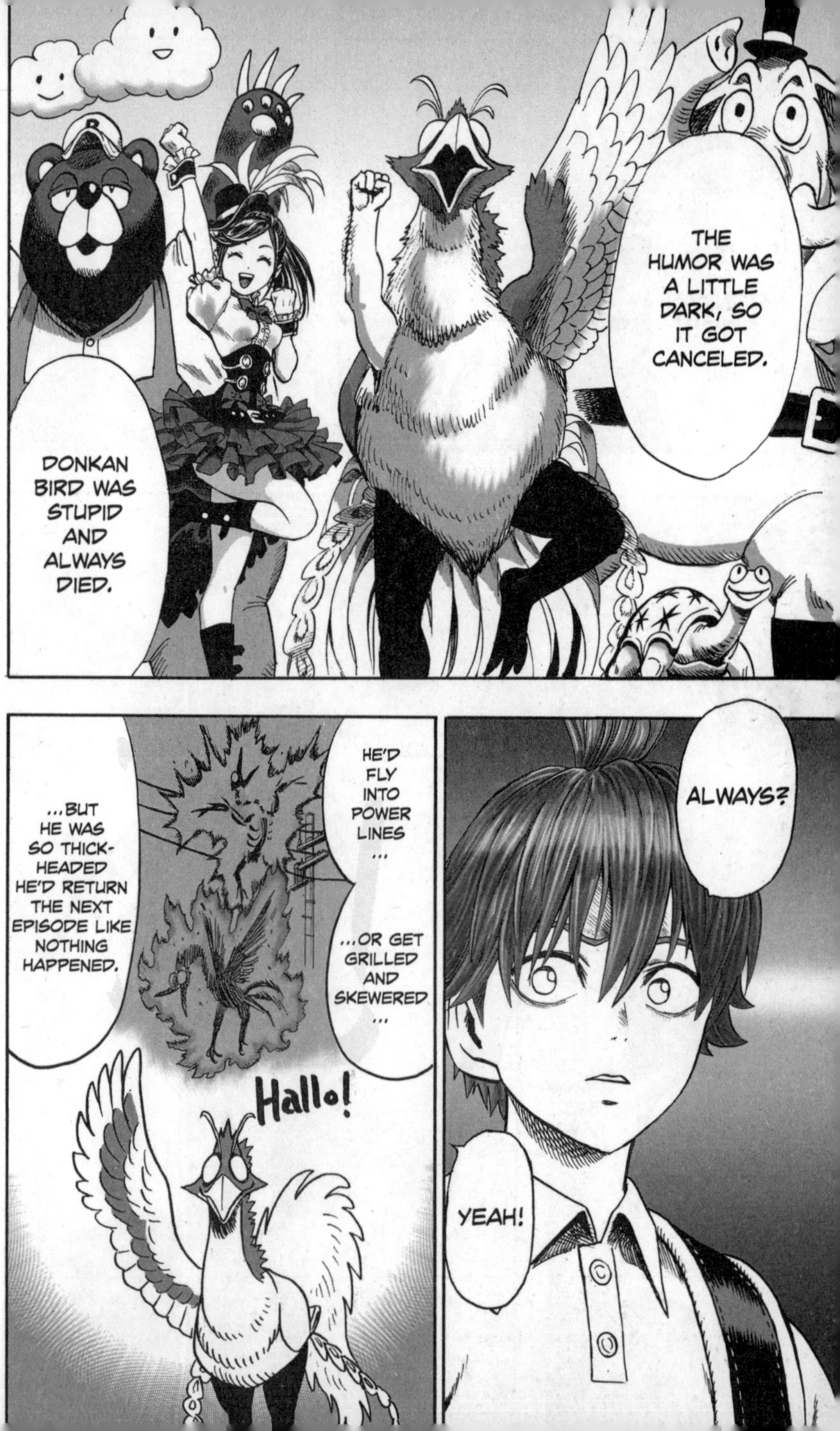
THE HUMOR WAS A LITTLE DARK, SO IT GOT CANCELED.
DONKAN BIRD WAS STUPID AND ALWAYS DIED.
ALWAYS?
YEAH!
HE'D FLY INTO POWER LINES ...
...OR GET GRILLED AND SKEWERED ...
...BUT HE WAS SO THICK-HEADED HE'D RETURN THE NEXT EPISODE LIKE NOTHING HAPPENED.
Hallo!

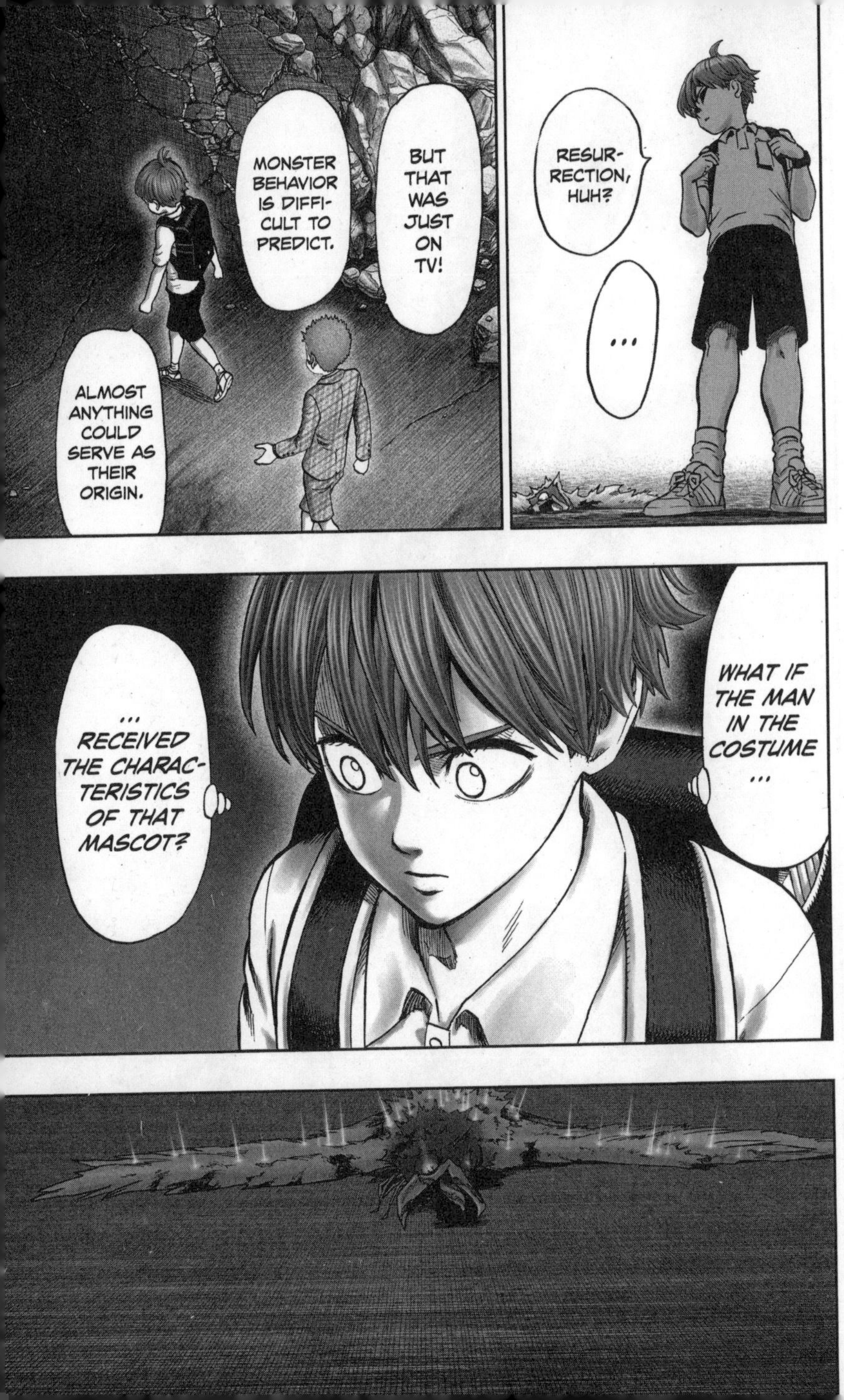
RESUR-RECTION, HUH?
...
BUT THAT WAS JUST ON TV!
MONSTER BEHAVIOR IS DIFFI-CULT TO PREDICT.
ALMOST ANYTHING COULD SERVE AS THEIR ORIGIN.
WHAT IF THE MAN IN THE COSTUME ...
... RECEIVED THE CHARAC-TERISTICS OF THAT MASCOT?

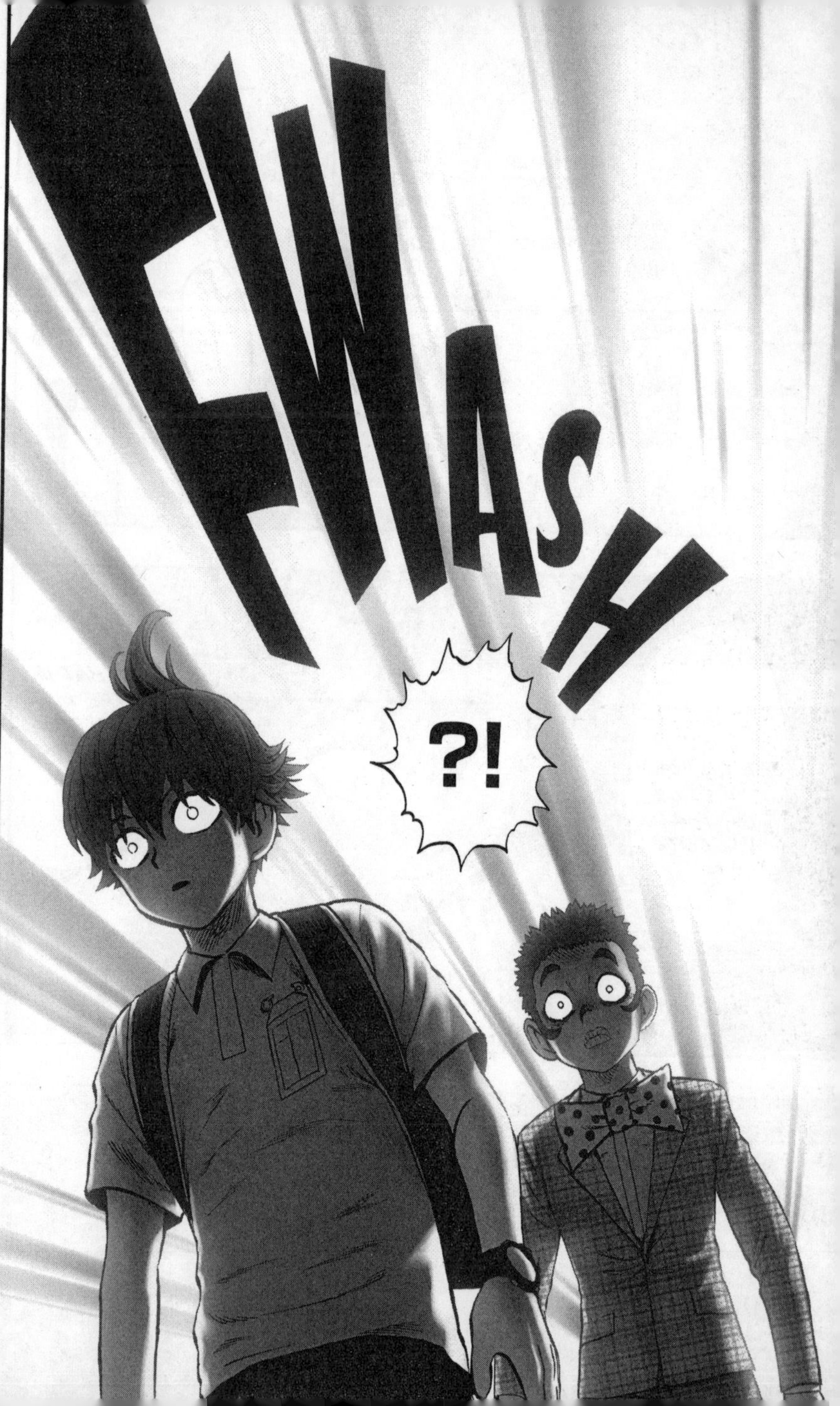
FWASH
?!

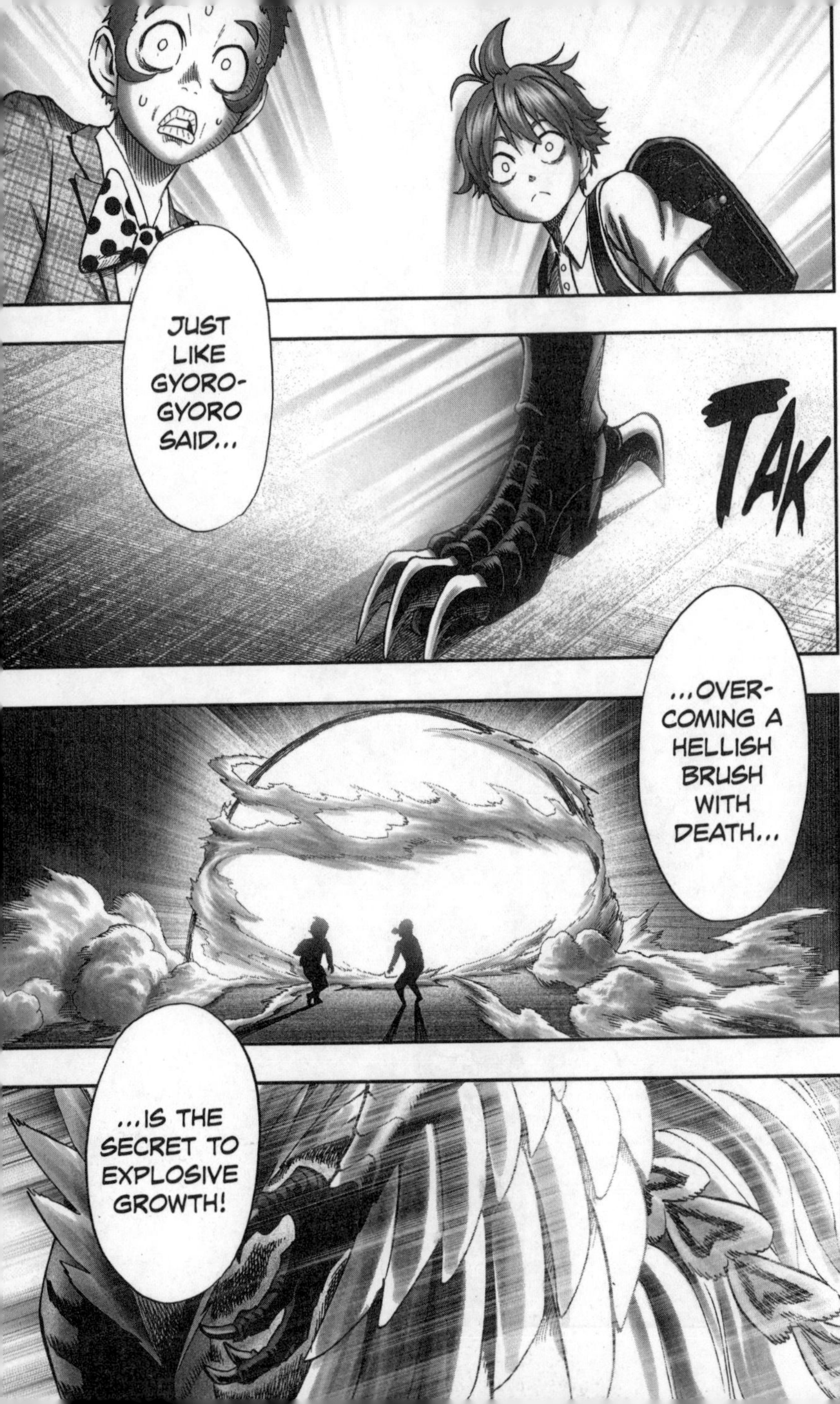
JUST LIKE GYORO-GYORO SAID...
TAK
...OVER-COMING A HELLISH BRUSH WITH DEATH...
...IS THE SECRET TO EXPLOSIVE GROWTH!

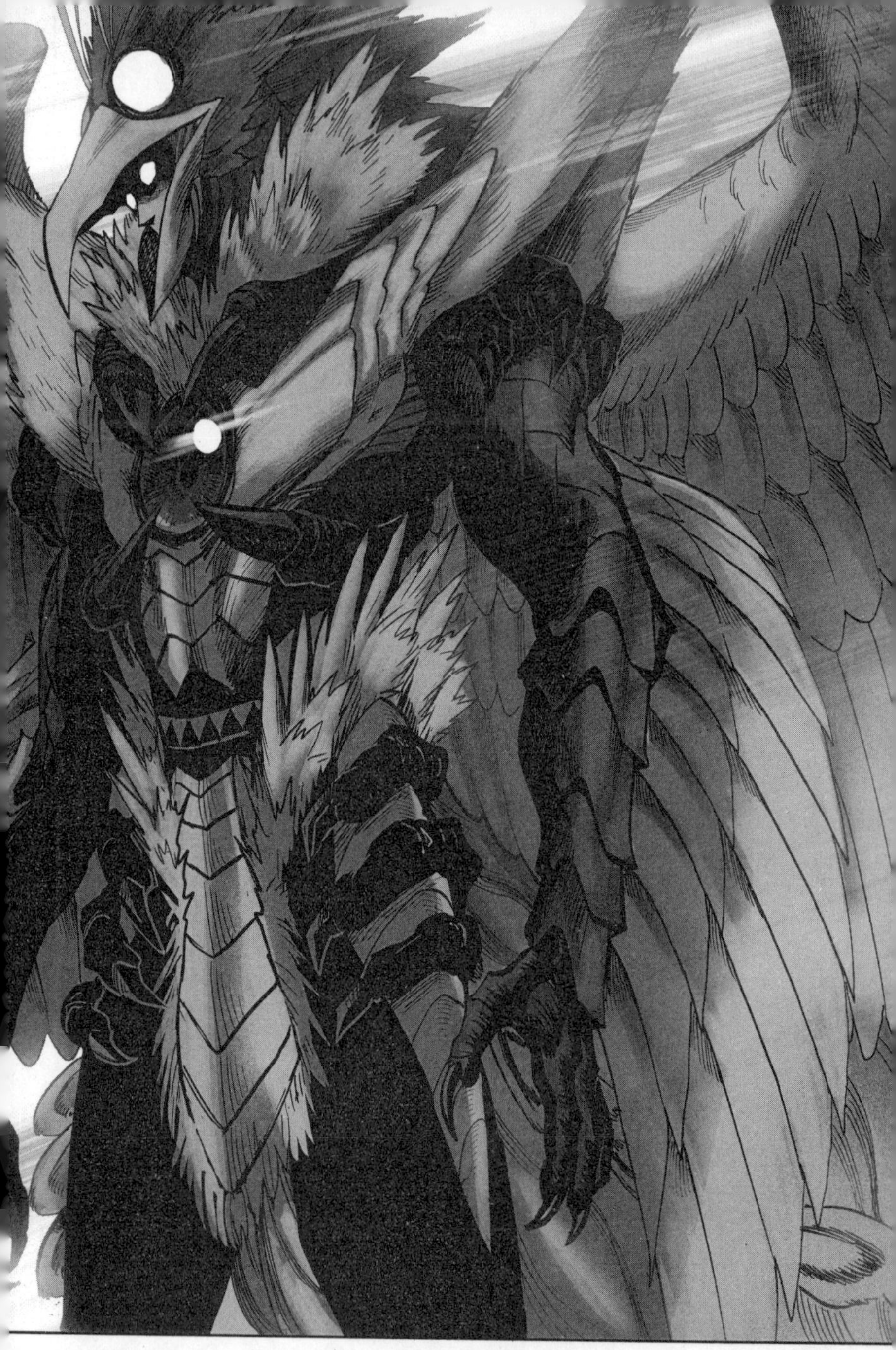

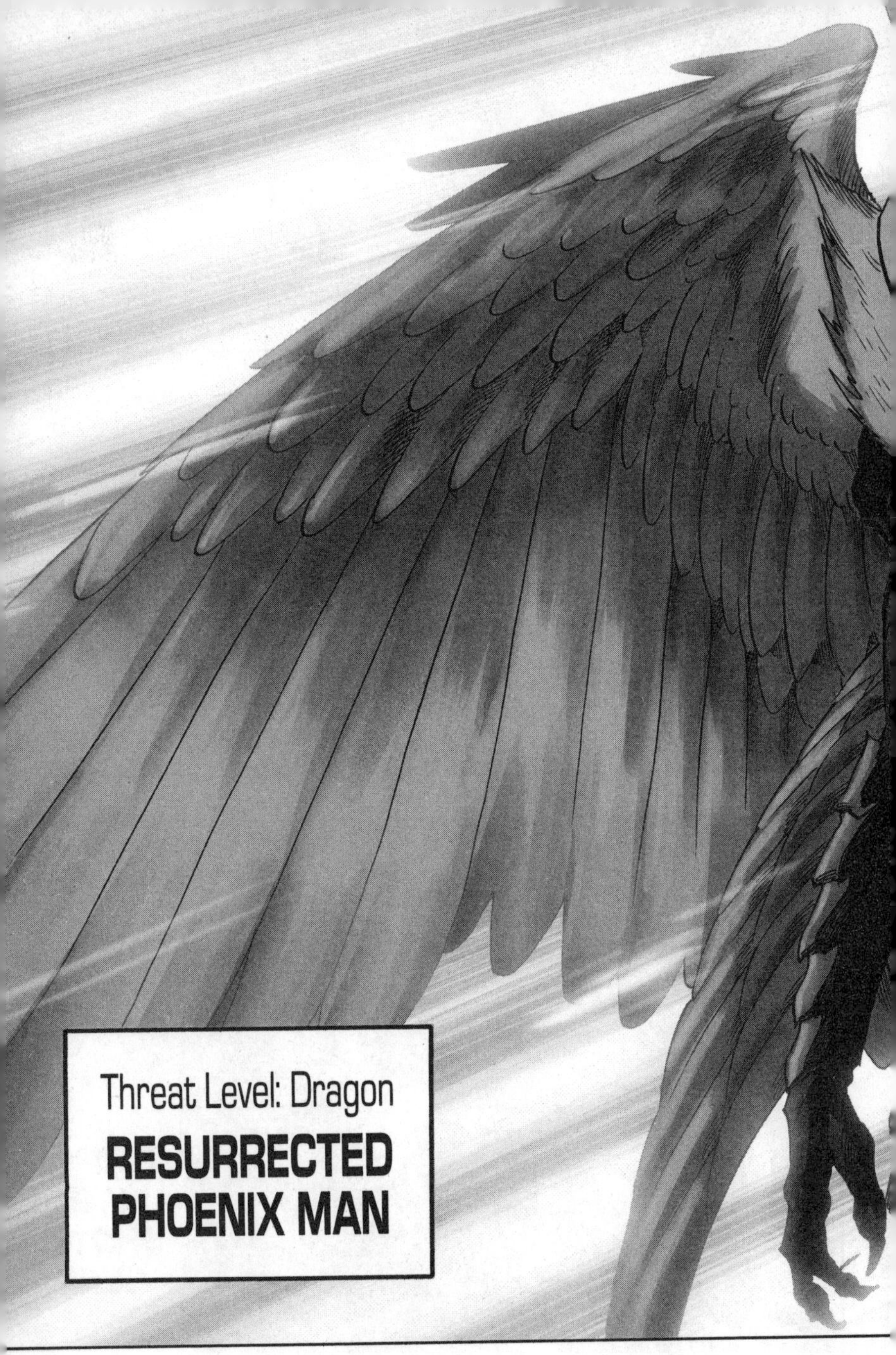
Threat Level: Dragon
RESURRECTED PHOENIX MAN

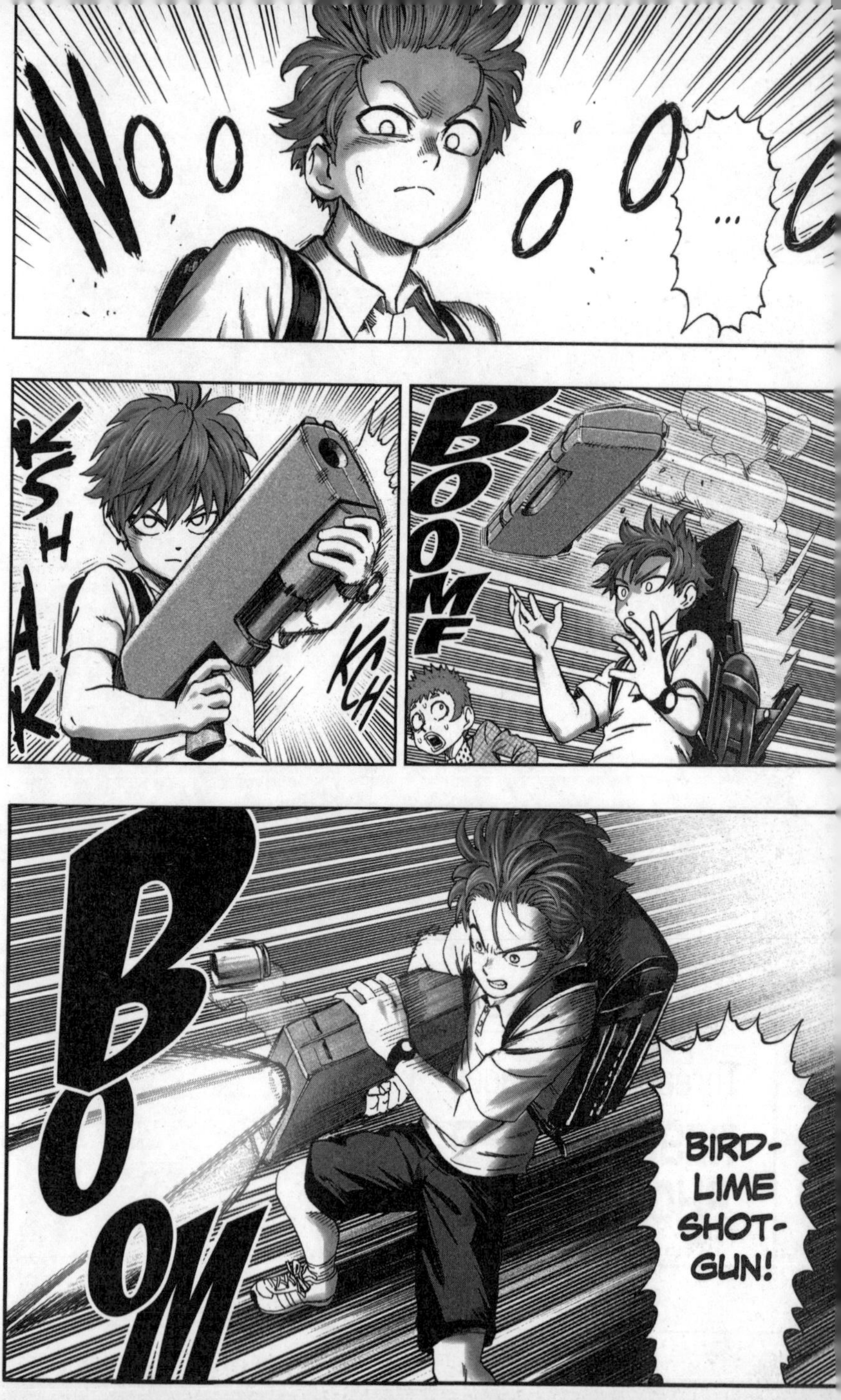
WOOOOOO
...
BOOMF
KSHAK
KCH
BIRD-LIME SHOT-GUN!
BOOM

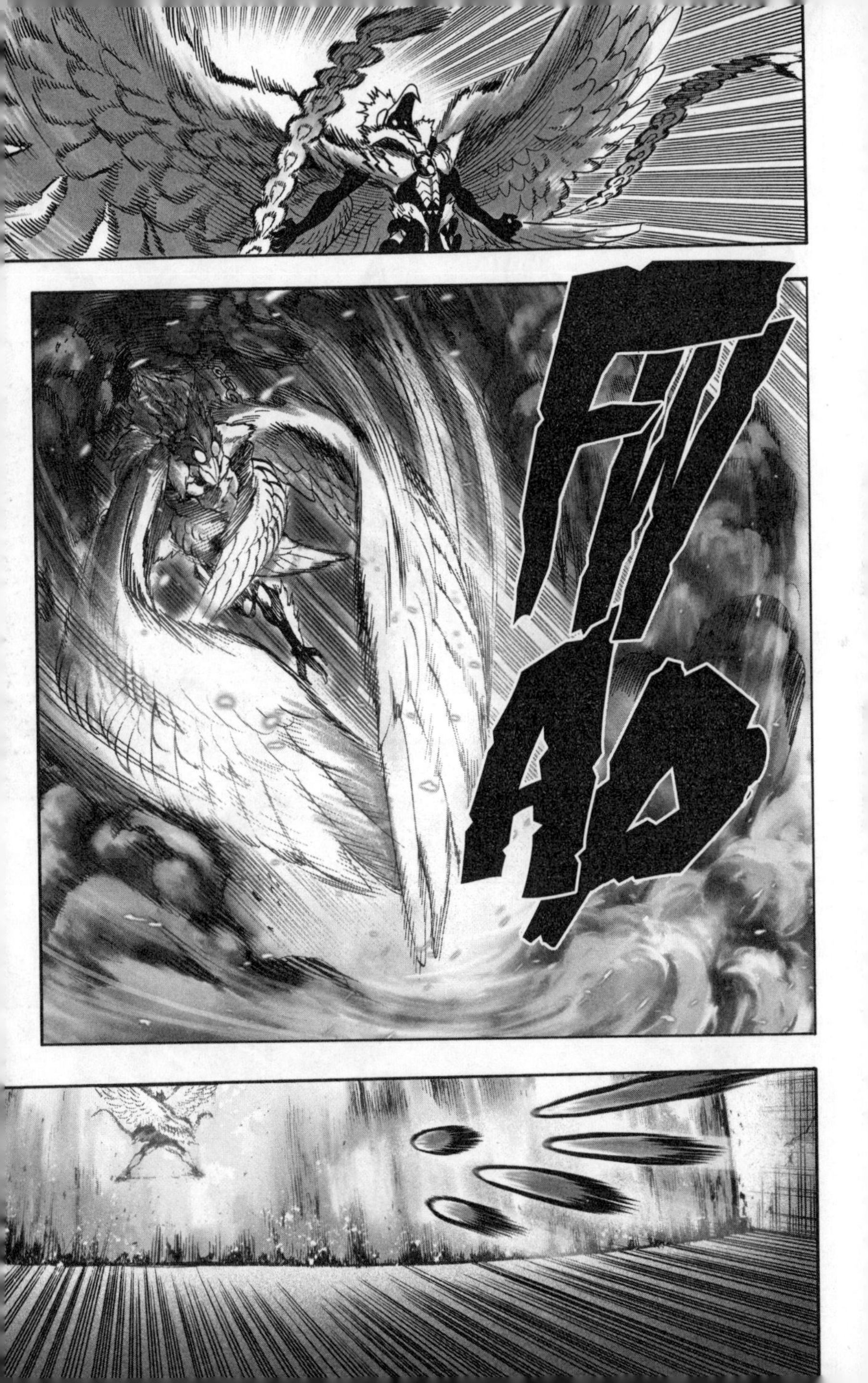

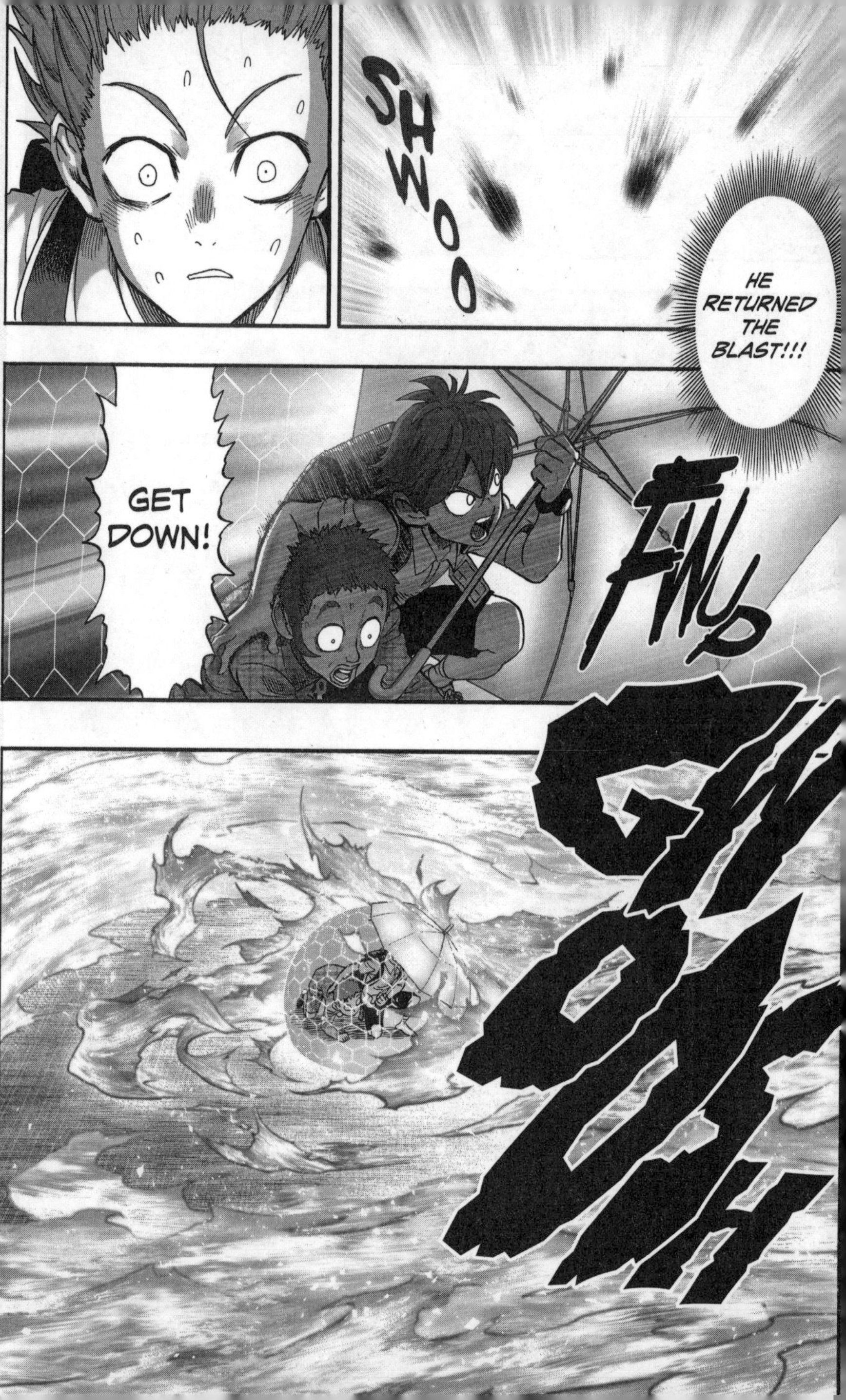
SHWOO
HE RETURNED THE BLAST!!!
GET DOWN!

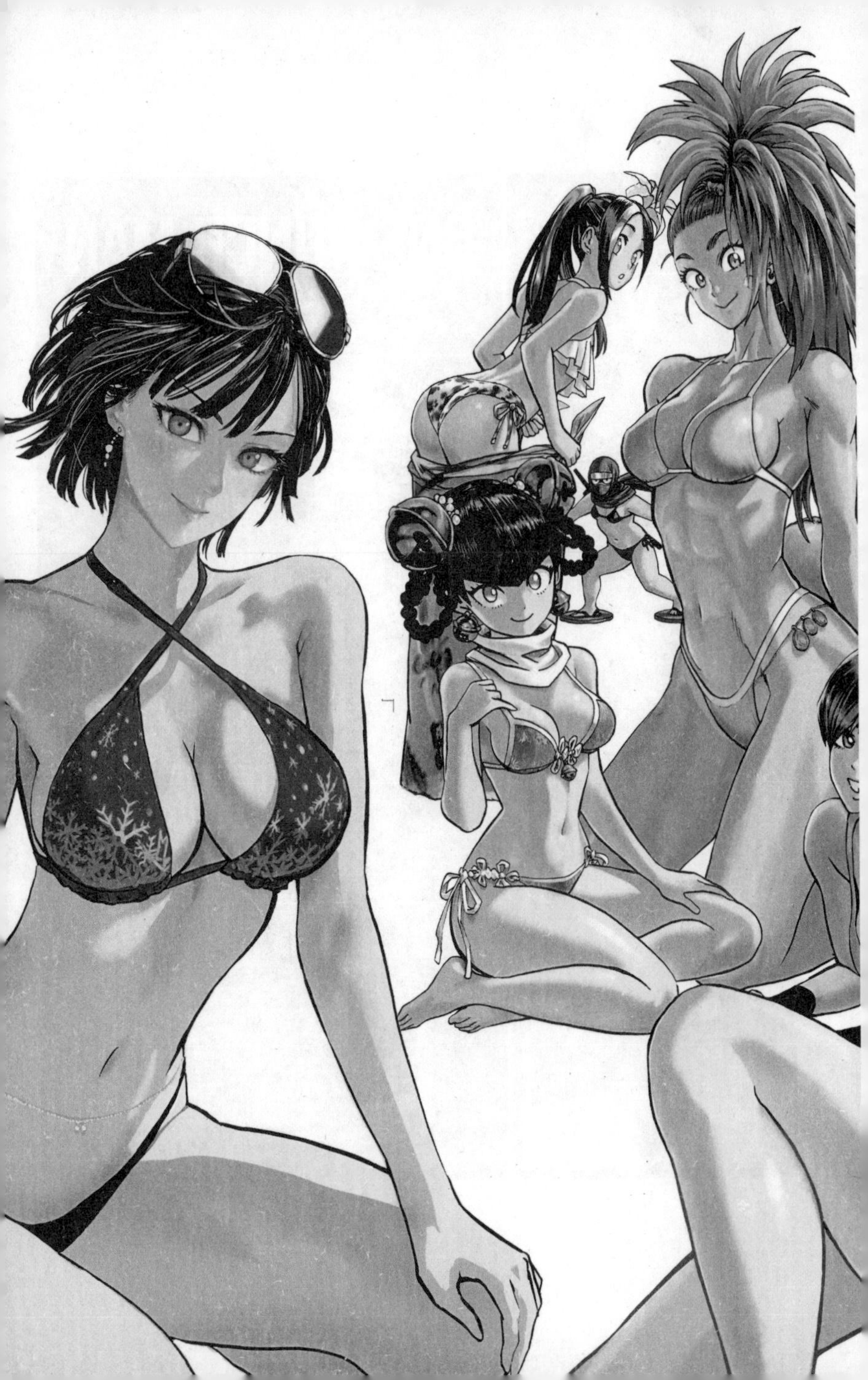

ONE-PUNCH MAN
VOLUME 21
SHONEN JUMP MANGA EDITION

STORY BY | **ONE**
ART BY | **YUSUKE MURATA**

TRANSLATION | JOHN WERRY
TOUCH-UP ART AND LETTERING | JAMES GAUBATZ
DESIGN | SHAWN CARRICO
SHONEN JUMP SERIES EDITOR | JOHN BAE
GRAPHIC NOVEL EDITOR | JENNIFER LEBLANC

ONE-PUNCH MAN © 2012 by ONE, Yusuke Murata
All rights reserved.
First published in Japan in 2012 by SHUEISHA Inc., Tokyo.
English translation rights arranged by SHUEISHA Inc.

The stories, characters and incidents mentioned in this
publication are entirely fictional.

No portion of this book may be reproduced or transmitted in any form
or by any means without written permission from the copyright holders.

Printed in Italy

Published by VIZ Media, LLC
P.O. Box 77010
San Francisco, CA 94107

viz.com

SHONEN JUMP

10 9 8 7 6 5 4 3
First printing, October 2020
Third printing, May 2022

ratings.viz.com

RATED
T
TEEN

PARENTAL ADVISORY
ONE-PUNCH MAN is rated T for Teen and
is recommended for ages 13 and up. This
volume contains realistic and fantasy violence.

DEMON SLAYER

KIMETSU NO YAIBA

Story and Art by

KOYOHARU GOTOUGE

In Taisho-era Japan, kindhearted Tanjiro Kamado makes a living selling charcoal. But his peaceful life is shattered when a demon slaughters his entire family. His little sister Nezuko is the only survivor, but she has been transformed into a demon herself! Tanjiro sets out on a dangerous journey to find a way to return his sister to normal and destroy the demon who ruined his life.

RATED TEEN **VIZ**

KIMETSU NO YAIBA © 2016 by Koyoharu Gotouge/SHUEISHA Inc.

A FUTURISTIC TALE OF SAMURAI ADVENTURE FROM THE CREATOR OF *NARUTO*!

SAMURAI 8
THE TALE OF HACHIMARU

Story by **Masashi Kishimoto**   Art by **Akira Okubo**

Becoming a samurai seems like an impossible dream for Hachimaru, a boy who can't even survive without the help of his father. But when a samurai cat appears before him, his whole life changes! The legendary creator of *Naruto* and a rising manga star come together to bring you this science fiction samurai epic!

SAMURAI8 HACHIMARUDEN © 2019 by Masashi Kishimoto, Akira Okubo/SHUEISHA Inc.

RATED TEEN   VIZ

Ruby, Weiss, Blake and Yang are students at Beacon Academy, learning to protect the world of Remnant from the fearsome Grimm!

RWBY

MANGA BY **Shirow Miwa**
BASED ON THE ROOSTER TEETH SERIES
CREATED BY **Monty Oum**

RWBY © 2017 Rooster Teeth Productions, LLC
© 2015 by Shirow Miwa/SHUEISHA Inc.

RATED
T
TEEN

VIZ
viz.com

ASTRA
LOST IN SPACE

CAN EIGHT TEENAGERS FIND THEIR WAY HOME FROM 5,000 LIGHT-YEARS AWAY?

It's the year 2063, and interstellar space travel has become the norm. Eight students from Caird High School and one child set out on a routine planet camp excursion. While there, the students are mysteriously transported 5,000 light-years away to the middle of nowhere! Will they ever make it back home?!

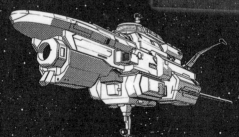

KANATA NO ASTRA © 2016 by Kenta Shinohara/SHUEISHA Inc.

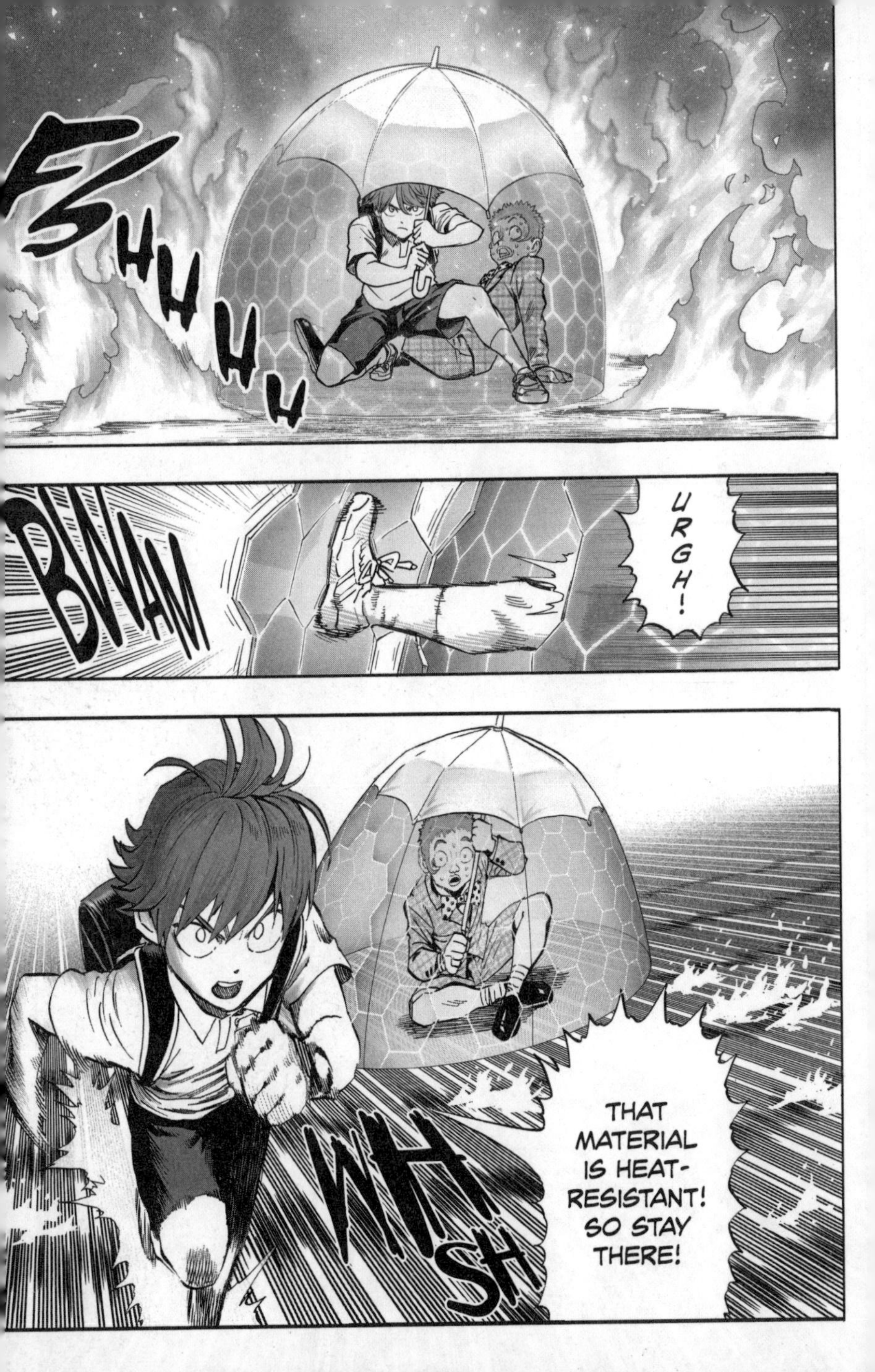
FSHHHHHH
URGH!
BWAM
THAT MATERIAL IS HEAT-RESISTANT! SO STAY THERE!
WHSH

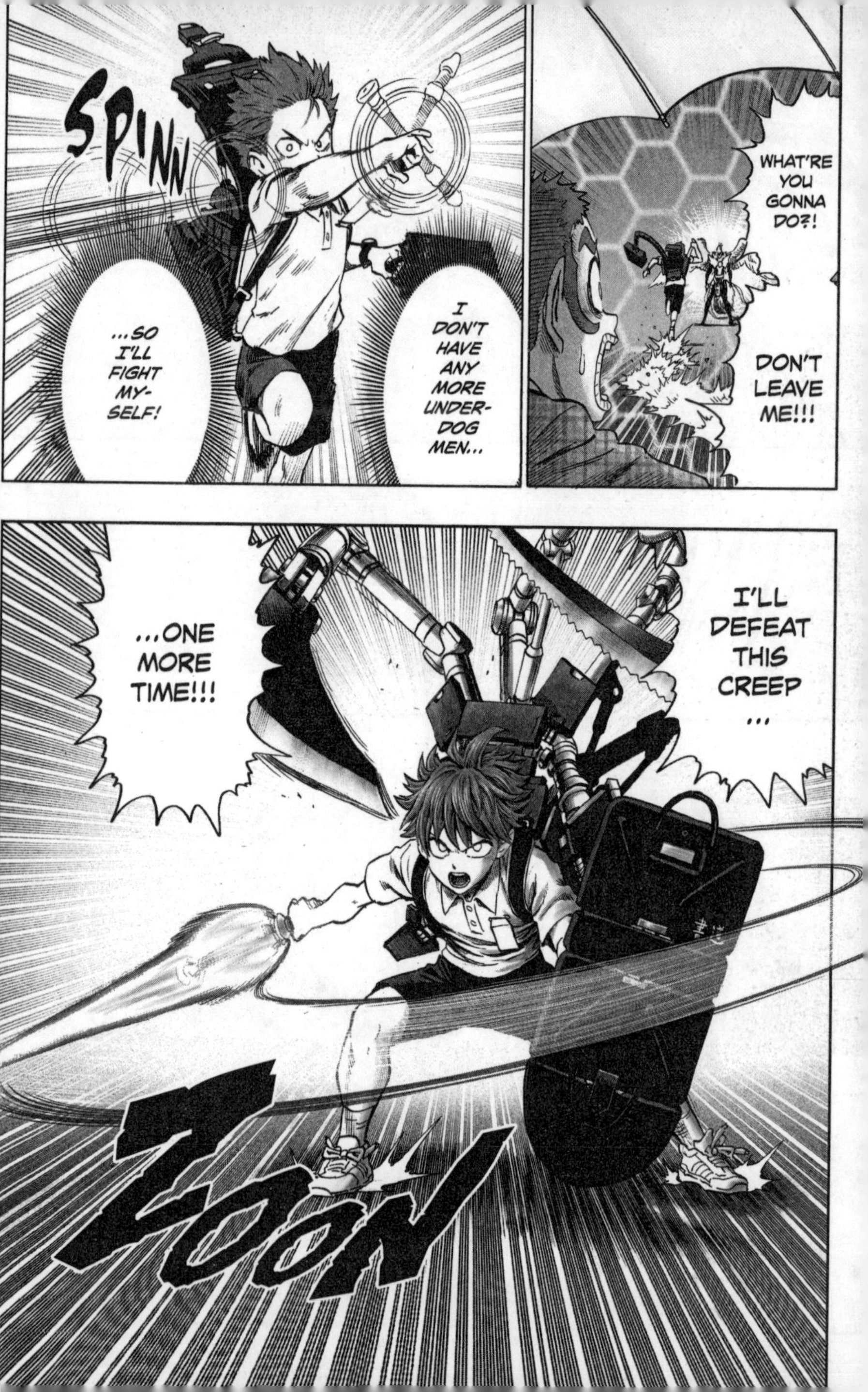
WHAT'RE YOU GONNA DO?!
DON'T LEAVE ME!!!
I DON'T HAVE ANY MORE UNDER-DOG MEN...
...SO I'LL FIGHT MY-SELF!
SPINN
I'LL DEFEAT THIS CREEP ...
...ONE MORE TIME!!!

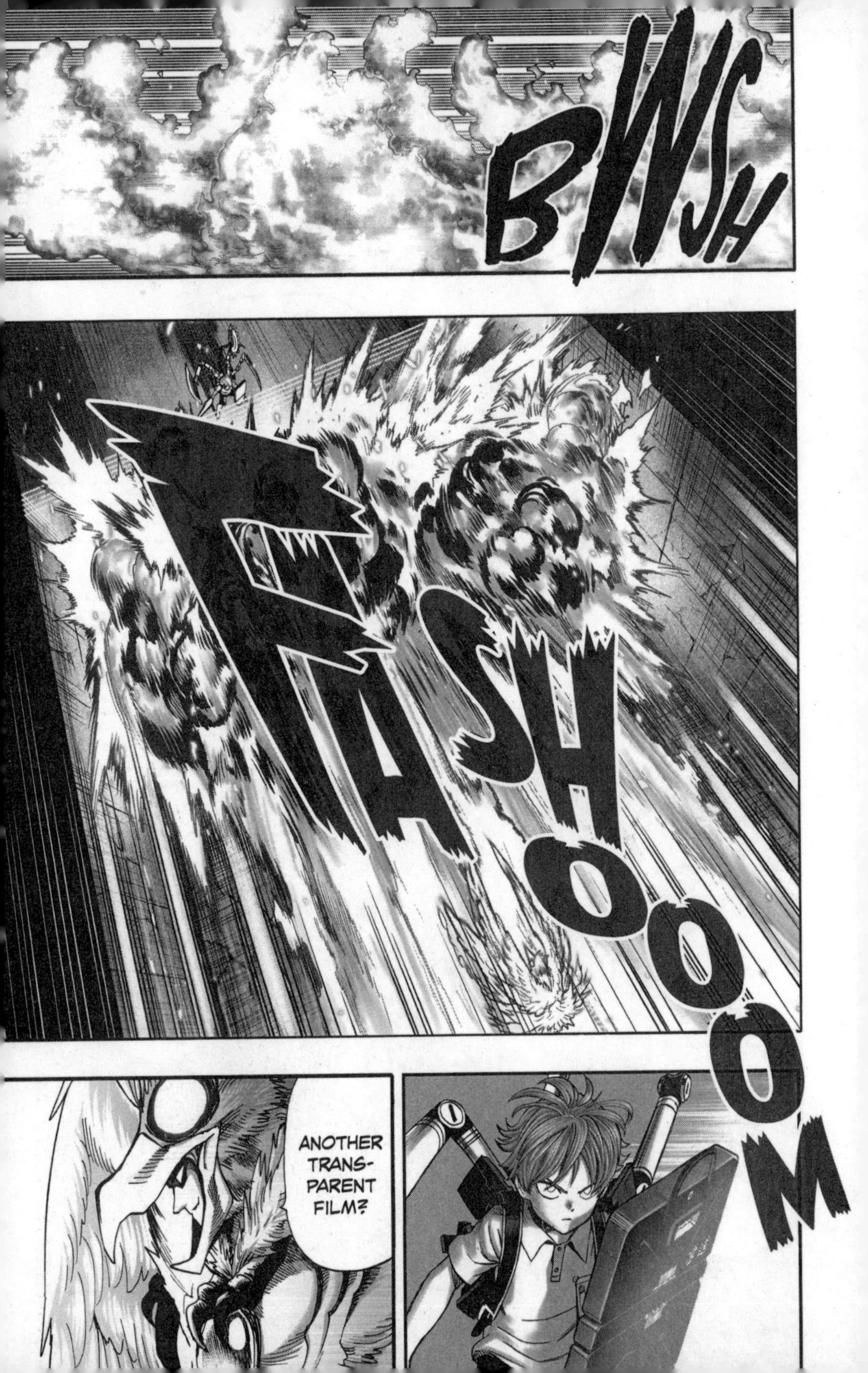
BWSH
FASHOOOOM
ANOTHER TRANS-PARENT FILM?

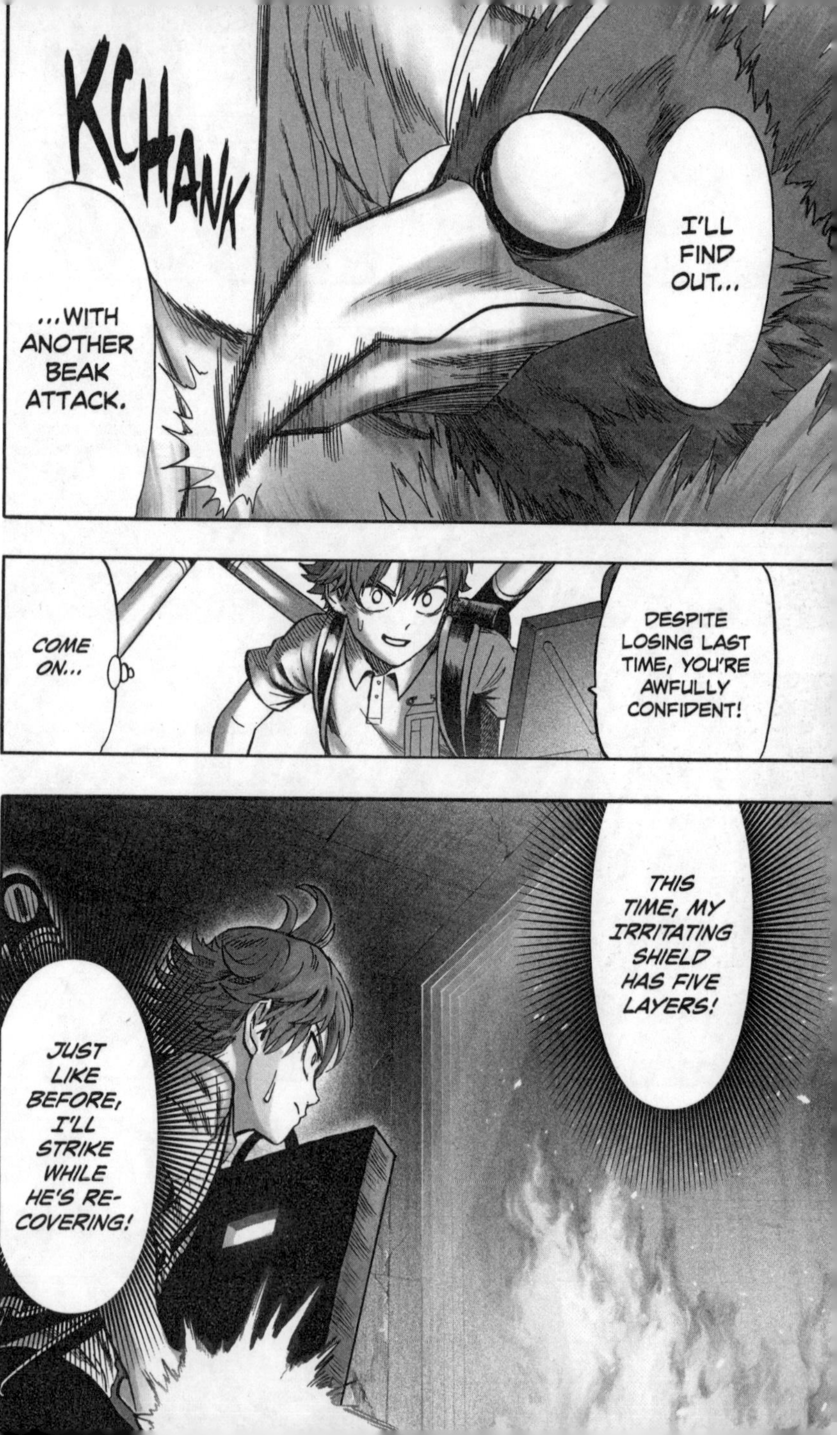
I'LL FIND OUT...
KCHANK
...WITH ANOTHER BEAK ATTACK.
DESPITE LOSING LAST TIME, YOU'RE AWFULLY CONFIDENT!
COME ON...
THIS TIME, MY IRRITATING SHIELD HAS FIVE LAYERS!
JUST LIKE BEFORE, I'LL STRIKE WHILE HE'S RE-COVERING!

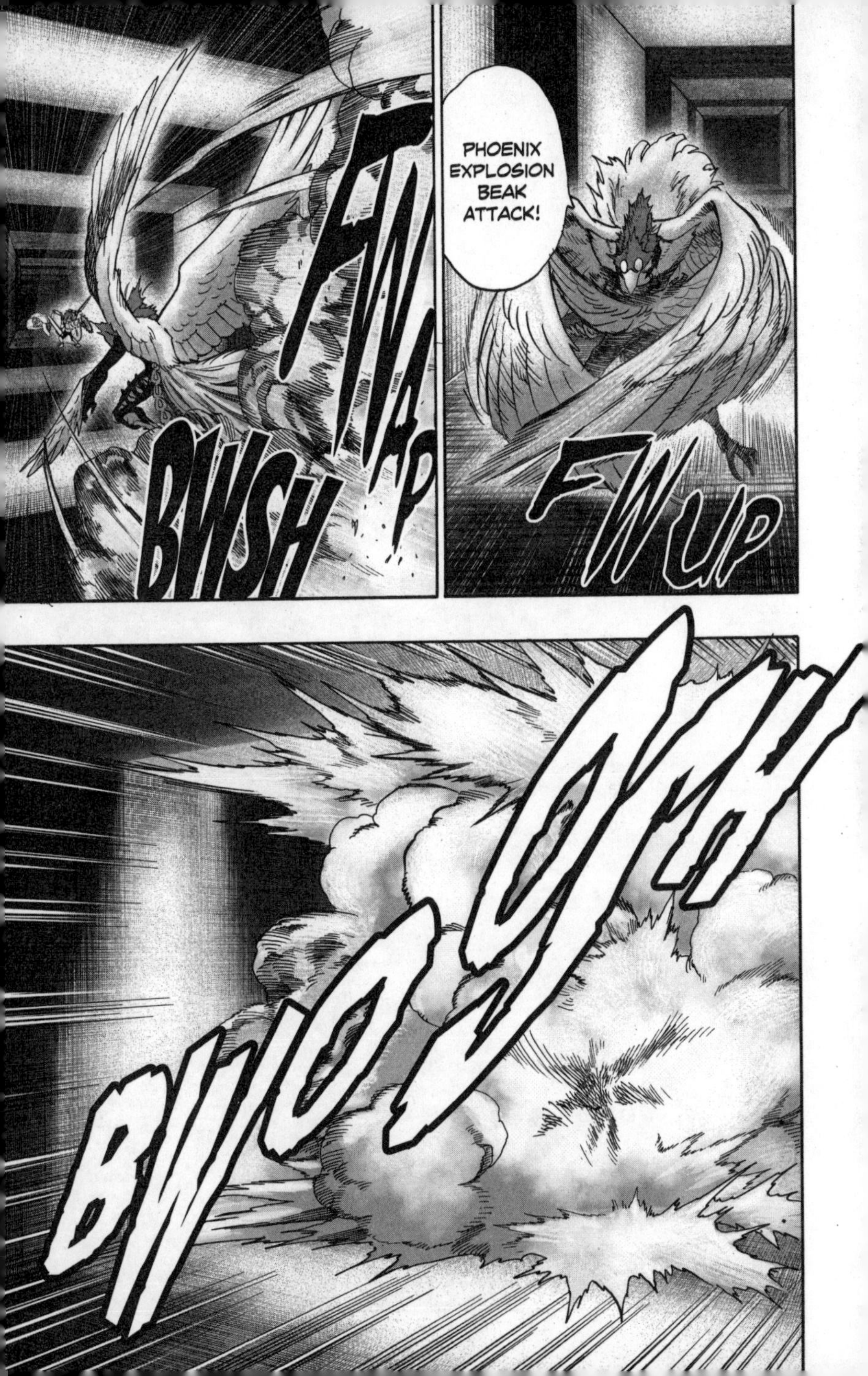
PHOENIX EXPLOSION BEAK ATTACK!
FWUP
FWAP
BWSH
BWOOM

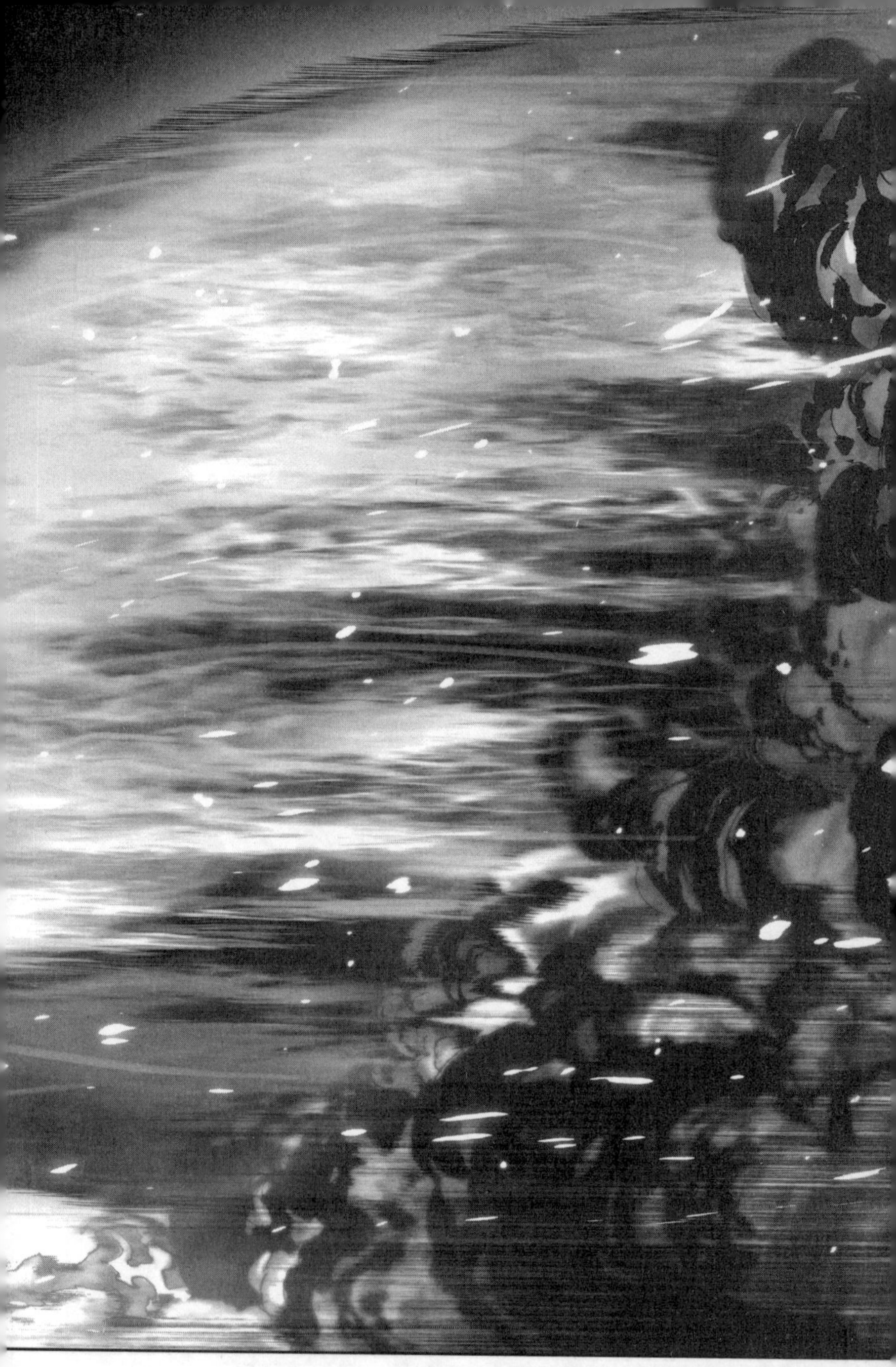

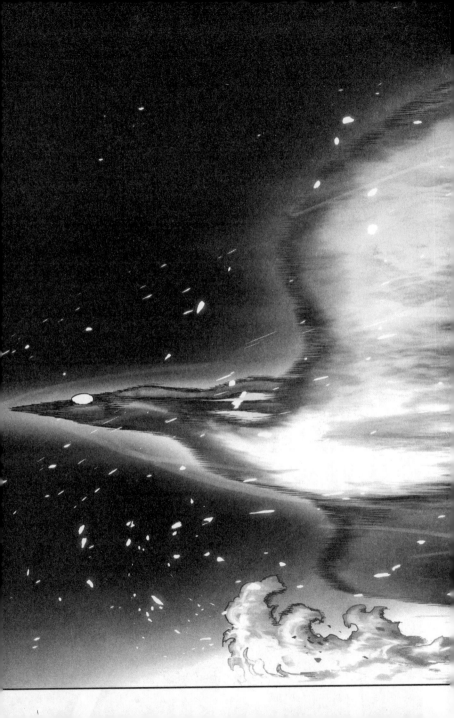

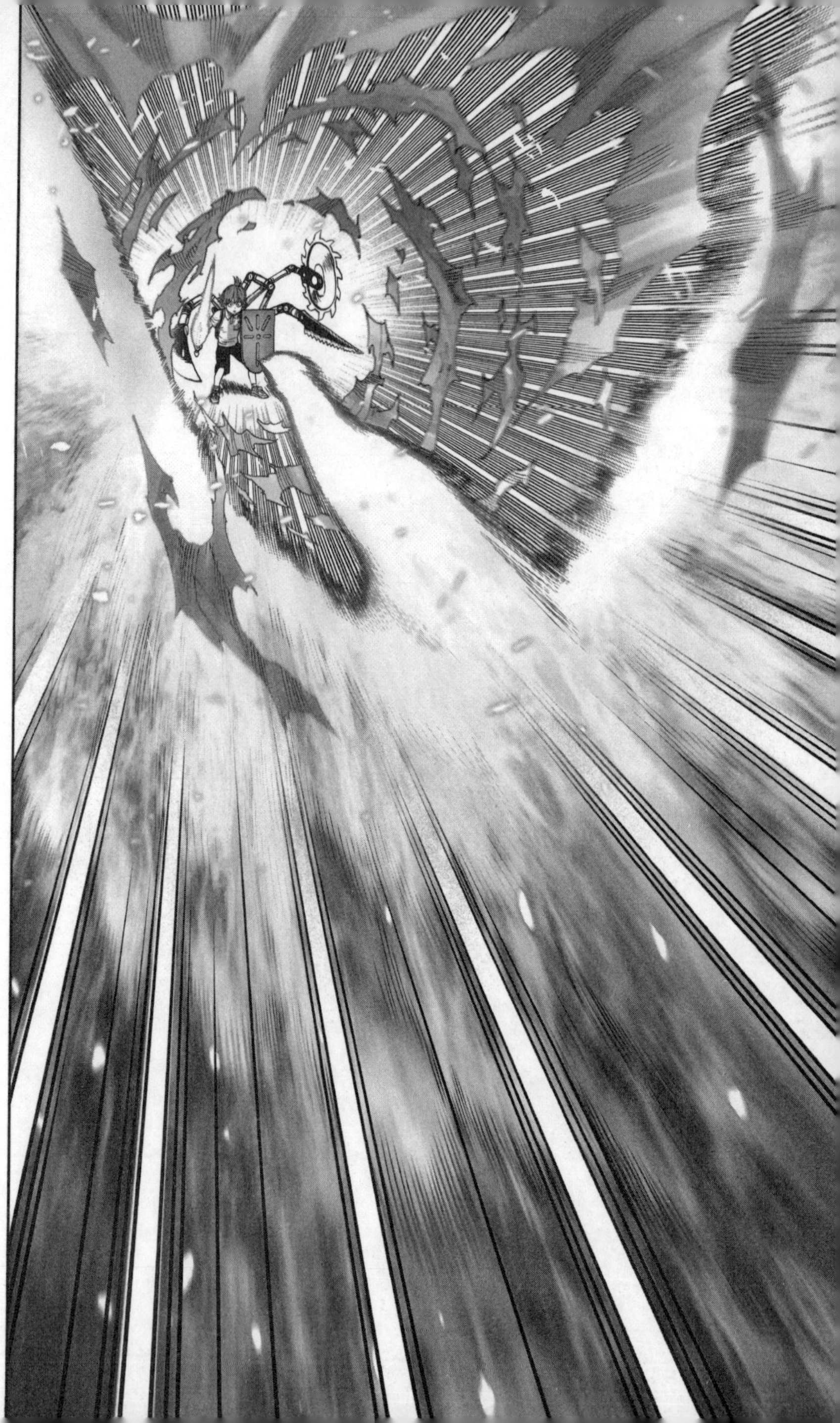

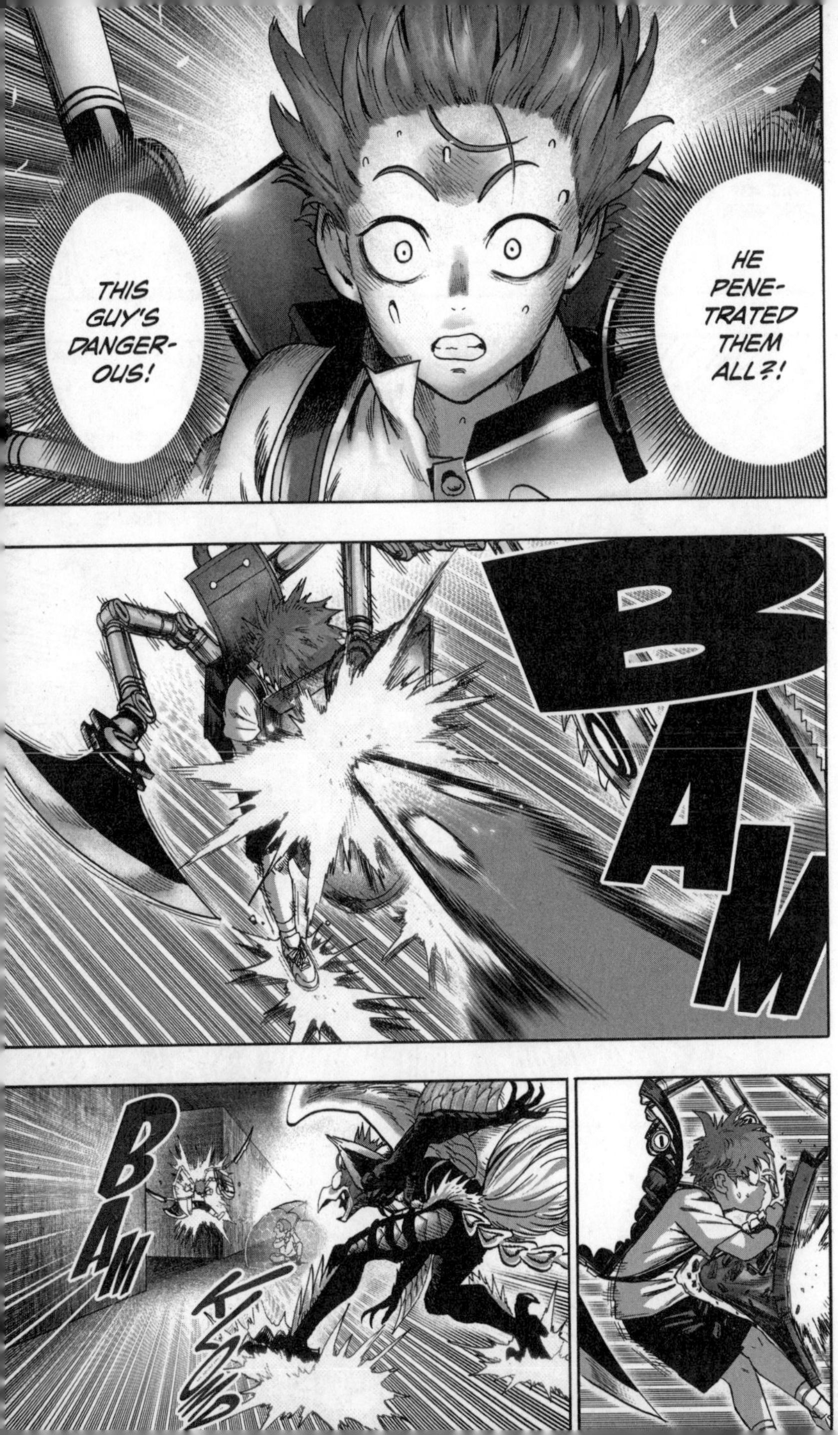
HE PENE-TRATED THEM ALL?!
THIS GUY'S DANGER-OUS!
BAM
BAM

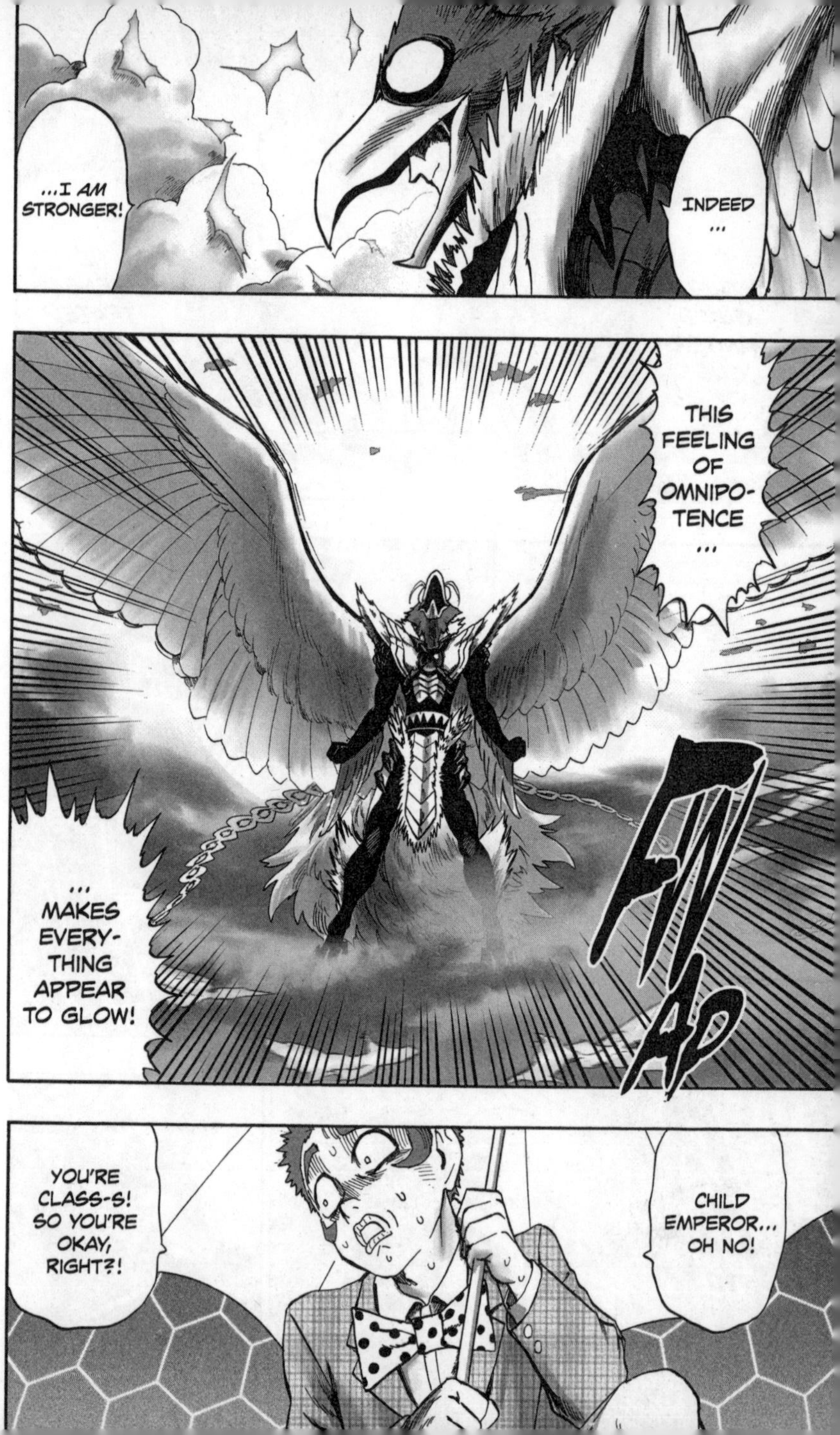
INDEED ...
...I AM STRONGER!
THIS FEELING OF OMNIPOTENCE ...
FWAP
... MAKES EVERYTHING APPEAR TO GLOW!
CHILD EMPEROR... OH NO!
YOU'RE CLASS-S! SO YOU'RE OKAY, RIGHT?!

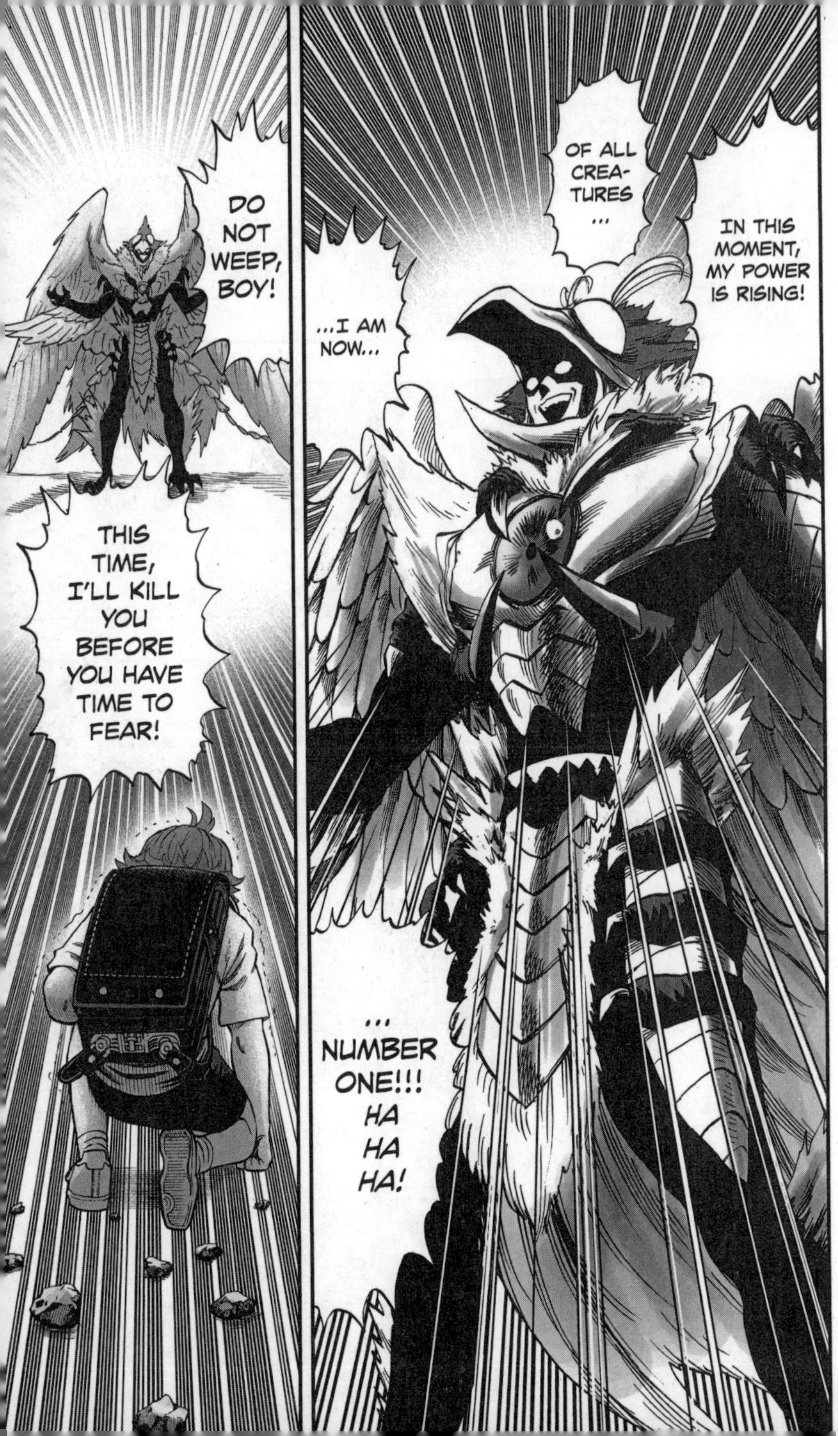
IN THIS MOMENT, MY POWER IS RISING!
OF ALL CREATURES...
...I AM NOW...
...NUMBER ONE!!! HA HA HA!
DO NOT WEEP, BOY!
THIS TIME, I'LL KILL YOU BEFORE YOU HAVE TIME TO FEAR!

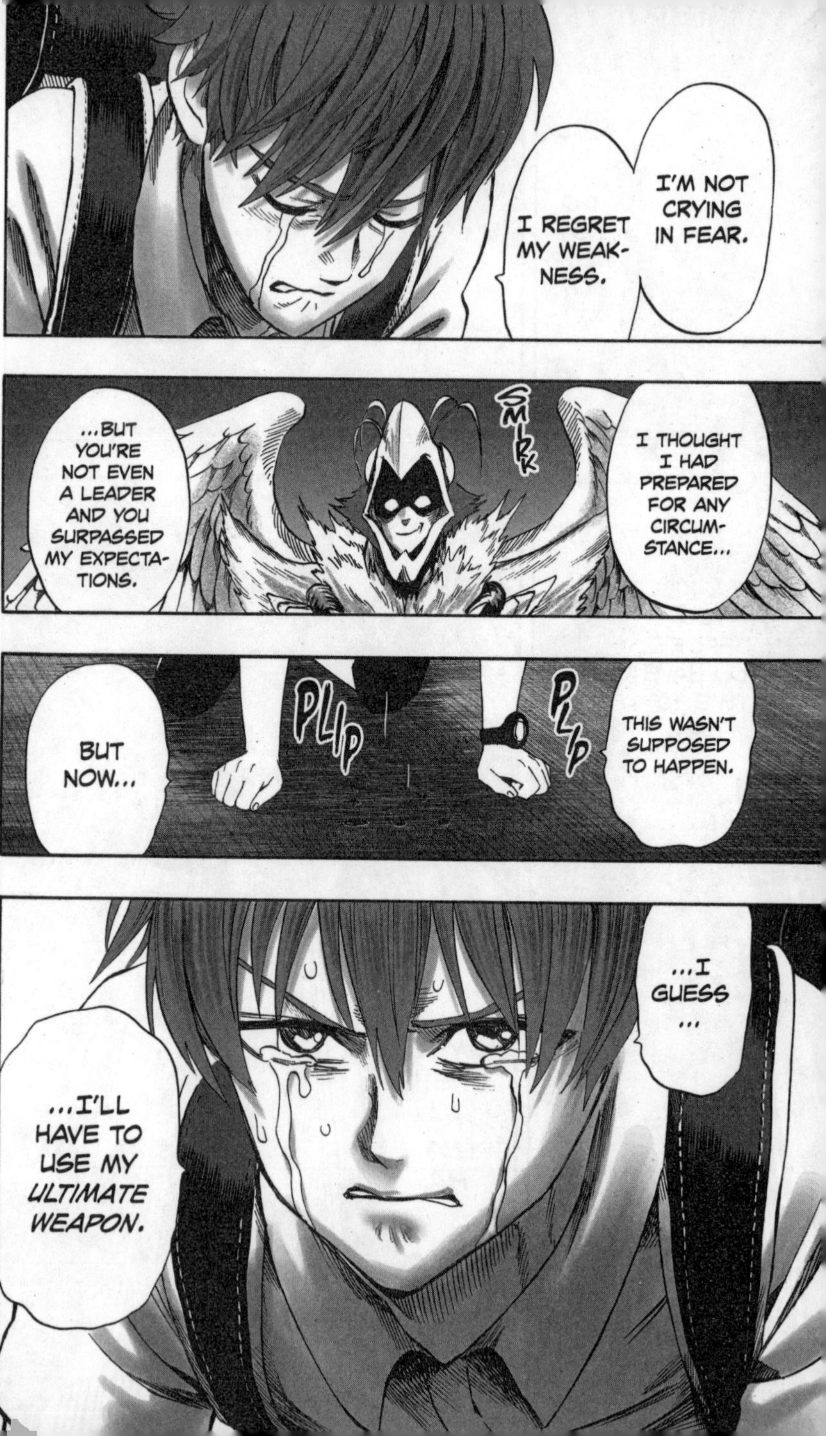
I'M NOT CRYING IN FEAR.
I REGRET MY WEAK-NESS.
I THOUGHT I HAD PREPARED FOR ANY CIRCUM-STANCE...
SMIRK
...BUT YOU'RE NOT EVEN A LEADER AND YOU SURPASSED MY EXPECTA-TIONS.
THIS WASN'T SUPPOSED TO HAPPEN.
PLIP
PLIP
BUT NOW...
...I GUESS ...
...I'LL HAVE TO USE MY ULTIMATE WEAPON.

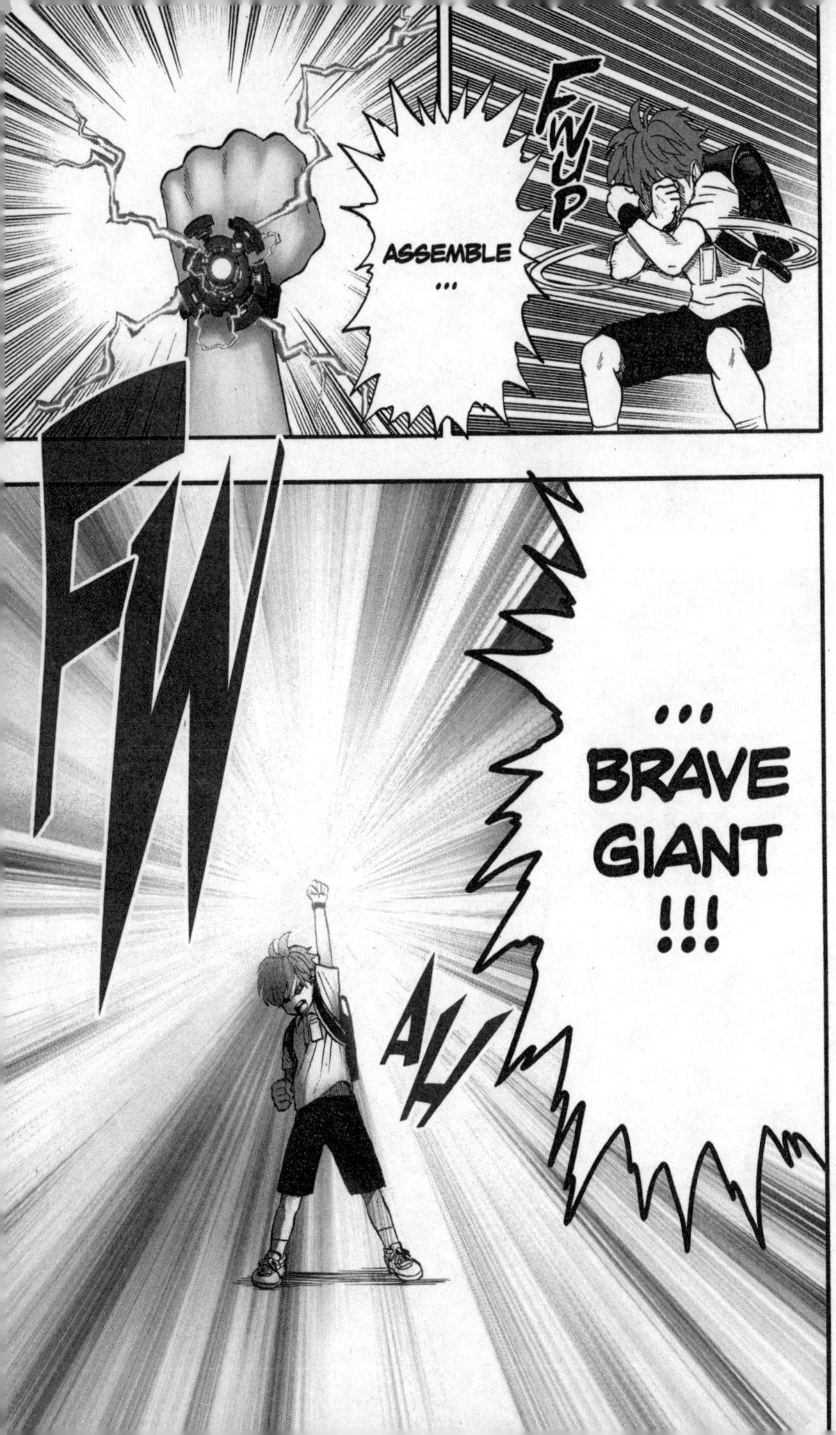
FWUP
ASSEMBLE ...
... BRAVE GIANT !!!
FW
AH

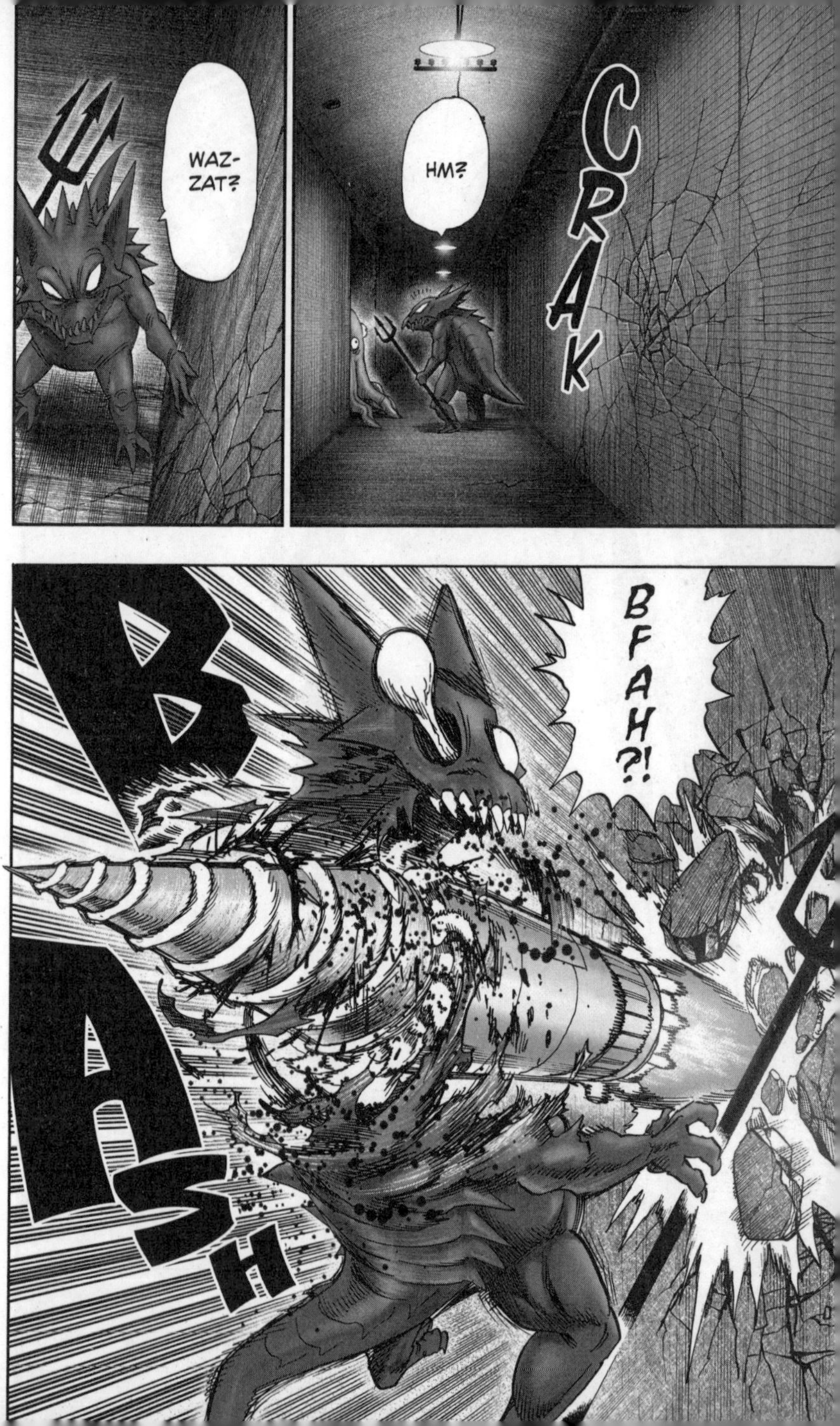
HM?
CRAK
WAZ-ZAT?
BFAH?!
BASH

NO...

MORE MON-STERS?!

WHOA!

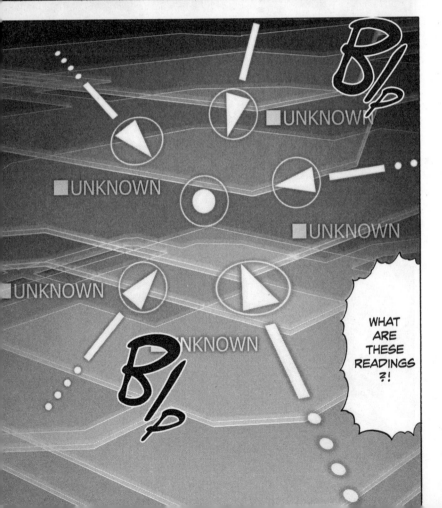

UNKNOWN

UNKNOWN

UNKNOWN

UNKNOWN

UNKNOWN

WHAT ARE THESE READINGS ?!

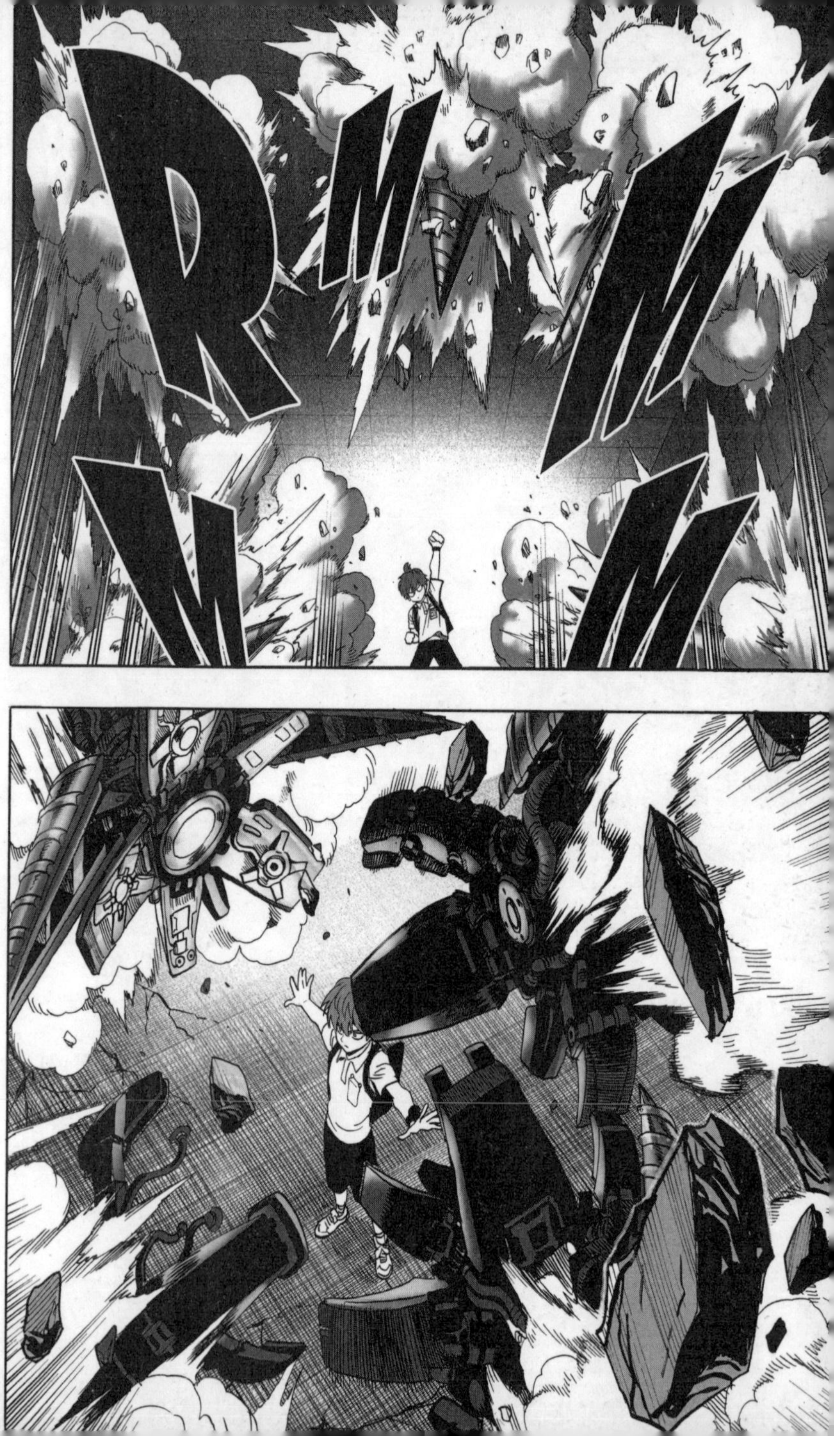

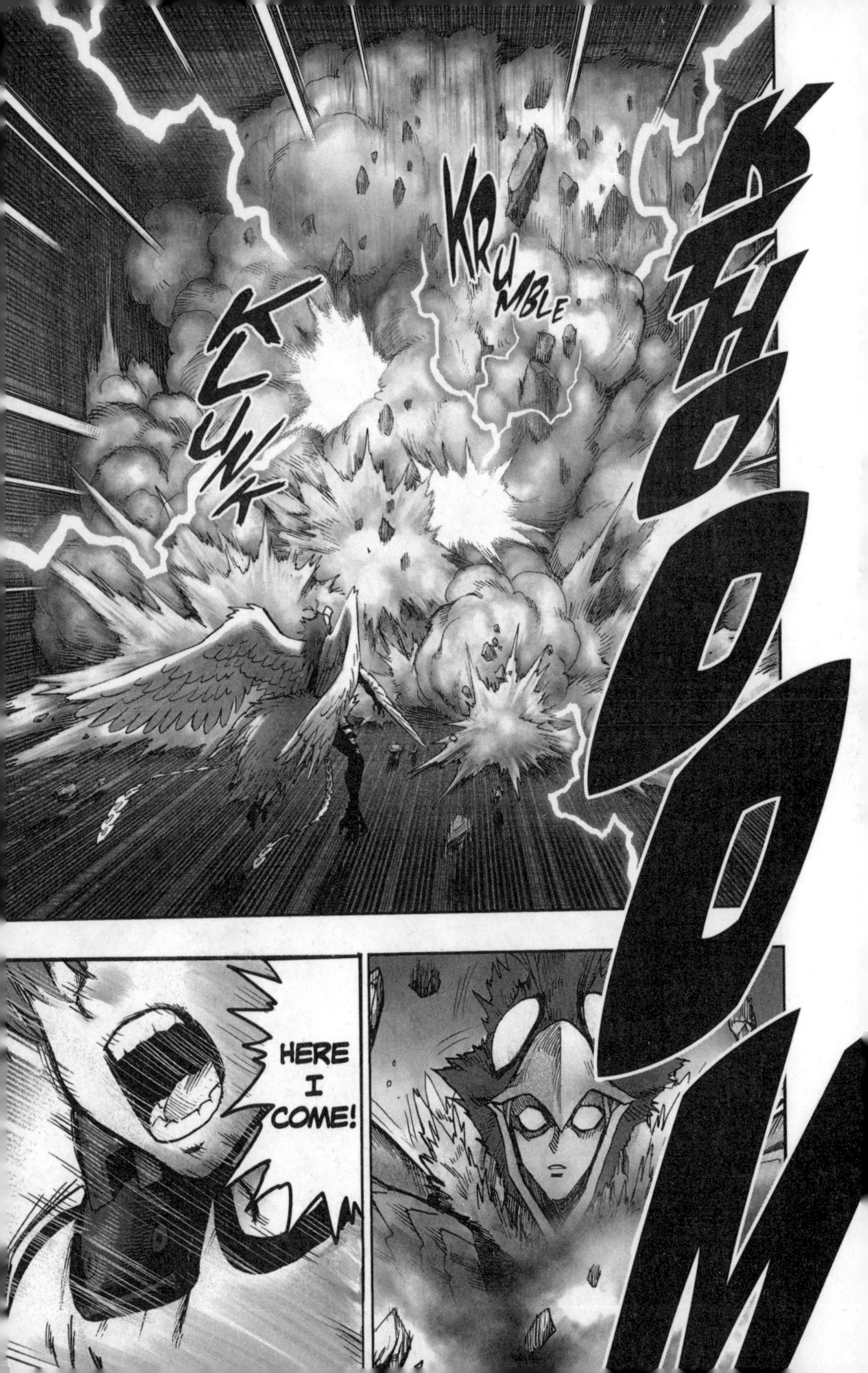
KABOOOM
KRUMBLE
KLUNK
HERE I COME!

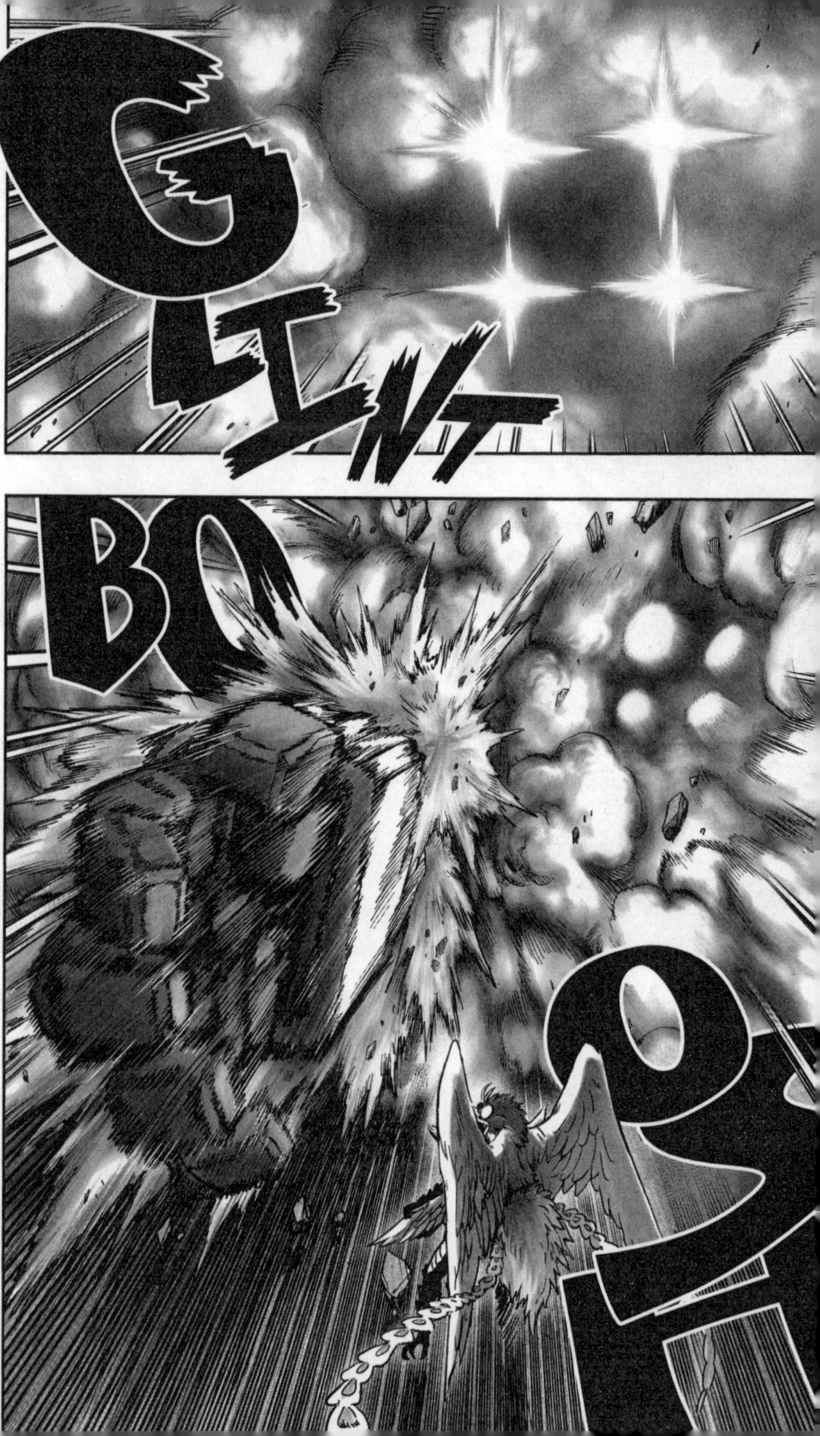
GLINT
BO

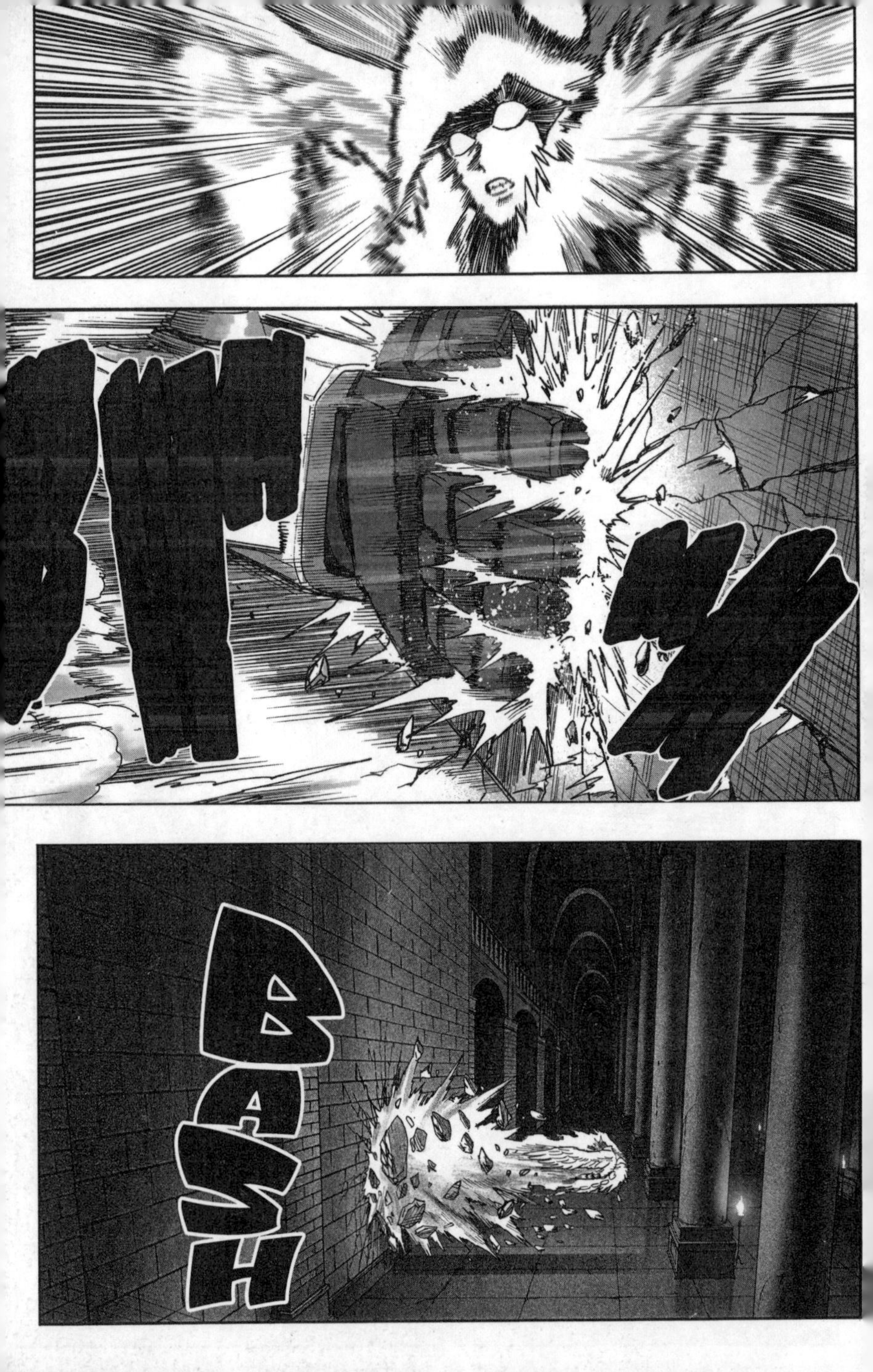
BASH

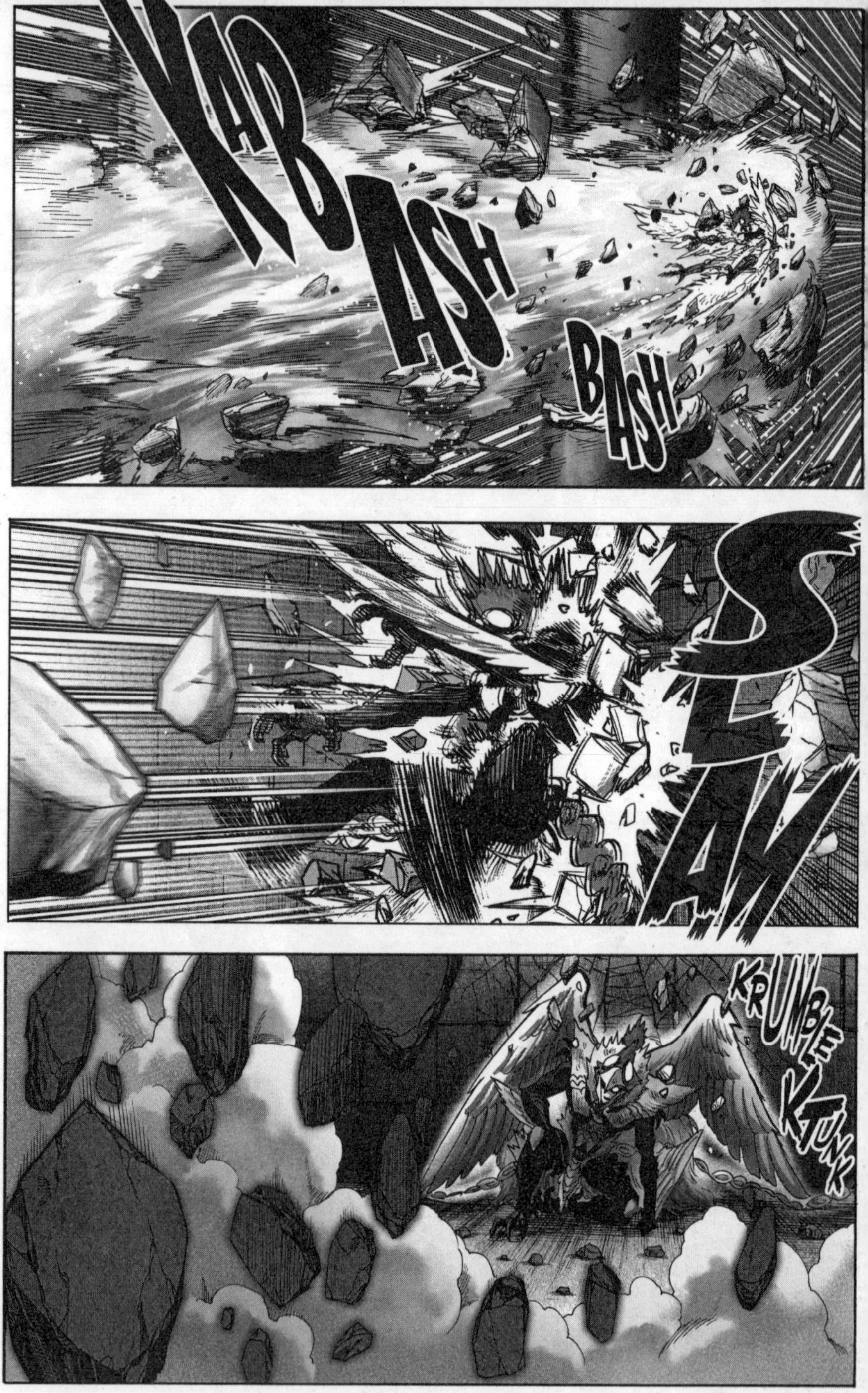
KABASH
BASH
SLAM
KRUMBLE
KTUNK

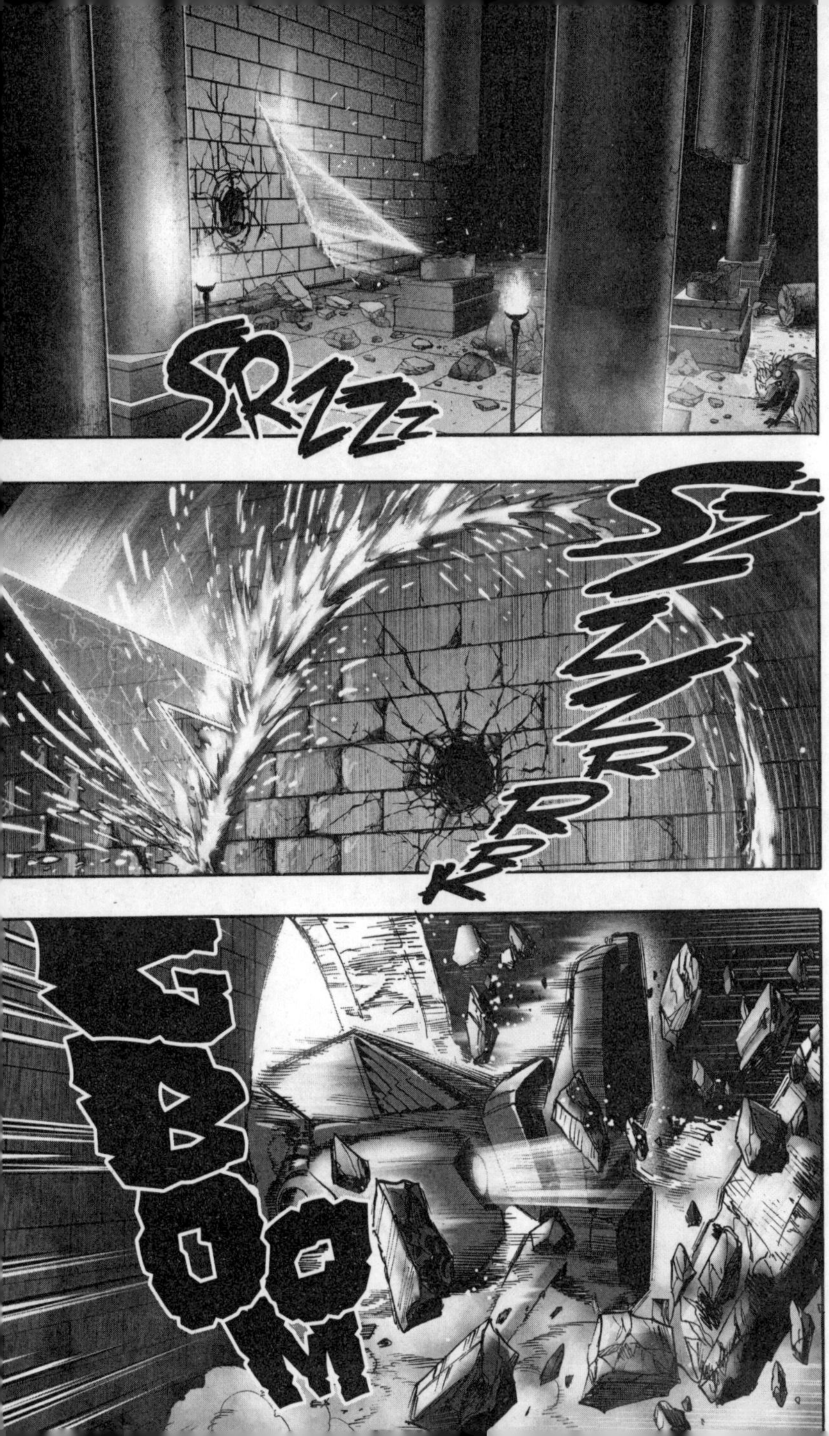
SRZZZz
SZZZRRRK
BOOM

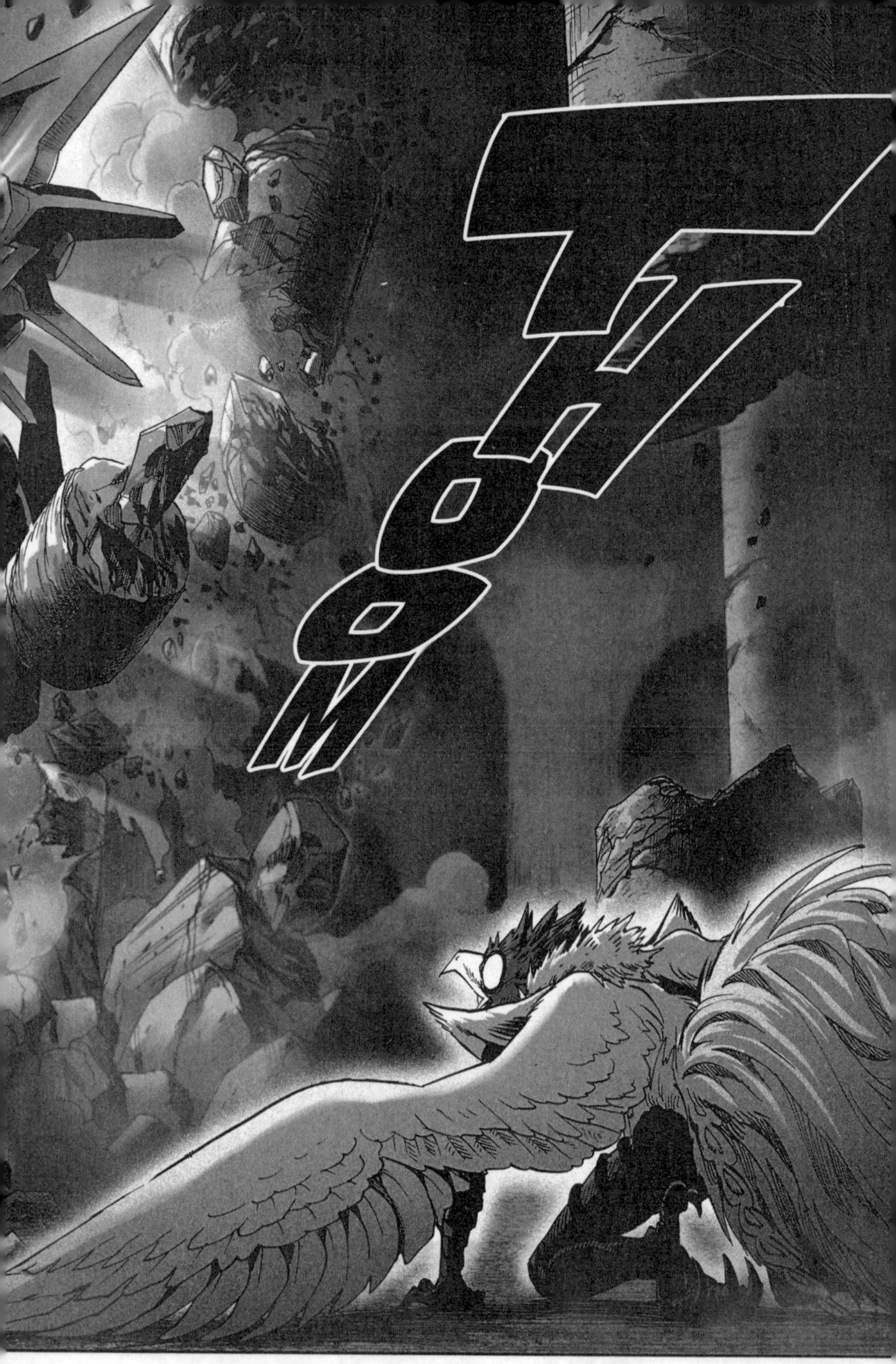
THOOM

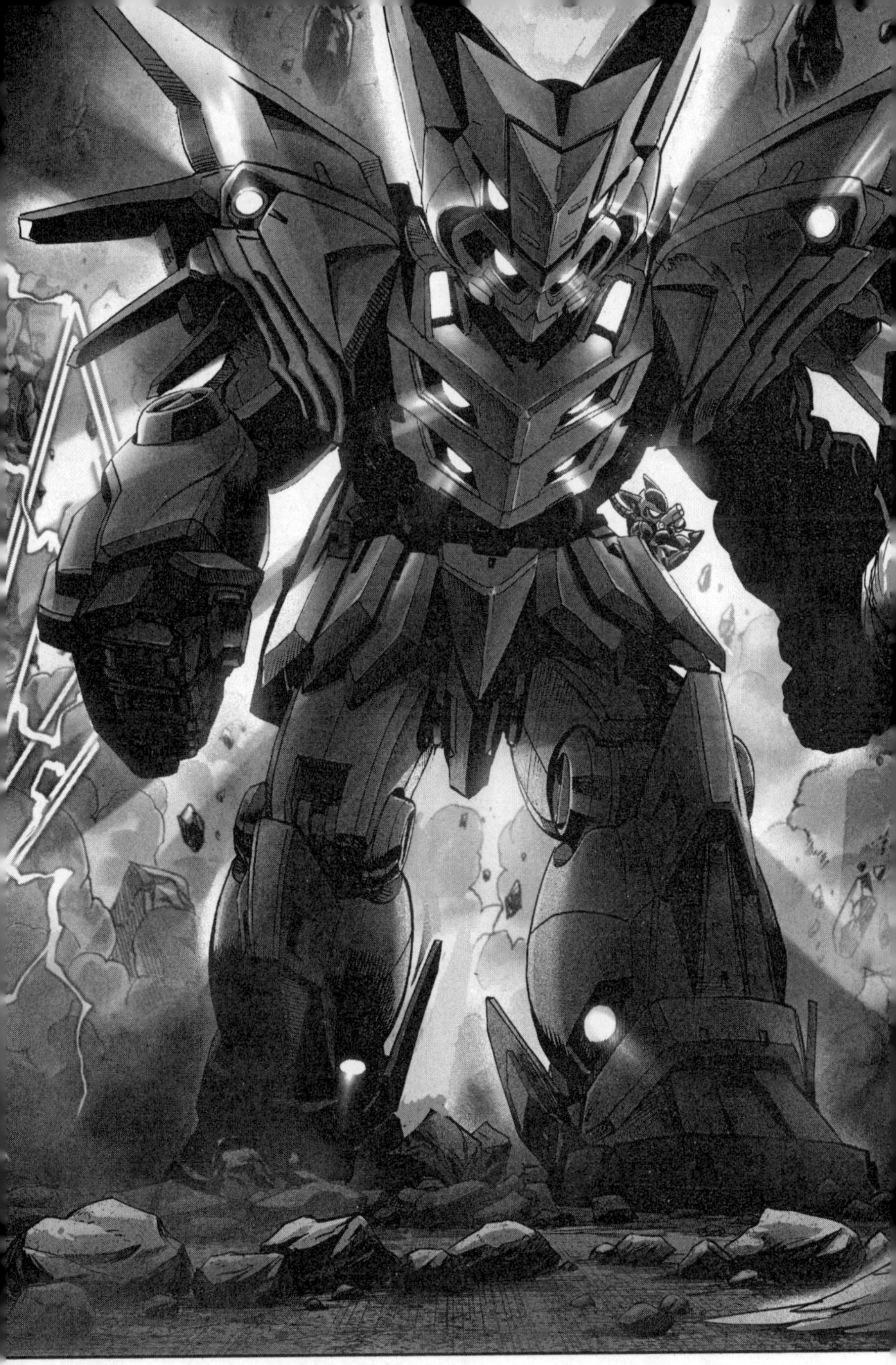

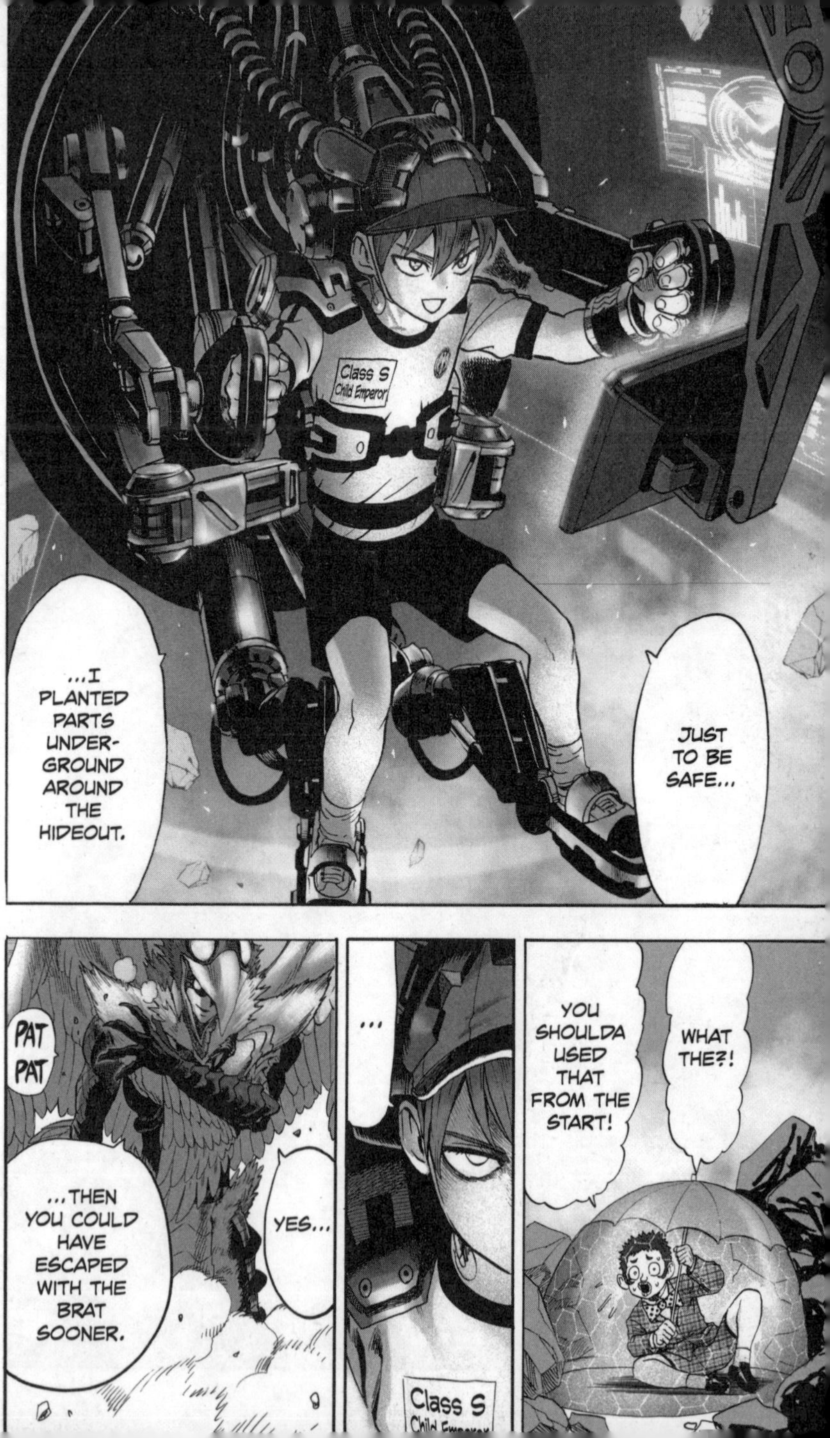
Class S
Child Emperor
JUST TO BE SAFE...
...I PLANTED PARTS UNDERGROUND AROUND THE HIDEOUT.
WHAT THE?!
YOU SHOULDA USED THAT FROM THE START!
...
Class S
PAT PAT
YES...
...THEN YOU COULD HAVE ESCAPED WITH THE BRAT SOONER.

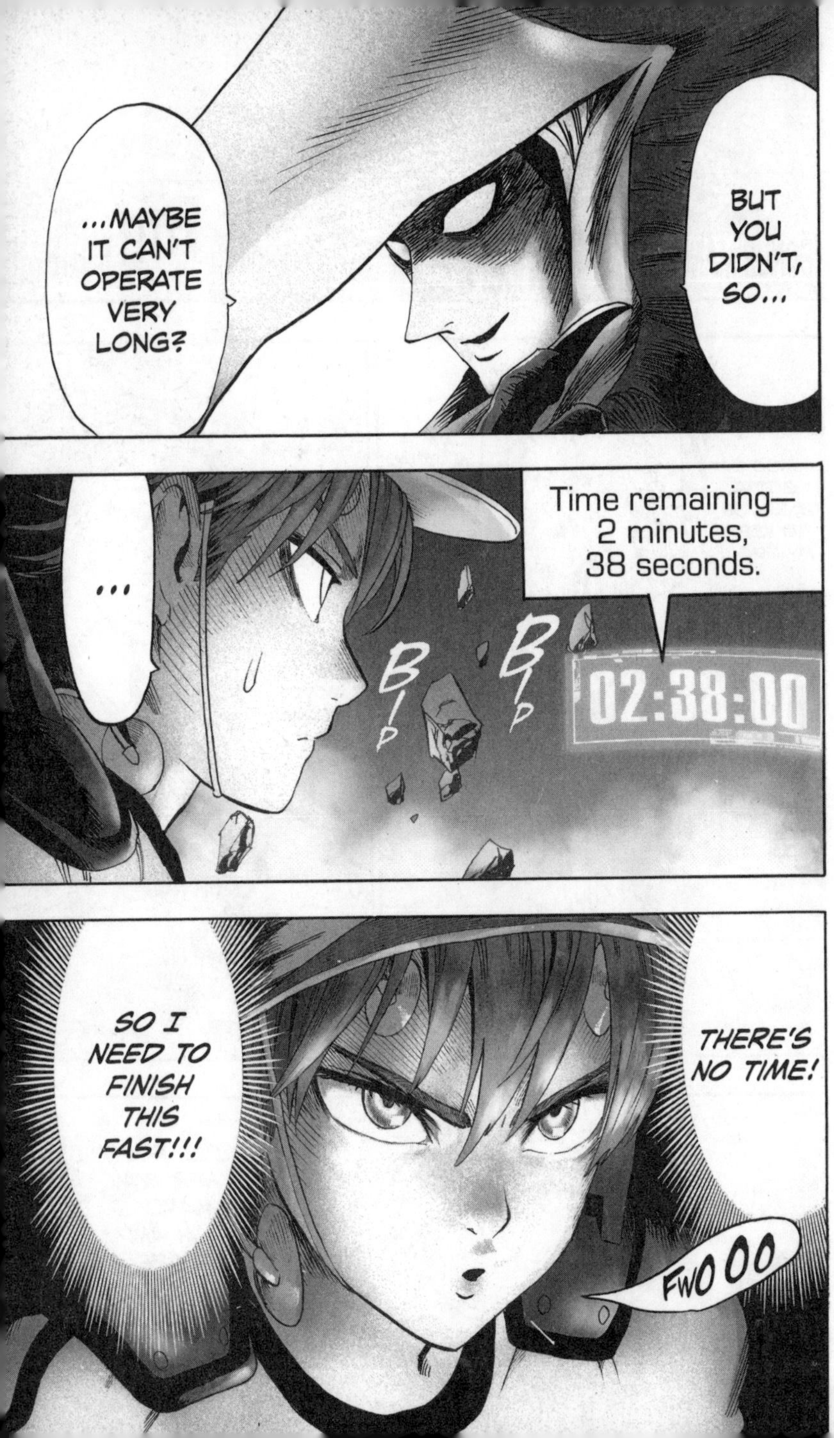
BUT YOU DIDN'T, SO...
...MAYBE IT CAN'T OPERATE VERY LONG?
Time remaining— 2 minutes, 38 seconds.
02:38:00
BIP
BIP
...
THERE'S NO TIME!
SO I NEED TO FINISH THIS FAST!!!
FWOOO

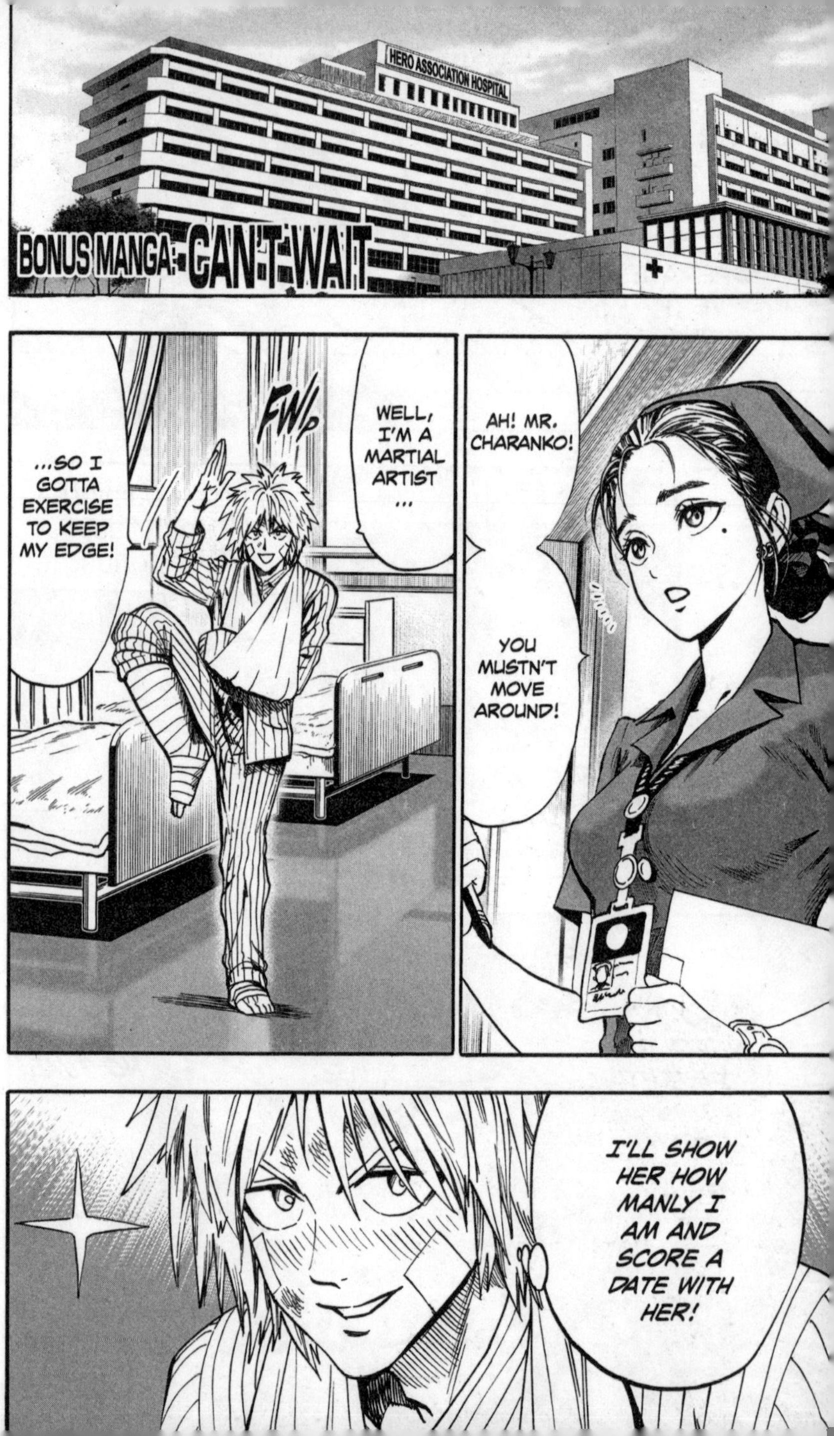
HERO ASSOCIATION HOSPITAL
BONUS MANGA: CAN'T WAIT
AH! MR. CHARANKO!
YOU MUSTN'T MOVE AROUND!
WELL, I'M A MARTIAL ARTIST ...
FW!
...SO I GOTTA EXERCISE TO KEEP MY EDGE!
I'LL SHOW HER HOW MANLY I AM AND SCORE A DATE WITH HER!

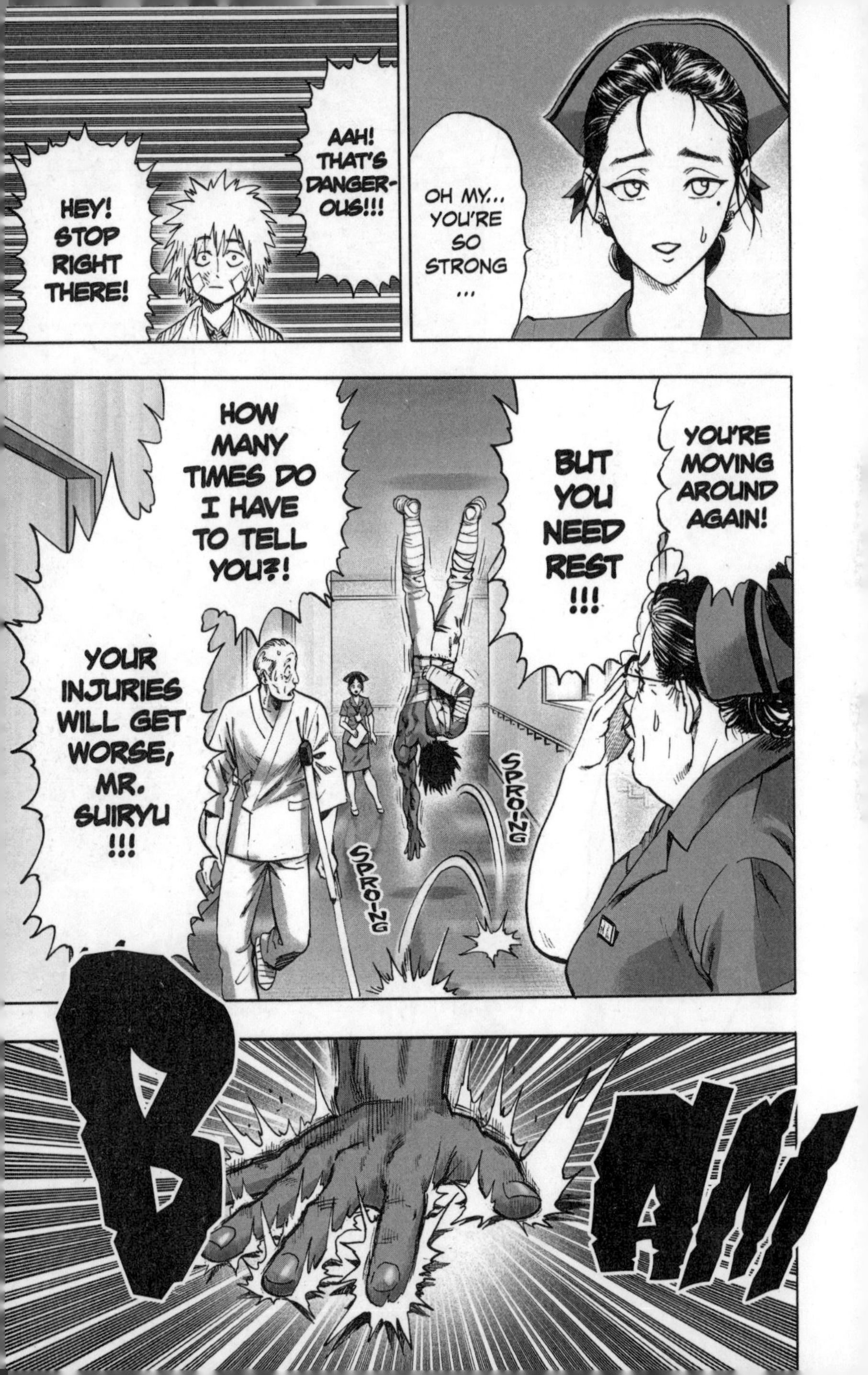
OH MY... YOU'RE SO STRONG ...
AAH! THAT'S DANGER-OUS!!!
HEY! STOP RIGHT THERE!
YOU'RE MOVING AROUND AGAIN!
BUT YOU NEED REST !!!
HOW MANY TIMES DO I HAVE TO TELL YOU?!
SPROING
SPROING
YOUR INJURIES WILL GET WORSE, MR. SUIRYU !!!
BAM

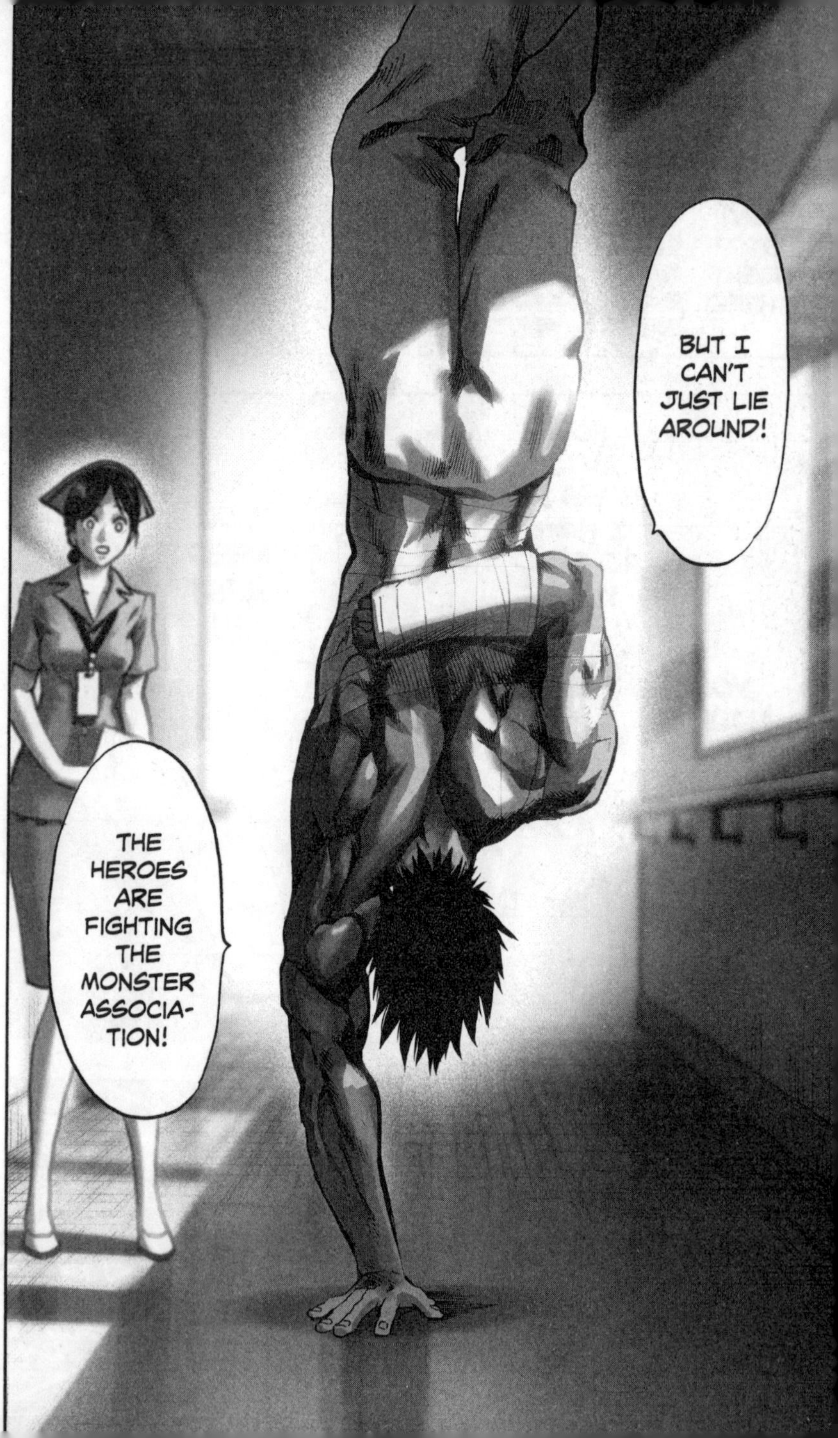
BUT I CAN'T JUST LIE AROUND!
THE HEROES ARE FIGHTING THE MONSTER ASSOCIA-TION!

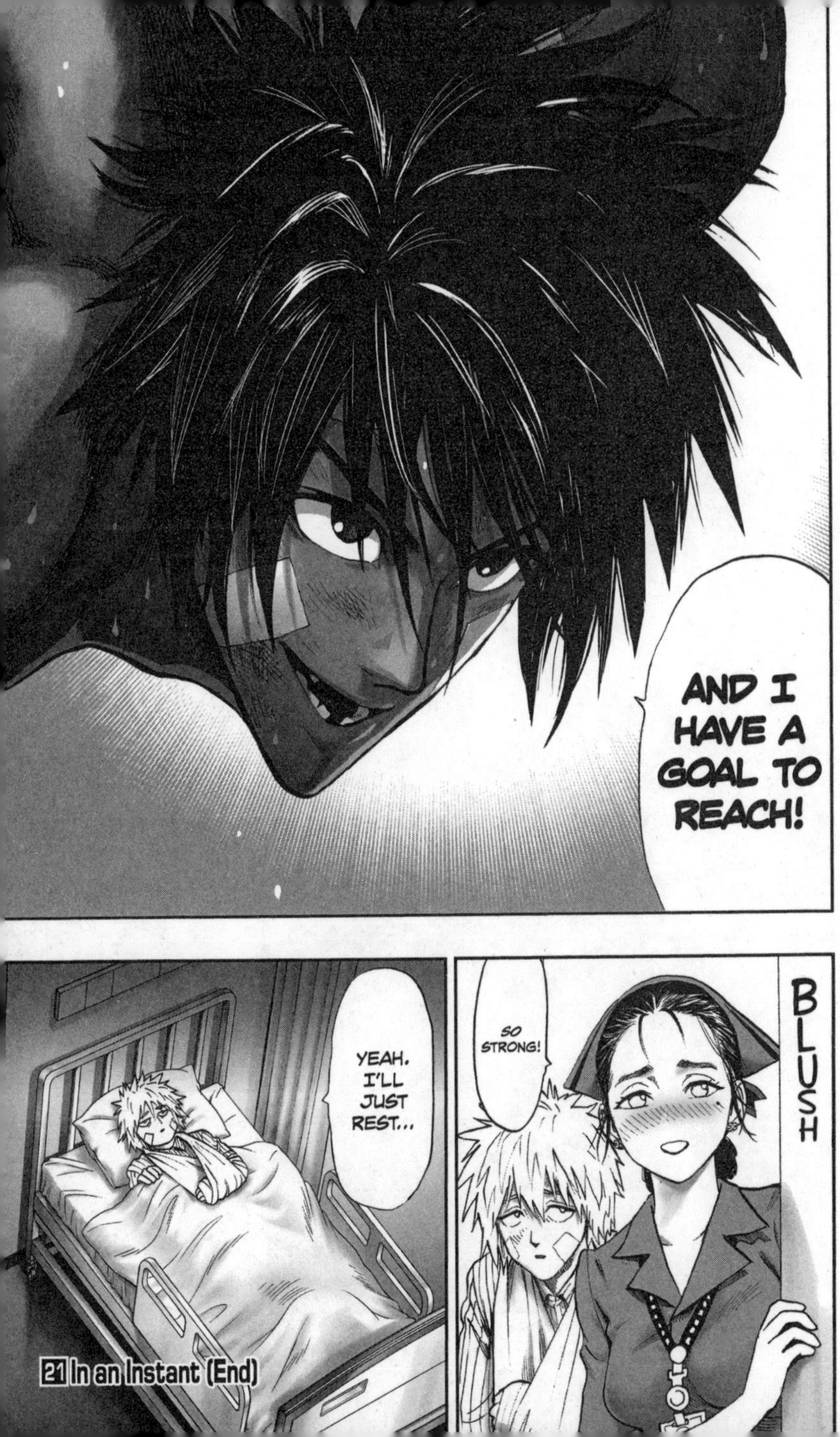
AND I HAVE A GOAL TO REACH!
SO STRONG!
BLUSH
YEAH. I'LL JUST REST...
21 In an Instant (End)

ONE-PUNCH MAN VOL. 19-21
FRONT COVER GALLERY

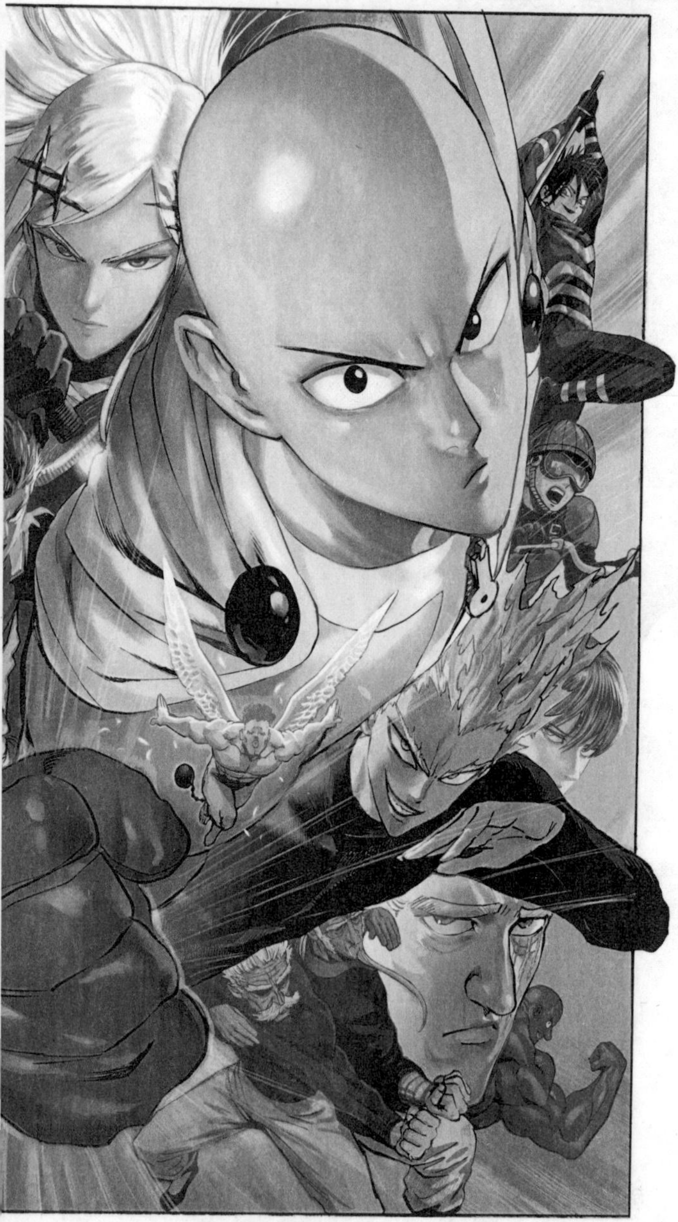

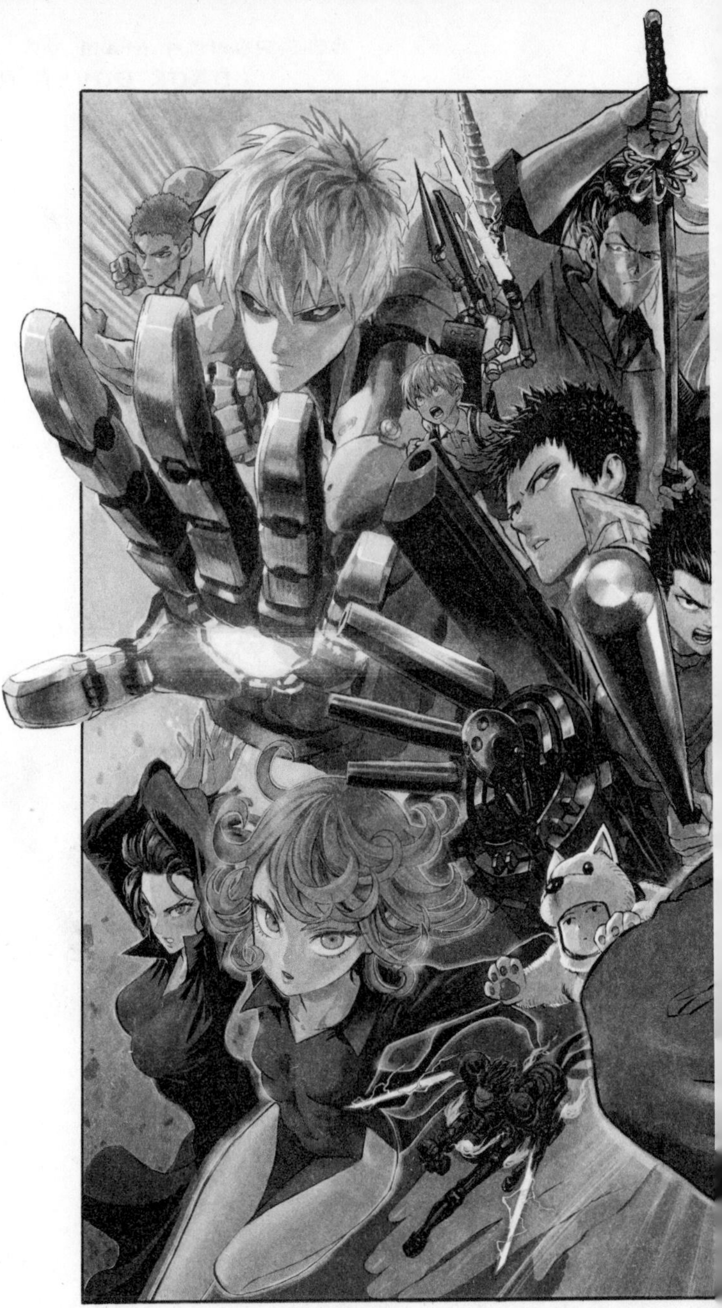

ONE-PUNCH MAN VOL. 19–21
BACK COVER GALLERY

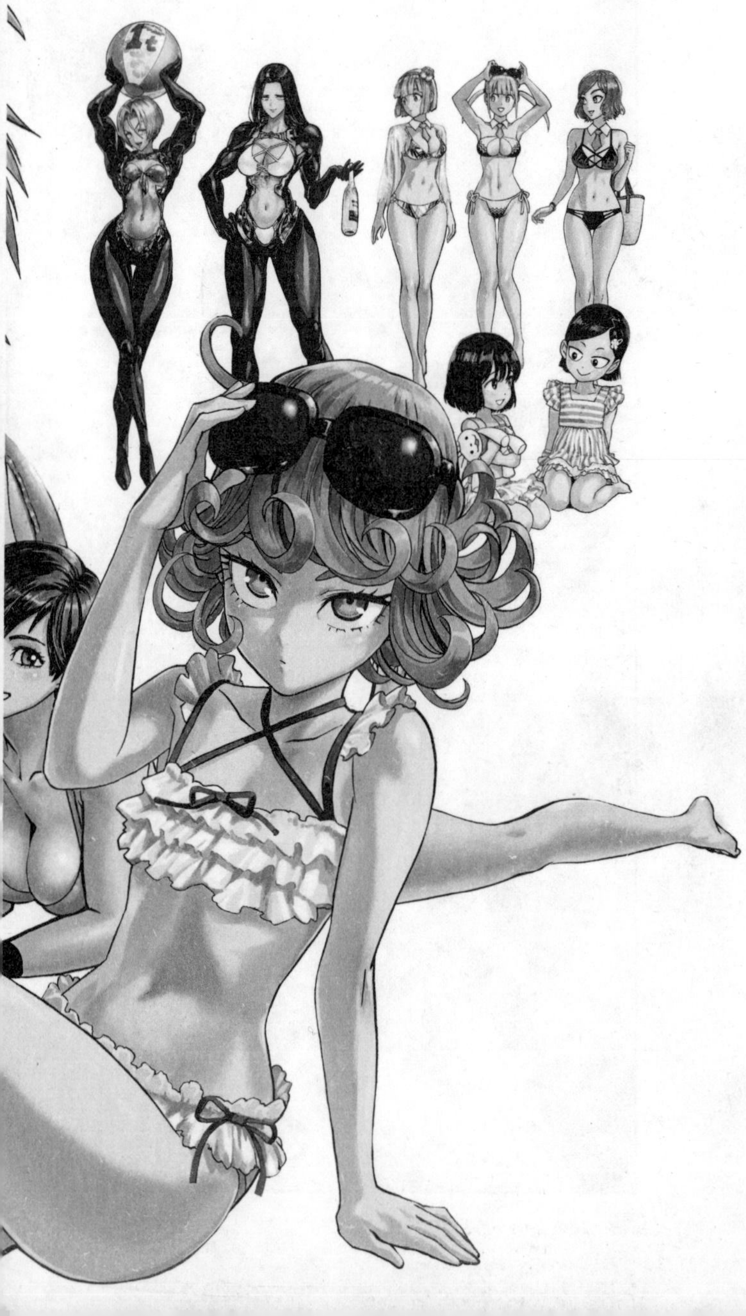

A Dragon Ball fan's greatest dream is getting to live in the Dragon Ball universe and fight alongside Goku and his friends! But one particular fan is in for a rude awakening when he suddenly dies and gets reincarnated as everyone's favorite punching bag, Yamcha!

Based on Dragon Ball by Akira Toriyama, Art by dragongarow LEE

DRAGON BALL GAIDEN: TENSEI SHITARA YAMCHA DATTA KEN
© 2017 by BIRD STUDIO, dragongarow LEE/SHUEISHA Inc.

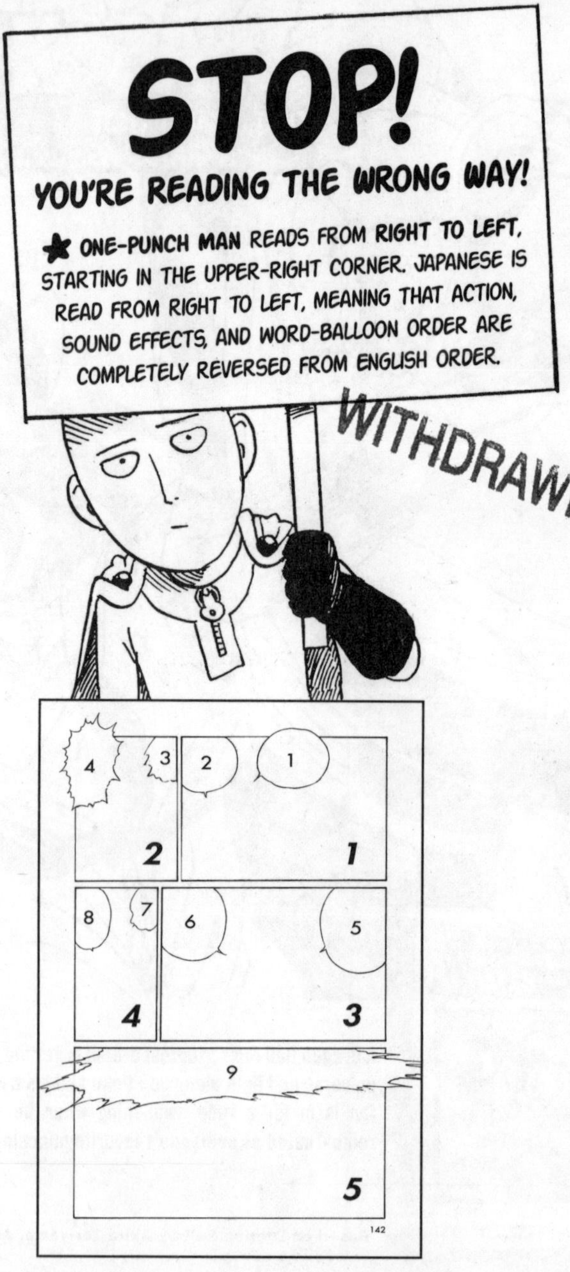
STOP!
YOU'RE READING THE WRONG WAY!
★ ONE-PUNCH MAN READS FROM RIGHT TO LEFT, STARTING IN THE UPPER-RIGHT CORNER. JAPANESE IS READ FROM RIGHT TO LEFT, MEANING THAT ACTION, SOUND EFFECTS, AND WORD-BALLOON ORDER ARE COMPLETELY REVERSED FROM ENGLISH ORDER.